Intersectionality and Context Across the Lifespan

COGNELLA SERIES ON FAMILIES AND SOCIAL JUSTICE

Intersectionality and Context Across the Lifespan

Readings for Human Development

FIRST EDITION

Written and Edited by J. Maria Bermudez

Series Edited by Katherine R. Allen

SAN DIEGO

Bassim Hamadeh, CEO and Publisher
Amy Smith, Senior Project Editor
Susana Christie, Senior Developmental Editor
Casey Hands, Production Editor
Emely Villavicencio, Senior Graphic Designer
Stephanie Kohl, Licensing Coordinator
Natalie Piccotti, Director of Marketing
Kassie Graves, Senior Vice President of Editorial
Jamie Giganti, Director of Academic Publishing

Cover image: Copyright © 2020 iStockphoto LP/anilakkus.

Printed in the United States of America.

cognella® | ACADEMIC PUBLISHING
3970 Sorrento Valley Blvd., Ste. 500, San Diego, CA 92121

This book is dedicated to my daughters, Lucia, Aida, and Giana, who give me hope for a better future

Contents

Foreword   xiii

Preface   xv

Acknowledgments   xix

CHAPTER 1   Introduction: Overview of Intersectionality, Context, and Lifespan   1

CHAPTER 2   Defining Self Across Time and Place   9

Introduction   9
Summary of Readings   10

Reading 2.1 The Complexity of Identity: "Who am I?"   12
Beverly Daniel Tatum

Reading 2.2 Ideology, Myth, and Magic: Femininity, Masculinity, and 'Gender Roles'   20
Allan Johnson

Reading 2.3 Place Matters Even More than We Thought: New Insights on the Persistence of Racial Inequality   33
Margery Austin Turner

Reading 2.4 The American Dream of Meritocracy   38
Heather Beth Johnson

Reflexive Questions   47

CHAPTER 3   Pregnancy and Childbirth   49

Introduction   49
Summary of Readings   50

Reading 3.1 The Colour of Loss   54
Elizabeth Ruth

Reading 3.2 Pregnant Behind Bars   64
Victoria Law

Reading 3.3 Culturally Competent Care for Aboriginal Women: A Case for Culturally Competent Care for Aboriginal Women Giving Birth in Hospital Settings   70
June Birch, Lia Ruttan, Tracy Muth, and Lola Baydala

Reading 3.4 Childbirth at the Global Crossroads   85
Arlie Hochschild

Reflexive Questions   91

CHAPTER 4   Infancy, Gender, and Culture   93

Introduction   93
Summary of Readings   94

Reading 4.1 Population & Societies: Masculinization of Births in Eastern Europe   98
Christophe Z. Guilmoto and Géraldine Duthé

Reading 4.2 'It's a … Does It Matter?': Theorising 'Boy or Girl' Binary Classifications, Intersexuality and Medical Practice in New Zealand   104
Geraldine Christmas

Reading 4.3 The Work of Breastfeeding   116
Cindy A. Stearns

Reflexive Questions   124

CHAPTER 5   Early Childhood   125

Introduction   125
Summary of Readings   126

Reading 5.1 Unequal At the Start: Early Childhood Programs Pay Dividends for Life   130
Ann O'leary

Reading 5.2 From Brilliant Baby to Child Placed At Risk: The Perilous Path of African American Boys in Early Childhood Education   133
Hakim M. Rashid

Reading 5.3 Indigenous Children: Their Human Rights, Mortality, and the Millennium Development Goals   144
Jane Freemantle

Reflexive Questions   150

CHAPTER 6   Middle Childhood   151

Introduction   151
Summary of Readings   153

Reading 6.1 Childhood Disability in Turkana, Kenya: Understanding How Carers
Cope in a Complex Humanitarian Setting   156
Maria Zuurmond, Velma Nyapera, Victoria Mwenda, James Kisia, Hilary Rono,
Jennifer Palmer, and Maria Zuurmond

Reading 6.2 What Constitutes a Quality Program for Children Who Are
Deaf?   171
J. Freeman King

Reading 6.3 NASP Position Statement Safe Schools for Transgender and Gender
Diverse Students   174
Reflexive Questions   183

CHAPTER 7   The Adolescent Years   185

Introduction   185
Summary of Readings   186

Reading 7.1 Schools and the Social Control of Sexuality   189
Melinda S. Miceli

Reading 7.2 Lost in the Shuffle: Culture of Homeless Adolescents   194
Joanne O'Sullivan Oliveira and Pamela J. Burke

Reading 7.3 Female Genital Cutting: Crossing Borders   210
Hazel Barrett

Reflexive Questions   222

CHAPTER 8   Emerging and Young Adulthood   223

Introduction   223
Summary of Readings   225

Reading 8.1 Agency and Error in Young Adults' Stories of Sexual Decision
Making   228
Katherine R. Allen, Erica K. Husser, Dana J. Stone, and Christian E. Jordal

Reading 8.2 Emerging Adults with Disabilities: Theory, Trends, and
Implications   246
Jill M. Meyer, Vanessa M. Hinton, and Nicholas Derzis

Reading 8.3 My Life as a Dreamer Who Acted Beyond the Barriers: From Growing Up "Undocumented" in Arizona to a Master's Degree from Harvard   260
Silvia P. Rodríguez Vega

Reflexive Questions   264

CHAPTER 9   Middle Adulthood   265

Introduction   265
Summary of Readings   267

Reading 9.1 Gender Pay Equity in Advanced Countries: The Role of Parenthood and Policies   270
Joya Misra and Eiko Strader

Reading 9.2 Is Anti-Aging Medicine the New Ageism?   279
Arlene Weintraub

Reading 9.3 A Midlife Transition   281
Heather Lamborn

Reflexive Questions   284

CHAPTER 10   Late Adulthood   285

Introduction   285
Summary of Readings   288

Reading 10.1 Equity and Social Determinants of Health Among Older Adults   292
Steven P. Wallace

Reading 10.2 Protecting and Ensuring the Well-Being of LGBT Older Adults: A Policy Roadmap   299
Robert Espinoza

Reading 10.3 America's Aging Society Problem: A Look to Japan for Lessons on Prevention   307
Ender Ricart

Reflexive Questions   310

CHAPTER 11   End of Life, Loss, and Bereavement   311

Introduction   311
Summary of Readings   314

Reading 11.1 Parents' Death and Adult Well-being: Gender, Age, and Adaptation to Filial Bereavement   317
Thomas Leopold and Clemens M. Lechner

Reading 11.2 Kin and Kindred: Death and Social Relations   326
Tong Chee-Kiong

Reading 11.3 Origins and Celebrations of El Día de Los Muertos   332
J. Rhett Rushing

Reflexive Questions   335

CHAPTER 12   A Call to Action: Being an Agent of Change   337

Introduction   337
Summary of Readings   339

Reading 12.1 Where Do We Go from Here? In Search of New Knowledge: Intersectionality   341
Patricia Hill Collins

Reflexive Questions   345

About the Author   347

Foreword

Katherine R. Allen, Virginia Tech

In this timely and relevant book, *Intersectionality and Context across the Lifespan: Readings for Human Development*, Maria Bermudez has created an educational resource that is intellectually challenging, globally informed, and personally engaging. Scrolling down the table of contents, the teacher in me is immediately excited by the diverse and comprehensive approach to lifespan human development within the context of family and society. The student in me is equally delighted to find that I am offered such compelling and wide-ranging readings with which to approach the diversity of human experience in all of its complexity. Finally! A lifespan human development book that upsets the "one size fits all" approach to how individuals live, love, parent, partner, and die in the family context—an arena that has private, public, and political dimensions. Each chapter presents critical readings about a variety of individual and family developmental issues across the lifespan, from infancy to old age. In each of the 12 chapters, Maria guides and inspires the reader by offering definitions and interpretations of the theoretical concepts that infuse this book as well as summaries of each of the readings. Given her commitment to helping students make life-changing connections with the ideas that inform their lives and spur them to action for justice in personal and social relations, Maria also provides challenging reflexive questions that ask students to think deeply about their own lived experiences with identity, intersectionality, privilege, and oppression. The materials are all here for a comprehensive resource that students and teachers will want to read and engage.

This book reveals the heart, mind, and soul of the teacher who is truly invested in transformative educational practice. From my earliest acquaintance with Maria when she was a graduate teaching assistant and I was her teaching supervisor in the late 1990s at Virginia Tech to her current position as a professor at the University of Georgia, I have witnessed in Maria a champion for global, feminist, and intersectional scholarship. Maria's approach to research and teaching resonates with those of us who have experienced marginalization. When interacting with Maria, we feel seen, listened to, and heard. The reflexive practice that Maria so effectively utilizes in this book is intimately tied to her expertise as a therapist and scholar. In this book, Maria raises the hard questions that wise teachers know students have grappled with and experienced. She provides us a book that is a gift to education as the practice of transformation, demonstrating how passionate scholarship is powerful, productive, and healing.

Preface

Upon over a decade of teaching a course on human development across the lifespan, I began to see the growing need to understand development beyond what was being presented in standard texts. While most texts on human development offer perspectives on diversity, it is often not possible for those texts to offer intersectional and contextual perspectives in greater depth. *Intersectionality and Context Across the Lifespan: Readings for Human Development* was created to supplement readings that are often missing from texts focusing on biopsychosocial perspectives. For me, this process was as challenging as it was meaningful.

Given the endless amount of research studies focused on diversity issues, it is indeed overwhelming to create a text focused on diversity. My challenge was to offer critical multiple perspectives, knowing that it is impossible for any given text to be exhaustive in its scope. In the end, my hope is that this anthology would help students and faculty in various ways. First, I hope that the reader will gain the ability to acknowledge and appreciate the complexity of diversity across and within cultures. Second, I hope the reader will critique and evaluate mainstream human development texts and challenge norms and assumptions that are presented as universal. Third, it is my aim that this book will help the reader examine the ways in which systems of privilege, power, and oppression shape developmental trajectories, specifically attending to nuances of those who are marginalized in society and those who are granted various unearned privileges. Lastly, I hope each person reading this text will be more attuned to the ways in which their own identities will remain constant and/or change across varying social contexts, places, and stages of life.

Theoretical Framework

Although I am influenced by many theories, the ones that guide this body of work mostly fall under critical social theories. These critical theories (e.g., social constructionism, intersectional and transnational feminism, standpoint theory, queer theory, critical race theory, decolonizing frameworks, and critical geography) serve as lenses to interpret and construct the meaning of theories related to human development across the lifespan. Critical theories serve to politicize social problems (e.g., poverty, sexism, heterosexism, etc.) by situating them in a historical context with the goal of liberating people from dehumanizing circumstances. The primary means of achieving this goal is through critiquing and changing dominant and oppressive societal structures. For example, early activists worked to politically mobilize women, racial, ethnic, and sexual minorities to gain the right to vote, own land, obtain formal education, gain access to reproductive health, and to legally marry. Such movements have ushered in changes in family and societal systems, shaping developmental trajectories (e.g., women working outside of the home, educational achievement, interracial and same-sex marriage, etc.).

Additionally, I am also informed by decades of research on resilience and cumulative disadvantage theory to help examine factors leading to social positions of privilege and oppression. For example, factors such as our social and cultural capital, race, skin tone, religion, nationality, political affiliation, immigration status, ability status, gender, age, culture, and sexual orientation all affect our lived experience at every age and life stage. Together, these factors work together to lead to cumulative access to advantages and opportunities; however, they can also lead to disadvantages and adversity over time. In essence, it is imperative that we continuously strive to examine how our theoretical frameworks, scientific knowledge, and contextual lives intersect to inform our understanding of the human experience.

Positionality Statement

Consistent with feminist-informed scholarship, I offer my positionality statement to situate myself as a scholar and writer in terms of my own intersectionality, context, and life stage. I believe that ignoring systemic oppression adversely affects individuals, families, and societies. Central to this framework is the notion that developmental milestones, interpersonal relationships, and notions of healthy and functional family forms cannot be conceptualized apart from historical and sociocultural contexts.

I am a middle-aged, able-bodied, heterosexual Latina woman who is a practicing Catholic. I am a professor of human development and family science and marriage and family therapy. For over twenty-five years I have taught undergraduate courses on human development across the lifespan, diversity and social justice, human sexuality, family dynamics, and women's studies, among other graduate-level courses. I am passionate about helping students gain an advanced appreciation of diversity, while also valuing their own cultures. I strive to help them examine and appreciate their own complexities as individuals who are also embedded in families and social systems. Additionally, because we also evolve as scholars, researchers, and teachers, it is important that I situate myself within the context of my life and this book. This is how I would describe myself at this point in time.

I have many brothers and sisters, thanks to my father, but I am the youngest of six children from both parents. My ancestors immigrated to Honduras from Austria/Hungary and the US and Spain and we were there for three generations before immigrating to the United States. I was only two years old, so by all accounts, I do not "look nor sound like an immigrant." I always appreciated being bicultural and I am proud of my *Latinidad* (my Latina culture and identity). At the same time, I was always reminded that I was a *gringa* (an American) who had blue eyes and White privilege. Like those who identify as biracial, bisexual, and bicultural, I too, experienced what it was like to live my life from multiple cultural lenses. Growing up, my mother and I traveled to Honduras to see my extended family and I developed an appreciation of culture, a deeper perspective on poverty, social class, and gender formation. My mother, Judith Perez, was born in 1930 who was an accountant by day and sewed clothing for her children by night. She was a feminist, the primary provider for her six children, and took care of many others she considered hers too.

She was married to my father, Rene Perez, who was born in 1916 and a skilled auto mechanic. He was a kind man, but maintained many of the *machista* roles prescribed by Honduran society. My mother was a competent and independent woman who anchored my family in this foreign land. I am the first in my family to graduate college and the only one to have an advanced degree. I owe much of my success to my amazing and loving family who have given me a solid foundation in my life and continuous support in all that I do. I am also a proud mother of three and a wife to a loving husband who is an incredible and devoted father to his three children.

Given the influence of my family and many others who served as teachers, mentors, colleagues, and friends, I have always been a collectivistic and systemic thinker and collaborative person. My research and writing focus on feminist-informed teaching, research and clinical practice, specifically in studying the risk and resilience among immigrant Latinx families. I acknowledge that due to many aspects of my identity that I hold contradictions that may be irreconcilable (e.g., being feminist and Catholic); however, despite these challenges, my aim is to be a lifelong learner and never fully arrive at "knowing" or being an expert. Cultural humility is especially necessary for understanding everything pertaining to diversity, the practice of couple and family therapy, and social science. My hope is that anyone who reads this text will maintain an open reflexive stance and envision what is possible in a compassionate and socially just society.

Acknowledgments

I would like to share my sincere appreciation and gratitude for my former undergraduate research assistants, Lauren Lauterbach, Ashton Quattlebaum, and Alexandra (Alex) Sausa, who delved into the Cognella University Readers library and reviewed hundreds of diversity-related readings to help select which readings to include in this text. Alex Sausa was especially instrumental in the development of this book. I sincerely appreciate her focused commitment to the project. She offered invaluable feedback regarding the reading choices. Alex read and summarized each one, edited the writing, and offered invaluable insights for engaging college students with this body of work. All three research assistants conducted a critically informed content analysis of the readings and examined them from intersectional and contextual perspectives across the lifespan. I would like to thank and acknowledge the University of Georgia's Center for Undergraduate Research Opportunities (CURO) for generously supporting these students in their participation in this project.

I am also indebted to my former doctoral student, Dr. Joshua Boe, recent graduate of the Department of Human Development and Family Science and the Marriage and Family Therapy Program at UGA. I sincerely appreciate their thoughtful contributions to this body of work.

I would also like to thank Dr. Katherine Allen, for writing such a beautiful foreword. Dr. Allen embodies what it means to live life as a passionate, feminist informed teacher, mentor, researcher, scholar, and activist. I continue to seek her guidance!

Thank you also to my beautiful family and lifelong friends for continuously being a source of love and support and for helping me live each stage of my life to the fullest. I love each one of you deeply and with all my heart! To my husband Romulo "Ronnie" Rama, thank you for your love and unwavering support in all that I do. It is a gift being your life partner and being on this journey together. To our amazing children Lucia, Aida, Giana, Meg, Nico, Eric, Leah, and Mandy—we cannot love you more than we do and we are so grateful for what your presence means in our lives.

Last but not least, I would like to thank and acknowledge my students and colleagues at the University of Georgia for continuing to walk alongside me on this long hard road toward social justice ... lifting as we climb.

CHAPTER 1

Introduction

Overview of Intersectionality, Context, and Lifespan

Human development is complex, and even with over a century of sociobiological science, there are still many unanswered questions. For example, what factors contribute to positive or negative outcomes for individuals, families, and communities? What is "optimal development," and how do people achieve it? Are the assumptions we make about gender, race, sexuality, and class the same worldwide? These questions require us to carefully examine how context and culture inform, guide, and shape development. For decades, we have studied how scholars like Bronfenbrenner and Vygotsky examined the importance of context and culture. Although family scholars consider the influence of context and culture, most textbooks on human development focus predominantly on biopsychosocial perspectives and less on issues related to culture and diversity. By contextualizing human development, we gain alternative standpoints through which we can understand, teach, and research development. It is my hope that by reading this book, students studying human development across the lifespan can gain a greater awareness and appreciation of the complexity of development as we age. Further, I hope students can resist relying on ethnocentric values, beliefs, and assumptions to guide their ideas about what is normative human development.

Throughout this text, my aim is to present diverse perspectives across each life stage. Although it is not possible to represent all cultures, groups of people, voices, worldviews, or definitions, the selected readings offer a small window into global and contextual perspectives from pregnancy to old age. I intentionally chose readings that focus on populations that are often underrepresented in lifespan textbooks. The text offers a glimpse of how issues related to gender, ability status, social class, race, culture, sexual orientation, nationality, and others are central to broadening our lens and lessening our impulse to primarily focus on cultures represented in the United States of America.

The Structure of this Anthology

There are a total of twelve chapters and 33 readings in this anthology. Within these chapters, I focus on the following developmental stages: 1) pregnancy and childbirth, 2) infancy and toddler years, 3) early childhood, 4) middle childhood, 5) adolescence, 6) emerging and young adulthood, 7) middle adulthood, 8) late adulthood, and 9) end of life and bereavement. The readings are from scholarly sources in peer-reviewed scientific journals, books, and magazines across many disciplines found in the Cognella library. Each chapter offers a brief overview of the life stage from intersectional and contextual perspectives, an introduction to the readings, and reflexive questions. These questions serve as prompts for reflection/process papers and class discussion to encourage students to examine their own beliefs, values, norms, and aspects of their identities across the various stages and contexts of their lives.

Situating Context and Intersectionality across the Lifespan

Before delving into the readings for each chapter, I present a brief introduction of context, intersectionality, and human development across the lifespan. I situate this writing in social constructionist and intersectional and transnational feminist ideas and practices that encourage family scholars, students, and practitioners to question and challenge ethnocentric and androcentric norms and representations of family and development across the lifespan (Lloyd, Few, & Allen, 2009).

Context

Societal context can be described as a dynamic interaction of social systems in which we situate our experiences (McDowell, Knudson-Martin, & Bermudez, 2018). Our context is the space and place in which we live our lives. Some spaces and contexts will pave the road for privilege and well-being, while others will set a course of disadvantage, creating barriers to optimal growth and well-being. It is important to note that many children and adults may occupy similar spatial settings, such as in homes, schools, hospitals, workplaces, courtrooms, and neighborhoods, but will receive differential treatment and have different experiences and outcomes based on how their multiple identities intersect to create their realities. For example, in the United States, we aspire to treat children of all genders and races fairly, to provide them with the same education, and to grant them equal access to safe environments and experiences that enable positive identity development and interpersonal relationships. The reality is that many children in the United States and many parts of the world experience gross inequities and barriers due to their social location: race, gender, social class, and physical abilities and differences. The myth of meritocracy would have us believe that we all have equal access to opportunities and resources (McNamee & Miller, 2004), but examples such as the school-to-prison pipeline in the United States and forbidding girls to attend school in Pakistan reminds us otherwise.

Additionally, I adopt McDowell, Knudson-Martin, and Bermudez's (2018) definition of culture as situated in context. Culture refers to "beliefs, values and traditions, ways of being and doing, collective meaning-making, shared knowledge and attitudes, and conceptual frameworks for understanding the universe including spirituality and religion" (p. 14). From this perspective, culture is a shared, socially constructed system of meaning-making and knowledge. Culture is fluid and shifts to adjust to changing circumstances. For example, lesbian and gay people were barred from marriage in many places in the United States until 2015, when the US Supreme Court ruled it a constitutional right. This shift occurred in large part due to political activism and cultural changes in the visibility and acceptance of lesbian, gay, and bisexual (LGB) people.

The very act of legalizing same-sex marriage is changing our culture in the United States as well as changing the culture of marriage and family. This change is beginning to loosen the grip of the mythical norm (Lorde, 2007) and dominant ideology of the standard North American family (SNAF) (Smith, 1993). Despite these gains toward marriage equality, many LGB and other queer-identified individuals continue to experience stigma, discrimination, fear, and relentless targeting for abuse and violence worldwide. Homophobia and transphobia persists, especially among LGBTQ+ people of color.

Intersectionality

Intersectionality is an important analytical tool from which to understand human development. Long before its coining, intersectionality was used by Black feminist scholars as a tool for analyzing the ways in which identity and systems of oppression are inextricably linked (Collins & Bilge, 2016). Our identities are complex, and no one has a singular way of describing or experiencing their identity. Although there are some aspects of our identity that may be more punctuated than others (i.e., woman, African American, hearing impaired), they are most salient when those aspects of our identities are "othered," subordinated, or targeted with the intent to dehumanize or oppress (Tatum, 1997). The issues of gender, social class, race, culture, sexual orientation, and nationality, among others, co-exist and co-influence one another to create unique matrices that benefit and harm us uniquely depending on varying contexts (Collins & Bilge, 2018; Creswell, 1989). According to Collins and Bilge (2016), intersectionality is situated in the following essential core elements: 1) social inequality, 2) power, 3) relationality, 4) social context, 5) complexity, and 6) social justice. They contend that power, for example, is mutually constructed by social identities that intersect. Given that there are no pure "isms," social identities gain meaning when they are in relation to one another. This interlocking system relates to the idea of relationality. Relationality rejects a binary understanding of either/or (i.e., female and male) and examines the both/and of social identities. Complexity arises from the interconnection among social inequality, power, relationality, and social context. To help illustrate this point, Crenshaw (1989) used the metaphor of a traffic intersection to highlight the complexities of identities that intersect to form our sense of self, challenging our assumptions of holding separate identities. In essence, no single part of our identity stands alone. For example, a transgender immigrant Latina's experience is the culmination of the unique intersection of her identities and cannot be *truly* understood by parsing out those identities and representing self in a fragmented way (Lorde, 2007). Additionally, her identity will also continue to evolve as she engages in multiple contexts and spaces as she ages.

Although intersectionality as a concept seems intuitive, it is complex from a theoretical and research perspective. Currently, a debate exists on whether intersectionality is a theory, paradigm, or method (Few-Demo, 2014). Collins and Bilge (2016) state that intersectionality has two organizing features: critical inquiry (research) and critical praxis (consciousness into action). As a framework and analytical tool, intersectionality helps us understand the complexity of human experience. Intersectionality as a theory explains identity in these ways: 1) they are not discrete but complex, which may cause conflict among identities (Crenshaw, 1993; Yuval-Davis, 2006);

2) they are grounded in ideologies (Crenshaw, 1993); 3) they are historically and contextually grounded (Crenshaw, 1993); and 4) although identities are embodied by individuals, they operate in complex intersecting power structures (Greenwood, 2008). In this vein, Few-Demo (2014) urges researchers to consider how people are situated by their social locations and how they negotiate systems of privilege and oppression and change across the lifespan.

As a methodology, intersectionality is currently underdeveloped (Hancock, 2007; Nash, 2008). This challenge of developing it as a methodology is in part due to the complexity of including multiple dimensions and categories of analysis (McCall, 2005). Hillsburg (2013) contends that while it is important to account for categories, they should not be relied upon too heavily to guide research. An intersectional methodology requires researchers to attend cautiously and critically to categories (i.e., race, class, gender) while resisting the idea that they are "natural" and hierarchical. An over-reliance on categories within the social sciences is problematic in that it essentializes people without taking into account oppression or power that cannot be easily understood at the individual level (Few-Demo, 2014; Hillsburg, 2013). Such a perspective requires us to study families and human development more comprehensively and to intervene at multiple levels of systems (i.e., individual/family, local, state, and federal) (Allen, Lloyd, & A. L. Few, 2009; Walker, 2009). It also requires us to understand that systems of power are never neutral, nor do they remain stagnant.

Lastly, scholars such as Collins and Bilge (2016) urge us to identify ways to use intersectionality as a form of critical praxis (consciousness in action). They contend that "for practitioners and activists, intersectionality is not simply a heuristic for intellectual inquiry, but it is also an important analytical strategy for doing social justice work ... and that both scholarship and practice are intimately linked and mutually inform each other" (p. 42). Additionally, removing intersectionality from its social justice roots and neglecting to give credit to Black feminist scholars for their development of this work negates important foundational tenets and serves to culturally appropriate this term and its use.

Human Development across the Lifespan

Consistent with most human development texts, the scholarly work presented here is informed by biopsychosocial perspectives. Aspects of human development, such as biological processes, genetics, epigenetics, cognitive and psychological processes, and interpersonal and social contexts, all inform and shape the science examining who we are and how we develop over time. Life-stage theories were important to the scientific inquiry of human development over time. Researchers such as Freud, Piaget, Kohlberg, Erikson, Bowlby, and Vygotsky continue to be influential today; however, the concept of universal life stages is controversial. Although these theories are still important to the study of human development, toward the end of the 20th century, theorists began questioning the validity of stage theories. Arnett (2016) contends that there should be a new approach focused on indigenous life-stage concepts, which he defines as stemming from local knowledge that comes from the course of cultural life. He offers a diverse range of life concepts that spans history and cultures while still using a biological framework for growth, maturity, and aging. Arnett contends that it is better to think of master narratives instead of life stages so as to better understand cultural nuances in how people understand development across the lifespan. It is also important to study the ways in which these master narratives function for individual identity development and across cultures.

In sum, it is necessary to study people within their sociocultural contexts. An understanding of context is crucial for deepening our awareness of how our lived experiences, overall health and well-being, and opportunities are shaped by factors such as our gender, race, abilities, financial resources, gender, sexual orientation, religion, and geography, among many others. These factors, alone and as they intersect, have a profound effect on how our identities are shaped, valued, and diminish over our lifetime. Consequently, given that there are major differences in the ways we are shaped by our social location, it is vital to have an international global perspective when studying human development across the lifespan. Not having a broader sociocultural perspective puts us at risk of reifying ethnocentric biases and colonizing agendas.

Terms Related to Identity, Privilege, and Oppression

Diversity-related concepts and terms are constantly changing, evolving, and shifting. Given how quickly these terms are changing, it is important for the readers of this text to consider the timing and context in which it is being written. These terms and concepts are highly contested, currently evolving, and will likely develop new meanings over time. Despite the risk of these terms and ideas being quickly outdated, for the goal of having common ground, I offer a table with a list of terms used to describe identity (i.e., age, gender, race, sexual orientation, etc.), specific forms of oppression (i.e., racism, sexism, classism, etc.) and social forces that can negatively affect a person's sense of self (i.e., heteronormativity, transgender oppression, white supremacy, etc.). Although this is not an exhaustive list, I hope that it invites you to add what is missing and critique what is there.

My hope is that the list of terms will help the reader reflect on how social forces affect our sense of identity within positions of privilege and oppression. For example, it is well known that children and teens are more vulnerable to the social forces that maintain forms of prejudice and oppression (Tatum, 1997). A child or teenager might have gained a strong, positive ethnic and racial identity at home, which is central to mental health and academic success (Wakefield & Hudley, 2007), but larger social forces of institutional racism and white privilege work together to create and maintain internalized racism. This process is similar to being a girl and receiving affirming and encouraging experiences at home, only to get older and experience the effects of external and internalized sexism and/ misogyny in education, work, politics, and society at large. As always, it is imperative that one understands how these aspects of identity intersect to inform our lived experiences (Crenshaw, 1989; Collins & Bilge, 2016; Lorde, 2007; 1984) and that one is cognizant of sensitive periods of development in which identity is shaped by multiple forces (Tatum, 1997).

TABLE 1.1 **Identity-Based Oppression and the Social Forces That Maintain Them**

Identity	Type of Oppression	Social Forces
Gender	sexism, misogyny, transphobia	patriarchy, male privilege, cisgender privilege
Sexual Orientation	homophobia	heteronormativity, religion, cultural values, patriarchy
Race	structural, systemic, and individualized racism, colorism	White supremacy, White privilege, forced assimilation, segregation, Anglo-Eurocentrism, White flight, colonization, color blindness, legacy of slavery
Ethnicity	Eurocentrism, racism	White supremacy, White privilege, color blindness
Socioeconomic Class (SES)	classism	myth of meritocracy, capitalism, poverty, class segregation, materialism, cumulative advantage and disadvantage
Ability	ableism	capitalism, normativity, perfectionism, intolerance and pathologizing of difference
Age	ageism, adultism	youth-oriented society, adult-centered norms, anti-aging norms, anti-aging messages and industries
Appearance	lookism, sizeism	pretty privilege, performances of toxic and hyper-masculinity and femininity, fat phobia, perfectionism, medical and beauty industry
Nationality	xenophobia, White nationalism, ethnocentrism	colonization, structural racism, imperialism, institutional and systemic racism, White nationalism, Eurocentrism, immigration policies
Religion	Islamophobia, anti-Semitism, anti-atheist, anti-indigenous	Christian-centric, colonialism, theocratic beliefs, White nationalism
Sex/Intersex	cisgender bias, transphobia, cissexism, cisgenderism	patriarchy, misogyny, sexual dualism, cisnormativity, heteronormativity, male privilege, medical industry ("corrective" surgeries)

Conclusion

Overall, my aim for this book is to curate a body of work that expands students' abilities to examine human development from intersectional and cross-cultural perspectives, as well as to gain a greater appreciation of the complexities of how we develop across the lifespan. As you read the introduction and selected readings for each chapter, I invite you to engage in a self-reflexive stance and think about your own social location, intersectionality identity, and worldviews, and consider the factors that shaped them and will continue to affect them throughout each stage of your life.

References

Allen, K. R., Lloyd, S. A., & Few, A. L. (2009). Reclaiming feminist theory, method, and praxis for family studies. In S. A. Lloyd, A. L. Few, & K. R. Allen (Eds), *Handbook of feminist family studies* (pp. 3–17). Sage.

Crenshaw, K. (1989). Demarginalizing the intersection of race and sex: A Black feminist critique of antidiscrimination doctrine, feminist theory, and antiracist politics. *The University of Chicago Legal Forum, 1989*(8), 139–167.

Collins, P. H., & Bilge, S. (2016). *Intersectionality.* Polity.

Combs, G. (2019). White privilege: What's a family therapist to do? *Journal of Marital and Family Therapy, 45*(1), 61–75. doi:10.1111/jmft.12330

Lorde, A. (2007). *Sister outsider: Essays & speeches by Audre Lorde.* Crossing Press.

Masten, A. S. (2018). Resilience theory and research on children and families: Past, present, and promise. *Journal of Family Theory and Review, 10*(1), 12–31. doi:10.1111/jftr.12255

McDowell, T., Knudson-Martin, C., & Bermudez, J. M. (2018). *Socioculturally attuned family therapy: Guidelines for equitable therapy and practice.* Routledge.

McNamee, S. J., & Miller, R. B. (2004). *The meritocracy myth.* Rowman & Littlefield Publishers.

Merton, R. K. (1988). The Matthew effect in science, II: Cumulative advantage and the symbolism of intellectual property. *isis, 79*(4), 606–623.

Tatum, B. D. (1997). *The Complexity of Identity: "Who am I?" Why are all the Black kids sitting together in the cafeteria?: And other conversations about race.* Basic Books.

Walsh, F. (2016). *Strengthening family resilience* (3rd ed.). Guilford Press.

CHAPTER 2

Defining Self Across Time and Place

Introduction

Simply stated, identity encompasses beliefs, values, memories, relationships, and experiences that shape and define who we are as individuals. Although many scholars contend that our temperaments and personalities remain relatively constant across our lifetimes (Harris, Brett, Johnson, & Deary, 2016), identity may be more fluid (Onorato & Turner, 2004), often being shaped by, and adapting to, endless multiple contexts throughout our lifetime. For example, a woman at midlife might identify with certain roles such as mother, partner, aunt, professional, etc., but may not have had those aspects of her identity in her younger years. Those aspects of her identity developed over time. Not only do experiences shape who we are, but our contexts clearly have an effect in shaping our sense of self, other's perceptions of us, and how we continue to evolve over time. Identity often can be carefully examined by the use of "I am" statements. For example, I am an immigrant Latina woman, a U.S. citizen, highly educated with White privilege, Catholic, heterosexual, cisgender, able-bodied, middle-class, professor, family therapist, middle-aged, mother, who has divorced and remarried. Some aspects of my identity have evolved; others have remained constant. Some aspects I was born with (e.g., sex, skin color), while others were shaped by my context and life stage (e.g., professor, family therapist, mother, immigrant status, social class, age).

According to social identity theory and identity theory, the concept of self is a reflexive process in which one can see self as an object and can categorize, classify, or name one's self in certain ways, especially as we relate to self in relation to other social categories or classifications (Stets & Burke, 2000). This process is called *self-categorization* in social identity theory (Turner, Hogg, Oakes, Reicher, and Wetherell, 1987) and *identification* in identity theory (McCall, George, & Simmons, 1978). It is believed that one's identity is formed through the process of reflexivity, self-categorization and/or identification. Nevertheless, the concept of identity has been challenged (Hall & du Gay, 1996). Hall and du Gay contend that identities, which have had a stabilizing force, no longer have the same stronghold, and new identities are altering our understanding of a "unified subject." What can be perceived as an identity crisis by some can be thought of as a broader process of change that is disrupting the central structures and processes. As certain parts of our identities are subjugated and marginalized by society (e.g., gay, African American, low socioeconomic status/SES), others reflect the values and privileges of the dominant group (e.g., male, Christian, U.S.-born citizen, able-bodied, financially secure). It is the power ascribed to our intersectionality that most often shapes and defines who we are (Collins & Bilge, 2019). In this spirit, the following readings were selected to showcase scholarship that introduces topics related to identity, gender, place, race, and social class.

Summary of Readings

It was indeed a challenge to select readings fitting for this chapter. There are countless readings that could help guide our understanding of what shapes our identities and development over time. The following readings were chosen with the hopes that they would help situate you, the reader, in ways to better engage in self-reflexivity.

In Beverly Tatum's classic essay "**The Complexity of Identity: 'Who Am I?'**" (1997), she asks us to examine the ways in which aspects of our identity align with dominant groups and ideologies in our society (those that hold the most power, privilege, and prestige) and subordinate groups within our society (those that are the most subjugated, disempowered, ignored, targeted, and marginalized). She invites us to examine which aspects of our identities hold the most or least amount of influence and how they intersect to shape who we are across time and diverse contexts. This framework has been central to my work as a professor and diversity scholar.

In the reading "**Ideology, Myth, and Magic: Femininity, Masculinity, and 'Gender Roles'**" (2014), Allan Johnson explores how gender roles perpetuate—even normalize—patriarchal oppression and male privilege. Johnson stresses the patriarchal obsession with gender, sex, and rigid ideas of "masculine" and "feminine" is not biologically ingrained, but rather societally conditioned, especially by the language we use. Stereotypes about masculinity and femininity are inherently male-centric and place girls and women in subordinate social positions. Worldwide, patriarchal concepts of gender make men the standard and cast women in the role of "other," perpetuating the idea that women are inherently less than men. Moreover, by rigidly contrasting what traits are "feminine" and "masculine" and defining women and men as polar opposites, we deny both women and men the opportunity to be well-rounded, capable, strong, and empathetic human beings.

In the reading "**Place Matters Even More than We Thought: New Insights on the Persistence of Racial Inequality**" (2014), Margery Austin Turner helps us understand the ways in which our different experiences of place affect our opportunities in life. Where we live greatly affects the advantages and disadvantages we experience, receive, and will be affected by throughout our lives. She contends that at the core, it is racial and economic segregation that engenders racial inequality. The effects of structural disadvantages strongly shape access to resources and opportunities. In the United States, race and place are conflated, meaning that it is hard to separate the two. This conflation is primarily due to the effects of structural and systemic racism (Tourse, Hamilton-Mason, & Wewiorski, 2018). In the societal context of racism, both race and place matter and cannot be disentangled from the other. However, in terms of educational and work opportunities, perhaps place (where we were raised and lived) is a stronger indicator of access to resources, which has lifelong consequences for our health and our relational and material lives.

In the final reading, "**The American Dream of Meritocracy**" (2008), Heather Beth Johnson dissects the fundamental facets of the American Dream and how it influences American perceptions and psychology. The American Dream is ultimately defined as the way Americans understand upward mobility. It is a concept that rests on the idea that America is a meritocracy that grants equal opportunity—with liberty and justice for all. Following this logic, any American can achieve their aspirations with hard work and determination. Consequently, status is something that is earned by the individual, as evidenced by the phrase "self-made man." By asserting that the individual earns status due to hard work and effort, the American Dream justifies the inequality of social positions. However, despite the American belief in meritocracy, in actuality, inherited wealth is a significant critical advantage passed on from generation to generation. Furthermore, this advantage is often unearned by the parents and their children. This is why scholars such as McNamee and Miller (2004) have referred to the *myth of meritocracy*, especially noting how race, gender, and social class intersect to create disparity and uneven playing fields from the start. Despite the reality of unequally distributed privilege, studies illustrate that the idea of the American Dream is deeply entrenched in the American psyche.

References

Collins, P. H., & Bilge, S. (2016). *Intersectionality*. Polity Press.

Hall, S., & du Gay, P. (Eds.) (1996). *Questions of cultural identity*. Sage Publications.

Harris, M. A., Brett, C. E., Johnson, W., & Deary, I. J. (2016). Personality stability from age 14 to age 77 years. *Psychology and aging, 31*(8), 862–874. http://dx.doi.org/10.1037/pag0000133

McCall, George J., & Simmons, J. L. (1978). *Identities and Interactions*. Free Press

McNamee, S. J., & Miller Jr., R. K. (2004). The American Dream: Origins and prospects. In *The Meritocracy Myth* (pp. 1–12). Rowman & Littlefield.

Onorato, R. S., & Turner, J. C. (2004). Fluidity in the self-concept: the shift from personal to social identity. *European journal of social psychology, 34*(3), 257–278. https://doi.org/10.1002/ejsp.195

Stets, J. E., & Burke, P. J. (2000). Identity theory and social identity theory. *Social Psychology Quarterly, 63*(3), 224–237.

Tourse, R., Hamilton-Mason, J., & Wewiorski, N. (2018). *Systemic Racism in America: Scaffolding as Social Construction*. Springer Publisher.

Turner, J. C., Hogg, M. A., Oakes, P.J., Reicher, S. D., & Wetherell, M. S. (1987). *Rediscovering the Social Group: A Self-Categorization Theory*. Basil Blackwell.

The Complexity of Identity

"Who am I?"

Beverly Daniel Tatum

The concept of identity is a complex one, shaped by individual characteristics, family dynamics, historical factors, and social and political contexts. Who am I? The answer depends in large part on who the world around me says I am. Who do my parents say I am? Who do my peers say I am? What message is reflected back to me in the faces and voices of my teachers, my neighbors, store clerks? What do I learn from the media about myself? How am I represented in the cultural images around me? Or am I missing from the picture altogether? As social scientist Charles Cooley pointed out long ago, other people are the mirror in which we see ourselves.[1]

This "looking glass self" is not a flat one-dimensional reflection, but multidimensional. Because the focus of this book is racial identity in the United States, race is highlighted in these pages. Yet, how one's racial identity is experienced will be mediated by other dimensions of oneself: male or female; young or old; wealthy, middle-class, or poor; gay, lesbian, bisexual, transgender, or heterosexual; able-bodied or with disabilities; Christian, Muslim, Jewish, Buddhist, Hindu, or atheist.

Abigail Stewart and Joseph Healy's research on the impact of historical periods on personality development raises the question, Who is my cohort group?[2] Am I a child of the Depression, a survivor of World War II, the Holocaust, the U.S. internment of Japanese Americans? A product of the segregation of the 1940s and 1950s, or a beneficiary of the Civil Rights era? Did I serve in the Vietnam War, or am I a refugee of it? Did I come of age during the conservatism of the Reagan years? Did I ride the wave of the Women's Movement?

Was I born before or after Stonewall and the emergence of gay activism? What historical events have shaped my thinking?

What has my social context been? Was I surrounded by people like myself, or was I part of a minority in my community? Did I grow up speaking standard English at home or another language or dialect? Did I live in a rural county, an urban neighborhood, a sprawling suburb, or on a reservation?

Who I am (or say I am) is a product of these and many other factors. Erik Erikson, the psychoanalytic theorist who coined the term *identity crisis,* introduced the notion that the social, cultural, and historical context is the ground in which individual identity is embedded. Acknowledging the complexity of identity as a concept, Erikson writes,

We deal with a process "located" *in the core of the individual* and yet also *in the core of his communal culture.* ... In psychological terms, identity formation employs a process of simultaneous reflection and observation, a process taking place on all levels of mental functioning, by which the individual judges himself in the light of what he perceives to be the way in which others judge him in comparison to themselves and to a typology significant to them; while he judges their way of judging him in the light of how he perceives himself in comparison to them and to types that have become relevant to him. This process is, luckily, and necessarily, for the most part unconscious except where inner conditions and outer circumstances combine to aggravate a painful, or elated," identity-consciousness."[3]

Triggered by the biological changes associated with puberty, the maturation of cognitive abilities, and changing societal expectations, this process of simultaneous reflection and observation, the self-creation of one's identity, is commonly experienced in the United States and other Western societies during the period of adolescence.[4] Though the foundation of identity is laid in the experiences of childhood, younger children lack the physical and cognitive development needed to reflect on the self in this abstract way. The adolescent capacity for self-reflection (and resulting self-consciousness) allows one to ask, "Who am I now?" "Who was I before?" "Who will I become?" The answers to these questions will influence choices about who one's romantic partners will be, what type of work one will do, where one will live, and what belief system one will embrace. Choices made in adolescence ripple throughout the lifespan.

Who Am I? Multiple Identities

Integrating one's past, present, and future into a cohesive, unified sense of self is a complex task that begins in adolescence and continues for a lifetime. The complexity of identity is made clear in a collection of autobiographical essays about racial identity called *Names We Call Home*.[5] The multiracial, multiethnic group of contributors narrate life stories highlighting the intersections of gender, class, religion, sexuality, race, and historical circumstance, and illustrating that "people's multiple identifications defy neat racial divisions and unidimensional political alliances."[6] My students' autobiographical narratives point to a similar complexity, but the less developed narratives of the late adolescents that I teach highlight the fact that our awareness of the complexity of our own identity develops over time. The salience of particular aspects of our identity varies at different moments in our lives. The process of integrating the component parts of our self-definition is indeed a lifelong journey.

Which parts of our identity capture our attention first? While there are surely idiosyncratic responses to this question, a classroom exercise I regularly use with my psychology students reveals a telling pattern. I ask my students to complete the sentence, "I am _____," using as many descriptors as they can think of in sixty seconds. All kinds of trait descriptions are used—friendly, shy, assertive, intelligent, honest, and so on—but over the years I have noticed something else. Students of color usually mention their racial or ethnic group: for instance, I am Black, Puerto Rican, Korean American. White students who have grown up in strong ethnic enclaves occasionally mention being Irish or Italian. But in general, White students rarely mention being White. When I use this exercise in coeducational settings, I notice a similar pattern in terms of gender, religion, and sexuality. Women usually mention being female, while men don't usually mention their maleness. Jewish students often say they are Jews, while mainline Protestants rarely mention their religious identification. A student who is comfortable revealing it publicly may mention being gay, lesbian, or bisexual. Though I know most of my students are heterosexual, it is very unusual for anyone to include their heterosexuality on their list.

Common across these examples is that in the areas where a person is a member of the dominant or advantaged social group, the category is usually not mentioned. That element of their identity is so taken for granted by them that it goes without comment. It is taken for granted by them because it is taken for granted by the dominant culture. In Eriksonian terms, their inner experience and outer circumstance are in harmony with one another, and the image reflected by others is similar to the image within. In the absence of dissonance, this dimension of identity escapes conscious attention.

The parts of our identity that *do* capture our attention are those that other people notice, and that reflect back to us. The aspect of identity that is the target of others' attention, and subsequently of our own, often is that which sets us apart as exceptional or "other" in their eyes. In my life I have been perceived as both. A precocious child who began to read at age three, I stood out among my peers because of my reading ability. This "gifted" dimension of my identity was regularly commented upon

by teachers and classmates alike, and quickly became part of my self-definition. But I was also distinguished by being the only Black student in the class, an "other," a fact I grew increasingly aware of as I got older.

While there may be countless ways one might be defined as exceptional, there are at least seven categories of "otherness" commonly experienced in U.S. society. People are commonly defined as other on the basis of race or ethnicity, gender, religion, sexual orientation, socioeconomic status, age, and physical or mental ability. Each of these categories has a form of oppression associated with it: racism, sexism, religious oppression/anti-Semitism,[7] heterosexism, classism, ageism, and ableism, respectively. In each case, there is a group considered dominant (systematically advantaged by the society because of group membership) and a group considered subordinate or targeted (systematically disadvantaged). When we think about our multiple identities, most of us will find that we are both dominant and targeted at the same time. But it is the targeted identities that hold our attention and the dominant identities that often go unexamined.

In her essay, "Age, Race, Class, and Sex: Women Redefining Difference," Audre Lorde captured the tensions between dominant and targeted identities co-existing in one individual. This self-described "forty-nine-year-old Black lesbian feminist socialist mother of two" wrote,

> Somewhere, on the edge of consciousness, there is what I call a *mythical norm,* which each one of us within our hearts knows "that is not me." In america, this norm is usually defined as white, thin, male, young, heterosexual, christian, and financially secure. It is with this mythical

norm that the trappings of power reside within society. Those of us who stand outside that power often identify one way in which we are different, and we assume that to be the primary cause of all oppression, forgetting other distortions around difference, some of which we ourselves may be practicing.[8]

Even as I focus on race and racism in my own writing and teaching, it is helpful to remind myself and my students of the other distortions around difference that I (and they) may be practicing. It is an especially useful way of generating empathy for our mutual learning process. If I am impatient with a White woman for not recognizing her White privilege, it may be useful for me to remember how much of my life I spent oblivious to the fact of the daily advantages I receive simply because I am heterosexual, or the ways in which I may take my class privilege for granted.

Domination and Subordination

It is also helpful to consider the commonality found in the experience of being dominant or subordinate even when the sources of dominance or subordination are different. Jean Baker Miller, author of *Toward a New Psychology of Women,* has identified some of these areas of commonality.[9]

Dominant groups, by definition, set the parameters within which the subordinates operate. The dominant group holds the power and authority in society relative to the subordinates and determines how that power and authority may be acceptably used. Whether it is reflected in determining who gets the best jobs, whose history will be taught in school, or whose relationships will be validated by society, the dominant group has the greatest influence in determining the structure of the society.

The relationship of the dominants to the subordinates is often one in which the targeted group is labeled as defective or substandard in significant ways. For example, Blacks have historically been characterized as less intelligent than Whites, and women have been viewed as less emotionally stable than men. The dominant group assigns roles to the subordinates that reflect the latter's devalued status, reserving the most highly valued roles in the society for themselves. Subordinates are usually said to be innately incapable of being able to perform the preferred roles. To the extent that the targeted group internalizes the images that the dominant group reflects back to them, they may find it difficult to believe in their own ability.

When a subordinate demonstrates positive qualities believed to be more characteristic of dominants, the individual is defined by dominants as an anomaly. Consider this illustrative example: Following a presentation I gave to some educators, a White man approached me and told me how much he liked my ideas and how articulate I was. "You know," he concluded, "if I had had my eyes closed, I wouldn't have known it was a Black woman speaking." (I replied, "This is what a Black woman sounds like.")

The dominant group is seen as the norm for humanity. Jean Baker Miller also asserts that inequitable social relations are seen as the model for "normal human relationships." Consequently, it remains perfectly acceptable in many circles to tell jokes that denigrate a particular group, to exclude subordinates from one's neighborhood or work setting, or to oppose initiatives which might change the power balance.

Miller points out that dominant groups generally do not like to be reminded of the existence of inequality. Because rationalizations have been created to justify the social arrangements, it is easy to believe everything is as it should be. Dominants "can avoid awareness because their explanation of the relationship becomes so well integrated *in other terms; they* can even believe that both they and the subordinate group share the same interests and, to some extent, a common experience."[10]

The truth is that the dominants do not really know what the experience of the subordinates is. In contrast, the subordinates are very well informed about the dominants. Even when firsthand experience is limited by social segregation, the number and variety of images of the dominant group available through television, magazines, books, and newspapers provide subordinates with plenty of information about the dominants. The dominant world view has saturated the culture for all to learn. Even the Black or Latino child living in a segregated community can enter White homes of many kinds daily via the media. However, dominant access to information about the subordinates is often limited to stereotypical depictions of the "other." For example, there are many images of heterosexual relations on television, but very few images of gay or lesbian domestic partnerships beyond the caricatures of comedy shows. There are many images of White men and women in all forms of media, but relatively few portrayals of people of color.

Not only is there greater opportunity for the subordinates to learn about the dominants, there is also greater need. Social psychologist Susan Fiske writes, "It is a simple principle: People pay attention to those who control their outcomes. In an effort to predict and possibly influence what is going to happen to them, people gather information about those with power."[11]

In a situation of unequal power, a subordinate group has to focus on survival. It becomes very important for the subordinates to become highly attuned to the dominants as a way of protecting themselves from them. For example, women who have been battered by men often talk about the heightened sensitivity they develop to their partners' moods. Being able to anticipate and avoid the men's rage is important to survival.

Survival sometimes means not responding to oppressive behavior directly. To do so could result in physical harm to oneself, even death. In his essay "The Ethics of Living Jim Crow," Richard Wright describes eloquently the various strategies he learned to use to avoid the violence of Whites who would brutalize a Black person who did not "stay in his place."[12] Though it is tempting to think that the need for such strategies disappeared with Jim Crow laws, their legacy lives on in the frequent and sometimes fatal harassment Black men experience at the hands of White police officers.[13]

Because of the risks inherent in unequal relationships, the subordinates often develop covert ways of resisting or undermining the power of the dominant group. As Miller points out, popular culture is full of folk tales, jokes, and stories about how the subordinate—whether the woman, the peasant, or the sharecropper—outwitted the "boss."[14] In his essay "I Won't Learn from You," Herbert Kohl identifies one form of resistance, "not-learning," demonstrated by targeted students who are too often seen by their dominant teachers as "others."

> Not-learning tends to take place when someone has to deal with unavoidable challenges to her or

his personal and family loyalties, integrity, and identity. In such situations, there are forced choices and no apparent middle ground. To agree to learn from a stranger who does not respect your integrity causes a major loss of self. The only alternative is to not-learn and reject their world.[15]

The use of either strategy, attending very closely to the dominants or not attending at all, is costly to members of the targeted group. Not-learning may mean there are needed skills which are not acquired. Attending closely to the dominant group may leave little time or energy to attend to one's self. Worse yet, the negative messages of the dominant group about the subordinates may be internalized, leading to self-doubt or, in its extreme form, self-hate. There are many examples of subordinates attempting to make themselves over in the image of the dominant group—Jewish people who want to change the Semitic look of their noses, Asians who have cosmetic surgery to alter the shape of their eyes, Blacks who seek to lighten their skin with bleaching creams, women who want to smoke and drink "like a man." Whether one succumbs to the devaluing pressures of the dominant culture or successfully resists them, the fact is that dealing with oppressive systems from the underside, regardless of the strategy, is physically and psychologically taxing.

Breaking beyond the structural and psychological limitations imposed on one's group is possible, but not easily achieved. To the extent that members of targeted groups do push societal limits—achieving unexpected success, protesting injustice, being "uppity"—by their actions they call the whole system into question. Miller writes, they "expose the inequality, and

throw into question the basis for its existence. And they will make the inherent conflict an open conflict. They will then have to bear the burden and take the risks that go with being defined as 'troublemakers.'"[16]

The history of subordinate groups is filled with so-called troublemakers, yet their names are often unknown. Preserving the record of those subordinates and their dominant allies who have challenged the status quo is usually of little interest to the dominant culture, but it is of great interest to subordinates who search for an empowering reflection in the societal mirror.

Many of us are both dominant and subordinate. Clearly racism and racial identity are at the center of discussion in this book, but as Audre Lorde said, from her vantage point as a Black lesbian, "There is no hierarchy of oppression. "The thread and threat of violence runs through all of the isms. There is a need to acknowledge each other's pain, even as we attend to our own.

For those readers who are in the dominant racial category, it may sometimes be difficult to take in what is being said by and about those who are targeted by racism. When the perspective of the subordinate is shared directly, an image is reflected to members of the dominant group which is disconcerting. To the extent that one can draw on one's own experience of subordination—as a young person, as a person with a disability, as someone who grew up poor, as a woman—it may be easier to make meaning of another targeted group's experience. For those readers who are targeted by racism and are angered by the obliviousness of Whites sometimes described in these pages, it may be useful to attend to your experience of dominance where you may find it—as a heterosexual, as an able-bodied person, as a Christian, as a man—and consider what systems of privilege you may be overlooking. The task of resisting our own oppression does not relieve us of the responsibility of acknowledging our complicity in the oppression of others.

Our ongoing examination of who we are in our full humanity, embracing all of our identities, creates the possibility of building alliances that may ultimately free us all. It is with that vision in mind that I move forward with an examination of racial identity in the chapters to follow. My goal is not to flatten the multidimensional self-reflection we see of ourselves, but to focus on a dimension often neglected and discounted in the public discourse on race.

Notes

1 See C. Cooley, *Human nature and the social order* (New York: Scribner, 1922). George H. Mead expanded on this idea in his book, *Mind, self, and society* (Chicago: University of Chicago Press, 1934).

2 A. J. Stewart and J. M. Healy, "Linking individual development and social changes," *American Psychologist* 44, no. 1 (1989): 30–42.

3 E. H. Erikson, *Identity, youth, and crisis* (New York: W.W. Norton, 1968), p. 22.

4 For a discussion of the Western biases in the concept of the self and individual identity, see A. Roland, "Identity, self, and individualism in a multicultural perspective," pp. 11–23 in E. P. Salett and D. R. Koslow (Eds.), *Race, ethnicity, and self: Identity in multicultural perspective* (Washington, DC: National MultiCultural Institute, 1994).

5 B. Thompson and S. Tyagi (Eds.), *Names we call home: Autobiography on racial identity* (New York: Routledge, 1996).

6 Ibid., p. xi.

7 *Anti-Semitism* is a term commonly used to describe the oppression of Jewish people. However, other Semitic peoples (Arab Muslims, for example) are also subject to oppressive treatment on the basis of ethnicity as well as religion. For that reason, the terms *Jewish oppression* and *Arab oppression* are sometimes used to specify the particular form of oppression under discussion.

8 A. Lorde, "Age, race, class, and sex: Women redefining difference," pp. 445–51 in P. Rothenberg (Ed.), *Race, class, and gender in the United States: An integrated study,* 3d ed. (New York: St. Martin's Press, 1995), p. 446.

9 J. B. Miller, "Domination and subordination," pp. 3–9 in *Toward a new psychology of women* (Boston: Beacon Press, 1976).

10 Ibid., p. 8.

11 S. T. Fiske, "Controlling other people: The impact of power on stereotyping," *American Psychologist* 48, no. 6 (1993): 621–28.

12 R. Wright, "The ethics of living Jim Crow" (1937), reprinted in P. Rothenberg (Ed.), *Race, class, and gender in the United States: An integrated study,* 3d ed. (New York: St. Martin's Press, 1995).

13 An article in the popular weekly magazine *People* chronicled the close encounters of famous Black men with White police officers. Despite their fame, these men were treated as potential criminals. Highlighted in the article is the story of Johnny Gammage, who was beaten to death by White police officers following a routine traffic stop in Pittsburgh. T. Fields-Meyer, "Under suspicion," *People* (January 15, 1996): 40–47.

14 Miller, "Domination and subordination," p. 10.

15 H. Kohl, "I won't learn from you: Confronting student resistance," pp. 134–35 in *Rethinking our classrooms: Teaching for equity and justice* (Milwaukee: Rethinking Our Schools, 1994), p. 134.

16 Miller, "Domination and subordination," p. 12.

Bibliography

Cooley, C. *Human nature and the social order.* New York: Scribner, 1922.

Erikson, E. H. *Identity, youth, and crisis.* New York: W.W. Norton, 1968.

Fiske, S.T. "Controlling other people: The impact of power on stereotyping." *American Psychologist* 48, no. 6 (1993): 621–28.

Kohl, H. "I won't learn from you: Confronting student resistance." Pp. 134–35 in *Rethinking our classrooms: Teaching for equity and justice.* Milwaukee: Rethinking Our Schools, 1994.

Lorde, A. "Age, race, class, and sex: Women redefining difference." Pp. 445–51 in P. Rothenberg (Ed.), *Race, class, and gender in the United States: An integrated study,* 3d ed. New York: St. Martin's Press, 1995.

Mead, G. H. *Mind, self, and society.* Chicago: University of Chicago Press, 1934.

Miller, J. B. "Domination and subordination." Pp. 3–12 in *Toward a new psychology of women.* Boston: Beacon Press, 1976.

Roland, A. "Identity, self, and individualism in a multicultural perspective." Pp. 11–23 in E. P. Salett and D. R. Koslow (Eds.), *Race, ethnicity, and self: Identity in multicultural perspective.* Washington, DC: National MultiCultural Institute, 1994.

Stewart, A. J., and J. M. Healy. "Linking individual development and social changes." *American Psychologist* 44, no. 1 (1989): 30–42.

Thompson, B., and S. Tyagi (Eds.). *Names we call home: Autobiography on racial identity.* New York: Routledge, 1996.

"Under suspicion." *People* (January 15, 1996): 40–47.

Wright, R. "The ethics of living Jim Crow." Reprinted in P. Rothenberg (Ed.), *Race, class, and gender in the United States: An integrated study,* 3d ed. New York: St. Martin's Press, 1995.

Ideology, Myth, and Magic

Femininity, Masculinity, and 'Gender Roles'

Allan Johnson

Why Make So Much of Gender?

Until the 1970s or so, the word 'sex' was used to refer to anything related to being biologically female or male—as in sex differences or sex change operation. 'Gender' was about grammatical constructions, which often had nothing to do with sex—such as classifying French and Spanish nouns as masculine or feminine. In French, for example, the gender of the noun 'table' is feminine, and the gender of the noun 'virus' is masculine. In practical terms, all this means is that adjectives used to modify the two kinds of nouns have different endings and the nouns take different articles—*le* and *la* in French (the masculine and feminine forms of 'the')—none of which has much of anything to do with being male or female.

This worked well enough until feminists pointed out the difference between biological and social factors that shape people's lives. From this they argued that male privilege and women's oppression are rooted in society, not biology, and therefore are neither inevitable nor immutable. Having a clitoris, for example, is a matter of biology. The nineteenth-century expectation that women were not supposed to enjoy sex, however, and the continuing practice in some areas of the world of removing women's clitorises to control their sexuality have nothing to do with biology and everything to do with women's position in patriarchal societies.[1] To make such distinctions clear, feminists appropriated 'gender' from the realm of grammar and gave it a new meaning focused on social aspects of being female or male. In the new version of things, *having* a clitoris is about sex, while ideas and practices *about* the clitoris are matters of gender.

Although the distinction between biological and social forces is important, it also creates problems by making it seem as though sex is not in any way social but rather exists as a concrete biological reality that we are simply naming in an objective way. Of course, the human body is not a cultural creation, but as Michel Foucault argues, how we think about the body certainly is.[2]

When girls reach puberty, for example, the biology of being female dictates that they will rapidly acquire most of their adult body weight. This includes a naturally higher percentage of fat than is usually found in males. By itself, this is not a problem, but in some patriarchal societies, male-identified standards of female beauty encourage pubescent girls to view their natural growth with a sense of alarm that can stay with them for their entire lives.[3]

This contrasts sharply with other cultures, including most of Europe, whose classical art is rich with full-bodied women (and where women today tend to gain far more weight during pregnancy than do women in the United States) or Western Samoa, where large women are admired for their erotic dancing during some public events. Even in the United States, it was not so long ago that 'sex goddesses' such as Marilyn Monroe were idolized for bodies that would be considered not thin enough by current Hollywood standards and the fashion industry. The obsession with female thinness—the denial of a natural body fullness rooted in biology—is nothing less than a cultural transformation of what it *means* to be female. In this sense, what a female actually *is* as a living being takes a backseat to the ideas a culture makes available for thinking *about* what she is.

Why cultures would include two categories—male and female—is not hard to see, since no society can continue without reproducing its population, and it takes males and females to do it. In other words, sex makes a distinction that is certainly relevant to human existence. But it is one thing to make a clear distinction and quite another to give it cosmic importance, as if who people are as female or male were at the core of their lives, the linchpin of personal identity, and the rock foundation of society and social life.

As Sam Keen tells it, for example, we are men and women before we are people, for "God did not make persons ... only men and women."[4] Robert Bly goes even further, into every cell where men's and women's bodies supposedly "vibrate" at different frequencies, "sing" different songs, and "dance" a different dance.[5] Jungians (who are especially popular with the mythopoetic men's movement)

see human existence as organized around a universal core of male and female archetypes—animus and anima—that presumably exist regardless of time or place.[6] And John Gray would have us believe that women and men are so completely and fundamentally different that they might as well come from different planets.[7]

From a strictly biological perspective, it's hard to see what all the fuss is about since what actually makes us male or female depends on a tiny bit of genetic information out of all other factors, genetic and otherwise, that shape who we are. Some would argue, though, that however simple sex differences may be, they are crucial and central to human life because of their role in reproduction. This has a lot of intuitive appeal, especially since reproduction brought each of us into the world. It cannot, however, carry the weight of explaining why humans have organized so much of social life around an obsession with gender. It cannot carry the weight because if we look closely, we find that human cultures assign less importance to reproduction than we think.

For thousands of years, societies worshipped fertility and used images of pregnant women as religious symbols. Studies of these traditions suggest, however, that the object of reverence and awe was not simply human regeneration or women's part in it but the seemingly miraculous process through which *all* forms of life are renewed and sustained. It is not at all clear that ancient people were obsessed with human reproduction per se rather than with the regeneration of life in general on which human survival depends. Goddess figures were associated with human mothers, for example, but, more important, they were also associated with the Earth and all the manifestations of its fertile abundance, much of which is plant based and essentially asexual. In short, before humans worry about reproducing themselves, they have to worry about the ability of all the species that provide food to reproduce *themselves* so that people who are already born can eat.

Of course there has to be a certain amount of human reproduction for social life to continue. This doesn't mean, however, that reproduction and gender are any more important than other necessary ingredients of human existence. This is especially so given that in its fullest sense, reproduction is a long and complicated process that doesn't end with birth. Human societies do not need babies in order to survive. They need fully functioning adults, and compared with what it takes to produce an adult, sexual reproduction is a walk in the park.

Some might argue that the socialization of children into adults lacks the grand mystery—and hence the fascination and importance—of sexual reproduction and, by extension, sex and gender. But why limit our capacity for wonder to that? I was awed when I saw my children being born, but my sense of wonder did not end there. I will never be able to account for the mysteries of children learning to speak and think and struggle with love, death, and loss. I will never be able to explain my feeling that my children are connected to my body and my soul even though I never carried them inside myself, neither birthed nor nursed them—indeed, like every father, had no body experience that unequivocally said they were mine. Is any of this less amazing, less mysterious, or less vital to the human condition and experience than the male-female coupling in sexual reproduction? And yet we attribute no cosmic importance to the amazing and difficult process through which people come into being or to the caring work that makes it possible—work that both men and women are capable of doing.[8]

Even reproduction in its fullest sense, however, is not much more important than numerous other human necessities. In fact, it may be less so if we judge from how children are actually treated. Throughout most of human history, the death of babies and infants has been a common and relatively uneventful occurrence, as have abortion and infanticide, and where infant mortality is high, babies are often left unnamed until they show that they are likely to survive beyond infancy. For children who do survive, the historical record of child care is unremarkable in much of the world. Children have a long history of being forced to work under appalling conditions or being killed, sold, bartered, and otherwise neglected and abused. This is especially true for females (who, one would think, would be cherished for their reproductive potential) in societies most obsessed with gender distinctions.

None of this means that reproduction doesn't matter. It does suggest, however, that the obsession with sex and gender is not based on some vital interest in human reproduction. What this obsession *does* serve are the interests of patriarchy, by anchoring the whole idea of a male-dominated, male-identified, and male-centered society. After all, if we were human beings first and women or men second, the patriarchal order wouldn't make much sense. Patriarchy, not some inherent human condition, requires that gender assume mythic proportions and take its place as the most defining and confining human characteristic, dwarfing all others by comparison. This is true of most systems of privilege: race distinctions, for example, would barely exist, much less matter, without their link to white privilege.[9]

Using gender to define the core of what makes us human creates huge contradictions by requiring us to define men and women as fundamentally different from each other and yet also as full human beings. On the one hand, this cannot be done, because as soon as human traits are made gender specific, each gender is encouraged to alienate itself from a substantial portion of what makes us human. On the other hand, patriarchy depends on such divisions, because there is no basis for men to dominate women if we see human beings in all their forms as fundamentally the same *as human*. And this is what sets up a contradiction that can be sustained only through some peculiar thinking.

This includes, for example, the notion that men's place in society is defined more by their manhood than their adulthood. What it means to be an adult is fairly constant across societies—the ability and willingness to take responsibility, to care for others, to be productive and contribute to family, community, and society; to be courageous, to live creatively and with awareness. Under patriarchy, however, manhood has to amount to more than this. It has to differ from adult *womanhood* enough to justify organizing social life in a male-identified, male-centered way. This calls for a vision of male adulthood based on a social, psychological, spiritual, and physical territory that men can identify with and defend as exclusively their own.

The only way to accomplish this cultural sleight of hand is to gender what are essentially human qualities by pretending they define manhood rather than adulthood. The idea of heroism, for example, has been assigned almost entirely to patriarchal manhood. From movies and television to literature to the nightly news, our ideas of who and what are heroic focus almost entirely on men and what they do. Where the cultural magic comes in is in the pretense that women are not heroic, which we can see when we look at what heroism actually

consists of. Sam Keen, for example, describes the "heroic male identity" as a capacity to feel outrage in the face of cruelty, to protect the powerless, and to heal those who are broken. This kind of real man knows how "to take care of the place to which he has been entrusted ... to practice the art of stewardship, to oversee, to make judicious use of things, and to conserve for the future ... to make a decision to be in a place, to make commitments, to forge bonds, to put down roots, to translate the feeling of empathy and compassion into an action of caring."[10]

These are all wonderful human qualities, but why should we associate them primarily with manhood and not adulthood? The answer is that gendering such qualities distinguishes and elevates men in relation to women. The falseness of this practice is even more striking when we consider that in many ways what Keen describes as heroic is more common among women than men. If anyone puts down roots, commits to relationships, and organizes a life around empathy, compassion, caring, healing, and even protecting the powerless, it is women. This is especially true in relation to children, whom many fathers seem all too willing to abandon and all too unwilling to provide for when the going gets rough. In contrast, women rarely feel they have a choice about whether to stay with and care for their children and usually will do whatever is necessary to hold families together. Why, then, is heroism gendered as an essential element of manhood even though men are no more heroic than women? The answer is that under patriarchy such beliefs perpetuate the ruse that women and men are fundamentally different and in the process elevates men by appropriating for them a valuable chunk of symbolic territory.

Robert Bly provides another example of such contradictions when he argues that for "soft" men to get in touch with the true spirit of the "wild man," they must overcome their fear of "wildness, irrationality, hairiness, intuition, emotion, the body, and nature."[11] Ironically, almost all of these traits are culturally associated with women, not men. In other words, Bly is telling men to become more like women as a key to being true wild men. He gets into the same kind of trouble when he complains about the suppression of the wild man, because even more striking is the suppression of wildness in women. It is women, not men, who shave the hair from their bodies, who feel compelled to deny their inherent juiciness lest they be accused of being sluts, who learn to look upon their own flesh as an enemy, who are taught that anger and rage are unbecoming in them. Women's potential wildness so threatens patriarchy that it has been suppressed and twisted to the point of being unrecognizable and shows itself on rare and predictably controversial occasions (such as in the film *Thelma and Louise*). Instead of female wildness, patriarchy churns out images of vengeful feminists, mass media caricatures such as Madonna, and the proverbial 'slut,' whose wildness, for all the myths about nymphomania, serves men's imaginations more than women's lives.

When we gender what are inherently human qualities, we lock ourselves in a web of unreality whose main consequence is to keep patriarchy going, for if society is to remain male dominated, male identified, and male centered, women and men must be seen as fundamentally different so that men can control women as 'other.' But the lie cannot abide the underlying truth that all people share a common biological, spiritual, and psychological core, and that qualities such as heroism, caring, and wildness are no more about maleness than they are about femaleness.[12] Rather than confront the contradiction,

we obsess about gender and define it as the core of social order and ourselves. And in struggling to hold the lie together, we keep ourselves from knowing what's really going on and what it's got to do with us. [...].

Patriarchy as Role: The Myth of Gender Roles

Talk about gender rarely goes on for long without involving the idea that femininity and masculinity are organized into gender (or sex) roles that almost magically account for most of what goes on regarding gender. As we see, this is a classic liberal perspective that reduces patriarchy to men and women enacting male and female roles that they learn in childhood, and that pins hopes for change on education and individual enlightenment.

The problem with this approach is that although it may help explain how people participate in patriarchy, it tells us little about the system itself. And what gender roles tell us about men and women as individuals does not amount to much, because as strange as it may seem, it is far from clear that such roles even exist. Many who study gender have all but abandoned the concept as a distraction from the core dynamics that make patriarchy work.[13]

The easiest way to see the problem is to consider what social roles are. Roles are sets of ideas about what is expected of people based on the positions they occupy in social relationships. Lawyer and client, for example, are positions in a relationship, and their associated roles shape how people participate in it. Clients are supposed to tell their lawyers the truth and lawyers are not supposed to betray the confidence. Similarly, mother and child are positions with roles attached—mothers are expected to love, nurture, and protect their children, and children are expected to love and obey their mothers.

Such expectations help define the terms of relationships between people who occupy various positions in social systems. In this, roles both identify people and locate them socially. Ask a woman who is spoon-feeding her child, "What role are you playing now?" and she'll say she's being a mother. But that same woman who is spoon-feeding her invalid mother will answer differently because although her behavior is the same, the relationship and her position in it are different. Notice, then, how roles are tied to identifiable positions in relationships. That is what counts more than anything else in understanding roles and social behavior.

If we now try to think of what a gender role might be, the first problem we run into is that 'male' and 'female' do not name positions in relationships in the way that 'lawyer' and 'client' or 'mother' and 'child' do. Rarely, if ever, would someone answer the question, "What role are you playing right now?" simply with "I'm being a man" or "I'm being a woman," because the mere fact of gender is never enough to tell us who someone *is* in a social situation. When a mother disciplines her child, is she playing the role of mother or the role of woman? And if we reply that they are one and the same, since you cannot be a mother without being female, what do we say about that same woman when she defers respectfully to her grandmother (as granddaughter) or heroically runs into a burning building to rescue her brother (as sister)? Is she playing the same role in each case, the female gender role? Since only females can be sisters, do we explain her risking her life to save her brother as conforming to the female role? No, because 'sister' tells us who she is socially in that situation, while 'female' does not.

It is true that we play many roles that are culturally *associated* with gender, but never are we simply being male or female. Men behave very differently as sons, brothers, uncles, husbands, grandsons, or fathers even though they are men in every case. They behave differently because although they are always men, none of those relationships is primarily about that. If they neglect or abuse an ill parent, for example, they fail in their role as sons, not as men, just as abandoning their children violates their role as fathers. It is true that failing at being fathers, mothers, employees, and such may seem to damage our standing as women and men, but this has more to do with adulthood than gender.

Having said all this, we cannot deny that whether we are identified as female or male has real and powerful effects on perceptions, feelings, and expectations. As I argue shortly, however, this takes the form of a general ideology that can be invoked as needed to help maintain male privilege and the patriarchal order.

Ideas about gender, for example, play an important part in how people are sorted into various social positions: the relative absence of women among scientists, motion picture directors, presidents, prime ministers, and corporate CEOs has much to do with how gender is used as a basis for hiring, firing, and distributing power and rewards. The same is true of the relative absence of men among secretaries, elementary schoolteachers, nurses, and day care workers.[14]

Ideas about gender also affect how people perform occupational and other roles and how others perceive and treat them. Sexual harassment on the job, for example, isn't part of any job description. There is nothing about working for a government official, studying with a college professor, or working on a construction site or serving in the military that remotely calls for sexual harassment. What *does* promote sexual harassment is the gendered inequality of power inherent in such situations and how power, sexuality, and a sense of male control and entitlement are linked together under patriarchy. When a male soldier interprets his authority as a legitimate basis for sexually coercing a woman whose rank is lower than his own, he draws on a patriarchal ideology that goes far beyond job descriptions.

In an important sense, then, gender is linked with ideas about people that shape our perceptions and expectations as we participate in role relationships. This means that while gender may have no direct connection to a given role, it nonetheless can have powerful indirect effects. This is true of many social characteristics such as race, age, ethnicity, and social class. There are no race roles or class roles, for example, but race and class relations are shaped by ideologies that profoundly affect how we perceive and treat ourselves and one another.

As concepts, then, femininity and masculinity play an important part in social life, but not as gender roles or ways of describing men and women as they actually are. Instead, they are a key element in perpetuating male privilege. In particular, they help control potential threats to patriarchy, manage men's competition with other men, and make oppression appear to be a normal part of everyday life.

Maintaining the Gender Order

In perpetuating patriarchy, femininity and masculinity are important tools for social control. This works primarily through people's investment in maintaining a socially acceptable gender identity. Everyone needs to have a relatively stable sense of who they are and a secure place in the world. Given the importance of gender identity in patriarchal societies, attacking people as being insufficiently masculine or feminine can do a lot to control them because it both challenges their sense of who they are and makes them feel like outsiders. This can be a serious enough threat to keep people from doing anything that might undermine or even question the status quo. Attacks on people's gender identities are also effective because masculinity and femininity are such sloppy, contradictory categories, much like insanity and sanity.

Sanity and insanity are vaguely defined concepts full of inconsistency when applied to people in everyday life, so much so that mental health professionals shun them in their work.[15] Whether someone is sane or insane is hardly a matter of scientific certainty (how, for example, would you *prove* you were sane?), and whether a particular behavior is regarded as evidence of insanity depends pretty much on who does it and the social situation. What is seen as 'eccentric' in a wealthy recluse might qualify as 'nuts' in a homeless person walking through a shopping mall, and what is considered pathological in one society or historical period may be seen as normal, inspired, brilliant, or even holy in another.

And yet, for all their arbitrary sloppiness, the categories of sane and insane can be used to devastate people's lives and grant enormous power to anyone authorized to decide who belongs in which. During the slavery era in the United States, for example, the legitimacy of recapturing escaped slaves was reinforced by the medical diagnosis of 'drapetomania,' defined as "an insane desire to run away."[16] In the former

Soviet Union, diagnoses of mental illness were often used to justify the imprisonment of political dissidents in 'mental hospitals.'[17] And throughout the last century, mental illness diagnoses have been used to pathologize and control women's unhappiness and rebellion against patriarchal constraints.[18]

Femininity, masculinity, sanity, and insanity are all concepts plagued by ambiguity, inconsistency, imprecision, and lack of clarity. This would not be a problem if it were not for what happens when they're used to attack someone. Since no one's masculinity or femininity can ever be proved conclusively, anyone can be challenged, and the more importance we give to gender in building a sense of who we are, the more anxious we are likely to feel about it. This is especially true for men, who, as members of the dominant gender group, have the most to lose, which helps explain why men typically get much more worked up over proving their manhood than women do over proving womanhood.

In this sense, femininity and masculinity are powerful weapons of social control that help maintain the patriarchal order. The truth of this is reflected in how inconsistently and unevenly they are applied, for they are invoked primarily when someone threatens patriarchy and its core values. Men and women often appear and behave in ways that do not fit masculine and feminine expectations but without anyone making an issue of it. With children, for example, women may be assertive and powerful and men may be emotionally expressive and tender without inviting criticism that they're being insufficiently feminine or masculine. But when appearance or behavior raises questions about the male-identified, male-dominated, male-centered, and control-obsessed nature of

patriarchy, the heavy cultural artillery comes rolling out, and gender identities get attacked left and right.

Nowhere is this more apparent than in the treatment of lesbian, gay, bisexual, and transgender people, much of whose oppression has relatively little to do with sexual behavior, identity, or orientation per se. Instead, they are attacked because they undermine the patriarchal model that defines manhood in sexual terms and sees male superiority as inherent in maleness itself.[19]

A key aspect of male privilege and women's oppression is rooted in heterosexual relations that subordinate women to men's right to sexual access and control. Gay men undermine this by not relating to women in this way,[20] as do lesbians who choose women rather than men as sexual partners. By the examples set by their own lives, lesbians and gays challenge basic patriarchal assumptions and arrangements. In the process, they often provoke feelings of fear, betrayal, and rage in men who depend on male solidarity and female acquiescence to feel secure in themselves and their privilege.

Transgender women and men also violate a deep assumption about the gender order. When someone who was sex-assigned as male at birth gender-identifies as a woman (a trans woman), or someone who was assigned as female gender-identifies as a man (a trans man, as in the film *Boys Don't Cry*), both violate the patriarchal principle that masculinity and manhood are inseparable from biological maleness. Without this assumption, there is no basis for claiming an inherent male superiority and the privilege that goes with it. It is no surprise, then, that transgender people have shared in little of the increased acceptance achieved by those who are gay, lesbian, or bisexual, and that trans women are especially likely to be victimized by men's violence.[21]

The role of LGBT* oppression in maintaining patriarchy is clear when we look at how it works in practice. When public attention was first focused on lesbians and gays, for example, it was common to stereotype couples as conforming to the model of patriarchal heterosexuality, with one partner in a dominant 'male' role ('butch') and the other in a subordinated 'female' role ('femme'). In part, the stereotyping was a way to dismiss same-sex relationships as merely mimicking heterosexual couples. But it also deflected a potential challenge to patriarchy by portraying gays and lesbians as *sexually* deviant but *socially* conforming to the most important element of patriarchal heterosexuality—the domination of one partner by the other and the identification of dominance with men and masculinity (hence the tendency to describe the 'dominant' partner in a lesbian relationship as masculine).

This has a long social history, as anthropologist David Gilmore notes in his study of masculinity. The ancient Greeks, for example, allowed a man to have male lovers without forfeiting his manhood *unless* he "accepted the passive or receptive role in the sex act, because then he surrendered the male prerogative of control or domination." Similarly, the Romans equated manhood with being sexually active, regardless of the lover's sex.[22] This dynamic is also reflected today in gay behavior among men in prisons, where heterosexual men do not see themselves as gay as long as they are dominant.

A related practice is the use of terms for lesbians and gays as insults against heterosexuals to control behavior or gain competitive advantage.

Among young men, for example, those called 'faggots,' 'fairies,' or 'queers' are often heterosexuals. Rarely is sexual behavior, identity, or orientation the issue, since many younger males know little about either. Instead, what occasions such attacks is often a reluctance to support male solidarity by playing the control and domination game, especially in relation to athletics and females. The target may be a boy who enjoys playing with girls, for example, or a young man who shuns aggressive behavior, who shows little interest in contact sports, who is reluctant to take a dare, who seems emotionally sensitive or vulnerable, or who holds back from joining in banter about women as objects of male sexual conquest. Whether he is gay is irrelevant, because it is only his solidarity with patriarchal values and other males that matters. Often the target of the attack is simply someone chosen more or less at random to be a foil against which other males can assert their claim to manhood. It also creates outsiders who heighten the feeling of being an insider. So a quiet boy in gym class may be taunted as 'queer' as a way to embody the 'other' and clarify and affirm the masculine standing of male classmates.

In this way, a man can elevate himself or make himself feel more secure simply by challenging other men's credentials as real men, like the stereotypical Old West tough guy picking a fight.[23] There seems to be no area of social life where this does not happen—from adolescent boys trading dares to national leaders going out of their way to foster images of toughness ("Bring it on") and dispel suspicion that they might be wimps or otherwise lacking in manly virtues. As most men learn early in life, this is almost every man's Achilles' heel in patriarchal systems, and the only sure protection is to find

---

* LGBT is an acronym for lesbian, gay, bisexual, and transgender. Some activists expand it to include 'queer' (LGBTQ) a general term that refers to those who, in various ways, reject, test, or otherwise transgress the boundaries of what is culturally regarded as normal in relation to gender, gender identity, or sexual orientation and expression. Some regard it as an umbrella term for the other four components of LGBT. 'Queer,' of course, is also routinely used as an insult directed at LGBT people.

a way not to care whether other men consider him masculine.

But this brings on a whole new set of risks that come with being identified as an outsider, if not a traitor to one's gender. As a result, for men who do not identify with patriarchal values, the path of least resistance is not to make a public show of it. When they are with other men, for example, and someone uses misogynist or heterosexist language to insult another man ('pussy,' 'faggot,' 'queer,' etc.), they may remain silent and thereby join in the collusion of male solidarity. Though they may be able to sustain inner lives and intimate relationships relatively free of patriarchal values, their public lives are a different story, especially in the company of men.

When women deviate from feminine expectations, the social response tends to be quite different in both quality and intensity. A woman who dons a tuxedo gets far less negative attention, for example, than a man who wears a dress. At the least he will provoke laughter—intentionally in the case of comedians—and at most he may be suspected of mental instability or risk being assaulted.

A major reason for this is that a woman in man's clothing is seen as dressing up in the uniform of her social superiors, a socially acceptable act of identifying with the dominant group. A man who dresses as a woman, however, will be seen either as making fun of women (which is culturally acceptable) or as identifying with women (which is not). Since solidarity with male dominance is at issue in either case, ambiguity is intolerable, and there is always a reaction of one sort or another. There is less ambiguity when women dress 'as men' because it is assumed they are identifying with men rather than making fun of them. This pattern repeats itself among all kinds of dominant groups, who tend to be blind to the idea that someone might actually ridicule them. This is why there are so few jokes about WASPs in Anglo-identified societies and why men are so hypersensitive when women make even the slightest fun of them *as men*.

Normalizing Privilege and Oppression

As elements of patriarchal culture, femininity and masculinity are part of a way of thinking that makes privilege and oppression seem acceptable and unremarkable—as simply the way things are in everyday life. They are used to portray women and men in ways that justify the oppression of one by the other, that make it seem normal that men should control women, and that give the various aspects of privilege and oppression a taken-for-granted, 'of course' quality that hardly bears notice, much less analysis or challenge.

This is common in all systems of privilege. In the heyday of colonialism, for example, white Europeans typically saw themselves as advanced and civilized compared to the 'primitive,' 'backward,' even 'subhuman' peoples of color whom they colonized. This made it seem only natural that 'superior' Europeans would control and exploit non-Europeans, much as they controlled and exploited domestic animals (also defined as 'other').[24] As Albert Memmi writes, much of colonial ideology is grounded not in real differences but in a racism rooted as deeply as the body itself: "Racism ... penetrates the flesh, the blood and the genes of the victim. It is transformed into fate, destiny, heredity. From then on, the victim's very *being* is contaminated, and likewise *every manifestation of that being*: behavior, body, and soul."[25]

Under patriarchy, gender is defined in similar ways with masculine and feminine imagery portraying male and female as two opposite sorts of human beings. In patriarchal ideology, each gender is assigned an immutable nature fixed in the body and permanently set apart from the other. This is to maintain an almost cosmic polarity on which the universe supposedly depends for balance and order. The fact that human variation does not take the form of opposites—that we are all fundamentally alike with far more in common than whatever distinguishes us—makes no difference at all when it comes to ideology.[26]

As a result, women are objectified and relegated to the position of other. And men, like any dominant group, become the standard against which others are evaluated, just as colonized peoples have been measured against European cultures. As under colonialism, a critical part of this process is the practice of identifying subordinate groups with nature and the Earth and of identifying dominant groups with civilization, science, and other institutional means of control.[27] In patriarchy, this is used to justify male dominance and to portray women as marginal to what really counts in the patriarchal view of civilization and how it works.

The concepts of femininity and masculinity also normalize privilege and oppression by creating images of men and women as harmonious, complementary, and equal, and therefore not involved in a system of privilege at all. We are encouraged to embrace images of women and men as yin and yang, as inherently incomplete beings whose only hope for wholeness lies in joining with the other. Each has a role to play in the life of the other if only we align ourselves in the proper way and accept our predestined positions in the gendered order of things. What this has to do with patriarchal control and male privilege is lost in a haze of longing and romantic cultural imagery.

A critical approach to femininity, masculinity, and gender does not mean we are the same and that ideas to the contrary are ideological props. It does mean, however, that we need to pay attention to how we think about gender as a cultural creation and what happens when we attach so much importance to it. The patriarchal vision of men and women as separate types of human beings whose differences assume cosmic importance in social life has little to do with who we are and everything to do with perpetuating patriarchy, its core values, and the consequences they produce.

Notes

1 This form of female genital mutilation is still common in many regions of Africa and the Middle East. See Fran P. Hosken, *The Hosken Report: Genital and Sexual Mutilation of Females*, 4th rev. ed. (Lexington, MA: Women's International Network News, 1994); and Anika Rahman and Nahid Toubia, eds., *Female Genital Mutilation: A Guide to Laws and Policies Worldwide* (London: Zed Books, 2000).

2 See Michel Foucault, *The History of Sexuality: An Introduction* (Harmondsworth, UK: Penguin, 1981).

3 See S. Bordo, *Unbearable Weight: Feminism, Western Culture, and the Body* (Berkeley: University of California Press, 1995); Kim Chernin, *The Obsession: Reflections on the Tyranny of Slenderness* (New York: Harper and Row, 1981); and Naomi Wolf, *The Beauty Myth: How Images of Beauty Are Used against Women* (New York: Morrow, 1991).

4 Sam Keen, *Fire in the Belly: On Being a Man* (New York: Bantam Books, 1991), 218. Biblical scholar Phyllis Trible has shown Keen to be quite wrong on this. Her translation of the book of Genesis reveals that God created a person named *ha'adam*, the Hebrew

word for *person* with no specification as to sex. Only when God saw the need for human affiliation did he create women and men. See Trible, *God and the Rhetoric of Sexuality* (Philadelphia: Fortress Press, 1978).

5 Robert Bly, *Iron John: A Book about Men* (Reading, MA: Addison-Wesley, 1990), 93–94.

6 See, for example, Eugene Monick, *Phallos: Sacred Image of the Masculine* (Toronto: Inner City Books, 1987); and Robert Moore and Douglas Gillette, *King, Warrior, Magician, Lover: Rediscovering the Archetypes of the Mature Masculine* (San Francisco: HarperCollins, 1990). I have much to say about the new men's movement in later chapters.

7 John Gray, *Men Are from Mars, Women Are from Venus* (New York: HarperCollins, 1993).

8 Sara Ruddick describes this as "maternal work" in her powerful and insightful book, *Maternal Thinking: Towards a Politics of Peace* (Boston: Beacon Press, 1995). She emphasizes that it can be performed by both women and men, although it is, of course, almost always women's responsibility.

9 See Theodore Allen, *The Invention of the White Race*, 2nd ed. (New York: Verso Press, 2012); and Audrey Smedley and Brian Smedley, *Race in North America: Origin and Evolution of a Worldview*, 4th ed. (Boulder, CO: Westview Press, 2011).

10 Keen, *Fire in the Belly*, 166, 180.

11 Bly, *Iron John*, 14.

12 See Bobbi J. Carothers and Harry T. Reis, "Men and Women Are from Earth: Examining the Latent Structure of Gender," *Journal of Personality and Social Psychology* 104, no. 2 (2013): 385–407.

13 For the best such statement that I have seen, see Carrigan, Connell, and Lee, "Hard and Heavy."

14 Although the association of gender with 'wife' and 'husband' may seem obvious, it is less so in light of the fact that in some societies women may marry other women, and even in the United States there is a growing recognition of marriage among gays and lesbians. One can be a woman's spouse without being a man, which means that the relationship between husbands and wives bears a particular relationship to gender—a relationship that varies from one society to another. We should also note that just as 'husband' has meaning beyond the confines of marriage, being a good wife has similar cultural connotations about caring, support, and self-sacrifice in relation to one's spouse that need not necessarily be confined to women. As Judy Syfers put it, "My God, who *wouldn't* want a wife?" "I Want a Wife," *Ms.*, December 1979.

15 Beyond informal everyday usage, 'sane' and 'insane' are primarily legal terms.

16 R. N. Proctor, *Racial Hygiene: Medicine under the Nazis* (Cambridge, MA: Harvard University Press, 1988).

17 See, for example, E. Stover and E. O. Nightingale, *The Breaking of Bodies and Minds: Torture, Psychiatric Abuse, and the Health Professions* (New York: St. Martin's Press, 1985).

18 This has been particularly true of the authority that the male-dominated health profession has used to determine what constitutes a healthy adult woman. See Phyllis Chesler, *Women and Madness* (New York: Doubleday, 1972); and Ehrenreich and English, *For Her Own Good*.

19 See Frank Browning, *The Culture of Desire: Paradox and Perversity in Gay Lives Today* (New York: Crown, 1993); Carrigan, Connell, and Lee, "Hard and Heavy"; and David Gary Comstock, *Violence against Lesbians and Gay Men* (New York: Columbia University Press, 1991).

20 This is not to say that gay men can't be misogynist.

21 Kristin Schilt, *Just One of the Guys? Transgender Men and the Persistence of Gender Inequality* (Chicago: University of Chicago Press, 2011).

22 See Gilmore, *Manhood in the Making*.

23 For an insightful discussion of such issues in the history of American manhood, see Rotundo, *American Manhood*.

24 See Frantz Fanon, *The Wretched of the Earth* (New York: Grove Press, 1963), 38–40.

25 Albert Memmi, *Dominated Man* (New York: Orion Press, 1964), 190.

26 For insightful criticism of dichotomous thinking about gender, see Anne Fausto-Sterling, *Myths of Gender: Biological Theories about Women and Men*, 2nd rev. ed. (New York: Basic Books, 1992); and Carole Pateman, *The Sexual Contract* (Stanford, CA: Stanford University Press, 1988).

27 The cultural association of women with nature is not universal in patriarchal societies, but whatever is associated with women tends to be devalued in favor of what is associated with men.

Place Matters Even More than We Thought

New Insights on the Persistence of Racial Inequality

Margery Austin Turner

Patrick Sharkey's new book, *Stuck in Place: Urban Neighborhoods and the End of Progress toward Racial Equality,* makes a huge contribution to both scholarship and policy debate about racial inequality and the role of neighborhood segregation. Like Denton and Massey's *American Apartheid* and Wilson's *The Truly Disadvantaged, Stuck in Place* marshals data and rigorous statistical analysis to reframe our understanding about these stubbornly complex problems. Sharkey sheds new light on the persistence of racial inequality, forcing us to confront our tragic lack of progress in closing the income gap between blacks and whites. He makes creative use of survey data that track parents and children over several decades, revealing new insights on intergenerational effects of living in severely distressed neighborhoods. And he applies these new insights to what's become a rather stale debate about "people versus place," articulating instead the need for "durable urban policies."

Persistence of Racial Inequality

We are all familiar with the discouraging evidence of persistent gaps in economic outcomes for whites and blacks. Sharkey shows that—although the U.S. made significant progress in narrowing those gaps during the 1960s and 70s—the gains since then have been minimal. And it's not just that a disproportionate share of blacks have been trapped in poverty while many others have achieved middle- and upper-income success. The share of blacks in the poorest fifth of the income distribution is only slightly lower today than it was in 1971, and the share in the richest fifth is only slightly higher. In fact, the cohort of blacks born after the end of legally sanctioned discrimination and segregation is actually doing worse economically than their parents' generation. While many whites who grew up in middle-income families have higher incomes than their parents did, the opposite is true for a majority of blacks.

Intergenerational Neighborhood Effects

Sharkey's biggest contribution comes from his analysis of neighborhood effects. Many scholars have addressed the question of how neighborhood conditions (like poverty, crime and unemployment) affect outcomes for individual adults and children. One of the most common criticisms of research on this topic is that it overstates the causal connection, because people with problems (like low incomes, weak job skills or criminal involvement) "choose"—or are constrained to—problem neighborhoods. If this is the case, the argument goes, conditions in the neighborhood may be caused by the characteristics of people living there, rather than vice versa. So researchers investigating neighborhood effects go to enormous lengths to control for individual and family characteristics to estimate the independent effects of neighborhood conditions.

Sharkey's analysis suggests that this kind of narrow, "all else being equal" analysis may obscure the most important effects of neighborhoods. He makes a compelling case that neighborhood conditions during childhood play a big role in explaining gaps between whites and blacks in income and wealth during adulthood, other things being equal. And neighborhoods may have even more long-lasting effects. Sharkey presents new evidence that living in a poor, segregated neighborhood undermines some outcomes not just for one generation, but across generations. For example, he shows that children whose families lived in poor neighborhoods for two generations score dramatically worse on reading and problem-solving tests than those whose parents grew up in non-poor neighborhoods, other things being equal. In fact, the parents' neighborhood exposure may be *more* important than the child's neighborhood exposure.

This new evidence suggests that conventional research methods actually understate the damage caused by neighborhood poverty and distress. And they also suggest that we may be too quick to declare policies that improve neighborhood conditions ineffective.

If the neighborhood experiences of parents play a big role in shaping the child's academic achievement, then improvements in the child's neighborhood environment might not pay off right away in his or her test scores. It may not be until the next generation that we begin to see substantial gains. If we give up too soon, abandoning our efforts to improve the neighborhoods in which black children grow up, today's daunting achievement gaps will persist for yet another generation.

Durable Urban Policies

By focusing on the persistence of inequality across generations and the long-lasting effects of neighborhood distress, Sharkey makes a compelling case that point-in-time interventions will inevitably fall short. What's required is sustained interventions operating at multiple levels that recognize the reciprocal effects between people and the places where they live. He calls this "durable urban policy."

One of the features I like most about Sharkey's analysis is that it underscores the need for effective policy at multiple geographic scales—federal, state, local and neighborhood. Narrowing the racial equity gap requires a healthy national economy, shaped by federal policies that expand decent-paying jobs with adequate benefits, offer reasonable work supports for low-wage earners, and provide a compassionate safety-net for the most vulnerable. But even the best federal policy solutions would fall short without contributions at the state level, like Medicaid expansion and alternatives to mass incarceration. The economic vitality of individual metros plays an essential role as well, reinforced by city and regional policies that promote growth, expand opportunities, and ensure equal access. And finally, even in vibrant metros, racial disparities will persist without targeted investments in the most distressed neighborhoods and intensive supports for struggling families. (Two new books from Brookings on the metro- and neighborhood-level policy challenges are well worth reading: *Confronting Suburban Poverty in America*, by Berube and Kneebone and *The Metropolitan Revolution* by Katz and Bradley).

Too often, the policymakers, advocates, and practitioners who devote their energies to one or two of these policy domains forget their interdependence. And as a consequence, policy debates too often pit one essential element against another. In my view, Sharkey's framing of "durable urban policy" should remind us how the success of policies and investments at every level depend upon what happens at other levels. And it puts another nail in the coffin of the tired debate about "people-based vs. place-based" policies. Sharkey makes it so abundantly clear that if we care about racial equity, we need a web of "place-conscious" policies that expand opportunities, ensure equal access, and provide supports for people and families.

Assisted Housing Mobility and Neighborhood Redevelopment

Sharkey gives special attention to the long-standing tension between assisted mobility interventions and neighborhood reinvestment strategies as tools for tackling the damaging concentration of poverty and social distress. I agree with his conclusion that we need both, that they can be mutually supportive, and that they must be pursued at a robust, "durable" level. Both of these approaches have proven ineffective when the help they deliver isn't sustained

for enough time or the investments they make are too shallow.

We've learned a lot in recent years about what works (and what doesn't) to help poor minority families escape from severely distressed environments and move to opportunity-rich neighborhoods. Building on encouraging findings from the Gautreaux demonstration, HUD launched the Moving to Opportunity (MTO) demonstration to find out whether poor families would be better off if they could move away from distressed, high-poverty housing projects to live in low-poverty neighborhoods. Last year, HUD released findings from its evaluation of MTO, answering the question: Are families that received the demonstration's experimental treatment (housing counseling and vouchers for rentals in low-poverty neighborhoods) better off than their counterparts in a control group? It turns out that, as a group, the MTO experimental families did enjoy significantly better health and mental health than the control group but not higher employment, incomes, or educational attainment.

Some scholars and policymakers have taken these findings to mean that where we live—and where our kids grow up—doesn't really matter. In fact, the evidence from MTO is much more consistent with Sharkey's diagnosis of neighborhoods' long-term effects. First, the health gains enjoyed by MTO's experimental families are hugely important. High rates of obesity, anxiety, and depression severely degrade a person's quality of life, employability, and parenting abilities. Nobody should understate the value of a policy intervention that helps tackle these chronic health risks.

Second, one likely reason that MTO gains were limited to health outcomes is that the special mobility assistance provided by the demonstration didn't enable the experimental families to sustain access to high-opportunity neighborhoods. Experimental families moved to better-quality housing and safer neighborhoods but few spent more than a year or two in low-poverty neighborhoods. My recent analysis of MTO data (*Benefits of Living in High-Opportunity Neighborhoods*) finds that families who lived for longer periods in neighborhoods with lower poverty did achieve better outcomes in work and school, as well as in health. Specifically, adults who spent more time living in lower-poverty neighborhoods were more likely to have jobs and earn more, other things being equal. And youth (both boys and girls) who spent more time in lower-poverty neighborhoods achieved higher English and math test scores.

This evidence suggests that assisted housing mobility strategies can play an essential role in a "durable urban policy" if they help families move to *and stay in* opportunity-rich neighborhoods. The latest generation of mobility programs reflect these lessons and include new elements like second-move counseling and hands-on help for families who need services and supports in their new neighborhoods. One of the things I admire most about advocates and practitioners working on these strategies is their openness to learning from research about what tools work—or don't work—and their willingness to refine and strengthen their strategies to reflect emerging evidence.

Over the years, we've also gained a lot of knowledge and experience about the effectiveness of efforts to revitalize the severely distressed neighborhoods that residential segregation, discrimination, and redlining created. These efforts implicitly aim for neighborhoods to function as "incubators" for their low-income residents—so that gradual improvements in employment, income, and education will transform the neighborhood as a whole. A recent volume from the Aspen Institute's Roundtable on Community Change (*Voices from the Field III*) acknowledges that although investments in neighborhoods targeted for this kind of revitalization have benefited individual residents who participated in new programs and helped build stronger community leadership and networks, few have produced the population-level transformation they sought.

One explanation for this disappointing outcome is that many of the forces that trap communities and families in distress are outside the control of neighborhood-level interventions—again highlighting the interdependence of policy at multiple scales. But consider an alternative vision of how neighborhoods should function for low-income residents: not as incubators but as launch pads. Like an incubator neighborhood, a launch pad would offer services and supports that poor people need to advance economically. But as families achieved greater economic security, they wouldn't be expected to stay in the neighborhood. Instead, many would move to more desirable (and expensive) neighborhoods, to be replaced by other needy families. Even though the neighborhood as a whole wouldn't show big gains in employment, income, or wealth, people would benefit from having lived there. Neighborhoods that have historically served as entry points for successive waves of immigrants perform in this way, and Sharkey's analysis of neighborhoods that became less distressed (and less damaging) during the 1980s and 1990s confirms that immigrant neighborhoods may be good models of launch pads for low-income families of color.

In the years ahead, policymakers, practitioners, and researchers who care about racial equity should work together to advance the effectiveness of both mobility and reinvestment strategies. We need to keep experimenting, learning, and adapting to make both these approaches more effective and more durable even though, in the near-term, political and fiscal constraints will keep the scale of investment tragically small.

Resources

Berube, Alan and Elizabeth Kneebone. 2013. *Confronting Suburban Poverty in America.* Washington, DC: Brookings Institution Press.

Katz, Bruce and Jennifer Bradley. 2013. *The Metropolitan Revolution: How Cities and Metros Are Fixing Our Broken Politics and Fragile Economy.* Washington, DC: Brookings Institution Press.

Kubisch, Anne C., Patricia Auspos, Prudence Brown and Tom Dewar. 2010. *Voices from the Field III: Lessons and Challenges from Two Decades of Community Change Efforts.* Washington, DC: The Aspen Institute.

Massey, Douglas S. and Nancy Denton. 1993. *American Apartheid: Segregation and the Making of the Underclass.* Cambridge, MA: Harvard University Press.

Turner, Margery Austin, Austin Nichols and Jennifer Comey. 2012. *Benefits of Living in High-Opportunity Neighborhoods: Insights from the Moving to Opportunity Demonstration.* Washington, DC: The Urban Institute, http://www.urban.org/publications/412648.html

Wilson, William Julius. 1987. *The Truly Disadvantaged: The Inner City, the Underclass, and Public Policy.* Chicago: The University of Chicago Press.

The American Dream of Meritocracy

Heather Beth Johnson

The American Dream has been continually re-invented over time, so that for each generation of Americans it has held different meanings. And since the phrase "the American Dream" could mean different things to every one of us, it might be more accurate to call it "the American Dreams." At its core, however, some aspects of the Dream (or Dreams) are consistently fundamental. Simply, the American Dream explains the logic of our country's social system. *It is a way (or perhaps the way) we are to understand how American society operates.* It is how we make sense of our particular social structure. The American Dream rests on the idea that, with hard work and personal determination anyone, regardless of background, has an equal opportunity to achieve his or her aspirations. The American Dream promises that our system functions as a meritocracy. *Within a meritocracy people get ahead or behind based on what they earn and deserve, rather than what circumstances they were born into.* This notion of is central to the American Dream, and is the central logic of how our system is supposed to operate. The American Dream, in many ways, defines us and sets our system apart from others.

Given the importance of the American Dream to our national identity, and the enormity of it in shaping our core ideologies, it is curious how little attention the idea has received in academe, especially in the social sciences. Until relatively recently, no one had traced the history of its origins, meanings, or cultural impacts. In the past decade, however, groundbreaking scholarship on the American Dream has yielded important understandings. We know, for example, that the principles of the American Dream were promoted by even the very first settlers to arrive from Britain. Later, the American Dream was central to the charter of the United States when the Declaration of Independence was created. And although the phrase "the American Dream" does not appear to have been coined until around 1931, it has quickly become recognizable the world over. The American Dream is, for better or for worse, the central creed of our nation.

As a creed, the American Dream represents a basic belief in the power and capacity of the individual. Deeply embedded in this belief is a particular notion of individual agency—the idea that over the course of our own lives we are each accountable for whatever position we find ourselves in. Full collective potential for this agency, though, depends on exactly that which the dream promises: A system of opportunity, so that regardless of background each individual has an equal chance to prosper. The American Dream promises that an egalitarian system will allow individuals to advance based on their own merit. This promise resonates throughout contemporary American society telling us—through multiple variations on a theme, through school assignments and television advertisements, through song lyrics and newspaper stories—that in a meritocratic process we rise or fall self-reliantly. So, despite differences across generations and regardless we each have unique hopes and dreams, we share the American Dream of meritocracy in common: That is, we are each subject—in one way or another—to our nationalist ideology of meritocracy.

Meritocracy explains not only how our society works but how inequality exists. The idea is that what we reap—good or bad—is merited; whatever we have, whatever our status, whatever our place in the social world, we earn. A system of meritocracy does not assert equality *per se*—within any social hierarchy some individuals will inevitably be positioned higher and some lower—rather, it justifies inequality of social positioning by the meritocratic process itself. Inequality of outcomes is justified and legitimized by equality of opportunity. This meritocratic idea has roots dating back to the British colonialists' aspirations for a society founded in a "natural aristocracy." In their vision upward mobility and prominence would be merited and achieved, rather than ascribed. For those first families settling from Europe, this vision was a defiant rebellion from other forms of social structure where social rank was inherited based on such distinctions as family lineage, royalty, and caste. Although they never precisely defined how merit should be measured, it was always clear how it should not be: achievement based on individual merit is not unearned advantage; it is not inherited privilege. A meritocratic system is contingent upon a societal commitment to fair competition so that no individual or group is advantaged or disadvantaged by the positions or predicaments of their ancestors.

The American Dream of meritocracy is at once a simple idea and a complex national ethos. For some people the American Dream may simply represent owning a home, while for others it might represent striking it rich. Although those may be part of what the American Dream means for many people, as a foundational ideology it is about more than material abundance or a place with streets-paved-with-gold. It is about opportunity—not just an opportunity, but equal opportunity. It is about not just a chance, but equal chances. In her landmark book, *Facing Up to the American Dream: Race, Class, and the Soul of a Nation*, political scientist Jennifer Hochschild explicates the American Dream and identifies its main tenets. She distinguishes key premises which interlock to form its philosophical foundation. These premises include meritocracy, the notion that in our social system upward and downward mobility is based on personal achievement so that people get ahead or behind based on merit; equal opportunity, the notion that all members of society are given equal opportunity for social mobility; individualism, the notion that each individual makes it on his or her own; and the open society, the notion that the United States is a free country, the melting pot of the world, the land of opportunity for all people. As Hochschild outlines, the American Dream is a set of deeply held beliefs, a particular mindset. It is a particular way of viewing the world, and it is a particular way in which we want the world to view us. For many Americans, the American Dream is a great source of pride. But even many who question it as an accurate portrayal of social life believe strongly in the egalitarian and inclusive principles for which it stands.

As a dominant ideology the American Dream echoes throughout our nation, it carries on through generations, and can cement in crystal form in our minds. But it can also be easily taken for granted. For as central the American Dream is to our national identity, we don't consciously reflect on it often. As historian Jim Cullen has noted, the American Dream is "an idea that seems to envelop us as unmistakably as the air we breathe." We can be reminded of it, without even being aware, every time we are told that we will achieve if we work hard enough, or that we could have achieved if we had only worked harder. The American Dream can inspire great aspirations and explain great achievements, and it can depress us as we ponder our regrets. It is malleable enough to fit in almost any social situation. We can use it to justify our accomplishments: I earned it on my own. This is the result of my hard work. I deserve this. And we can feel the sting of it as we question ourselves: Should I have worked harder? Could I have gone farther? Why am I not where he is? And, we can use it to question others' social standing: Why doesn't she try harder? Doesn't he want more? Why don't they make better choices? The American Dream is all around us, and, in many ways it is in us.

Ultimately, the American Dream is an explanation for the hierarchical ordering of our class positions in our social world. It explains our relative rank as the result of solely our own doing, not as the result of social forces or the circumstances we find ourselves in. It is not surprising, then, that Americans might genuinely believe that they independently earn and deserve their class positions—the dominant ideology of our culture tells them so. This internalized sense of class positioning has been

the subject of scholarly research, especially in regards to working-class and poor families. In Richard Sennett and Jonathan Cobb's pivotal book *The Hidden Injuries of Class*, for example, they discuss the "hidden injury" of the internal class conflict experienced among working-class men. They wrote that "Every question of identity as an image of social place in a hierarchy is also a question of social value. ... This is the context in which all questions of personal and social legitimacy occur." The American Dream helps to sustain these "hidden injuries" by bombarding people with the message that their social place—and their social value, their self-worth—is directly and exclusively the result of their own actions.

In their interviews for this book, people spoke in depth and at length about the American Dream, despite the fact that in the first 182 interviews the families were not even asked about it. Those parents were told that the project was to study assets and inequality, and during the interviews they were asked to speak about the communities they lived in, their children's schools, and their families' financial histories. Over and over, however, the focus of the interviews turned to beliefs in meritocracy as families repeatedly brought up the subject and wove it into the conversations. I must admit that I myself was surprised with the extent to which the interview findings were so ideological in nature. And I was even more surprised when interviews—including those interviews from the second phase which did directly ask people about their thoughts on the American Dream—revealed the depths of people's commitment to, and belief in, meritocracy as a real and valid explanation for how contemporary American society operates. People from all walks of life spoke forthrightly of their belief in meritocracy, not just as rhetoric, but as an accurate explanation of our social system.

Trying to confirm these findings has been frustrating due to the lack of qualitative studies that have asked people in-depth about their perspectives on the American Dream. Curiously, even in terms of quantitative studies, surprisingly few public opinion polls have been conducted on the subject of the American Dream. However, related social survey data that do exist reflect that Americans overwhelmingly believe that their country operates as a meritocracy. Indeed, after his review of the data political scientist Everett Carl Ladd concluded that survey research "shows Americans holding tenaciously and distinctively to the central elements of their founding ideology." He found Americans' belief in the American Dream to be more intense, pervasive, and firmly entrenched than generally recognized. Very recent qualitative research on post-civil rights views also finds that in in-depth interviews people are remarkably insistent in their beliefs that the playing field is level, that meritocracy is real. While these findings are definitely in line with my own, perhaps the most compelling affirmation for me has been to discover that other sociologists doing in-depth interviewing on subjects not explicitly focused on the American Dream are finding, as I have, that respondents consistently evoke the American Dream—specifically the notion of meritocracy—as their own theme in interviews. In the 200 interviews conducted for this study, what families said, their views, their decisions, and their experiences, were explicitly framed by their belief in meritocracy. These families' perspectives give a vivid account of the place and significance of the American Dream in contemporary life.

The reality of wealth in America though—the way it is acquired, distributed, and the way it is used—is a direct contradiction to these fundamental ideas. In interviews with American families we have seen a way how that plays out. Examining school decision-making (just one arena wherein families potentially experience the ramifications of wealth inequality), those parents from backgrounds of even moderate wealth had a significant advantage over parents with family histories of wealth poverty. Disproportionately white, wealth-holding parents used the financial assistance, intergenerational transfers, and security of their family wealth to help access schools for their own children that were viewed as advantageous by all of the parents. Meanwhile, parents without family wealth to rely upon, who were disproportionately black, were navigating the same arena unaided, with relatively limited resources and constrained capacities. *A central incongruity surfaces when families' school decisions are considered in the context of the American Dream: the assets that the wealth-holding families had owned, relied upon, and utilized in choosing schools had most often originated from non-merit sources.* Inherited wealth and the security of family wealth were critical advantages being passed along to the next generation—advantages often unearned by the parents themselves, and always unearned by their children.

A foundational conflict exists between the meritocratic values of the American Dream and the structure of intergenerational wealth inequality. Simply, advantageous resources inherited and passed along in families are not attained through individual achievement. Although wealth can, of course, be earned by an individual entirely independently, in the case of the families we spoke with it had not. This is the aspect of family wealth that concerns us here. Family wealth generates unearned advantages for those who have it. It is a form of privilege. In light of their beliefs in the American Dream, how do those families who present the most transparent contradiction to the idea of meritocracy—families with wealth privilege—understand their positioning and the unearned advantages they pass along to their children?

We could presume that as with other forms of privilege (such as race privilege or gender privilege) wealth privilege would generally appear invisible and be taken for granted by those who have it. However, one of the most striking aspects of the interviews was the acknowledgement of wealth privilege on the part of wealth-holding families. The parents who had benefited from family wealth acknowledged a structure of wealth inequality that grants privilege to some families and disadvantage to others, and they acknowledged the advantages they were passing along to the next generation through the schools that they chose. [...].

Conviction in Meritocracy: Hard Work or Lack Thereof

Carter: The fact of the matter is because you get some assistance from your parents doesn't mean that you haven't primarily achieved anything on your own. The fact of the matter is getting a down payment on a house means you were able to get a house sooner, but you still have to make the payments on the house, you still have to do everything necessary to maintain that house. So yeah, it's a help, but it's not the overriding factor.

Int: You think the overriding factor is your own—

Carter: Your own psyche. ... At the end of the day, hard work is the most important ingredient—in anybody's success.

Int: Think so?

Carter: Yes. The determination to be successful is like the tide, you know? You can't stop it.

Faith & Carter Martin,
Homemaker & Attorney,
White, Washington, D.C.

Tracei Diamond, a black single mother from St. Louis, spent much of her interview answering "no" to every question regarding any financial assistance she might have received and explaining the lack of any family financial resources available to her. As a full time banquet waitress at a private country club, Tracei's annual income was $24,000, she had zero net financial assets, and held only a high school degree. Tracei talked about how she sees the members of the country club at functions and events and thinks about how they and their children had advantages that she and her three children simply did not have. She spoke at length, for example, about how the schools "out there" (where the country club was located) were "good schools," how the teachers "really work with them" (the students), and how overall "the education is better." In Tracei's view, for as much as she would like to be able to give her kids those same kinds of opportunities, she simply cannot afford the move to such an area. On top of supporting her three children on her own (she was receiving no child support), Tracei also was doing whatever she could to financially support her younger sister and their mother.

Tracei's interview was typical in that she articulated clear recognition of a structured inequality amongst families that blatantly and categorically translates into unequal educational opportunities for children of different family wealth backgrounds. Yet also typical was Tracei's outright rejection of this inequality and of unequal opportunity. Tracei recognized it and rejected it at the same time. After Tracei had talked about how "wealthy families" get the "better schools," she was asked about how a family's wealth plays a factor in their children's access to quality education. She replied: "It really doesn't have an impact on it. I guess pretty much it depends on you, as far as what kind of life you will have for your child." When she was asked if wealth has any impact, she said "I don't really look at it like that. So, like I say, money definitely doesn't have anything to do with it." When asked to explain further, Tracei did: "It's basically what the parents want or whatever, that's the only thing I really can see. It just depends on how they raise them really." Despite their perspectives that class inequality structures life chances, Tracei and the other families maintained their belief that merit—not money—is what matters; they maintained with conviction their belief in meritocracy.

It was striking to hear disadvantaged parents talk so vehemently about meritocracy, to hear them assert repeatedly that positions in society are earned entirely through hard work and personal achievement, and to hear them deny family wealth inequality as a legitimate explanation. But considering that many of these parents had no direct experience with wealth privilege, that they had no awareness of the extent to which wealthy families are using and extending intergenerational transfers of assets, that they did not know for sure how much others are advantaged by unearned resources, then it makes sense how they clung so resolutely to the dominant ideology. What was most remarkable, however, is that those parents with family wealth who had spoken openly of their unearned advantages, who had so plainly seen and felt and known wealth privilege in motion in their own lives, were, at the same time, insistent that meritocracy is an accurate and realistic explanation for social stratification in America. In an interview in St. Louis, Briggette and Joe Barry spoke in detail of the financial help they had received from their parents. *They openly declared that these resources had allowed for a lifestyle they would not otherwise have had. After listing extensive financial assistance, the security of family wealth, and the many advantages they have had, the Barrys insisted that the way they had earned their assets was through hard work.*

The Barrys were not atypical of the white middle-class families interviewed; on the contrary, they portrayed the sentiments of families like them in the sample. Their socioeconomic positions were due, in large part, to the inheritance and accumulative advantages of family wealth, yet at the same time they were adamant that they singlehandedly earned and deserved their places in society. These families' insistence that they had, "worked their butts off" for what they had was astonishing. They listed in detail the help they had received from their families: Financial assistance with major purchases, down payments on houses, school tuition for children, "loans" that were later forgiven, etc. They catalogued the gifts they had received from family members for birthdays, graduations, weddings, and births of children. They discussed the numerous ways their extended families had been financially generous over the years by providing used cars, old furniture, flight tickets home for holidays, family vacations, dining out, kids' back-to-school clothes, and groceries, to name a few. They described the "push" and the "safety net" that comes with family wealth: Feeling that they have had "a head start" or "an edge" over others, knowing they would have something to fall back on in a financial pinch, and the expectation of future inheritances. While they talked about, listed, and described these things when asked, they repeatedly emphasized how hard they had worked for all that they owned and how much they deserved their stations in life.

Regardless of background, families used the American Dream of meritocracy to explain their assertion that anyone can be anything and do anything and get anywhere with hard work. They stressed that hard work or lack thereof was the determinant of each individual's position in society. But for those with family wealth, what was most notable was how they implied, implicitly and explicitly, that their own advantages as well as the advantages they were passing along to their children were earned and deserved autonomously—through hard work, perseverance, and determination alone.

Another example comes from our interview with Chris and Peter Ackerman, a white couple in their early thirties who lived in a white suburb of St. Louis. They had three kids, ages six, three, and two. They had been married for ten years and both worked in management positions on the staff of a local university. Their combined annual income was $83,000, their net worth $210,000, and their net financial assets totaled $91,500. This couple owned savings accounts, savings bonds, small trust funds for each child, and a boat worth $12,500. They had received significant financial assistance from their families, including help with a down payment on their first home, which they bought when they married. The equity from that house was later used as a down payment for an upgraded home when they had their children. Chris and Peter's parents financed their college educations; they never had to take out student loans; their children regularly received cash gifts and savings bonds from their grandparents on holidays and birthdays; Chris's parents had often paid for the family to vacation with them; Peter's parents had bought many of their major household appliances for them, as well as their car; and so on. They talked about how appreciative they were of all this help, about how they would not be in the position that they are without it. Despite this acknowledgement, Chris and Peter continually insisted that their wealth had been achieved single-handedly:

> Int: How did you acquire the assets you own?
>
> Chris: By working.
>
> Peter: Saving, working.
>
> Chris: Working and saving, working and saving. That's basically how we do it.

The Ackermans and many of their peers simultaneously acknowledged the power of their wealth privilege and avowed that it does not really matter. They were resolute in their explanation that hard work and determination had gotten them to where they are. For as much as they were upfront about the structure of wealth, they also depicted social positioning as independently earned and deserved. As one young mother from just outside of New York City put it, "You know—and I'm not bragging, I'm not saying anything—but it just comes from setting your priorities straight, and taking care of business!" In discussing hard work and individual achievement people often spoke louder, quicker, and sometimes at a higher pitch. People leaned forward or moved in toward the tape recorder's microphone as if to want to be sure they were heard clearly on this. They spoke with fervor and conviction when crediting themselves with their own success. For example, in talking with Lily and Jonathan Boothe, a white wealthy family from the New York City area, Jonathan had been quite serene throughout the interview. However, when we began talking about the Boothes' perspectives on success and achievement, Jonathan became noticeably more vivacious.

Just as people with wealth credited themselves for their success, conversely, those who lacked family wealth blamed themselves. Conviction in meritocracy worked both ways, and meritocracy could justify both positions. The themes of "sticking to one's ideals," "being focused," "motivated," and "willing to work hard" were as consistent in interviews with working-class and impoverished families as they were in affluent families. People blamed themselves for their inability to attain what they wished for and wanted for themselves and their children, even when they were starting from the most disadvantaged backgrounds. One parent from Boston explained that, compared to others, she comes up short because "I did a lot of fooling around." A mother from St. Louis said, "I would say that I am a little bit limited. But it's nobody's fault but my own. So I can't complain." And still another parent lamented, "If I was to make more, better, wiser decisions along the way, I wouldn't have the debt that I have now."

Most people have regrets in life, and maybe if the families who were struggling to make ends meet had made "more, better, wiser decisions along the way," things would have turned out differently for them. Maybe not. But one of the things that stood out the most about this explanation was that many of these families had in fact done extraordinarily well for themselves. More often than not, however, the fruits of unaided self-achievement simply paled in comparison to the results of self-achievement combined with the advantages of family wealth. Still, throughout the interviews, parents from poor and working-class family backgrounds compared themselves to more "well-off" others, blamed themselves, and legitimized their situations by saying they should have worked harder. While to some extent they understood that a structure of wealth inequality existed, and while they recognized the real advantages for those with family wealth, they simultaneously blamed themselves for not having worked harder and done better than they had.

The interviews also show the power of hope. For these families the American Dream was hope. It held out hope that what is wanted will happen, and that what is wanted can be expected. It held out hope that children's life chances were all equally unconstrained. It held out hope that the world is just. To think otherwise (to think that the world is not just) would be heart-breaking to any parent. And, I believe, many parents fear that to think otherwise (to think that the world is not just) could potentially—if conveyed to children—break the spirit of any child. So they hold on to the American Dream, they hold on to their hope. This hope was reflected in the parents' perspectives regarding themselves, the social system they are acting on and within, and—most importantly—their children.

Discussion Questions

1. What makes the idea of meritocracy so compelling to Americans that people believe in it, even when it is contradicted by evidence all around them?
2. How would the members of your family explain their economic situation to themselves and to others? As the result of hard work and talent alone?
3. Why do you think none of the respondents talked about the role of luck in their own successes and failures?
4. Do you think that the American Dream can survive the increasing economic inequality which has is transforming American society? Why or why not?

References

Hochschild, Jennifer. 1995. *Facing Up to the American Dream: Race, Class, and the Soul of a Nation*. Princeton, NJ: Princeton University Press.

———. 1981. *What's Fair? American Beliefs about Distributive Justice*. Cambridge, MA: Harvard University Press.

Schwartz, John E. 1997. *Illusions of Opportunity: the American Dream in Question*. New York: W. W. Norton.

Sennett, Richard & Cobb, Jonathan. 1972. *The Hidden Injuries of Class*. New York: W. W. Norton.

Reflexive Questions

1. How has your gender, race, culture, social class, ability status, and sexual orientation shaped your identity and who you have become today?

2. How do these aspects of your identity intersect and work together to develop your sense of self?

3. If you had to choose one aspect of your identity that has most strongly shaped you, which one would it be and why? If certain aspects were not there or were taken away (e.g., gender, race, religion), how would that affect your life?

4. What aspects of your identity do you attribute more to nature (your genetic inheritance), and which ones do you attribute more to your nurture (your upbringing and socialization)?

5. When you think about yourself, what aspects of your identity seem to work in your favor (privilege) and which ones work against you (disadvantage)?

6. Which social forces affect you either positively to afford you advantages or negatively to afford you disadvantages?

7. How do the above aspects of identity shift when you are in different contexts (e.g., home, work, college, another city or country, with a certain group of people)?

8. How did your culture, religion, and place where you grew up shape who you are today?

9. What is one thing about you that has caused you to experience the most discrimination? How has that affected your sense of self and your relationship to others?

10. What does it mean to develop well across each life stage? What do you think are the most important factors for positive development? Which factors can derail a person's positive development?

CHAPTER 3

Pregnancy and Childbirth

Introduction

Worldwide, there are countless values, beliefs, and practices that reflect the complexity of pregnancy. Some pregnancies are planned, while others are not. The factors that influence this decision, or lack thereof, are complex and often due to people's access to resources such as information, contraception, and healthcare. Through an intersectional analysis, one can see how societal structures impact this access. For example, economic stability, religious, cultural, and traditional gender norms influence girls and women's control of their bodies. Furthermore, womanhood is often tied to reproduction and relationships to others. In many parts of the world, a woman's worth is tied to her ability to reproduce and raise children. Although family scholars consider gender and how it influences developmental outcomes, we rarely engage in the much-needed analysis of how pregnancy can potentially become a site of oppression.

One way in which pregnant women face oppression relates to legislation and debates on abortion and reproductive rights. Central to such debates is the controversial issue of whether the fetus has personhood (Himma, 2005). On the one hand, those who are pro-life consider the fetus a moral person, while on the other hand, those who are pro-choice do not often position the fetus as such. Positioning the fetus as a being with subjective experiences makes abortion a moral dilemma. That is, many question whether abortion is akin to murder. Although it may seem tempting to engage with this dilemma, we often fail to notice how the personhood of the fetus and the personhood of the woman are held in opposition. When seen in this vein, abortion debates continue to question the personhood of women.

Another example is centered around how issues of biocapital influence the lives of women. Biocapitalism refers to the process through which materials are derived from human and nonhuman bodies and assigned monetary value (Lettow, 2018). An example of biocapital is reproduction. Assisted reproductive technologies (i.e., egg and sperm donation and surrogacy) allow women to comodify their bodies in exchange for selling a service, having little to no claim of the product—the child (Vora, 2009). Because women experience higher rates of poverty than men (e.g., the feminization of poverty), reproduction can become a source of labor. For example, women receive monetary compensation for donating eggs, offering the child for adoption, or for being a commercial surrogate; however, market conditions affect the level of compensation they receive (Kenney & McGowan, 2004). Furthermore, assisted reproductive technologies have implications for transnational issues, leading to complexity of bioethics and global economies (Sarojini, Marwah, & Shenoi, 2011). In fact, human egg donation becomes a site of racialization and White supremacy, especially in the market value of the fertility industry (Deomampo, 2019).

Good nutrition, health care, and a positive and safe environment are essential for optimal health of the mother and unborn baby. However, when family scholars engage in an intersectional analysis, pregnancy and prenatal development become more nuanced as a developmental phase. Measures need to be taken to ensure an infant's health and viability; however, when considering international context and power structures, the commercialization of reproduction can be harmful to women and place infants at risk. The readings selected for this chapter do not necessarily address women's personhood, abortion debates, or biocapitalism, but they provide the reader with another perspective, as factors related to intersectionality and context continue to be core issues affecting women, pregnancy, and the socioeconomics of becoming a parent. The readings in this chapter offer a glimpse at some of the challenges and struggles related to sexual orientation, race, immigration status, and social class as they intersect with fertility, pregnancy, and the birthing process.

Summary of Readings

In the first reading, "**The Colour of Loss,**" Elizabeth Ruth writes her first-person account of the discrimination she experienced as a lesbian seeking reproductive technologies to help her become pregnant. She brings to light the biased and prejudiced nature of the medical industry, especially as it relates to reproductive health care among same-gender couples. A lack of medical knowledge prevents women from making informed choices about their health. This lack of knowledge includes contradicting information, blatant misinformation, and a lack of research on fertilization procedures and fertility drugs. Moreover, when it comes to medical procedures related to conception, heterosexual couples have inherent heteronormative privilege, and lesbian couples face obstacles due to homophobia and heteronormative bias.

The second reading, "**Pregnant Behind Bars: The Shameful Lack of Prenatal Care in U.S. Prisons and Jails**" by Victoria Law, offers a glimpse of the challenges of pregnant women who are incarcerated. Many pregnant women in the prison system face challenges such as lack of medical care, hunger, restraint during labor, separation from the infant after 48 hours, risk of gestational diabetes from poor nutrition, and an increased risk of future diabetes. The author mentions several examples of injustices faced by pregnant women in prison. For example, one woman was not believed when she described her bodily changes, like lower back pain, cramps, and heavy discharge, and when she gave birth without assistance, her infant died. Another woman was shackled while giving birth to her twins. Later, she was told that her twins died due to a treatable infection. Another woman was told that her mother would not be allowed guardianship of her infant, and she was not informed about what happened to her child. These abuses led to a class-action lawsuit filed by the state of Arizona, the ACLU, and the Prison Law Office in 2012. The author states that places like Delaware have implemented group homes for incarcerated pregnant women and their children so that the mothers can care for their children and the children do not have to be separated from their mothers. This reading helps us reflect more on the needs of women often facing a multitude of vulnerabilities (e.g., poverty, systemic racism, sexism), many of which led them to the prison system.

The third reading, "**Culturally Competent Care for Aboriginal Women: A Case for Culturally Competent Care for Aboriginal Women Giving Birth in Hospital Settings**" by Birch et al., emphasizes the need for cultural sensitivity in the healthcare of Aboriginal women. They discussed the need to examine how Aboriginal beliefs about health intersect with Western healthcare systems in Canada. The authors discuss the importance of educating healthcare providers on the needs of Aboriginal women giving birth in order to offer culturally competent care. Aboriginal women participate in a Holistic health approach, which is a balance of physical, mental, spiritual, and emotional needs. The women typically rely on traditional healing medicines such as herbs, tobacco, etc., and think that giving birth in hospital settings with technology is foreign. The reading discusses the importance of healthcare providers understanding these cultural practices and needs so that they can be supportive and offer an atmosphere of respect that many Aboriginal women do not receive. In contrast to the Western, individualistic view of health that emphasizes a binary of mind and body, Aboriginal concepts of health are more holistic; wellness means balancing mental, emotional, physical, and spiritual health. Understanding cultural differences between Western and Aboriginal cultures is crucial to providing culturally competent care. By appreciating cultural nuances, Canadian healthcare providers can create an atmosphere of respect and empowerment for Aboriginal women and their families.

The last reading, "**Childbirth at the Global Crossroads**" by Arlie Hochschild, brings to light how issues related to social class (poverty and wealth), gender, and power intersect to create a commercial surrogate service. In this reading, we can take a closer look at the personal narratives of Indian women who are paid to be surrogate mothers, live in a group home for nine months, often with their children, and abide by the rules of the home/agency. The factors that influence this type of business/service are complex. The author helps elucidate the effects that commercial surrogacy has on the lives of women involved in this reproductive industry. The very process of conception, caring for herself and the fetus as it forms and develops inside of her, and giving birth, is a deeply personal and intimate process. Yet, given the economic needs of these women and families, it is evident that the short-term benefits of food, shelter, and money help ensure their survival, despite the emotional toll it may have on them.

In sum, it is our hope that these readings will help students reflect on the personal, structural, and financial complexities related to pregnancy and the business of making and having a child. While these processes are deeply personal, they are also transnational, financial, and commercialized. As Collins (1990) reminds us, our social location, such as our gender, race, class, and other systems, operates as a "matrix of domination" that exploits the labor and restricts the citizenship rights of people. This ability to have access or restrict access to resources depends on how we are situated in relation to major social structures. Given the above-mentioned processes related to context and intersectionality, it is vital that we critically evaluate and question how our social locations affect women's, men's and gender non-conforming people's access to reproductive information, rights, health, and processes.

References

Deomampo, D. (2019). Racialized Commodities: Race and value in human egg donation. *Medical anthropology, 7*(38), 1–14. https://doi.org/10/1080/0145974.2019.1570188

Himma, K. E. (2005). A dualist analysis of abortion: personhood and the concept of self qua experiential subject. *Journal of Medical Ethics, 31*(1), 48–55. doi:10.1136/jme.2002.000828

Kenney, N. J., & McGowan, M. (2014). Egg donation compensation: ethical and legal challenges. *Medicolegal & Bioethics, 9.* http://dx.doi.org/10.2147/MB.551328

Lettow, S. (2018). Biocapitalism. *Krisis, 2,* 13–14. Retrieved from http://proxy-remote.galib.uga.edu:80/login?url=https://search.proquest.com/docview/2291069960?accountid=14537

Sarojini, N., Marwah, V., & Shenoi, A. (2011). Globalisation of birth markets: a case study of assisted reproductive technologies in India. *Globalization and health, 7*(1), 27–36. http://www.globalizationandhealth.com/content/7/1/27

Vora, K. (2009). Indian transnational surrogacy and the commodification of vital energy. *Subjectivity, 28*(1), 266–278. https://doi.org/10.1057/sub.2009.14

ILLUSTRATION Jaime Drew

The Colour of Loss

Elizabeth Ruth

I know something of missed opportunities, stunted and misweven cells, futures undone. I know relentless, raging optimisms, babies not yet wished into being. Yes, I know all too well these trying, trying times that so many face, because, for almost five years, my partner and I have watched younger women with buoyant, hopeful energy push double strollers through fertility clinic doors and flip the pages of glossy magazines while we wait for blood draws and ultrasounds, and a successful pregnancy. We've celebrated friends and family as they gave birth to their second children, while we experienced miscarriages and continued trying for our first. They are everywhere, the fresh, naive faces. They don't look haggard, weary, defeated. How I've hated them for their blind privilege, and especially for their optimism. Not being able to bear a child will break your heart, but hopes raised and dashed, month after month, will bleed all joy from living.

Flesh of my flesh,

Blood of my blood, who will I be without you?

Who would I have been if you'd stayed?

More than a decade ago, at the University of Toronto, I concentrated my graduate studies in the areas of women's reproductive and mental health, researched the history of various cutting-edge drug treatments and pored over recommendations made by the Royal Commission on New Reproductive And Genetic Technologies. I wrote papers on the ethics of anonymous sperm and egg donation and argued, from a feminist point of view, for regulation. I investigated potential long-term side effects of pills like Clomid, both on women who took them and on the offspring produced. I learned that very little research had been done in the area. There are still no long-term studies—which is why doctors are able to tell me, with great assurance, that there's no link between the fertility drugs so many of us now swallow and inject, and the cancers all women fear.

So, when I decided, on my 35th birthday, to have a child, I wasn't naive about the history of the Western medical model responding to women's health. I knew other drugs deemed safe had later been proven dangerous and taken off the market. I believed our bodies, especially our hormonal bodies, are routinely perceived and treated as defective, or in need of control and management, and that childbirth itself has become a state of emergency in North America, with C-sections and early interventions fast becoming the norm. I also expected that, because I was old, reproductively speaking, and because my partner was a woman, I'd find myself in a doctor's office. At the very least, I had a sperm access issue. What I couldn't envision then, and swore I'd never do, was to give over control of my body. Of course, that's exactly what I ended up doing.

I conceived without drugs on our first attempt, using frozen sperm from an anonymous donor. I was optimistic, with no visible stress in my life. I knew it wouldn't be long before I was pregnant. The procedure was a simple, non-invasive insemination (sperm deposited in the vagina, at the opening of the cervix) and not, as it would be for years subsequently, the highly touted, invasive and more expensive intrauterine insemination (IUI). I was certain I was pregnant within hours, though people told me it wasn't possible to know so soon. Two weeks later, the pregnancy was confirmed with a blood test. Unfortunately, I miscarried at eight weeks. Despite reassurances to the contrary, I wondered whether my hypothyroidism was a factor.

My thyroid, previously regulated with a prescription medication, had spiralled out of control the instant I became pregnant. I searched for answers online, in bookstores, and at the library as to why this might've been and how to prevent it happening again. Though I can never know for certain what caused that miscarriage, the doctor doubted it was my thyroid. (Another fertility doctor was adamant that it probably *had* been the cause.) What exactly is the relationship between hypothyroidism and miscarriage? I still don't know. I was told to grieve and move on, because miscarriage is common, and an easy first conception is a sign of fertility. I tried for another year without success.

That first doctor had many lesbian patients, yet her receptionist routinely asked for my husband's health card number. The doctor, a walking infomercial who answered our questions before we had a chance to finish asking them, never spent more than 10 minutes with us. She told us she wouldn't speak with my partner, as I was the patient, so that's how it was for almost a year—both of us at morning ultrasounds and blood draws (10 days per month), both at scheduled information appointments, and both at two monthly inseminations—but only one of us invisible. I only understood this to be discriminatory after a straight couple I knew began seeing the same doctor and, though they were also using anonymous donor sperm, the male partner in that couple was actively involved in conversations and decisionmaking. That first doctor was a gynecologist and reproductive specialist, but not an endocrinologist, which is the reason I finally left. I was willing to put up with discrimination because I wasn't sure the situation would be different at another clinic, and finding a new doctor meant being on a waiting list for months.

My second fertility doctor, reportedly one of the best in city, was extensively renovating his multimillion-dollar Toronto clinic while we dug ourselves deeper into debt, stepped through plaster dust and suffered summers in the attic waiting room without air conditioning. My thousand dollars a month for two inseminations wouldn't buy the leather chair I sat on while I waited. This specialist recommended fertility drugs to us on my first visit because of my age, he said, and because I was a lesbian, not because any tests showed me to be infertile. "Fertility drugs will save time," he told us. He looked me up and down. "My guess is you'll respond best to injectables."

His plan was the usual—to have me inject gonadotropins and carpet-bomb my uterus with multiple eggs each cycle, thereby increasing the likelihood of conception with our frozen sperm. I wondered whether his reputation and his stats (and, perhaps, research funding) were dependent upon high success rates. Would I lower those success rates if I took too long to conceive? If I took a natural amount of time to conceive? So I said no to fertility drugs. For two more long years I said no.

"What does yes really mean in a system where saying no feels impossible?"

Definitions of infertility have shifted dramatically in the past decade, arguably since drugs have been more accessible. Whereas once a woman would be referred to a specialist after two years of unsuccessfully trying with her male partner, now many doctors refer after one year, and increasingly after only six months of consecutive attempts. Why? Have women's bodies changed? Or, perhaps our eggs are a new cash crop?

Refusing drugs was not easy. I secretly wondered if I shouldn't give in, if I wasn't denying myself because of ideological principles, and overinflating the potential unknown risks. It was harder to say no when most of my friends, many of them lesbian, had said yes without similar reservations. My partner was becoming anxious about our mounting debt. It was also a monthly struggle with the doctor, who, at each insemination, while he sat with his face between my legs and deposited sperm into my uterus, would remind me of how low my chances of conceiving were without drugs. He'd remind me of how relatively ineffective frozen sperm was, compared with fresh, despite the fact that we had no access to fresh—he said he would not treat us with a known donor. Once, he told me that my becoming pregnant a second time would be the equivalent of winning the lottery.

We tried to find a doctor who would allow us to do IUIs with a known donor's sperm, but we were plainly told, by three, that they weren't legally permitted to have a known donor's sperm washed and inseminated in me. Was it, as one specialist claimed, because if I contracted an STI the clinic would be liable? Or, as another claimed, because they worried our known donor might be gay, and gay men are not allowed to donate sperm? The third specialist told me bluntly that it was because I was a lesbian and he wasn't comfortable. We pointed out that heterosexual patients could also contract STIs and that I should have an equal right to the donor of my choice. Those conversations left my partner and I frustrated, confused and angry, but apparently powerless, since doctors' hands were tied because of legislation. For anyone to be willing to wash and inseminate me with this better, fresher sperm of a known donor, they'd have to be convinced I was in a sexual relationship with that donor. In other words, I'd have to lie. I've known of lesbian couples who've done this, at great cost to their personal relationships, their anxiety levels and their senses of self.

Interestingly, The Assisted Human Reproduction Act and Health Canada are clear that no distinction is to be made between semen from a known donor (including men who are not a patient's sexual partner) and semen from anonymous donors. Further, according to Dr. Leah Steele and Dr. H Strotmann, in their May 2006 article for *Canadian Family Physician,* doctors shouldn't use fresh semen in their offices, and "any physician planning therapeutic donor insemination is legally obliged to use semen that's been cryo preserved for six months." What we initially thought was denial of service to us because of paternalistic legal barriers was, in fact, something more subtle and insidious. Our doctors weren't willing to bend the rules for us, but they'd routinely do so for their heterosexual clients, and hide their bias behind a misleading veil of legality. Meanwhile, we continued to purchase frozen sperm each month, at a cost of $500 per sample, plus $150 to the specialist and a $50 delivery charge to the cryobank.

Watching friends conceive through the same clinics and with the same doctors was difficult, but knowing that some had an edge on us because they were straight was infuriating. We learned that by not doing IVF (in vitro fertilization) we were moving through a second-rate treatment model. Had I wanted to, IVF was not something we could have afforded. The costs are staggering, ranging from between $6,000 to $10,000 per cycle. But the odds are better. With IVF, a woman receives gonadotropin injections to stimulate her follicles to produce multiple eggs, which are then surgically retrieved from her body, fertilized in a laboratory and reimplanted in that same woman—or in another woman. Our friends used their relatives' cashed-in RRSPs to do IVF with frozen sperm and, afterwards, told us the attention they received as IVF patients was better than when just doing intrauterine inseminations; they'd felt like a priority. We never felt like anyone's priority. In fact, we felt like a nuisance. Those friends conceived on their second IVF attempt, after years of doing exactly what we were still stuck doing.

One of the many mornings when I was at the clinic to cycle monitor (psycho monitor I call it), I met a patient who was also a GP. We broke the unwritten code of silence in the waiting room and exchanged details about our treatments. By this point, I'd grown desperate and had, against my own judgment, agreed to three cycles of fertility drugs. My partner's insurance plan offered partial coverage for a limited number of attempts. The GP-patient told me that in her private practice, because of anecdotal research, she advises women not to take gonadotropin injections or Clomid, even for the recommended period of less than six months, but that she had been taking Clomid for eight months and was terrified of what she was doing to her body. Most of all, she was fearful of what she was willing to do. Like me, she'd entered the process with a bottom line that was continually shifting, so she no longer trusted herself to be able to stop. Would she end up with ovarian cancer in 10 years? Would it all be worth it if she conceived?

Clomiphene, a.k.a. Clomid and Serophene, is a relatively inexpensive drug (about $60 per month) taken from day four or five of your cycle through to near ovulation. It's meant to promote regular ovulation. Injectable gonadotropins are synthetic or (originally) distilled from menopausal women's urine, and they push your body to mature multiple eggs. They cost us, on average, $1,700 per month. Both classes of drugs have common side effects compromising the likelihood of conception: thinning of cervical fluids in the case of Clomid and ovarian hyperstimulation syndrome in the case of injectables.

Why are there no long-term studies? Who benefits from not tracking such information? Would being fully informed stop women from taking fertility drugs? Probably not. But it would guide our decision-making, as more of us might decide against drug treatments altogether, or disentangle from them earlier. Knowing the actual risks to long-term health would, at the very least, make our consent to treatment legitimate. What does yes really mean in a system where saying no feels impossible?

There are known short-term side effects of the drugs (read the packaging). On injectables,

I experienced headaches, skin rashes, racing heart, chest pain, numbness in my toes, anxiety and ovaries hyperstimulated to many times their natural size, making it dangerous for me to do physical activity (like riding my bicycle), lest they rupture. Each week, after a pregnancy test would come back negative and my hormones would drop from artificially high to normal again, acute depression would set in. I skipped months of cycles after each round, waiting for my ovaries to return to normal size. On Clomid, I had a steady migraine, weight gain and anxiety. All of this is routine. And the treatments are unsuccessful just as often as they are successful. Even with technology, the doctor is, at best, guessing what dose of drug might produce the desired number of follicles in a given woman.

Women who take fertility drugs feel like we're making decisions largely in the dark, leaping at fate, hoping to land softly, babe in arms. We feel uniquely unsuccessful when the drugs don't bring the desired result, and overexposed as we share personal information with myriad professionals who use terms like "poor egg quality," "incompetent uterus" and the present-day scarlet letters, "advanced maternal age." We make martyrs of ourselves, but no one notices because the very cultural definition of motherhood is tangled up in martyrdom.

After all, fertility has always been a life-and-death matter—women have been dying for their children for centuries, or been expected to do so. In some parts of the world, women still die in childbirth or because of related complications. But in wealthy nations, like ours, where "choice" can be purchased on VISA or paid for in cash, the notion of dying to be mom isn't something doctors or patients are willing to acknowledge.

We can't, because admitting that we are, in effect, guinea pigs in a field with less than

"Sometimes we forget that our bodies, that we, are there at all.

scientific diagnostics and treatments, and maybe putting our lives in danger, might mean stopping. Doctors can't admit to undocumented risks without calling their purpose into question.

After another year and thousands of dollars more debt, I walked away from the second doctor, too. I came to see that the stress and treatment were anathema to my well-being. It became clear one day, as my partner and I waited almost half an hour for the doctor to perform the intrauterine insemination. Our sperm was thawed and we began to panic—after 20 minutes of being exposed to air, frozen sperm begins to die. My partner found the doctor and asked him to please hurry. He waved her off. Again, five minutes later, my partner went to fetch him. This time he came with the nurse, but was obviously angry. He ignored my greeting and briskly told me to lie down. I was already undressed, my feet in the stirrups. As he threaded the catheter through my cervix, an unpleasant, if not painful experience, he raised his voice and reprimanded us: "You people think you know best. If I tell you the sperm is fine, it's fine. This'll never work if you don't trust me. You ask too many questions. Next month I'll prepare cue cards and hold them up so I don't have to keep repeating myself!"

I should've kicked him in the face, but of course I was desperate to get the sperm into me as quickly as possible. When it was done, I stared at the beige ceiling I'd stared at for so long and knew I couldn't harm myself in this way any longer. Perhaps it was my lack of belief in the drugs and biomedical model, but I would never succeed at a clinic. Leaving was scary, too, for it meant being willing to risk the unknown, believing more in my intuition about my body being healthy than in "expert" advice. Possibly, it meant never becoming pregnant.

I sought out an experienced traditional Chinese doctor who performed acupuncture on me several times a month and reminded me at each hour-and-a-half-long visit that there was nothing fundamentally wrong with me, that I was still young enough, healthy enough and deserving enough to become somebody's mother. Each time I left her office, I felt more at home in my own skin, like myself again. More than three years of paying doctors to tell me I was defective, show me statistics on rates of pregnancy for my age group and push drugs as the only hope for success produced no pregnancy. Three months within a traditional Chinese model, and I was pregnant for the second time.

North American boomers who saw the advantages of the pill were weaned on the nebulous concept of freedom of reproductive choice, and that limited perspective has filtered down to us, their children. You'd think that having greater reproductive options (assuming you can pay) would be easy. But, of course, it's not.

Having choice means bearing the burden of responsibility for our yeses and our nos and that's a heavy burden to carry when the outcome is so profound. In fact, it requires superhuman strength to say no to drugs, or exploratory surgery, or even daily ultrasounds, without feeling you're potentially closing off your option of having children, without doubting yourself and being judged as treatment-resistant. So what if there are side effects? Our second doctor told me that if I wanted to be a mother badly enough, I'd take a second mortgage on our home and increase my odds by doing IVF.

I was a new homeowner who barely scraped into the market. (We ultimately sold the house.) What about women who don't own homes or can't even pay their rent? What about people who can't imagine doing what we did: maxing out credit cards and overdraft? What about the more logical option of having both my partner and I try, thereby doubling our monthly egg pool and odds, without drugs?

I met a young lesbian couple on Pride Day one year, pushing a double stroller. They'd tried to conceive without technology, when, perhaps out of frustration, or because of the financial stress of paying for anonymous sperm, they'd agreed to gonadotropin injections. "Whatever happens to you," one mother told me, "don't do it." Their twins had been born premature and one baby needed several emergency surgeries because part of his intestine was sitting outside his body. He'd have lingering health problems as an adult. The couple was drained, emotionally and financially, and had spent their first year as new parents separate, each caring for one baby, both worried for their gravely ill newborn.

"But it worked out," I said. "I mean those are the chances all parents take, right?"

"Maybe," said the other mother. "We love the boys. ..." She spoke with the honesty of a stranger and the raw wisdom that only comes from surviving a trauma. "But we wouldn't do it again if we knew." I smiled politely, envying them their children, despite their arduous journey. I dismissed it as an unusual case, exceptional, and made their situation rare. But stress on prospective parents' relationships, massive debt, pregnancy and delivery complications, high rates of multiple births, lack of social support for same-sex parents trying to have a family, lack of support in general for all people within the fertility machine—these are the norm.

A free-choice analysis of the present-day fertility model is short-sighted and stops at easy, non-threatening questions about over-medication and equal access. It doesn't extend to an institutional critique of the industry, which would look at how profit-driven motives might be guiding or defining (in)fertility. There have been other feminist critiques of the new reproductive and genetic technologies before now, but what's new today is that lesbians and single women of all sexual orientations—those who need access to safe sperm, women who are not by any objective measure infertile—are using these technologies in great numbers. As a result, more women in Canada are being referred to fertility clinics and undergoing drug treatments when they've failed to conceive fast enough. We ought to be challenging how the fertility machine participates in—or prevents—the creation of non-traditional families, and we must demand an honest examination of the relationship between pharmaceuticals and fertility doctors. We might even want to talk about the social construction of infertility itself. What frightens me most isn't the actual drug treatments, though they may indeed prove dangerous, but the culture of uncritical thinking and denial in which we willingly submit to them.

Yet, women are not passive, ignorant, dupes. We're simply pressed to keep trying under our doctor's hand by our own deep desires, pushed on by those who want us to be happy, or by a medically driven society that believes in taking drugs the way other people, in less secular times, believed in God. We're just plain frightened at the prospect of never being anyone's mother. Above all, we

become disembodied through the process of being poked and prodded, and treated under the assumption that we're defective. We stop believing in our bodies, and eventually stop listening to them and begin following directions. Sometimes we forget that our bodies, that *we,* are there at all. After a time, we see with blinkers, registering only the minority of women for whom the drugs work, holding them up as beacons of hope. We search out those in clinics and on television with whom we might identify, and all the while we're tempted, painfully tempted, by that candy dangling before us—a baby, a healthy baby, our baby.

It is possible to have too many choices.

I know the denial, minimization and myopia that are required when on a mission to conceive. My partner and I know the repeated disappointment, anguish over what life might look like if pregnancy never happens, and how these fears cause you to begin to welcome the drugs despite risks, to welcome anything that brings a baby, so hey—even twins begin to sound great. After all, two babies are better than none. We patients grow into this mindset because we must contort, intellectually and emotionally, to fit a model of treatment that's inflexible, pathologically negative and refuses to see us in holistic terms. Should we hear only the stories of those who succeed? Are *they* not perhaps the most biased, the least likely to question their treatments? Don't they just need to get on with the business of parenting?

I don't wish to demonize individual women who opt for fertility drugs, or argue against the existence of actual infertility, but I want to remind us all that, in our brave new world, the interpretation of infertility and the need for fertility treatments is always political. We must think critically. Are the drugs dangerous? Are there alternatives, such as acupuncture, that could be explored first? Are queers in a uniquely vulnerable position within the system, and if so, how is that being played out? But most significantly, is the model for treatment itself generating or exacerbating the very problem it purports to rectify? Can infertility or subfertility be an iatrogenic disorder? In other words, can childlessness result from the inherent stress and negativity of Western infertility treatments?

"We stop believing in our bodies, and eventually stop listening to them, and begin following directions."

I conceived the first time when I'd not yet become embroiled in the medicalization of my own fertility, when I was making the decisions, had no debt or stress, and before I came to believe my body was too old and defective to bear a child. I conceived the second time only when I disentangled from the medical model, took back control of my body and the process, and was therefore able to trust both. Finding an encouraging, supportive, traditional Chinese doctor who engaged with my questions and fears made a difference. She didn't dismiss me as irrational or uneducated, because the model she works from teaches that there *is* a connection between the mind and body, and that the body is something to be respected, not only corrected. Instead of statistics and percentages, she offered stories of success. She also told me openly that I might never become, or stay, pregnant.

Despite all that's happened, I still find myself alone by the blue-note light of the Alberta moon listening to k.d. lang sing

"Helpless" while I write this and miscarry, for a second time. My thyroid, once more shocked into overdrive by pregnancy, failed to respond to aggressive treatment. Again, doctors tell me it probably had nothing to do with the miscarriage, but this time I don't believe them. I think of the incredible debt I've accumulated paying for something I once swallowed for free, the books I might've written all these years, the trips my partner and I might've taken had every penny not been going towards buying sperm and paying for inseminations. I think of other undiscovered dreams, secondary for so long, that never had a chance to materialize. And I think it's time to stop. Yes, there comes a final, terrible point of clarity for any woman trying in vain to have a child, where the choice that matters most becomes the choice between the life before us now and the life we so desperately imagine creating.

Again, I wonder what sins I've committed to draw such bad luck my way? I see my future laid out before me, and that future may be too quiet, free of obligation. Perhaps there'll be no new love. I'm alone tonight but I'm only one of many childless mothers watching cradles rock empty, seemingly banished for no reason from the club that is motherhood. This is all I know: Reproductive technology offers queers options we couldn't have dreamed decades ago, but we're not the intended or desired recipients. And, there is no meant to be. Babies are random gifts from gods, as well as measured reproductive science, bestowed upon the undeserving just as often (though it seems to me now, more often) as the deserving. Trying to become pregnant for a long time is like swimming in molasses, a dark curse that grows more powerful with each negative pregnancy test, each appointment, invasive procedure or injection. So while a tiny beam of light fades from me tonight, a clawing, crystalline sense of frustration also fades. The struggling and trying and hoping and waiting feels as though it's finally coming to an end. Even the world beyond my keyboard seems to be slipping away. In some senses it's a relief. Yet, tomorrow I'll pick up the phone and call my partner, who's at home in Toronto, naive and still hopeful, and I'll read her this story I don't want to tell. My story. Our story. And I'll ask:

If red is the colour of love, what colour is loss?

A year after this article was written, my partner and I are thrilled to be expecting a baby in December. Ignoring the advice of three fertility doctors, my partner conceived without using fertility drugs.

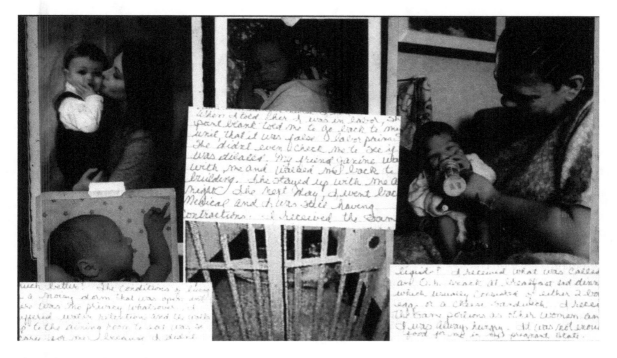

Photos/Letters Via Victoria Law

Photos, clockwise from top L: Sierra Watts in her only visit with her son, Oak Lee, before he was adopted; Minna Long's son Noah; Michelle Barton with her daughter, Semaj, in February 2014, hours after birth; the mattress in the Wichita County Jail cell where Nicole Guerrero gave birth, June 12, 2012; Noah's twin brother. Joseph. Excerpts from a 2015 letter from a pregnant prisoner in Oklahoma.

Pregnant Behind Bars

Victoria Law

The shameful lack of prenatal care in U.S. prisons and jails

AT 5 A.M, ON JUNE 12, 2012, lying on a mat in a locked jail cell, without a doctor, Nicole Guerrero gave birth.

Guerrero was eight-and-a-half months pregnant when she arrived 10 days earlier at Texas' Wichita County Jail. The medical malpractice lawsuit Guerrero has filed—against the county, the jail's healthcare contractor, Correctional Healthcare Management, and one of the jail's nurses, LaDonna Anderson—claims she began experiencing lower back pain, cramps, heavy vaginal discharge and bleeding on June 11. The nurse on duty told her there was no cause for concern until she had bled through two sanitary napkins. Several painful hours later, Guerrero pushed the medical emergency button in her cell.

At 3:30 a.m., more than four hours later, Guerrero was finally taken to the nurse's station. Guerrero says she showed Anderson her used sanitary pads filled with blood and fluids, but was not examined. Instead, she was taken to a one-person holding cell with no toilet, sink or emergency call button, known as the "cage." At 5 a.m., her water broke. She called out to Anderson, but, Guerrero says, Anderson refused to check on her. Shortly after, Guerrero felt her daughter's head breach. A passing guard stopped to assist her, and Guerrero, unable to keep from pushing, gave birth on a blood and pus-covered mattress.

The baby was dark purple and unresponsive, with the umbilical cord wrapped around her neck. When Anderson arrived minutes later, she did not attempt to revive the baby, Guerrero says. The EMTs got there after 20 minutes and rushed the baby to the hospital. Guerrero remained in the cage, where she delivered the placenta. At 6:30 a.m., the baby was pronounced dead.

No Data, No Problem

The number of women who cycle through U.S. jails is increasing by approximately 1.6 percent each year, to 109,100 in 2014, while the number of women in prisons has risen nearly tenfold in the past 40 years, to 111,300 in 2013. Though the United States accounts for only 5 percent of the world's women, it has 33 percent of the world's women prisoners.

There is no current data on how many of those women are pregnant. In 2004, a Bureau of Justice Statistics survey found that 3 percent of women in federal prisons and 4 percent of those in state prisons were pregnant upon arrival. The statistics on pregnancy in local jails is older—a 2002 survey found that 5 percent of women entered local jails pregnant. At those rates, approximately 9,430 pregnant women are incarcerated annually.

There is even less data on what kind of care pregnant prisoners receive: their nutrition, pre-natal check-ups and medical attention, which can be a matter of infant life or death in cases like Guerrero's. Nor do we hear much about the trauma of pregnancy and childbirth under prison conditions, or the heartbreak of having an infant taken away hours after birth.

In a six-month investigation, *In These Times* reached out to dozens of incarcerated women, activists and advocates, seeking to reach women who had been pregnant behind bars. Twelve came forward to share their stories.

In These Times then requested information about pregnancy care and policies from the prisons and jails where the women were incarcerated. Only four of eight complied. Correct Care Solutions, a contractor that provides healthcare at Nashville's Davidson County Jail, refused, declaring that private companies do not need to open their records to public scrutiny. Those that did provide records typically took months to do so, and the data was often poor. Phoenix's Maricopa County Jail records live births, miscarriages and abortions, but not stillbirths. Washington's Clark County Jail keeps track of the number of medical visits by pregnant women (42 in 2014), but not the number of pregnant women incarcerated.

However, from the 12 individual women's accounts, a picture began to emerge. Many received no medical care or experienced long waits. Most were constantly hungry. Others were restrained during labor, delivery or postpartum recovery, even in states that ban the practice. The majority of those who gave birth in custody had their infants taken away within 48 hours.

Care and Loathing

Medical neglect can endanger the lives of pregnant women as well as fetuses.

Diana Claitor, executive director of the Jail Project of Texas, says she interviewed a young woman whose complaints of extreme pain were dismissed by a jail doctor as morning sickness. But "it was because her fetus had been dead for some time," says Claitor, who also examined the woman's medical records. "She was very ill and could have died." The woman was finally taken to the emergency room, where she delivered the dead fetus.

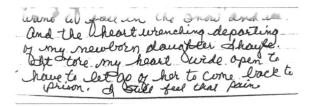

Letter from a pregnant prisoner in Oklahoma, 2015

Bridgette Gibbs says that, despite telling staff of her history of miscarriages, she received no medical attention in two months of pregnancy at the Westchester County, N.Y., jail. She still hadn't been examined when, early in her second trimester, she went into labor. Before being taken to the hospital, she was strip-searched and shackled at the hands, waist and ankles. She gave birth to twins handcuffed to the bed, and was still handcuffed there hours later when she learned that her premature newborns had died. The hospital told her that the early labor was the result of a treatable infection. (The Westchester County Department of Correction could not confirm or deny her story, saying that it no longer has Gibbs' records.)

In Arizona, complaints about prison medical care prompted the ACLU and the Prison Law Office to file a class-action suit in 2012. An accompanying investigation uncovered two incidents in the summer of 2013 when officials at the state prison in Perryville dismissed women's claims that they were going into labor. One woman said that it took two hours to convince the guards to transport her to the hospital. She gave birth 20 minutes after arrival. The other said nurses refused to believe her water had broken even after it tested positive for amniotic fluid. Officers sent her to the hospital only when she began screaming.

'It Hurts to Be Hungry Like That'

Pregnant women especially need nutrient-rich food. It's typically recommended that they eat three or more servings of fresh fruits, vegetables, dairy and protein each day, as well as several servings of whole grain breads or other complex carbohydrates. Nutritional deficits can, for example, increase the risk of gestational diabetes, which can cause a fetus's trunk and shoulders to become too big for vaginal birth.

"Withholding healthy food from a pregnant woman is withholding medical care," says Tess Timoney, a certified nurse-midwife and director of women's HIV services at New York's Bronx-Lebanon Hospital.

In jails and prisons, meal times, foods and portions are limited. More than half of the dozen women interviewed by *In These Times* recalled an overwhelming, unrelenting hunger.

Some jails and prisons specify a special pregnancy diet and an additional snack. But women report that these foods are often inadequate.

Twenty-three-year-old Minna Long was pregnant with twins when she entered the Clark County jail in Washington state in 2010. She received an extra 8-ounce carton of milk with all three meals, but, she recalls, "There were countless times the milk was expired and sour and I couldn't drink it." Her pregnancy also caused her to feel revulsion toward many of the foods served. During her four months in jail, she subsisted on milk, fruit and cold cereal, as well as commissary purchases of donuts, candy, trail mix, meat and cheese sticks, and flavored popcorn.

> My most memorable experience is realizing adoption was my only choice. The best experience is when I got to prison and would be able to eat better.

Letter from Jackie, who gave birth while incarcerated and is still in prison

Kandyce (who is still incarcerated, and asked that her last name not be used and her prison not be specified, for fear of retaliation) says that when she was pregnant in prison in 2014, between breakfast and dinner was a 12-hour wait. "It hurts to be hungry like that," she says.

'I don't Ever Want to Be Pregnant Again'

Even when medical care is adequate, the restrictions and confinement inherent in prisons can make pregnancy and birthing traumatic. It is standard policy in U.S. prisons and jails to strip search prisoners upon entering and exiting, including a squat and cough, with no exceptions for pregnant or postpartum women.

A five-year study by the nonprofit Correctional Association of New York found that while there were delays in pregnancy care upon arrival, most women in state prisons then received prenatal care at roughly the frequency recommended by the U.S. Department of Health. Waiting for those visits, however, was often painful. Women were seated for up to five hours on a narrow wooden bench with no food or water. Though pregnant women are supposed to move around frequently to ease muscle tension and prevent fluid build-up, the women were not allowed to stand, and were often threatened with disciplinary tickets if they leaned back.

Kandyce saw a doctor regularly during her pregnancy, but the nurses, she says, strictly enforced the prison's policies and often refused her doctor's requests. For instance, her doctor asked for a wedge pillow and an extra mattress to supplement the thin prison mattress. "As you get bigger, they get thinner," Kandyce recalls. "I'm already heavyset and being pregnant was even worse—I couldn't really breathe if I wasn't propped up." The nurses denied her the pillow but allowed extra blankets. Those were confiscated by officers in the monthly room search, however, and each time, Kandyce had to go to the sergeant to get them back. "By the time I was eight months pregnant, I was really frustrated," she said.

Medical staff told Kandyce that she needed a caesarean section. The night before, she was placed in the prison's Inpatient Unit. "You're in a room by yourself—no TV, no book, no nothing," she recalls. "All you do is sit in this room by yourself. You know that you're about to have your baby [and] that you're going to have to give your daughter up. All you have time to do is think about it." By 11 a.m., when officers arrived to transport her to the hospital, she no longer wanted to go through with it. "I just wanted to keep my baby with me."

Normally, caesarean sections require only regional anesthesia, but when Kandyce arrived at the hospital, she was so stressed and anxious that the doctor—a man she had never met—decided to put her to sleep. "My daughter was going to be here and everything was wrong," she recalls thinking. Her daughter was born healthy, but the entire experience was so devastating that Kandyce says, "I don't ever want to be pregnant again."

Each time Minna Long went to court, jail staff placed her in handcuffs, ankle cuffs and a waist chain, a practice known as shackling. Then, they stopped. Washington had become the seventh state to pass legislation restricting the shackling of pregnant women. That was in 2010; fourteen states have followed suit.

But advocacy groups in California, Massachusetts, New York, Pennsylvania and Texas have found that the practice persists despite bans. Sierra Watts, 37, incarcerated in Washington state just after the law went into effect, learned this firsthand. While she was allowed to give birth without restraints, she was then cuffed to the bed. Her son was placed in a cradle next to her. "I just had to lean over to get him out, but it's harder when you can't move that far," she says.

The Washington State Department of Corrections says that "a post-incident review determined she was not supposed to be cuffed."

Sierra's Choice

For Sierra Watts, the worst part wasn't the shackling, but what followed. Although she had granted her mother temporary guardianship, child welfare workers told her that they would not send her son to live with his grandmother. After spending 24 hours with her newborn, Watts was taken back to prison without knowing her son's fate. Because he was born on a Friday, he was to remain in the hospital until child welfare offices opened on Monday.

As Watts tells this story, her eyes fill with tears. "He was going to stay in the hospital with nobody holding him, nobody knows where he's going, nobody's even going to tell me where he's going," she says. "Nobody said [to me], 'It's going to be okay. We're going to watch him. We won't let anything happen to him.'" She did not learn where he was placed until the following Tuesday. The next—and last—time she saw him in person was during a prison visit one year later, shortly before he was adopted.

Under the 1997 Adoption and Safe Families Act, if a child is in foster care for 15 of 22 months, the state must begin proceedings to terminate parental rights. Watts says that she initially fought to maintain custody, but finally signed away her rights. "They told me that if I was to take it to trial and lose, then I wouldn't be able to get photos or hear how he's doing or send him cards or anything," she says. She receives photos of her son, age 3, several times a year, but never sees or speaks to him.

That's relatively common for incarcerated women who give birth; two other women interviewed by *In These Times* arranged for their babies to be adopted.

By contrast, when Michelle Barton, 37, gave birth in an Oklahoma prison in 2013, she knew that her baby would be safe with her sister-in-law, who was already taking care of Barton's 3-year-old son until her release from prison.

But she still cried when it was time to leave the hospital. Upon her return to prison, she was reminded how little motherhood means there. A nurse had given her a piece of paper with her daughter's footprint. The officer who strip-searched her upon arrival threw it away. "Getting strip searched is nothing," Barton says, but watching her daughter's footprint tossed into the garbage "just tore my heart out."

Another Way

Michelle Barton's daughter was 18 months old when Barton was released from prison in August. She boarded a bus to Oklahoma City with only the clothes on her back. Although she has a job lined up at Church's Chicken, she is homeless and cannot reclaim her two young children from her sister-in-law until she finds affordable housing.

The Mabel Bassett Correctional Center spends $14,800 per year to incarcerate each woman. Barton was there for nearly two years. What if that $29,600 had been spent directly on resources for her and her family?

Oklahoma's incarceration cost is dramatically low. At the Washington Corrections Center for Women, incarcerating each woman costs $44,400 per year. Sierra Watts was sentenced to 40 months. What if the $148,000 spent to imprison her had instead been spent to help her stay out of the prison system?

The UN Rules for the Treatment of Women Prisoners and Non-custodial Measures for Women Offenders, known as the Bangkok Rules, recommend that for a pregnant woman or a child's primary caregiver, "non-custodial measures should be preferred where possible and appropriate." But pregnancy and parenting are rarely taken into consideration in the U.S. legal system. Across the nation, more than 120,000 mothers and 1.1 million fathers of children under 18 are behind bars. Approximately 10 million children have had a parent incarcerated at some point in their lives.

Recognizing that maternal incarceration can devastate children, some states are exploring alternatives. In November 2014, the Delaware Department of Correction created New Expectations, a group home for pregnant women with drug addictions who would otherwise be imprisoned. The home provides meals, prenatal vitamins, clothing, toys, intensive substance abuse counseling, and classes on infant care, parenting, breastfeeding, nutrition and budgeting. But the facility is run by the Department of Corrections and its healthcare provider, Connections Community Support Programs, and the doors are locked and alarmed.

Bridgette Gibbs and her daughters

James Trory

By contrast, New York City's Drew House and JusticeHome operate independently of the prison system. To be eligible, mothers must plead guilty to felony charges—but the charges are dismissed once they complete the program. In the meantime, they avoid prison, and their children avoid foster care.

Olgita Blackwood's youngest child was barely a week old when she was arrested. "I was so worried about my kids," she told the Associated Press. "They depend on me. They asked for me every day." The 24-year-old was sent to Drew House instead of prison, enabling her to stay with her three children. Nearly two years later, as she prepared to take her GED, she said that the program made her independent. "I can make decisions on my own, raise my kids. I can't imagine it any other way now."

What if such alternatives to incarceration were available everywhere?

The Bangkok Rules recognize that women's needs are unmet in a prison model designed for men and that women's incarceration is often a result of layers of gender discrimination. In addition to recommending non-custodial measures for pregnant women, the UN urges countries to establish alternatives to imprisonment for *all* women.

If the United States took these ideas seriously—or at least took seriously its basic healthcare responsibilities in its prisons and jails—today, Nicole Guerrero might be watching her 3-year-old daughter, Myrah Arianna, scamper around the playground.

Culturally Competent Care for Aboriginal Women

A Case for Culturally Competent Care for Aboriginal Women

Giving Birth in Hospital Settings

June Birch, B.A., Research Assistant, Misericordia Child Health Clinic, Misericordia Community Hospital, Edmonton, Alberta

Lia Ruttan, Ph.D., Research Associate, Misericordia Child Health Clinic, Misericordia Community Hospital, Edmonton, Alberta

Tracy Muth, M.Ed., Department of Educational Psychology, University of Alberta, Edmonton, Alberta

Lola Baydala, M.D., M.Sc., F.A.A.P., F.R.C.P., Associate Professor, Department of Pediatrics, University of Alberta, Edmonton, Alberta

Abstract

Increasing numbers of Aboriginal women are using urban hospital settings to give birth. Culturally competent care, including an understanding of cultural, emotional, historical, and spiritual aspects of Aboriginal Peoples' experience and beliefs about health and healthcare, is important to the provision of quality care. While there is a body of literature on culturally competent care, no models specific to Aboriginal women giving birth in hospital settings exist. This article explores Aboriginal peoples' historical experience with western health care systems, worldviews and perspectives on health and healing, and beliefs regarding childbirth. Some of the existing models of culturally competent care that emphasize provision of care in a manner that shows awareness of both patients' cultural backgrounds as well as health care providers' personal and professional culture are summarized. Recommendations for the development of cultural competency are presented.

Acquisition of knowledge, self-awareness and development of skills are all necessary to ensure quality care. It is essential that—at both systemic and individual levels—processes are in place to promote culturally competent health-care practices. Recommendations include: partnering with Aboriginal physicians, nurses, midwives and their representative organizations; conducting community-based research

June Birch, et al., "Culturally Competent Care for Aboriginal Women: A Case for Culturally Competent Care for Aboriginal Women Giving Birth in Hospital Settings," *Journal of Aboriginal Health*, vol. 4, no. 2, pp. 24–34. Copyright © 2009 by Aboriginal Health Research Networks Secretariat (AHRNetS). Reprinted with permission. Provided by ProQuest LLC. All rights reserved.

to determine labour and delivery needs; identifying and describing Aboriginal values and beliefs related to childbirth and its place in the family and community; and following Aboriginal women's birth experiences in hospital settings with the overarching goal of informing institutional practices.

Keywords

Aboriginal women, culturally competent care, hospital birth, obstetrics

Giving birth is a major life event for Aboriginal[1] women and their families. The experience can be positively or negatively affected by the care received, (Callister, 2004; Carlton, Callister & Stoneman, 2005; Matthews & Callister, 2004; Ottani, 2002), which can affect subsequent interactions with health care providers (Carlton et al., 2005). Culturally competent care, pre-natally, during the birthing experience, and post-natally, is critical to the provision of quality care (Callister, 2001; Edgecombe, 1996; Foster, 2006; Martin-Misener & Black, 1996; Matthews & Callister, 2004; Ottani, 2002; Smith, Varcoe & Edwards, 2005). Social, political and cultural changes that Aboriginal women in Canada have faced have negatively affected their education and cultural identity and traditional values, as well as their health (Adelson, 2005; Carroll & Benoit, 2001; Dion-Stout, Kipling & Stout, 2001). Culturally competent care is more likely to be successful than culture-blind care in addressing population health disparities, including gestational diabetes, high birth weights and higher post-natal death, including Sudden Infant Death Syndrome (SIDS) (Adelson, 2005; Smylie, 2001b). Given the history of negative experiences with mainstream health care institutions and the impact these factors have had on health outcomes of Aboriginal women, providing culturally competent care is particularly important for Aboriginal women who are giving birth in Canadian hospitals.

Aboriginal includes First Nations, Inuit, and Métis Peoples of Canada

Over the past 30 to 40 years, increasing numbers of Aboriginal women have given birth in large urban hospital settings. For many communities, this change began in the 1970s when the Canadian government established an evacuation policy for women living in remote northern communities (Hiebert, 2001; Inuit Tapiriit Kanatami, 2004; Kaufert, Koolage, Kaufert, & O'Neil, 1984; Smith, 2003; Smith et al., 2005). To give birth in urban facilities, women are often required to leave their families and communities, usually for several weeks at a time (Couchie & Sanderson, 2007). With the closing of many small, rural hospitals, women from reserve communities also give birth in large urban hospitals. In addition, half of all Aboriginal people in Canada now live in urban centres, adding another dimension to the picture of Aboriginal birthing. A needs assessment conducted by the National Aboriginal Health Organization (NAHO) (2006) found that 93 per cent (27 of 29) of the First Nations and Inuit women who completed the assessment questionnaire gave birth in a hospital setting. Efforts are being made to renew Aboriginal midwifery and birthing in homes or community-based facilities. In the meantime, the majority of Aboriginal women, currently give birth in hospital settings (NAHO, 2006). While there is a rich body of literature on the general topic of cultural competence, little has been written about applying this concept to healthcare professionals working with Aboriginal women giving birth in Canadian hospital settings. The purpose of this article is to summarize the issues involved and to illustrate the need for increasing culturally competent care with Aboriginal women giving birth in hospital settings.

Models of Culturally Competent Care

The concept of culturally competent care dates back to the mid-twentieth century and was used by increasing numbers of nurses and other health professionals throughout the 1980s (Leininger, 1988). Several nursing scholars have formulated models and frameworks of culturally competent care to guide practice and research (e.g., Campinha-Bacote, 2002; Davidhizar & Giger, 2001; Leininger, 1988; Purnell, 2002; Schim, Doorenboos, Benkert, & Miller, 2007; Spector, 2002; Suh, 2004). The development of these models was influenced not only by the needs of historically marginalized communities but by the increasing variety of immigrant ethnic communities in health service populations in Western countries. In Canada, an increasingly vocal indigenous critique of health care practices and the colonial practices endemic in western-based health systems contributed to the development of culturally competent care practices (Dion-Stout et al., 2001). The literature on models of culturally competent care is extensive and ongoing (Shen, 2004).

Leininger's (1988, 2002) culture care model, an early approach to culturally competent care, is also known as "the sunrise model." With the aim of facilitating, enabling or maintaining well-being through transcultural care decisions and actions, it promotes nursing care that matches the worldview and experience of the patient through a process of cultural assessment (Shen, 2004). In another model, Spector (2002) integrates concern for what she refers to as heritage consistency (the degree to which people's lifestyles reflect their traditional culture), HEALTH traditions (the balance of all facets of a person, physically, mentally

and spiritually, within a context that includes a person's family, culture, work, community, history, and environment), and a range of cultural phenomena. Spector draws on Davidhizar and Giger's (2001) six cultural phenomena that vary among cultural groups and affect health care: environmental control, biological variations, social organization, communication, space and time orientation. In another model, Campinha-Bacote (2002) emphasizes that gaining cultural competence must be understood as an ongoing process consciously carried out to provide effective care to patients, while keeping in mind the variations that occur within ethnic groups. Campinha-Bacote suggests this process includes: developing cultural awareness, cultural knowledge, cultural assessment skills while engaging in cultural encounters, and having what she refers to as cultural desire or personal motivation to engage—with humility—in cultural learning.

These models have in common a focus on healthcare delivery in which the provision of care shows awareness of both the client's cultural background and one's own personal and professional culture. Culturally competent care is more than simply a matter of cultural sensitivity or awareness, culturally competent care is actions that change policy and procedure (Brach & Fraserirector, 2000).

Models for culturally competent care were initially developed to address appropriate care for immigrant populations. Studies specific to Aboriginal women giving birth in hospital settings are limited. Available literature suggests serious concerns about the lack of both cultural sensitivity and respect by non-Aboriginal people (Baker & Daigle, 2000; Browne, 1995). The term, culturally competent care, is, therefore, a generic term that was not designed for Aboriginal women. Because no hospital-based models exist specifically for Aboriginal women giving birth in hospital settings, research in this area is necessary to respond effectively to the health care needs of this population.

Implications from Recent Research

In considering the importance of culturally competent care, health care providers must be able to understand the vulnerability people feel and the potential loss of dignity they experience upon admission to hospital (Matthews & Callister, 2004). Respect, dignity, choice and empowerment, some of the characteristics that comprise quality care, decrease the influence of learned helplessness, increase autonomy and enhance health care outcomes (Waller, 2002). These factors are even more important when delivering healthcare to patients from diverse and marginalized cultures (Matthews & Callister, 2004; O'Brien, Anslow, Begay, Pereira, & Sullivan, 2002). Beliefs, practices and perceptions regarding pregnancy, birth and postnatal care vary worldwide. Particularly meaningful is an understanding of who should attend the birth, the gender of the physician, the role of the nurse as information provider or simply as comforter, the experience of pain, and of the degree of technology involved (Callister, Khalaf, Semenic, Kartchner, & Vehvilainen-Julkunen, 2003; Carlton et al., 2005; Raines & Morgan, 2000). The post-partum period is often particularly sensitive and includes culturally-based differences regarding who is the primary focus of attention following birth, whether the mother and baby should be kept cool or warm, issues related to sleeping, breast feeding, the need for rest, the meaning and role of visitors, appropriate food, the need for prayer, and when to leave the hospital (Banks, 2003; Cioffi, 2004; Kim-Godwin, 2003; Raines & Morgan, 2000).

For Aboriginal women in North America, particularly salient issues include aspects of the holistic world view of Native American culture (Lowe & Struthers, 2001). Seven dimensions identified by Lowe and Struthers as useful in the development of nursing practices with Aboriginal people include spirituality, respect, trust, caring, traditions, connection, and holism. Spirituality, in the Aboriginal context, is the most important of the dimensions discussed, and yet is probably the least understood by health care providers. Traditionally, the relationship with the child is understood to begin before birth. Preparations for a good birth and a healthy baby include avoiding stress, listening to teachings of older women, remaining physically active, connecting with the child, and caring for oneself in a spiritually healthy way (L. Bill, personal communication, May 15, 1990; Long & Curry, 1998; Paulette, 1990, 1999; Sokoloski, 1995). In the context of health care and especially of birthing, cultural competence for Aboriginal women means that the whole person(s), both mother and baby, must be considered not only physically, but also spiritually, emotionally, culturally, and historically (Foster, 2006).

A recent study examining women's birthing experiences found that while the quality of the childbirth experience is enhanced by a sense of empowerment gained through the patient's involvement in decisions and interventions, the respect received from health care providers is even more important (Matthews & Callister, 2004). Respect must be understood in Aboriginal terms and applied to all interactions (Browne, 1995; Ellerby, 2001; Foster, 2006). Browne (1995) studied the meaning of respect in the context of interactions between Cree-Ojibway patients and health care providers. Respect was seen as a reciprocal process that acknowledges in word and action the equality of individuals and communities; respect was communicated through behaviours such as active listening, making genuine efforts to understand the patient's perspective, providing clear explanations and through demonstrations of personal integrity. In later work in Northern British Columbia, Browne, Fiske and Thomas (2000) confirmed this concern for respect and found that First Nations women's experiences were enhanced when practitioners allowed for active engagement in health care decisions, projected genuine caring and affirmed respect for personal and cultural identity.

In their study involving interactions with health care providers and Indigenous women in Ontario, Manitoba and the North central United States, Dodgson and Struthers (2005) found three areas of concern: the experience of historical trauma as a continuing lived marginalization; the demands of biculturalism as marginalization; and the difficulties involved in interacting in complex health care systems. Concerns raised included experiencing a lack of understanding of Aboriginal decision-making processes, experiencing disrespectful treatment and hesitating in informing health care providers of sensitive details. Trust and the lack of it was a major issue and, in the case of some younger women living in urban settings, lack of trust meant they avoided health care services altogether (Dodgson & Struthers, 2005).

Mi'kmaq hospital patients in Eastern Canada also reported dilemmas related to bicultural issues stated as differences between "our ways, their ways" (Baker & Daigle, 2000). Current research being conducted with Mi'kmaq women by Whitty-Rogers (2006) will provide further insight. A common source of conflict is the definition of a family member –and who is considered to be one—that comes up when large numbers of hospital visitors present as family members. What made a difference in women's hospital experiences was respect and personalized care, treatment as equals of and as equals

to non-Aboriginal patients and importantly, acceptance of often large numbers of visitors (Baker & Daigle, 2000; Sokoloski, 1995).

Other concerns involved discomfort with the degree of technological interference experienced; for example, induction and fetal monitoring, as well as choice regarding birthing positions and gender of physicians (Sokoloski, 1995). Concerns related to the proper care, rather than disposal of the placenta have been noted (Paulette, 1999). Avoiding conflict over the assumptions of hospital staff regarding the proper roles of mother and grandmother in postnatal care is important. For example, physicians and nurses may not realize that for some families the grandmother holds the baby first. Beliefs regarding appropriate weight gain during pregnancy and weight loss while breast-feeding may also be quite different from those held by medical staff and judgmental attitudes must be avoided (Vallianatos et al., 2006).

Effective communication is essential to culturally competent care. In order for Aboriginal people to be fully involved in their own care, services must be available in Aboriginal languages (Smylie, 2001b). Foster (2006) notes that, "cultural and language differences can lead to miscommunication, misdiagnoses and inappropriate treatments" (p. 28). Understanding non-verbal communication is also important (Ottani, 2002). For example, norms for eye contact or the absence of it, tone of voice, and degree and forms of participation in discussion and decision-making vary across cultures, and are often misinterpreted (Davidhizar & Bechtel, 1998; Ellerby, 2001). As noted by Ellerby (2001), avoiding eye contact and speaking softly, both signs of respect in Aboriginal cultures, are often misperceived by western professionals as avoidance. To communicate effectively, it is important for health care providers to allow for the time, pacing and acknowledgement of nonverbal communication that may be needed for the patients to express their questions comfortably (Dobbelsteyn, 2006).

Dissatisfaction with service provision was found in mothers who perceived a lack of support, control and communication throughout their birthing experiences (Fowler, as cited in Matthews & Callister, 2004). Taylor and Dower's (1997) study also found dissatisfaction with services due to lack of cultural sensitivity by health care providers. Loneliness, misunderstandings of cultural or spiritual beliefs, and fear are also cited as maternity experiences for Indigenous women worldwide (Watson, Hodson, Johnson, & Kemp, 2001). Cultural needs not being met may result in women avoiding utilization of a health care system during pregnancy until critically necessary, followed by early leave taking (Browne et al., 2000; Kaufert et al., 1984; Petten, 2002; Rankin & Kappy, 1993). Browne (2005) describes how popular societal discourses, which marginalize Aboriginal Peoples, influence the perceptions and attitudes of nursing staff. Aboriginal women are often represented in medical discourses both as having easy births and as being high risk, in each case differentiating them from the mainstream population. These stereotypes must be examined as such.

The need for culturally competent care for Aboriginal women to develop an understanding of Aboriginal Peoples' worldviews on health and western healthcare, it is necessary to consider the following issues: (a) respect for health, healthcare and childbirth beliefs and practices (Davidhizar & Bechtel, 1998; Milligan, 1984a); (b) diversity of perspectives within and between Aboriginal communities; and (c) potential for conflict in cross-cultural interactions. Healthcare providers must also develop greater awareness of their own assumptions regarding health, illness and appropriate care (Dobbelsteyn, 2006; Edgecombe, 1996; Foster, 2006; Kulig et al., as cited in Leipert & Reutter, 1998; Lowe & Struthers, 2001; Mattson, as cited in Callister, 2001; Spector, 2004).

Spector (2004) points out that "to understand health and illness beliefs and practices, it is necessary to see each person in his or her own unique sociocultural world" (p. xiv). Many Aboriginal people tend to view health holistically, as the balanced interaction of the whole person including physical, mental, spiritual and emotional aspects (L. Bill, personal communication, May 15, 1990; Dobbelsteyn, 2006; Mussell, Nicholl & Adler, as cited in Health Canada, 2001; Paulette, 1999; Waldram, Herring & Young, 2006). In this context, health does not stop at the individual; it includes the relational aspects of life in community. Good or poor health occurs within the experience of family and community health and relationships.

Prior to colonization, Aboriginal people relied on their own beliefs, knowledge systems, practices and practitioners for health and healing. Results of a NAHO telephone survey with First Nations Peoples across Canada suggest that these traditional practices still exist. In this survey, 51 per cent of respondents had relied on traditional Aboriginal healers or medicine over the past 12 months, 72 per cent of the respondents agreed with the statement, "I trust the effects of traditional medicines or healing practices," and 68 per cent indicated they "would use traditional medicines or healing practices more often if they were available through [the] local health centre" (NAHO, 2004, p. 99). Acknowledging and showing respect for traditional beliefs, practices and healers would enhance the cultural competency of current health care systems (Chen, 1999). Canadian examples exist in which health care institutions have successfully integrated both traditional and western medical philosophies (Smylie, 2001b). While keeping in mind that not all Aboriginal patients have the same history or the same preferences, Smylie describes "the use of traditional medicines, including the burning of sage, cedar, sweetgrass or tobacco in the hospital setting" (p. 8). By supporting cultural practices and healing, conditions of safety, respect and prayer are created.

A traditional Indigenous understanding of health is developed from a collective standpoint (Mussell et al., as cited in Health Canada, 2001) where "one's position and relationships in society and one's surroundings determine the state of one's health" (Eby, 1996, p. 64). Culturally competent care during childbirth is important not only because it is a major life event, but also, more importantly, because childbirth practices are rooted in culture (Ottani, 2002). Where and how one is born has an important impact on who one is and who one may become (Paulette, 1999). Health care providers who understand and show respect for cultural beliefs and practices are much better equipped to understand the cultural meanings of life events, including birth (Browne, 1995; Davidhizar & Bechtel, 1998). From an Aboriginal point of view, childbirth is a significant but normal event; it is a matter of wellness, not illness, and should not be unduly interfered with (Sokoloski, 1995). Many Aboriginal women have their own knowledge systems, traditional competencies, preferences and methods for prenatal care and birthing (Long & Curry, 1998; Paulette, 1999). Pregnancy involves taking care of oneself and the baby by eating the right foods, being active, avoiding stress and focusing on the developing relationship with the baby rather than on external issues (L. Bill, personal communication, May 15, 1990).

Postnatal care occurs as a part of everyday life and involves the extended family; mothers and their newborns are cared for by older women and family members (Kaufert et al., 1984; Milligan, 1984a; Sokoloski, 1995; Vallianatos et al., 2006).

Hospitalization for the purpose of giving birth is a foreign and often isolating event for many Aboriginal women. For example, the shift from family and community control of the childbirth experience to hospital births in far away urban centres, without family members present, has had far reaching implications for the Inuit community (Douglas, 2006). Chamberlain and Barclay (2000) explored the psychosocial outcomes of Inuit women who were required to leave their communities to give birth. The most frequently cited stressor among these women was enforced separation from family, culture and community. Mothers reported being bored, homesick and lonely in unfamiliar surroundings, and concerned for the well-being of other children left behind; they wished family members were there to participate in the birth.

It is paramount that health care providers understand and appreciate the importance that family and community play in the lives of Aboriginal Peoples. The Society of Obstetrics and Gynecology Canada (SOGC) policy document points out that "the concept of family is culturally specific." For example, in Aboriginal culture, "aunts, uncles, grandparents, cousins, and older siblings may play a role comparable in significance to the western European 'parent'" (Smylie, 2001b, p. 7). The role of mothers and grandmothers as essential to maintaining the cultural nature of birthing, and pre- and post-natal care cannot be overemphasized.

A diversity of perspectives exist within and between Aboriginal communities. Creating environments where traditional practices are accepted is important, but it is also important to acknowledge that Aboriginal Peoples and their beliefs, experiences and values are not homogeneous (Callister, 2001; Ellerby, 2001; Foster, 2006; Seideman, Haase, Primeaux, & Burns, 1992). "Aboriginal Peoples in Canada embody approximately 50 culturally diverse groups, the roots of which are found in distinct languages and land bases" (Smylie, 2000b, p. 5). Further, members of any one Aboriginal community vary in the degrees to which they identify with indigenous or western belief systems. To develop a truer perspective of patients and their families, individual life experiences and the meaning of those life experiences within variable cultural settings must be understood (Callister, 2001; Smith et al., 2005). Care must be taken to avoid stereotypes and to evaluate individual beliefs and practices regardless of cultural background (Davidhizar & Bechtel, 1998; Ottani, 2002).

The potential for conflict in cross cultural interactions must be acknowledged. Spector (2004) warns that "extreme events … can occur when two antithetical cultural belief systems collide within the overall environment of the health care delivery system" (p. 4). Jones and Spector (as cited in Callister, 2001) remark that health care involves three perspectives: the culture of the health care provider, the culture of the woman and her family, and the culture of the health care delivery system. Assumptions from within any single standpoint may result in cultural blindness (Callister, 2001), which may then lead to potential conflict when interacting with persons who hold other perspectives. Tensions are inevitable when individuals come together in a specific health care situation lacking understanding of others' points of view. Conflicts can arise from different cultural views on health care (Callister, 2001; Milligan, 1984a);

strongly held expectations regarding what constitutes appropriate birthing practices and a good birth can heighten this dilemma. These differences can result in the patient feeling isolated, disrespected and disempowered (Paulette, 1999; Smylie, 2001b).

Holistic views on health—in which one works towards balance to maintain or achieve health, and an illness is often thought to represent an imbalance in one or more areas—are common among many Aboriginal Peoples (Eby, 1996; O'Brien, et al., 2002; Stevenson, as cited in Health Canada, 2001). Wellness requires a commitment to work towards correcting imbalance through spiritual, mental, physical and emotional processes. The western view on health is individualistic and emphasizes a mind/body dualism. In addition, western health care systems and service providers have traditionally seen the health care provider as the expert and decision maker. Ellerby (2001) reminds us that "socio-political power relationships are epitomized and maintained through cultural dominance of Western medical practitioners" (p. 7). This situation often exacerbates the power dynamic with people whose voices have already been marginalized (Eby, 1996). In addition to developing a greater understanding one's own beliefs and practices on health, as well as a greater understanding of Aboriginal beliefs and practices, exploring the larger social and political influences on different health models and practices is key to becoming truly culturally competent (Eby, 1996; Foster, 2006; O'Brien et al., 2002).

Recommendations

The provision of culturally competent care for Aboriginal people must include an understanding of the history and impact of colonization (Adelson, 2005; Browne, Smye & Varcoe, 2005; Polashek Wood & Schwass, as cited in Smith et al., 2005; Smylie, 2000a). As Smith et al. (2005) stress, "health status and experiences like pregnancy and parenting must be seen within a broad understanding of the impact of colonization on Aboriginal people" (p. 55). This includes sending children away from parents and communities as experienced in residential schooling and the placement of many children in non-Aboriginal foster or adoptive homes in a phenomena referred to as "the sixties scoop." Moreover, it is important to understand the various terms used to refer to Aboriginal people and the legal and cultural implications associated with such terminology. Understanding the difference between status and non-status, treaty and non-treaty would enhance the development of culturally competent practices and reduce stereotypes (Smylie, 2001b).

Only 56 per cent of respondents of the NAHO (2004) poll agreed that "Aboriginal peoples are treated, as well as non-Aboriginal people in the health care system" (p. 129). In fact, 15 per cent of respondents reported unfair or inappropriate treatment "by a health care provider because they are Aboriginal" (p. 16). Understanding the roots of respondents' views is important. Much can be learned from situations where there has been a lack of cultural sensitivity or appropriateness; these cases should be highlighted and discussed with an eye to effecting change (Kaufert et al., 1984).

There is ample support in the literature for the benefits of developing cultural competency in health care providers (Callister, 2001, 2005; Davidhizar & Bechtel, 1998; Martin-Misener & Black, 1996; O'Brien et al., 2002; Ottani, 2002; Smith et al., 2005; Spector, 2004; Taylor & Dower, 1997; Watson et al., 2001). This is particularly important, considering the historical experiences of Aboriginal people in Canada with health care systems, health care providers and differential health care legislation. Cultural competency can be enhanced through acquiring knowledge, examining attitudes, engaging in new experiences, changing behaviour, and developing appropriate skills. A variety of methods are available to do this. Learning through open experiences with patients is probably one of the most important. Another method, described by Edgecombe (1996), is the use of value orientation profiles, which provide information on how individuals or groups rank-order the values in their society. This tool could be utilized in learning both about healthcare practitioners' own values and about other culturally-based value systems in order to recognize potential areas of misunderstanding. Similarly, completion of a cultural assessment model, as Leininger advocates, can give health care providers insight into their own beliefs and practices related to health and illness, as well as those of their patients (Mattson, as cited in Callister, 2001).

Providing cross-cultural education to healthcare providers is another means of moving forward (Baker, Findlay, Isbister, & Peekeekoot, 1987; Foster, 2006; Petten, 2002; Rankin & Kappy, 1993). Reading literary works that address cultural beliefs, practices, and issues at staff meetings (Callister, 2001), participating in cultural events, and attending workshops would enhance the education of health care providers (Ellerby, 2001; Smylie, 2001b). Following up initial educational activities with mentoring could precipitate learning through role modeling while providing opportunities to discuss experiences, and reinforcing good practice.

However, while increasing cultural sensitivity is necessary, it is insufficient if it does not lead to behaviour change; staff must be supported systemically at all levels in using knowledge gained to change practice. Particular systemic interventions may include using cultural brokers, partnering with traditional healers, developing culturally appropriate teaching practices and materials, initiating and maintaining training programs for all staff, and recruiting professionals who have relevant background and experience in policy development (Callister, 2005; Brach & Fraserirector, 2000).

Partnering with Aboriginal health care providers (Hart-Wasekeesikaw, 1999) including the Aboriginal Nurses Association of Canada (ANAC), the National Indian and Inuit Community Health Representatives Organization (NIICHRO), the Indigenous Physicians Association of Canada (IPAC), the Native Mental Health Association of Canada (NMHAC), the Institute of Aboriginal Peoples' Health (IAPH), and the National Aboriginal Health Organization (NAHO) can provide valuable connections for learning about ways of implementing cultural approaches to healthcare and, also, about common areas of sensitivity (Smylie, 2001b). Engaging in two-way knowledge translation and capacity building activities with these and other organizations is important (Smylie et al., 2004).

The need for more research in this area is evident (Whitty-Rogers, 2006). In their review, Brach and Fraserirector (2000) indicate more research on the beneficial impact of culturally competent techniques on outcomes, including the reduction of health inequity, is needed to determine if the practice of culturally competent care actually makes a difference in the experience of patients. Another recommendation is to conduct culturally appropriate community-based research to discover knowledge deficits, determine best practices and explore the healthcare delivery experience and needs of Aboriginal women (Kuptana, 1996; Petten, 2002; Smylie et al., 2004). Narrative inquiry and other qualitative methods are appropriate for exploring Aboriginal women's birth experiences in hospital settings and can be instrumental in informing institutional practices (Callister, 2004; Matthews & Callister, 2004; Watson et al., 2001). As well, further research to determine whether changes in staff and organizational attitudes and behaviours have indeed occurred will be necessary following the implementation of culturally competent practice policies (Brach & Fraserirector, 2000).

Conclusion

As the literature reveals, a key component in the provision of quality health care practices is the development of cultural competency. Culturally competent care includes honouring the birthing practices respected by each culture (Matthews & Callister, 2004). Health care providers must be willing to "integrate traditional practices or approaches to health care when the client needs or wants them" (Dobbelsteyn, 2006, p. 34). However, care must be taken to acknowledge the diversity that exists amongst Aboriginal Peoples in order to avoid engaging in further stereotyping. Incorporating a reflective and learner-based approach in health care delivery would greatly assist health care providers in achieving culturally competent practices. Recognition of the influence on any one health care provider of the biomedical "provider culture" (Spector, 2002, 2004) with its own normalized beliefs and assumptions regarding appropriate health choices is also essential.

Although models for culturally competent care exist, research outcomes on culturally competent practices for Aboriginal women giving birth in hospital settings in Canada are sparse. Additional research on the needs of Aboriginal women delivering babies in hospital settings is vital not only to informing health care policies and practices, but to address gaps and barriers that prevent access or effective access to the health care system. Culturally competent care is important; developing and using cultural sensitivity and relevant practice skills is critical to good care, as is institutional responsiveness to this issue. Moreover, understanding the historical and sociopolitical dynamics involved is an essential component of respect and may influence not only current encounters but women's willingness to engage in health services during both the pre- and postnatal periods. Forming partnerships with Aboriginal communities and professionals to develop policy and conduct research on these issues is important; doing so may assist in addressing the power imbalances between Aboriginal peoples and those working in the health care system. While awareness of the issues discussed in this article is increasing among health professionals, it continues to be critically necessary to develop a dialogue resulting in policy change and the application of strategies and practices that will promote an increased level of culturally competent care for Aboriginal women in hospital labour and delivery wards.

References

Adelson, N. (2005). The embodiment of inequity: Health disparities in Aboriginal Canada. *Canadian Journal of Public Health, 96,* S45–S61.

Baker, C. & Daigle, M. C. (2000). Cross-cultural hospital care as experienced by Mi'kmaq clients. *Western Journal of Nursing Research, 22,* 8–28.

Baker, F. W., Findlay, S., Isbister, L., & Peekeekoot, B. (1987). Native health care: An alternative approach. *Canadian Medical Association Journal, 136,* 695-696.

Banks, J. W. (2003). Ka'nisténhsera Teiakotihsniés: A Native community rekindles the tradition of breast-feeding. *AWHONN Lifelines, 7*(4), 340–347.

Brach, C. & Fraserirector, I. (2000). Can cultural competency reduce racial and ethnic disparities? A review and conceptual model. *Medical Care Research and Review, 57*(I), 181–217.

Browne, A. J. (1995). The meaning of respect: A First Nations perspective. *Canadian Journal of Nursing Research, 27,* 95–109.

Browne, A. J. (2005). Discourses influencing nurses' perception of First Nation patients. *Canadian Journal of Nursing Research, 37*(4), 62–87.

Browne, A. J., Fiske, J. & Thomas, G. (2000). *First Nations omen's encounters with mainstream health care services and systems. Women's Health Reports.* Vancouver, B.C.: British Columbia Center of Excellence for Women's Health.

Browne, A. J., Smye, V. L. & Varcoe, C. (2005). The relevance of postcolonial theoretical perspectives to research in Aboriginal health. *Canadian Journal of Nursing Research, 37*(4), 16–37.

Callister, L. C. (2001). Culturally competent care of women and newborns: Knowledge, attitude, and skills. *Journal of Obstetric, Gynecologic, and Neonatal Nursing, 30*(2), 209–215.

Callister, L. C. (2004). Making meaning: Women's birth narratives. *Journal of Obstetric, Gynecologic, and Neonatal Nursing, 33*(4), 508–518.

Callister, L. C. (2005). What has the literature taught us about culturally competent care of women and children? *MCN, 30*(6), 380–388.

Callister, L. C., Khalaf, I., Semenic, S., Kartchner, R., & Vehvilainen-Julkunen, K. (2003). The pain of childbirth: Perceptions of culturally diverse women. *Pain Management Nursing, 4*(4), 145–154.

Campinha-Bacote, J. (2002). The process of cultural competence in the delivery of healthcare services: A model of care. *Journal of Transcultural Nursing, 13*(3), 181–184.

Carlton, T., Callister, L. C. & Stoneman, E. (2005). Decision making in laboring women: Ethical issues for perinatal nurses. *Journal of Perinatal & Neonatal Nursing, 19*(2), 145–151.

Carroll, D. & Benoit, C. (2001). Aboriginal midwifery in Canada: Blending traditional and modern forms. *Canadian Women's Health Network Magazine, 4*(3). Retrieved October 14, 2006, from http://www.cwhn.ca/network-reseau/4-3/4-3pg2.html

Chamberlain, M. & Barclay, K. (2000). Psychosocial costs of transferring indigenous women from their community for birth. *Midwifery, 16*(2), 116–122.

Chen, Jr., M. S. (1999). Informal care and the empowerment of minority communities: Comparisons between the USA and the UK. *Ethnicity & Health, 4*(3), 139–151. Retrieved July 6, 2006, from Health Source: Nursing/Academic Edition.

Cioffi, J. (2004). Caring for women from culturally diverse backgrounds: Midwives' experiences. *Journal of Midwifery & Women's Health, 49*(5), 437–442.

Couchie, C. & Sanderson, S. (2007). A report on best practices for returning birth to rural and remote aboriginal communities. *Journal of Obstetrics and Gynaecology Canada, 29*(3), 250–260.

Davidhizar, R. & Bechtel, G. (1998). A model to enhance culturally competent care. *Hospital Topics, 76*(2), 22–26. Retrieved July 5, 2006, from Health Source: Nursing/Academic Edition.

Davidhizar, R. & Giger, J. N. (2001). Teaching culture within the curriculum using the Giger-Davidhizar model of transcultural nursing assessment. *Journal of Nursing Education, 40*(6), 282–284.

Dion-Stout, M., Kipling, G. D. & Stout, R. (2001). *Aboriginal Women's Health Research Synthesis*. Ottawa: Centres of Excellence for Women's Health.

Dobbelsteyn, J. L. (2006). Nursing in First Nations and Inuit communities in Atlantic Canada. *Canadian Nurse, 102*(4), 32–35.

Dodgson, J. E. & Struthers, R. (2005). Indigenous women's voices: Marginalization and health. *Journal of Transcultural Nursing, 16*(4), 339–346.

Douglas, V. K. (2006). Childbirth among the Canadian Inuit: A review of the clinical and cultural literature. *International Journal of Circumpolar Health, 65*(2), 117–132.

Eby, D. (1996). Traditional healing and allopathic medicine: Issues at the interface. In R. Fortuine, G.A. Conway, C.D. Schraer, M.J. Dimino, C.M. Hild & J. Braund-Allen (Eds.), *Circumpolar Health 96: Proceedings of the Tenth International Congress on Circumpolar Health: Vol. 57* (pp. 62–66). Anchorage, AK: American Society for Circumpolar Health.

Edgecombe, N. A. (1996). Value orientation of the Copper Inuit. In R. Fortuine, G.A. Conway, C.D. Schraer, M.J. Dimino, C.M. Hild & J. Braund-Allen (Eds.), *Circumpolar Health 96: Proceedings of the Tenth International Congress on Circumpolar Health: Vol. 57* (pp. 55–61). Anchorage, AK: American Society for Circumpolar Health.

Ellerby, J. H. (2001). *Working with Aboriginal Elders*. Winnipeg, Canada: University of Manitoba Native Studies Press.

Foster, C. H. (2006). What nurses should know when working in Aboriginal communities. *Canadian Nurse, 102*(4), 28–31.

Fry, S. T. (1992). The role of caring in a theory of nursing ethics. In H. B. Holmes & L. M. Purdy (Eds.), *Feminist Perspectives in Medical Ethics* (pp. 93–106). Bloomington, IN: Indiana University Press.

Hart-Wasekeesikaw, F. (1999). Aboriginal health nursing –a cultural approach. *Aboriginal Nurse, 14*(2), 3.

Health Canada. (2001). *It Takes a Community: Framework for the First Nations and Inuit Fetal Alcohol Syndrome and Fetal Alcohol Effects Initiative.* Ottawa, ON: First Nations and Inuit Health Branch, Health Canada.

Hiebert, S. (2001). The utilization of antenatal services in remote Manitoba First Nations communities. *International Journal of Circumpolar Health, 60*(1), 64–71.

Inuit Tapiriit Kanatami. (2004). *Evaluation of models of health care delivery in Inuit regions.* Retrieved July 4, 2006, from http://www.itk.ca/publications/200403-healthcare-evaluation.pdf

Kaufert, J. M., Koolage, W. W., Kaufert, P. L., & O'Neil, J. D. (1984). The use of "trouble case" examples in teaching the impact of sociocultural and political factors in clinical communication. *Medical Anthropology, Winter,* 36–45.

Kim-Godwin, Y. S. (2003). Postpartum beliefs and practices among non-Western cultures. *MCN, American Journal of Maternal Child Nursing, 28*(2), 74–78.

Kuptana, R. (1996). Address by the president of the Inuit Circumpolar Conference. In R. Fortuine, G.A. Conway, C.D. Schraer, M.J. Dimino, C.M. Hild & J. Braund-Allen (Eds.), *Circumpolar Health 96: Proceedings of the Tenth International Congress on Circumpolar Health: Vol. 57* (pp. 6–9). Anchorage, AK: American Society for Circumpolar Health.

Leininger, M. M. (1988). Leininger's theory of nursing: cultural care diversity and universality. *Nursing Science Quarterly, 1*(4), 152–60.

Leininger, M. (2002). Culture care theory: A major contribution to advance transcultural nursing knowledge and practices. *Journal of Transcultural Nursing, 13*(3), 189–92.

Leipert, B., & Reutter, L. (1998). Women's health and community health nursing practice in geographically isolated settings: A Canadian perspective [Electronic version]. *Health Care for Women International,* 19(6), 575–588.

Long, C. R. & Curry, M. A. (1998). Living in two worlds: Native American women and prenatal care. *Health Care for Women International, 19,* 205–215.

Lowe, J. & Struthers, R. (2001). A conceptual framework of nursing in Native American culture [Electronic version]. *Journal of Nursing Scholarship, 33*(3), 279–283.

Martin-Misener, R., & Black, J. (1996). Using the evaluation of the Dalhousie Outpost Nursing Program for responsive social action. In R. Fortuine, G.A. Conway, C.D. Schraer, M.J. Dimino, C.M. Hild & J. Braund-Allen (Eds.), *Circumpolar Health 96: Proceedings of the Tenth International Congress on Circumpolar Health: Vol. 57* (pp. 96–99). Anchorage, AK: American Society for Circumpolar Health.

Matthews, R. & Callister, L. C. (2004). Childbearing women's perceptions of nursing care that promotes dignity. *Journal of Obstetric, Gynecologic, and Neonatal Nursing, 33*(4), 498–507.

Milligan, B. C. (1984a). Nursing care and beliefs of expectant Navajo women (part 1). *American Indian Quarterly, 8*(2), 83–101.

National Aboriginal Health Organization (NAHO). (2004). *What First Nations think about their health and health care.* Ottawa, ON: Author.

National Aboriginal Health Organization (NAHO). (2006). *Exploring models for quality maternity care in First Nations and Inuit communities: A preliminary needs assessment.* Ottawa, ON: Author.

O'Brien, B. L., Anslow, R. M., Begay, W., Pereira, S. B. A., & Sullivan, M. P. (2002). 21st century rural nursing: Navajo traditional and western medicine. *Nursing Administration Quarterly, 26*(5), 47–57.

Ottani, P. A. (2002). Embracing global similarities: A framework for cross-cultural obstetric care. *Journal of Obstetric, Gynecologic, and Neonatal Nursing, 31*(1), 33–38.

Paulette, L. (1990). The changing experience of childbirth in the western N.W.T. In J. D. O'Neil & P. Gilbert (Eds.), *Childbirth in the north: Epidemiological, clinical and cultural perspectives* (pp. 45–50). Winnipeg, Manitoba: Northern Health Research Unit, University of Manitoba.

Paulette, L. (Speaker). (1999). *Ethics and cultural diversity in northern birthing. 11th Annual Canadian Bioethics*

Society Conference: Expanding the Boundaries of Ethics. Edmonton, AB: Kennedy Recordings.

Petten, C. (2002). Aboriginal women badly served by health care. *Windspeaker, 20*(5), 26.

Purnell, L. (2002). The Purnell model for cultural competence. *Journal of Transcultural Nursing, 13*(3), 193–196.

Raines, D. A. & Morgan, Z. (2000). Culturally sensitive care during childbirth. *Applied Nursing Research, 13*(4), 167–172.

Rankin, S. B. & Kappy, M. S. (1993). Developing therapeutic relationships in multicultural settings. *Academic Medicine, 68*(11), 826–827.

Schim, S. M. Doorenbos, A., Benkert, R., & Miller, J. (2007). Culturally congruent care: Putting the puzzle together. *Journal of Transcultural Nursing, 18*(2), 103–110.

Seideman, R. Y., Haase, J., Primeaux, M., & Burns, P. (1992). Using NCAST instruments with urban American Indians. *Western Journal of Nursing Research, 14*(20), 308–321.

Shen, Z. (2004). Cultural competence models in nursing: A selected annotated bibliography. *Journal of Transcultural Nursing, 15*(4), 317–322.

Smith, D. (2003). Maternal-child health care in Aboriginal communities. *Canadian Journal of Nursing Research, 35*(2), 143–152.

Smith, D., Varcoe, C. & Edwards, N. (2005). Turning around the intergenerational impact of residential schools on Aboriginal people: Implications for health policy and practice. *Canadian Journal of Nursing Research, 37*(4), 38–60.

Smylie, J. (2000a, December). *A guide for health professionals working with Aboriginal peoples: Executive summary* (SOGC Policy Statement No. 100). Retrieved February 16, 2006, from http://www.sogc.org/guidelines/index_e.asp

Smylie, J. (2000b, December). *A guide for health professionals working with Aboriginal peoples: The sociocultural context of Aboriginal peoples in Canada* (SOGC Policy Statement No.100). Retrieved February 16, 2006, from http://www.sogc.org/guidelines/public/100e-ps2-december2000.pdf

Smylie, J. (2001b, February). *A guide for health professionals working with Aboriginal peoples: Cross cultural understanding* (SOGC Policy Statement No.100). Retrieved February 16, 2006, from http://www.sogc.org/guidelines/index_e.asp

Smylie, J., Kaplan-Myrth, N., Tait, C., Martin, C. M., Chartrand, L., Hogg, W., et al. (2004). Health sciences research and Aboriginal communities: pathway or pitfall? *Journal of Obstetrics and Gynecology Canada, 26* (3), 211–216.

Sokoloski, E. H. (1995). Canadian First Nations women's beliefs about pregnancy and prenatal care. *Canadian Journal of Nursing Research, 27*(1), 89–100.

Spector, R. E. (2002). Cultural diversity in health and illness. *Journal of Transcultural Nursing, 13*(3), 197–199.

Spector, R. E. (2004). *Cultural diversity in health & illness* (6th ed.). Upper Saddle River, NJ: Pearson-Prentice Hall.

Suh, E. E. (2004). The model of cultural competence through an evolutionary concept analysis. *Journal of Transcultural Nursing, 15*(2), 93–102.

Taylor, D. & Dower, C. (1997). Toward a women-centered health care system: Women's experiences, women's voices, women's needs. *Health Care for Women International, 18*(4), 407–422. Retrieved July 5, 2006, from Health Source: Nursing/Academic Edition.

Vallianatos, H., Brennand, E. A., Raine, K., Stephen, Q., Petawabano, B., Dannenbaum, D., et al. (2006). Beliefs and practices of First Nation women about weight gain during pregnancy and lactation: Implications for women's health. *Canadian Journal of Nursing Research, 38*(1), 102–119.

Waldram, J. B., Herring, D. A. & Young, T. K. (2006) *Aboriginal Health in Canada: Historical, Cultural, and Epidemiological Perspectives* (2nd ed.). Toronto: University of Toronto.

Waller, B. N. (2002). The psychological structure of patient autonomy. *Cambridge Quarterly of Health Care Ethics, 11*(3), 257–265.

Watson, J., Hodson, K., Johnson, R., & Kemp, K. (2001). The maternity experiences of Indigenous women admitted to an acute care setting. *Australian Journal of Rural Health, 10*, 154–160.

Whitty-Rogers, J. (2006). Mi'kmaq women's childbirth experiences: Summary of literature review and proposed study for master's thesis. *Pimatisiwin, 4*(1), 68–93.

End Notes

1　For the purposes of this study, women's health is defined as mental and emotional health, physical health, and social well-being. When health is defined as mental, physical and social well-being, and not merely the absence of disease and infirmity, cultural and social practices become critical contributing factors to health (Arctic Council, 2004).

2　Obstetric evacuation is a mandatory practice in most Nunavut communities, except for Iqaluit where there is a hospital, and Rankin Inlet, where a low-risk delivery birthing centre is located.

3　Inuktitut word meaning "people of Nunavut."

4　Inuit is the Inuktitut word for "people." Inuk is the singular form meaning "person."

Childbirth at the Global Crossroads

Arlie Hochschild

Women in the developing world who are paid to bear other people's children test the emotional limits of the international service economy.

The auto-rickshaw driver honks his way through the dusty chaos of Anand, Gujarat, India, swerving around motorbikes, grunting trucks, and ancient large-wheeled bullock-carts packed with bags of fodder. Both sides of the street are lined with plastic trash and small piles of garbage on which untethered cows feed. The driver turns off the pavement onto a narrow, pitted dirt road, slows to circumvent a pair of black and white spotted goats, and stops outside a dusty courtyard. To one side stands a modest white building with a sign that reads, in English and Gujarati, "Akanksha Clinic."

Two dozen dainty Indian women's sandals, toes pointed forward, are lined along the front porch. For it is with bare feet that one enters a clinic housing what may be the world's largest group of gestational surrogates—women who rent their wombs to incubate the fertilized eggs from clients from around the globe. Since India declared commercial surrogacy legal in 2002, some 350 assisted reproductive technology (ART) clinics have opened their doors. Surrogacy is now a burgeoning part of India's medical tourism industry, which is slated to add $2 billion to the nation's gross domestic product by 2012. Advertisements describe India as a "global doctor" offering First World skill at Third World prices, short waits, privacy, and—important in the case of surrogacy—absence of red tape. To encourage this lucrative trend, the Indian government gives tax breaks to private hospitals treating overseas patients and lowers import duties on medical supplies.

In his 2007 book, *Supercapitalism,* Robert B. Reich argues that while industrial and clerical jobs could be outsourced to cheaper labor pools abroad, service jobs would stay in America. But Reich didn't count on First World clients flying to the global South to find low-cost retirement care or reproductive services. The Akanksha clinic is just one point on an ever-widening two-lane global highway that connects poor nations in the Southern Hemisphere to rich nations in the Northern Hemisphere, and poorer countries of Eastern Europe to richer ones in the West. A Filipina nanny heads north to care for an American child. A Sri Lankan maid cleans a house in Singapore. A Ukrainian nurse's aide carries lunch trays in a Swedish hospital. Marx's iconic male, stationary industrial worker has been replaced by a new icon: the female, mobile service worker.

We have grown used to the idea of a migrant worker caring for our children and even to the idea of hopping an overseas flight for surgery. As global service work grows increasingly personal, surrogacy is the latest expression of this trend. Nowadays, a wealthy person can purchase it all—the egg, the sperm, and time in the womb. "A childless couple gains a child. A poor woman earns money. What could be the problem?" asks Dr. Nayna Patel, Akanksha's founder and director.

But despite Patel's view of commercial surrogacy as a straightforward equation, it's far more complicated for both the surrogates and the genetic parents. Like nannies or nurses, surrogates perform "emotional labor" to suppress feelings that could interfere with doing their job. Parents must decide how close they are willing (or able) to get to the woman who will give birth to their child.

As science and global capitalism gallop forward, they kick up difficult questions about emotional attachment. What, if anything, is too sacred to sell?

I FOLLOW A KINDLY embryologist, Harsha Bhadarka, to an upstairs office of the clinic to talk with two surrogates whom I will call Geeta and Saroj. (Aditya Ghosh, a journalist with the *Hindustan Times,* has kindly offered to join me.) The room is small, and the two surrogate mothers enter the room nodding shyly. Both live on the second floor of the clinic, but most of its 24 residents live in one of two hostels for the duration of their pregnancy. The women are brought nutritious food on tin trays, injected with iron (a common deficiency), and supervised away from prying in-laws, curious older children, and lonely husbands with whom they are allowed no visits home or sex.

Geeta, a 22-year-old, light-skinned, green-eyed beauty, is the mother of three daughters, one of whom is sitting quietly and wide-eyed on her lap. To be accepted as a surrogate, Akanksha requires a woman to be a healthy, married mother. As one doctor explains, "If she has

children of her own, she'll be less tempted to attach herself to the baby."

"How did you decide to become a surrogate?" I ask.

"It was my husband's idea," Geeta replies. "He makes *pav bhaji* [a vegetable dish] during the day and serves food in the evening [at a street-side fast-food shop]. He heard about surrogacy from a customer at his shop, a Muslim like us. The man told my husband, 'It's a good thing to do,' and then I came to madam [Dr. Patel] and offered to try. We can't live on my husband's earnings, and we had no hope of educating our daughters."

The Global Marketplace: Surrogate mothers, serving clients from around the world, wait for their checkups at Dr. Nayna Patel's clinic in Anand, Gujarat.
All Photos: Ajit Solanki/AP Images

Geeta says she has only briefly met the parents whose genes her baby carries. "They're from far away. I don't know where," she says. "They're Caucasian, so the baby will come out white." The money she has been promised, including a monthly stipend to cover vitamins and medications, is wired to a bank account that Patel has opened in Geeta's name. "I keep myself from getting too attached," she says. "Whenever I start to think about the baby inside me, I turn my attention to my own daughter. Here she is." She bounces the child on her lap. "That way, I manage."

Seated next to Geeta is Saroj, a heavy-set, dark woman with intense, curious eyes, and, after a while, an easy smile. Like other Hindu surrogates at Akanksha, she wears *sindoor* (a red powder applied to the part in her hair) and *mangalsutra* (a necklace with a gold pendant), both symbols of marriage. She is, she tells us, the mother of three children and the wife of a vegetable street vendor. She gave birth to a surrogate child a year and three months ago and is waiting to see if a second implantation has taken. The genetic parents are from Bangalore, India. (It is estimated that half the clients seeking surrogacy from Indian ART clinics are Indian and the other half, foreign. Of the foreign clients, roughly half are American.) Saroj, too, knows almost nothing about her clients. "They came, saw me, and left," she says.

Given her husband's wages, 1,260 rupees (or $25) a month, Saroj turned to surrogacy so she could move to a rain-proof house and feed her family well. Yet she faced the dilemma of all rural surrogates: being suspected of adultery—a cause for shunning or worse. I ask the women whether the money they earn has improved their social standing. For the first time the two women laugh out loud and talk to each other excitedly. "My father-in-law is dead, and my mother-in-law lives separately from us, and at first I hid it from her," Saroj says. "But when she found out, she said she felt blessed to have a daughter-in-law like me because I've given more money to the family than her son could. But some friends ask me why I am putting myself through all this. I tell them, 'It's my own choice.'"

Since Dr. Patel began offering surrogacy services in 2004, 232 surrogates have given birth at Akanksha. A 2007 study of 42 Akanksha surrogates found that nearly half described themselves as housewives and the rest were a mix of domestic, service, and manual laborers. Hindu, Muslim, and Christian, most had seventh- to 12th-grade educations, six were illiterate, and one—who turned to surrogacy to pay for a small son's heart surgery—had a bachelor's degree. Each surrogate negotiates a different sum: One surrogate carrying twins for an Indian couple discovered she was being paid less (about $3,600) than a surrogate in the next bed who was carrying one baby for an American couple for about $5,600.

Observers fear that a lack of regulation could spark a price war for surrogacy—Thailand underselling India, Cambodia underselling Thailand, and so on—with countries slowly undercutting fees and legal protections for surrogates along the way. It could happen. Right now international surrogacy is a highly complex legal patchwork. Surrogacy is banned in China and much of Europe. It is legal but regulated in New Zealand and Great Britain. Only 17 of the United States have laws on the books; it is legal in Florida and banned in New York.

In India, commercial surrogacy is legal but unregulated, although a 135-page regulatory law, long in the works, will be sent to Parliament later this year. Even if the law is passed, however, some argue it would do little to improve life for women such as Geeta and Saroj. For example, it specifies that the doctor, not the surrogate, has the right to decide on any "fetal reduction" (an abortion). Moreover, most Indian federal laws are considered "advisory" to powerful state governments, and courts—where a failure to enforce such laws might be challenged—are backlogged for years, often decades. Dr. B.N. Chakravarty, the Calcutta-based chair of the surrogacy law drafting committee, says that the growth of the industry is "inevitable," but it needs regulating. Even if the law were written to protect surrogates and then actually enforced, it would do nothing to address the crushing poverty that often presses Indian women to "choose" surrogacy in the first place.

For N.B. Sarojini, director of the Delhi-based Sama Resource Group for Women and Health, a nonprofit feminist research institute, the problem is one of distorted priorities. "The ART clinics are posing themselves as the answer to an illusory 'crisis' of infertility," she says. "Two decades back, a couple might consider themselves 'infertile' after trying for five years to conceive. Then it moved to four years. Now couples rush to ARTs after one or two. Why not put the cultural spotlight on *alternatives?* Why not urge childless women to adopt orphans? And what, after all, is wrong with remaining childless?"

But Dr. Patel, a striking woman in an emerald green sari and with black hair flowing down her back, sees for-profit surrogacy as a "win-win" for the clinic, the surrogate, and the genetic parents. She also sees no problem with running the clinic like a business, seeking to increase inventory, safeguard quality, and improve efficiency. That means producing more babies, monitoring surrogates' diet and sexual contact, and assuring a smooth, emotion-free exchange of baby for money. (For every dollar that goes to the surrogates, observers estimate, three go to the clinic.) In Akanksha's hostel, women sleep on cots, nine to a room, for nine months. Their young children sleep with them; older children do not stay in the hostel. The women exercise inside the hostel, rarely leaving it and then only with

permission. Patel also advises surrogates to limit contact with clients. Staying detached from the genetic parents, she says, helps surrogate mothers give up their babies and get on with their lives—and maybe with the next surrogacy. This ideal of the de-personalized pregnancy is eerily reminiscent of Aldous Huxley's 1932 dystopian novel *Brave New World,* in which babies are emotionlessly mass-produced in the Central London Hatchery.

A lack of regulation could spark a price war for surrogacy—undercutting fees and legal protections along the way.

Patel's business may seem coldly efficient, but it also has a touch of Mother Teresa. Akanksha residents are offered daily English classes and weekly lessons in computer use. Patel arranges for film screenings and gives out school backpacks and pencil boxes to surrogates' children. She hopes to attract donations from grateful clients to help pay children's school fees as well. "For me this is a mission," Patel says.

In light of appalling government neglect of a population totally untouched by India's recent economic boom, this charity sounds wonderful. But is it wonderful enough to cancel out concerns about the factory?

AFTER LEAVING ANAND, I head to Dr. Nandita Palshetkar's office in Mumbai. With Alifiya Khan, another journalist from the *Hindustan Times,* I meet with Leela, a lively 28-year-old who gave birth to a baby for Indian clients about six months ago. Like Geeta and Saroj, Leela had been desperate for money, but her experience of pregnancy was utterly different. On the day I meet her, she is dressed in a pink sari, hair drawn back from her olive-skinned face into a long black braid. She leans forward, smiling broadly, eager to talk about her baby, his genetic parents, and her feelings about being a surrogate mother.

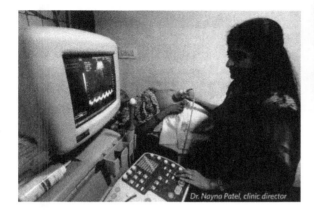

Dr. Nayna Patel, clinic director

At age 20, Leela married a fellow worker at a Mumbai-based company canteen. "I didn't know he was alcoholic until after we married," she says. "My husband ran up a $7,000 debt with the moneylender who sent agents to pressure him to repay it. … We couldn't stop the moneylender from hounding us. I decided to act. I heard from my sister-in-law that I could get money for donating my eggs, and I did that twice. When I came back to do it a third time, madam [Dr. Palshetkar] told me I could earn more as a surrogate."

Was she able to pay off the debt? Leela lowers her head: "Half of it."

She ate better food during her paid pregnancy than during her other pregnancies and delivered the baby in a better hospital than the one where she delivered her own children. Unlike others I spoke with, Leela openly bonded with her baby. "I am the baby's *real* mother," she says. "I carried him. I felt him kick. I prayed for him. At seven months I held a celebration for him. I saw his legs and hands on the sonogram. I suffered the pain of birth."

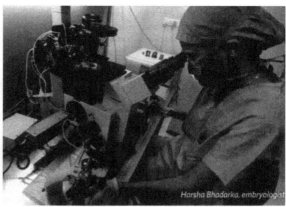

Harsha Bhadarka, embryologist

The baby's genetic parents, Indians from a nearby affluent suburb, kindly reached out to Leela. The genetic mother "sees me as her little sister, and I see her as my big sister," Leela says. "They check in with me every month, even now, and call me the baby's 'auntie.' They asked if I wanted to see the baby. I said 'yes' and they brought him to my house, but I was disappointed to see he was long and fair, not like me. Still, to this day, I feel I have three children." A friendship of sorts arose between the two mothers, although Leela's doctor, like Patel, discouraged it. "I deleted their phone number from my list because madam told me it's not a good thing to keep contact for long," she says.

Even if you can separate the genetic parents from the surrogate, you cannot separate the surrogate from her womb.

In a November 2008 *New York Times Magazine* article titled "Her Body, My Baby," American journalist Alex Kuczynski describes searching through profiles of available surrogates. "None were living in poverty," she writes. Cathy, the woman she eventually chose to carry her son, was a college-educated substitute teacher, a gifted pianist, and fellow fan of Barack Obama. They shared a land, a language, a level of education, a political bent—coming together to create a baby didn't seem like such a giant leap. But when the surrogate and genetic mother come from different corners of the globe—when one is an Indian woman who bails monsoon rains from her mud-floor hut and the other is an American woman who drives an SUV and vacations at ski resorts—the gap is more like a chasm. And as one childless American friend (rendered infertile through a defective Dalkon Shield intrauterine device) told me, "If I had hired a surrogate, I'm not sure how close I'd want to be to her. How open can you keep your heart when it's broken? Sometimes it's better not to touch unhealed wounds." A code of detachment seems almost necessary to circumvent the divide.

But detachment isn't so easy in practice. Even if you can separate the genetic parents from the surrogate, you cannot separate the surrogate from her womb. One surrogate mother told the sociologist Amrita Pande, "It's my blood, even if it's their genes." Psychologists tell us that a baby in utero recognizes the sound of its mother's voice. Surrogates I spoke with seemed to be struggling to detach. One said, "I try to think of my womb as a carrier." Another said, "I try not to think about it." Is the bond between mother and child fixed by nature or is it a culturally inspired fantasy we yearn to be true?

I asked Dr. Chakravarty if he thought that some children born of surrogacy would one day fly to India in search of their "womb mothers."

(The proposed regulation requires parents to reveal to an inquiring child the fact of surrogacy, though not the identity of the surrogate.) "Yes," he said. But chances are such an 18-year-old would not find her womb mother. Instead, she might come to realize she had been made a whole person by uniting parts drawn from tragically unequal worlds.

In a larger sense, so are we all. Person to person, family to family, the First World is linked to the Third World through the food we eat, the clothes we wear, and the care we receive. That Filipina nanny who cares for an American child leaves her own children in the care of her mother and another nanny. In turn, that nanny leaves her younger children in the care of an eldest daughter. First World genetic parents pay a Third World woman to carry their embryo. The surrogate's husband cares for their older children. The worlds of rich and poor are invisibly bound through chains of care.

Before we leave the Akanksha clinic in Anand, the gentle embryologist, Bhadarka, remains across the table from Aditya and me after Geeta and Saroj have left the room. I ask Bhadarka if the clinic offers psychological counseling to the surrogates. "We explain the scientific process," she answers, "and they already know what they're getting into." Then she moves her hands across the table and adds softly, "In the end, a mother is a mother, isn't that true? In the birthing room there is the surrogate, the doctor, the nurse, the nurse's aide, and often the genetic mother. Sometimes we all cry."

Reflexive Questions

1. How do systems of power and advantage influence concepts such as contraception, pregnancy, abortion, prenatal care, and childbirth?

2. What values and beliefs affect whether same-gender couples or queer individuals have the same rights to access reproductive technologies and healthcare as heterosexual couples and individuals?

3. Should medical professionals be allowed (in their code of ethics and professional standards) to act in a prejudiced or discriminatory manner based on their personal values about same-gender parenthood, relationships, and marriage?

4. What are the effects of treating patients differently based on their identity or immigration/residential status?

5. Before the reading about pregnant women who are incarcerated, had you ever thought about what it was like for a woman to be pregnant and incarcerated? What comes to mind when you think about it?

6. Consider what you have learned about prenatal development in terms of optimal outcomes for the infant and mother (attachment, nutrition, emotional health, etc.). What factors would be necessary for the health and well-being of the mother and fetus?

7. Considering that prisons were designed for men, do you think incarcerated pregnant women should be in a different type of facility? Why or why not?

8. What legal parenting rights should women have if they give birth while incarcerated?

9. Have you or a family member ever been treated in a disrespectful way by medical personnel? If so, was it based on race, social class, gender, culture, or immigration status? If not, why not? What aspects of your identity lend themselves to either advantage or disadvantage?

10. Based on your knowledge of infant and child development and the needs of pregnant women, how would you train medical professionals (doctors, midwives, nurses) to work with low-income immigrant women? How would you help them prevent having attitudes and actions that reflect systemic and structural racism, xenophobia, and sexism? Why is this important?

11. What cultural values are embedded in the medicalization of childbirth? How can medical settings reflect both cultural and clinical competence?

12. What are your thoughts and feelings about commercial surrogacy? What influences your perspective or worldview about it?

13. What social factors influence a woman's decision to be a paid surrogate mother?

14. What are other similar services/industries provided by women, whereby men are often the primary financial beneficiaries? How do power, social class, and gender intersect to create this tiered financial system?

CHAPTER 4

Infancy, Gender, and Culture

Introduction

Cultural values inform our meanings and understandings of gender. Given the saliency of gender, it becomes one of the first identities to shape how children define themselves and their gender-related appearance behaviors and preferences (Halim et al., 2014). Consider the question people often ask someone during pregnancy, "Are you having a boy or a girl?" At first glance, this question seems benign, but if we examine it more closely, we start to reveal assumptions of gender. First, gender matters a lot. This importance can be seen in the prevalence of "gender-reveal" parties and celebrations (Gieseler, 2018; Guignard, 2015). Gieseler states that these reveals/celebrations will prompt parents to begin generating gender-based expectations and assumptions onto their unborn infant and to enact them in digital, social, and public ways. Additionally, there is a worldwide preference for male infants (Prakash & Valdamannati, 2019), although there is some evidence that this preference is decreasing in countries such as the United States (Blau et al., 2020; Dahl & Moretti, 2008). Ultimately, the preference for males creates a trajectory of gender inequality among children and reinforces the belief that men are more valuable than women in society.

Second, gender is perceived as an "innate human condition," meaning that we are born with a gender. Once families "know" the "gender" of the fetus, they begin to construct narratives of the fetus's future life, personality, looks, temperament, and most often in stereotypically gendered ways. While the infant's sex may or may not be apparent at birth, we *assign* the infant's gender at birth based on their biological sex. Furthermore, researchers find families treat infants differently based on whether they perceive the infant to be a boy or a girl. Parents are more likely to engage in rough and tumble play with male infants and toddlers, and they are more likely to engage in gentler forms of play with female infants and toddlers (Lindsey & Mize, 2000, 2001). Beyond play, families tend to hold gender stereotypical beliefs about their children. For example, mothers tend to hold implicit assumptions of gender (e.g., girls should have long hair and bows), whereas fathers tend to hold explicit assumptions (e.g., telling boys that they should have short hair and to be tough) (Endendijk et al., 2013).

Lastly, there are only two acceptable and valid gender identities: boy/man and girl/woman. Even though our definitions of gender are expanding, we continually observe how gender is constrained by this binary. Our adherence to the gender binary has implications for intersex, transgender, and gender non-conforming/gender-expansive children. The definition of intersex is context-specific, relying on both cultural and scientific knowledge (Dreger, & Herndon, 2009). Intersex refers to a variation in congenital sex anatomy that is considered atypical for females or males (Dreger & Herndon, 2009). With the medicalization of gender, children born with "ambiguous" genitalia often undergo "corrective" (i.e., intersex genital mutilation) surgery (Davis et al., 2015). Unfortunately, such medical practices can be dangerous and will often negatively affect sexual pleasure in later life (Dayner et al., 2004). Another potential risk is that a child may feel as though the wrong gender was assigned to them. Although one can empathize with parents who want to help their child feel "normal" and not suffer the effects of being "different," it begs the question why we must change our anatomy to conform to societal beliefs and expectations, instead of expanding our definitions of what is "normal" and appreciating and embracing our physical differences.

This medicalization affects transgender people as well. Transgender is an umbrella term to encompass people who do not identify with the gender and/or sex assigned to them at birth (GLAAD, 2014). Some transgender people may seek gender affirming treatment such as hormone replacement therapy or gender-affirming surgeries (Coleman et al., 2012). Ultimately, it is common for parents to have strong expectations that their infant will grow up to be gender conforming (Coyle, Fulcher, & Trübutschek, 2016; Malpas, 2011; Pyne, 2014). Scholars such as Pyne (2014) argue that there needs to be a societal paradigm shift that is more affirming, non-pathologizing, and a positive approach to gender diversity among gender-independent children. The readings in this chapter help us closely examine the effects of gender and culture during birth and infancy, as well as take a closer look at breastfeeding as a form of bodywork and maternal care that influences the division of child care.

Summary of Readings

In the first reading, "**Masculinization of Births in Eastern Europe**" (2013), Christophe Guilmoto and Géraldine Duthé examine the prevalence and causes of sex-selective abortion in the Western Balkans and the Southern Caucasus region of Europe and Asia. This reading reviews the implications of sex-selective abortions and the high demand for males versus females. Throughout history, males have been the prize possession of families because a boy meant the continuation of the family lineage. Due to the rise in medical technology, it is now easier to determine the sex of infants before birth, leading to a rise in sex-selective abortion.

Technology has allowed medical personnel to determine the sex of an unborn child. Blood testing and other preconception methods that encourage sex selection have become common. Sex-selective abortions have created skewed sex ratios and have long term consequences for a society—as we have seen in China, India, and in certain countries in Eastern Europe. This sex imbalance is largely attributed to a belief in male superiority, leading to a preference for sons. Because Eastern European families are still traditionally based on male lineage and have strong patriarchal values and beliefs, many couples desire male children over female ones, and at least one boy at all costs. The authors discuss the social implications for the preference for males.

In the second reading, "'It's a … Does It Matter?' Theorizing 'Boy or Girl' Binary Classifications, Intersexuality, and Medical Practice in New Zealand" (2013) by Geraldine Christmas, the author examines the medical management of intersexuality in New Zealand, as well as the stigma surrounding intersexuality and the support available to intersex individuals and their families. The author points out how the small population size of New Zealand has important implications for intersexuality research. Not only is there little research on intersexuality in New Zealand, but the lack of anonymity in such a small country may discourage intersex individuals from participating in research. Furthermore, a distrust of the medical community—and its frequent dehumanization and embarrassing treatment of intersex people, including treating them like "research objects"—likely makes intersex people wary of research initiatives.

Additionally, the author discusses the silence around intersexuality. Although New Zealand is often considered a country with egalitarian gender roles, stigma and a lack of understanding still ensure that intersexuality is not something an intersex individual can openly discuss. The relentless reinforcement of a gender binary in childhood years further isolates intersex people. To combat this isolation and vulnerability, the author offers suggestions for how to better support intersexed children and their parents. Perhaps more importantly, support organizations help empower intersex individuals to be accepting and comfortable with who they are.

In the last reading, "The Work of Breastfeeding" (2009), Cindy Stearns discusses breastfeeding as a time- and labor-intensive form of bodywork and maternal care that influences the division of childcare. Stearns discusses the altered body practices that come with breastfeeding and carefully monitoring food and water intake to produce "quality" milk. Breastfeeding not only changes a mother's routine, but also comes with a learning curve. Stearns also examines the exclusivity of breastfeeding, which has unique implications for how mothers feel about breastfeeding. Some women report pleasure and pride in their ability to breastfeed and provide their child with sustenance in a way no one else can. Other women worry about their ability to produce enough milk. Additionally, some fathers may feel left out of the child-rearing process, while still others see breastfeeding as an excuse to opt out of infant care. Stearns concludes her reading by emphasizing the need for more empirical research on breastfeeding. By researching breastfeeding, scholars can learn more about the effects of the physically and emotionally demanding nature of this form of bodywork. Another important area to research is how we perceive lactating women who nurse infants other than their own. How do gender, culture, and socioeconomic status intersect to shape this practice?

In sum, similar to the readings in chapter 2, it is my hope that these readings will help the reader reflect on how gender is theorized, selected, enacted, and enforced, oftentimes even before the infant is born. I agree with many scholars and practitioners that there needs to be a worldwide movement to accept sex and gender independence and variability. This movement would be liberating and transformative and would free children from needing to rigidly adhere to oppressive gender scripts that unnecessarily create limitations for their development. Additionally, I hope readers will reflect on the importance and complexities of breastfeeding and how attitudes about breastfeeding are culturally informed and reinforced.

References

Blau, F. D., Kahn, L. M., Brummund, P., Cook, J., & Larson-Koester, M. (2020). Is there still son preference in the United States? *Journal of Population Economics, 33*, 709–750. https://doi.org/10.1007/s00148-019-00760-7

Brailey, C. D., & Slatton, B. C. (2019). Women, work, and inequality in the US: Revising the second shift. *Journal of Sociology, 7*(1), 29–35. https://doi.org/10/15640/jssw.v7n1a4

Coleman, E., Bockting, W., Botzer, M., Cohen-Kettenis, P., DeCuypere, G., Feldman, J., Fraser, L., Green, J., Knudson, G., Meyer, W. J., Monstrey, S., Adler, R. K., Brown, G. R., Devor, A. H., Ehrbar, R., Ettner, R., Eyler, E., Garofalo, R., Karasic, D. H., ... Zucker, K. (2012). Standards of care for the health of transsexual, transgender, and gender-non-conforming people, version 7. *International Journal of Transgenderism, 13*(4), 165–232. https://doi.org/10.1080/1553 2739.2011.700873

Coyle, E. F., Fulcher, M., & Trübutschek, D. (2016). Sissies, mama's boys, and tomboys: Is children's gender non-conformity more acceptable when nonconforming traits are positive? *Archives of Sexual Behavior, 45,* 1827–1838. doi:10.1007/s10508-016- 0695-5

Dahl, G. B., & Moretti, E. (2008). The demand for sons. *The Review of Economic Studies, 75*(4), 1085–1120. https://doi. org/10.1111/j.1467-937X.2008.00514.x

Davis, G., Dewey, J. M., & Murphy, E. L. (2016). Giving sex: Deconstructing intersex and trans medicalization practices. *Gender & Society, 30*(3), 490–514. https://doi.org/10.1177/0891243215602102

Dayner, J. E., Lee, P. A., & Houk, C. P. (2004). Medical treatment of intersex: parental perspectives. *The Journal of Urology, 172*(4), 1762–1765. doi.org/10.1097/01/ju.0000138519.12573.3a

Dreger, A. D., & Herndon, A. M. (2009). Progress and politics in the intersex rights movement: Feminist theory in action. *GLQ, 15*(2), 199–224. doi:10.1215/10642684-2008-134

Endendijk, J. J., Groeneveld, M. G., van Berkel, S. R., Hallers-Haalboom, E. T., Mesman, J., & Bakersman-Kraneburg, M. J. (2013). Gender stereotypes in the family context: Mothers, fathers, and siblings. *Sex Roles, 68*, 577–590. doi:10.1007/s11199-013-0265-4.

GLAAD. (2014). GLAAD media reference guide: Transgender issues. Retrieved from http://www.glaad.org/reference/transgender

Gieseler, C. (2018) Gender-reveal parties: performing community identity in pink and blue, *Journal of Gender Studies, 27*(6), 661–671. doi:10.1080/09589236.2017.1287066

Guignard, F. R. (2015). A gendered bun in the oven: The gender-reveal party as a new ritualization during pregnancy. *Studies in Religion, 44*(4), 479–500. doi:10.1177/0008429815599802

Halim, M. L., Ruble, D. N., Tamis-LeMonda, C. S., Zosuls, K. M., Lurye, L. E., Greulich, F. K. (2014). Pink frilly dresses and the avoidance of all things "girly": Children's appearance rigidity and cognitive theories of gender development. *Developmental Psychology, 50*(4), 1091–1101.

Lindsey, E. W., & Mize, J. (2000). Parent-child physical and pretense play: Links to children's social competence. *Merrill-Palmer Quarterly, 46* (4), 565–591. doi:10.1037/t58344-000.

Lindsey, E. W., & Mize, J. (2001). Contextual differences in parent-child play: Implications for children's gender role development. *Sex Roles, 44* (3/4), 155–176. doi:10.1023/A:1010950919451.

Malpas, J. (2011). Between pink and blue: A multi-dimensional family approach to gender nonconforming children and their Families. *Family Process, 50*(4), 453–470.

Pyne, J. (2014). Gender independent kids: A paradigm shift in approaches to gender non-conforming children. *The Canadian Journal of Human Sexuality, 23*(1), 1–8. doi.org/10.3138/cjhs.23.1.C01

Prakash, N., & Vadlamannati, K. C. (2019). Girls for sale? Child Sex Ratio and Girl Trafficking in India. *Feminist Economics, 25*(4), 267–308. doi:10.1080/13545701.2019.1666212

Walker, A. J. (2009). A feminist critique of family science. In S. A. Lloyd, A. L. Few, & K. R. Allen (Eds.), *Handbook of feminist family studies* (pp. 18–27). Sage.

Population & Societies

Masculinization of Births in Eastern Europe

Christophe Z. Guilmoto[1] and Géraldine Duthé[2]

Sex-selective abortion is not specific to Asia. Christophe Guilmoto and Géraldine Duthé explain why European countries in the Western Balkans and Southern Caucasus are affected too. Although the problem was described for the first time more than ten years ago, it is only now that the authorities in these countries and in Europe are starting to show concern.

The sex ratio at birth is said to be "skewed" when it exceeds the norm of 105 boys per 100 girls, as has been the case for more than 20 years in China and parts of India (Box 4.1.1). Excess male births resulting from sex-selective abortion of female fetuses is an issue generally associated with Asia. [1] But prenatal sex discrimination is by no means limited to that continent alone. [2] Evidence of sex imbalances at birth has been found elsewhere in the world, notably in the Asian diaspora (Box 4.1.1), but also in several countries of Eastern Europe where it has so far attracted less attention.

Twenty Years of Excess Male births in Certain Eastern European Countries

In two regions of Eastern Europe –the Southern Caucasus and the Western Balkans around Albania –the sex ratio at birth is between 110 and 117 (Table). For the three Caucasian countries, it increased in the 1990s (Figure 4.1.1, Table) [4.1.3, 4.1.4, 4.1.5] to reach levels even higher than the current estimates for the whole of India. It is highest in Azerbaijan (close to 117), which now ranks second in the world behind China among countries with the largest sex ratio imbalance.

In the other cluster of countries, located in Southeast Europe and centred around Albania but also including Kosovo, Montenegro and western Macedonia, the observed levels are lower, at around 110-111 male births per 100 female ones, but their regularity over time shows that the imbalance is real (Table, Figure 4.1.1).

---

1   Ceped-Institut de recherche pour le développement.
2   Institut national d'études démographiques.

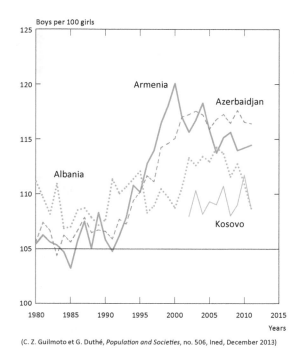

Boys per 100 girls

(C. Z. Guilmoto et G. Duthé, *Population and Societies*, no. 506, Ined, December 2013)

FIGURE 4.1.1 Sex ratio at birth in Albania, Armenia, Azerbaijan and Kosovo, 1980–2011
SOURCE: Vital records.

Despite pioneering demographic research, [4, 5] the rising sex ratio in these countries went unnoticed for more than a decade, with some seeing it as an artefact linked to the poor quality of vital records. It is true that these countries have seen major socio-political upheaval since 1991 due to the dismantling of the socialist system, combined in some cases –as in Kosovo, Georgia and Armenia –with internal or international conflicts. Yet while their statistical systems have inevitably been disrupted, the latest censuses in all these countries confirm the increasing share of male children, [6, 7] as do the national demographic and socioeconomic surveys conducted on representative population samples.[3, 5]

Understanding the Masculinization of Births

The increase in sex ratio at birth is attributed to three factors: a traditional preference for boys, access to technologies for prenatal sex selection

BOX 4.1.1. THE SEX IMBALANCE AT BIRTH IN ASIA

The emergence of a sex imbalance at birth was first observed in the early 1980s in Asia. By the mid-1990s it had reached 115 boys per 100 girls in South Korea and China (Figure 4.1.3). The trend has since reversed in South Korea, falling to a level of 106 today. This "return to normalcy" can be explained by improvements in women's status and by government measures to eradicate sex-selective abortion.

In China, on the other hand, the sex ratio at birth has continued to rise, reaching a level of 120 boys per 100 girls. The problem has also spread to other countries, such as Vietnam – where the sex ratio has risen over the last decade to reach 112 in 2012–and Nepal, the region of Kathmandu especially. In India, despite improvements in the most affected north-western states (Punjab, Haryana, Rajasthan), the 2011 census shows that sex selection has taken hold in several other previously untouched states such as Uttar Pradesh or Maharashtra. Not all Asian countries are concerned however. Iran, Thailand, Japan and Indonesia, for example, have normal sex ratios at birth.

TABLE 4.1.1 **Demographic indicators of countries with a high sex ratio**

Country	Sex ratio at birth[1]	Fertility (children per woman)[2]	Population size (millions)[3]
Asia			
China	117.8	1.7	1359.8
Vietnam	111.2	1.8	89.0
India	110.5	2.5	1205.6
Southern Caucasus			
Azerbaijan	116.8	1.9	9.1
Armenia	114.8	1.7	3.0
Georgia	111.8	1.8	4.4
Southeast Europe			
Albania	111.7	1.8	3.1
Kosovo	109.7	2.3	1.8
Macedonia (North-west)	110.9	1.5	0.3
Montenegro	109.8	1.7	0.6

Notes: [1] boys per 100 girls circa 2010, [2] in 2010-2015, [3] in 2010.

Sources: The sex ratios in Europe are calculated from vital records for Albania, Armenia, Azerbaijan, Georgia, Kosovo, Macedonia and Montenegro. Estimates are based on various sources for the other countries. The other indicators come from the United Nations Population Division and the World Bank (Kosovo). Northwestern Macedonia corresponds to the Polog region, for which we estimated the corresponding fertility level.

(1) Abortion was widely used for many years as a birth control method in the former socialist countries (Soviet Union and Yugoslavia). The only exception was Albania, where abortion was prohibited during the Communist era for pronatalist reasons. It was not legalized until 1995.

(mainly ultrasound screening and abortion), and the compounding effect of low fertility. [1, 8]

Fertility in Eastern Europe has fallen dramatically since the 1990s in response to political upheaval and rapidly changing living conditions. With the exception of Kosovo, fertility in all the countries of Eastern Europe affected by masculinization of births is below two children per woman (Table 4.1.1).

If a woman has two children, there is a 25% statistical chance that both will be girls. So in the absence of alternative sex selection methods, or of a freak biological phenomenon that alters the sex ratio at birth in these countries, the imbalance must be due to the abortion of female fetuses. In other words, couples wishing to have at least one son can undergo sex-selective abortion to avoid giving birth to a girl. This does not guarantee success, however, since the next pregnancy will not necessarily be a boy either; several successive pregnancies and abortions may precede a male birth.

Modern prenatal sex selection methods have become available in eastern European countries since the opening of their borders and the development of a market economy. Although abortion has been available in most of these countries for many years, often under excellent conditions of hygiene and safety,(1) ultrasound equipment did not exist in the past, or was based on obsolete Soviet technology producing poor-quality images that were difficult to interpret. When the borders were opened in the early 1990s, more advanced equipment could be imported and private clinics offering reproductive health services for future mothers sprang up across the region.

At Least One Boy at All Costs

Son preference is the main explanation for the high sex ratio at birth. In most European countries, low fertility and access to technology do not lead to distortions of this type. In the Western Balkans and the Southern Caucasus, however, decades of socialism which had eradicated many of the most flagrant forms of gender discrimination in society (in employment, education or socio-political autonomy) did little to reduce inequalities within the family unit. The family is still based upon the traditional male lineage, and the presence of sons, who often live with their parents after marriage, further strengthens family bonds. These strongly patrilineal and patrilocal structures not only remained robust throughout the Communist era, but even grew in strength after the fall of the Soviet regime. [9] In the ensuing period of widespread upheaval, the rapid withdrawal of state control led to a breakdown in solidarity and to mass unemployment that shook the fabric of society. The family structure was the social institution most resilient to such change. It provided its members with guaranteed security, financial support and housing, and offered a substitute for the shrinking state bodies and the immature market mechanisms

BOX 4.1.2. SKEWED SEX RATIOS IN THE DIASPORA

Excess male births have been observed in Europe and elsewhere in diaspora populations, notably among migrants of Asian origin. This is the case for populations of Indian origin in England, for example, among whom a sex ratio of 113 boys per 100 girls has been observed for third births. [12] A similar phenomenon has been reported among Chinese populations in Italy, Indians in Norway and among Albanian immigrants in Greece and Italy. It has also been observed in the United States, with sex ratios of around 110 for third births among the Chinese, Korean and Indian populations. There is no way of knowing if the problem exists in France due to the absence of data by ethnic origin.

In countries where prenatal sex selection is practically non-existent, these populations of immigrant origin account for a very small proportion of total births, so national sex ratios are barely affected. However, the existence of these preferences in the Asian diaspora populations, far from their countries of origin, shows that sex selection is linked more to the cultural attitudes brought by migrants to their host country than to the circumstances of the origin country (such as restrictive birth control policies like those enforced in China). These practices are likely to wane among populations of immigrant origin who settle permanently in industrialized countries, as patriarchal norms become progressively weaker and the status of women improves.

that were incapable of regulating economic activity during the socioeconomic transition period. However, it is difficult to understand why no sex imbalance is observed in neighbouring countries with comparable social and historical backgrounds and with similar patriarchal values (Northern Caucasus and Central Asia for example).

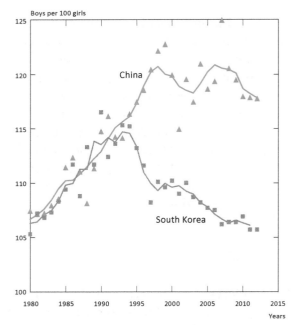

(C. Z. Guilmoto et G. Duthé, *Population and Societies*, no. 506, Ined, December 2013)

FIGURE 4.1.3   Sex ratio at birth in South Korea and China, 1980–2012
SOURCE: Vital records.
NOTES: ▲ ■ observations ══════ : smoothed curves.

Conclusion

The countries of Eastern Europe affected by a skewed sex ratio are sparsely populated, with a total population of just 23 million, equivalent to that of Shanghai, where the sex ratio at birth is also abnormally high. Asian diasporas are even smaller, so the effect of prenatal sex selection on the future demography of Europe is hardly comparable with the massive impact of such practices on the Asian giants. Moreover, certain countries such as Albania and Armenia are losing large numbers of young adults, mainly men, who are emigrating to Italy or Russia, thereby attenuating the effects of excess male births.

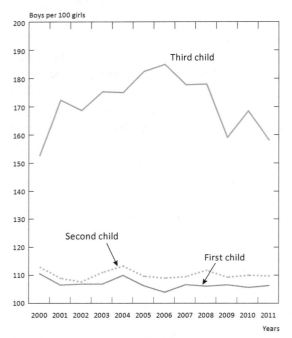

(C. Z. Guilmoto et G. Duthé, *Population and Societies*, no. 506, Ined, December 2013)

FIGURE 4.1.2   Sex ratio at birth by birth order in Armenia, 2000–2011
SOURCE: Vital records.

In countries where sex selection is practiced, the probability of having a third child tends to double or even triple if the first two are girls, and the sex ratio at birth increases sharply for third births, often exceeding 120 or 130. In the 2000s, the ratio even reached 185 for third births in Armenia, probably a world record (Figure 4.1.2). [2]

The discriminatory practices made possible by modern technologies are viewed as a practically "normal" feature of demographic choice in these countries, and reveal the true extent of gender inequalities. With technological progress, it will perhaps become even easier to determine the sex of an unborn child using a fetal blood test or other preconception methods, thus further encouraging sex selection. These methods are now at the centre of a new Europe-wide bioethical debate. [10] In the meantime, East European populations characterized by strong patriarchal values are testing a system of demographic laissez-faire on a local scale. Governments and civil society have paid little attention to this question, often to due relative ignorance of the problems associated with skewed sex ratios at birth. Recent efforts to understand the phenomenon stem more from international concern [11] than from local awareness, and have not yet given rise to any practical response in the form of campaigns to prevent sex-selective abortion or more far-reaching policies to restore gender equality within the family.

References

1. Gilles Pison, 2004, "Fewer births, but a boy at all costs: selective female abortion in Asia", *Population and Societies*, 404, 4 p.

2. UNFPA, 2012, *Sex Imbalances at Birth. Current Trends, Consequences and Policy Implications*, UNFPA, Bangkok.

3. Géraldine Duthé et al., 2012, "High sex ratios at birth in the Caucasus. Modern technology to satisfy old desires", *Population and Development Review*, 38(3), pp. 497–501.

4. Rube Yeganyan et al., 2001, "Life expectancies in two Caucasian Countries", *Demographic Research*, 5, pp. 217–244.

5. France Meslé et al., 2007, "A sharp increase in sex ratio at birth in the Caucasus. Why? How?", In Watering the Neighbour's Garden. *The growing female demographic deficit in Asia*, I. Attané and C.Z. Guilmoto, (eds.), Paris: CICRED, pp. 73–89.

6. UNFPA, 2012, *Sex Imbalances at Birth in Albania. Current Trends, Consequences and Policy Implications*, UNFPA, Tirana.

7. UNFPA, 2013, *Sex Imbalances at Birth in Armenia. Demographic Evidence and Analysis*, UNFPA.

8. Christophe Z. Guilmoto, 2009, "The sex ratio transition in Asia", *Population and Development Review*, 35(3), pp. 519–549.

9. Karl Kaser, 2008, *Patriarchy after Patriarchy. Gender Relations in Turkey and in the Balkans 1500-2000*, Vienna, LIT Verlag, 328 p.

10. Wybo Dondorp et al., 2013, "ESHRE Task Force on ethics and Law 20: Sex selection for non-medical reasons", *Human Reproduction*, 28(6), pp. 1448–1454.

11. Doris Stump, 2011. *Prenatal Sex Selection. Report, Committee on Equal Opportunities for Women and Men*, Council of Europe, Strasbourg.

12. Sylvie Dubuc and David Coleman, 2007, "An increase in the sex ratio of births to India-born mothers in England and Wales: Evidence for sex-selective abortions", *Population and Development Review*, 33(2), pp. 383–400.

13. James FX Egan et al., 2011, "Distortions of sex ratios at birth in the United States; Evidence for prenatal gender selection", *Prenatal diagnosis*, 31(6), pp. 560–565.

'It's a … Does It Matter?'

Theorising 'Boy or Girl' Binary Classifications, Intersexuality and Medical Practice in New Zealand

Geraldine Christmas

Abstract

This paper presents findings from my doctoral research on the medical management of intersexuality in New Zealand, as well as the type of support for intersex New Zealanders and their families. Specifically, I discuss the implications of New Zealand's small population on both medical management and undertaking research on what can be considered a rare condition and sensitive topic respectively. One such implication is that clinicians in New Zealand hospitals encounter a smaller number of intersex births compared to Australia, for example, and therefore have little experience or awareness of intersex conditions. Another implication is the difficulty of maintaining confidentiality in a small population. In New Zealand, providing anonymity is difficult compared to larger-populated countries such as the USA. I also discuss poststructuralist theorising about power structures in society—particularly in New Zealand, where there appears to be a connection amongst every New Zealander. And while New Zealand boasts about being an accepting, egalitarian nation, my findings show that judgemental attitudes towards a lesser-known condition still exist in parts of New Zealand society. I argue that New Zealanders' connectedness contributes to maintaining power structures to silence and isolate individuals for the fear of being found out—because their anatomies do not meet societal assumptions of male and female (binary) norms.

Key Words

intersexuality, medicalisation, methodology, communities, gender identity

Introduction

This article presents my findings from my recently-completed doctoral research on the medical management of intersexuality in New Zealand, and support for intersex New Zealanders and their families. It also presents material which was not included in the final version of my doctoral thesis.[1] My research includes

---

1   My doctoral thesis can be accessed online at http://researcharchive.vuw.ac.nz/handle/10063/2845

Geraldine Christmas, Selections from "It's a … Does It Matter? Theorising 'Boy or Girl' Binary Classifications, Intersexuality and Medical Practice in New Zealand," *Women's Studies Journal*, vol. 27, no. 1, pp. 25-26, 28-35. Copyright © 2013 by The New Zealand Women's Studies Association. Reprinted with permission. Provided by ProQuest LLC. All rights reserved.

findings from recorded interviews with five intersex New Zealanders, six parents of intersex children, three registered nurses, two specialist clinicians, a midwifery programme director, four community/support organisation representatives (one of whom is also a parent), a counsellor and a former MP.

Intersexuality is a biological variation, in which an individual with an *intersex condition* is often born with ambiguous genitalia which do not appear typically male or female. Individuals are also born with either a combination of male and female internal sex organs—as with *true hermaphrodites* (Grumbach, Hughes & Conte, 2003, pp. 908–909), or internal sex organs which are discordant with their external genitalia—as with *male* and *female pseudohermaphrodites* (Forest, 2001, pp. 1986–1989, 1997).

The following questions form the basis of my arguments, analysis and conclusions:

What are the medical rationales for managing intersex conditions with regard to health concerns, and how do traditional assumptions about gender and sexuality relate to medical decision-making?

What are the understandings of intersex people, parents, clinicians, nurses and community/support organisation representatives in New Zealand about clinical procedures and gender?

What are the understandings of the aforementioned people about support and acceptance of intersexuality in New Zealand, especially with its small population and apparent connectedness?

What are the links between my findings, and feminist and gender theories?

Specifically, I will discuss the implications of New Zealand's small population size on the research process itself, the medical management of intersexuality, and support for intersex New Zealanders and their families. I will also discuss an issue that emerges from my findings: *privacy in small communities*, which compel some people to remain silent about a lesser-known condition. [...].

Narratives About Medical Management in New Zealand

Because of New Zealand's small population, the number of babies born with intersex conditions per year is small compared to countries such as the USA, for example. Plastic surgeon Chris McEwan remarks that the Mayo Clinic in the USA, where he worked for three years, '[has] a significant practice in intersex' (McEwan, 2010, interview). The Mayo Clinic itself states that it is 'one of the few institutions specialising in a multidisciplinary approach to the treatment of more comprehensive urologic disorders' which include intersex conditions (Mayo Clinic, 2013). The Children's Hospital Boston also has a multidisciplinary clinic which specifically focuses on intersex conditions, and assists transgender children and young people considering medical procedures (Children's Hospital Boston, 2007). Compared to the USA, my findings suggest that some New Zealand clinicians may have never encountered a child with an intersex condition, and therefore may have little experience or awareness of intersexuality. A mother recalls a New Zealand hospital's apparent lack of experience when her newborn child's sex was questioned by a registrar:

He [registrar] said, 'I'm not quite sure, but I have...'—he had printed off a couple of pieces of paper, and he said to me, 'I think what your baby may have is CAH [congenital adrenal hyperplasia][2] ...' ... He said, 'I don't know much about it myself, but I've gone back and I've photocopied some papers.' So he gave me the papers to look at, and I was just like... what's going on? ... he said to me, 'At this stage we don't know what the sex of the baby is.' And he said, 'No one knows what to do from here.' (*Anonymous 1, 2010, interview*).

New Zealand's smaller number of intersex cases also has implications for New Zealand paediatric/urological surgeons, compared to such surgeons at American hospitals who may encounter intersex cases more frequently. Consequently New Zealand children are commonly referred to Royal Children's Hospital in Melbourne, in our neighbouring country Australia, which is regarded amongst the New Zealand medical community as a centre of excellence (P. Hofman, personal communication, 25 February 2010). Jacqui (pseudonym), a woman with CAH, remarks that, while she has 'nothing against' clinicians in New Zealand, New Zealand's smaller population—and smaller number of CAH individuals—can be problematic for the establishment of specialised surgical procedures:

... and that's why I think it's so important to keep those communication lines open with Australia—especially for us CAH girls. (*Jacqui, 2010, interview*).

Jacqui, who underwent about four (she cannot confirm the exact number) surgeries during infancy, childhood and adolescence, underwent her last surgery in 2007 at the Royal Mercy Hospital in Melbourne:

... it's [gynaecological surgery] just so, so worth it. I mean, had I not had that surgery I couldn't have had my son [who was delivered via caesarean section] ... Just very, very lucky to have the most understanding husband in the world, who—we were engaged for six or seven years before that, and we've basically a nil sex life so how many guys put up with that! So yeah I was very, very lucky with that. And then we went over [to Melbourne] and we got it sorted, and it was very successful. (*Jacqui, 2010, interview*).

Paediatric endocrinologist Professor Paul Hofman and another specialist clinician appear to recognise that New Zealand's small population has implications on establishing specialised medical care for intersex conditions. The clinician and his New Zealand colleagues have been liaising with their counterparts in Australia

---

2 *Congenital adrenal hyperplasia* (CAH) occurs during prenatal development in genetic males (46,XY) and females (46,XX), and results from deficiencies in specific enzymes in the adrenal glands (Forest, 2001, pp. 1986, 1997; Grumbach et al., 2003, p. 917). Genetic females with CAH are commonly born with masculinised genitalia with clitoral enlargement (Forest, 2001, p. 1997), while enzyme deficiencies in genetic males with CAH impairs the synthesis of testosterone to produce male sexual characteristics (ibid., p. 1986). A health concern for all CAH individuals is salt loss which can be life-threatening, and mineralocorticoid and glucocorticoid replacement medication is often prescribed (ibid.; pp. 1988–1989, 1997).

which, because of its larger population, has a greater number of intersex diagnoses:

> We have been in negotiation with Australia as well, because they have as many if not more problems than we have at this moment with the management of DSDs. I wouldn't be surprised if it expanded to form an Australasian group in due course. (*Anonymous clinician, 2010, interview*).

'What's That?'—Parents' Experiences and Strategies in Close-Knit Communities

Feminist poststructuralist theory analyses how power works by not only forcing people 'into particular ways of being', but by making those ways 'desirable' so that people adopt them as their own (Davies & Gannon, 2005, p. 318). In relation to this theoretical perspective, in this section I discuss how New Zealand's connectedness maintains power structures by compelling parents, for example, to keep silent about their children's intersex conditions for the fear of being found out. I will also discuss parents' experiences and strategies when dealing with prurient or judgemental attitudes from others.

While New Zealand boasts about being an accepting, egalitarian nation, my findings show that judgemental attitudes towards a lesser-known condition still exist in parts of New Zealand society. Bronwyn (pseudonym), a mother of four children—the two eldest of whom have intersex conditions, strongly advises parents to 'remain firm' against pressure from people asking about a newborn baby's sex—particularly in a small rural community:

> Be strong for the future's [*sic*] sake of your child because later on that child is going to grow up—in our case, in a very small community where everybody knows, and they will then have to face the fact that you said that you didn't know what sex it was, or you didn't know, or you announced male when it was female or whatever. And that child is going to grow up—unless you're going to move away—in that community. So stay strong—don't announce it. And for your child's future don't announce it—no matter how much pressure you get, because it will matter one day. At the moment, to you, well it may not matter, but in the future that child will have to face—and somebody will say, when you're at a very vulnerable age: 'My mum said there was this story, when you were born you were a boy. Are you a boy?' So hold out, stick to your guns and don't announce it. (*Bronwyn, 2010, interview*)

Bronwyn's view reflects her experience about wanting to protect her second child from stigmatisation—particularly hurt caused by gossip and rumours. Because of society's ingrained binary sex/gender system, many people only acknowledge the categories of male and female which makes it difficult for them to understand gender fluidity. Many people are also simply unaware about a relatively lesser-known condition compared to Down's syndrome, for example. Bronwyn's comment about being asked a potentially personal question 'at a very vulnerable age' echoes the issue of silence—that intersexuality is something never to tell to anyone (Chase, 1998, p. 211).

After being 'assured' by a paediatrician that their second child was male, Bronwyn and her husband Murray (pseudonym) placed a birth notice in their local newspaper that they had had a son (Murray, 2010, interview). Two weeks later a chromosome test confirmed that their child's sex chromosomes were female (46,XX) and a second test confirmed the same result (Bronwyn, 2010, interview). Murray recalls his feelings during this waiting period:

> So I guess from that, that was a pretty traumatic time when you've then got to tell your community—a close-knit community, that "We've had a boy but now we've actually got a girl". (*Murray, 2010, interview*).

Murray's comment that the time of the confirmed test results was 'traumatic', when he and Bronwyn had already publicly announced that their child was male, suggests a lack of awareness about intersexuality in their community. However, many people in other New Zealand locations (both rural and urban) and overseas only assume a male/female binary system. Information on Murray and Bronwyn's children's conditions, particularly during the time when their two eldest children were born, may have not only been scarce but difficult to access which may have exacerbated their stress. Visiting a library (the internet was non-existent then) in the nearest town—a considerable distance from their farm—would have been difficult because of Murray and Bronwyn's busy roles as farmer and mother of two then small children (she now farms alongside her husband), respectively.

While Bronwyn comments on 'what a corny society we live in' and that 'we are all on a [gender] continuum anyway', she maintains that society's pressure to be male or female is particularly reinforced during childhood:

> As a child you're wearing a girl's school uniform or a boy's school uniform ... you have to be one or the other. Every single child in New Zealand—and when they are growing up alongside other little children, every child knows that everybody's either a boy or a girl. Children are black and white. Adults can be grey as much as they want to, but children are not. (*Bronwyn, 2010, interview*).

Hofman also commented about societal attitudes towards intersex conditions associated with 'major ambiguity':

> [There is] ignorance in society, particularly amongst parents who feel isolated—they don't want to talk about it. I think support is fragmented, no parents want the school to know their child is different, such as a cubicle or changing room situation [e.g. for sports or swimming]. (*P. Hofman, personal communication, 25 February 2010*).

Hofman's comments suggest that other parents, like Bronwyn, want to protect their children from societal prejudices towards difference. Concerns about teasing and bullying compel parents to keep silent about their children's variance, which relates to poststructuralist theorising on how societal power structures are maintained. Bronwyn also recalled a midwife who was particularly helpful when her children were small, and her comments suggest there was an undercurrent of prurience in a local Plunket group:

> She helped me in practical ways to "face" the other young mothers—that is, being aware that

nappy-changing needed to be done away from the [Plunket] group, as I didn't feel comfortable having curious eyes looking on—if something is seen, it imprints on the brain, and I wanted to protect our daughters from that. (*Bronwyn, 2010, interview*).

Prurience also maintains societal power structures which again compel some parents to conceal their children's differences—though this is understandable as some parents want to protect their children from being the subject of gossip. Jo, another mother of an intersex child, told me her strategy of dealing with prurience:

> ... you get the odd morbid fascination from people, who every time you see them they go "What's your daughter got again?!" And it's like [sighs] ... but you just deal with those people. I just make sure I use the most complicated terms possible when I'm dealing with them, so that they feel a bit thick ... (*Jo, 2010, interview*).

Some people's prurience towards intersexuality also echoes its 'circus freak' connotations (HRC, 2007, p. 81)—the assumption that intersexuality is a supposedly unfortunate condition. Other findings, however, suggest that having an intersex condition is not as bad as some people or media sources convey. A woman with CAH remarked that:

> It's [intersex condition] not as bad as people say it is, it's the way people I guess comprehend the meaning of it. If they actually understood and had the information then maybe they'd

be more supportive. (*Anonymous 3, 2010, interview*).

Anonymous 1 offered a similar narrative. While she was stressed when her newborn baby's sex was not immediately confirmed by clinicians, and while her now-older child undergoes regular health-related tests because of her intersex condition, Anonymous 1 enthused about her child's energetic activities:

> Every time my child has one of her registrar appointments we do the bloods and our endocrinologist sits down, and she said to me, "CAH children are sometimes sickly children but ..." My child is one of those children who's really full of life, she plays rugby league, she won the cross-country, she's won everything in athletics, she's one of those really highly competitive girls.

> When you watch her on the rugby league field she's just—oh my God, she's just out there! Compared to other girls her age she's just really into it, and she loves sports ... (*Anonymous 1, 2010, interview*).

Support in New Zealand

My findings show that the work of support organisations is of particular importance in New Zealand. This is not only with regard to advice about sensitive matters of a sexual nature, but support appears to be particularly crucial for adolescents who may feel vulnerable amongst their peers. Sarah (pseudonym), who founded a support group for parents of intersex children,[3] talked about the difficulties that teenage girls can encounter after undergoing vaginal surgery, and how her support organisation helped one girl who lived in a rural part of New Zealand:

> So say they have top-up [genital] surgery as an adolescent and say they get a set of dilators,[4] which you have to order specially and, you know, it's all embarrassing for a teenager. … this girl I'm thinking of, who would have been in her late teens, had a set of dilators … she could find no one to teach her how to use them because she lived in the wops.[5] She was trying to insert them, and she was actually inserting them into the urogenital sinus rather than the vagina … So she was getting excruciating pain using these dilators, couldn't make them work … She's not in Melbourne [where surgery was performed]— like, she's a million miles away from Melbourne, there's nobody there for follow-up.
>
> …
>
> So you can see that even if they might go over to Melbourne and have excellent care, then gaps occur because we don't get follow-up care. … you might need counselling and there aren't people. … that's one of the functions of our [support] group … that at least they can ring and say, "Hey this is happening,

what do you think?" I'll say, "It's tricky, I don't have an answer, and what I'm wondering about is can you build up a relationship with a GP … gently build up a relationship with someone who could help you with this?" That's what this girl did, and it worked. (*Sarah, 2010, interview*).

This finding shows that New Zealand's small population can be problematic on establishing specialist medical care for a relatively rare condition, which Jacqui commented about previously. However, this finding also shows how a support group can counter the implications of New Zealand's small population and apparent lack of specialised medical care. A single telephone call to a support group contact person, who has *first-hand experience* of intersex issues, can indeed help someone overcome barriers of silence and embarrassment in relation to sexual issues. While the internet has enabled instant access to extensive information in the privacy of one's own home, and has enabled support networks to be more easily-accessible, the information that someone posts on a website can be difficult or even impossible to verify as legitimate (see Portelli, 1991, p. 51). Lisa (pseudonym), a woman with CAH, cautioned that information on the internet should not be regarded as gospel:

> Yeah, it's [internet] good but it can also be … it can lead you astray too. I've done a little bit of looking before and you've got to be careful not—to take everything as a grain of salt and, like, what is good and what's actually

---

3   As requested by Sarah, the name of this organisation has been withheld.
4   Individuals who have undergone vaginal surgery (either to construct a vagina or 'open up' a vaginal cavity) are often prescribed a set of dilators in different widths to prevent the vagina from narrowing or closing up.
5   *Wop-wops*, or *wops* (NZ slang): an isolated or remote area, especially a rural area far away from a town or city.

not good, so what's proper research and what's just hearsay.

[*I ask Lisa to elaborate*]

I think the thing with the internet is it's very hard to know, the person who's written that, what are their qualifications and—like it could be just a name, and it's so easy just to put information on the internet, which looks just as official as someone official. … like you're a research student, you know how to research—you'll research the name before you research the research … whereas for Joe Bloggs, they will just say, "Oh it's on the internet, it must be correct." So it's very easy just to get information there which hasn't actually got much standing, it's just someone with just their point of view, which is OK but you've got to be aware that there's scientific information and there's points-of-view information, which is …

GC: *'Just some people's opinions.'*

Yeah that's exactly it and it's that sort of thing which you've got to be careful with what you're doing. I think that's probably more what I was more relating to … is it actually good proper information or is it something else? There are good websites out there like the CAH [support organisation][6] website, it has got links to the research which they know is good and proper and stuff like that. (*Lisa & Geraldine, 2010, interview*).

Indeed, as I only interviewed five intersex people I visited online discussion forums in order to view other intersex people's narratives. However, echoing Portelli's (1991, p. 51) argument, it was impossible to determine which online discussion forums and websites on intersex issues were legitimate. While I used extensive word searches on the Google search engine, with words such as 'intersex', 'gender', 'surgery' and 'discussion', many search results appeared fetish-like, voyeuristic and pretentious.

Jacqui recommended that there should be more psychological-type support services in New Zealand:

There needs to be more—I think this is the right word, psychological support. … They're [clinicians] excellent in dealing with the physical stuff, they are not that great with dealing with the emotional side of things. Now over in Melbourne I was offered that extra support if I wanted it, and I was staunch in whatever enough then—I said, "I'm fine, I don't need that." … There needs to be open information for parents of kids, and that's becoming more and more, especially with the CAH support group … (*Jacqui, 2010, interview*).

She also remarked that such support is particularly important during adolescence:

Yes, yes, and around the major events—you know, like the surgeries and things. I've suffered from

---

6   In order to ensure confidentiality I have withheld details about this support group.

depression on and off for a number of years, and I think that's probably because of that. I'm free of it again at the moment and hopefully it will remain, but that probably started to become an issue when I—it might have been when I was little, still at home. But when I left home ... I had the most awesome parents who were very, very supportive, but I think there needs to be that—maybe counselling available, *easy* to get hold of, and not to dump you in a—as a psych case basically ... (*Jacqui, 2010, interview*).

The issue of stigma emerges from Jacqui's last comment, which suggests that she may have had negative experiences with a counsellor or psychologist. This also shows that psychological support or counselling should *empower* individuals, instead of making them feel that they 'have a serious problem' and that 'there is something wrong with me'.

Rogena commented that counselling and support is also important for *parents* of intersex children:

One, they [parents] need to be taught what causes this—the fact that it's naturally occurring. Actually this has been occurring since time began and there's nothing abnormal. Two, they need to be given counselling as to how to support, how to love that child. OK, it could be a bit of a grieving time because they're expecting... but if they're given the counselling and support they can overcome this. And three, the education of how to fight the little battles or big battles that are going to come in the future, but if they're given that support they can then overcome it. And four, how to overcome their religious beliefs to enable them to accept the child—if that's an issue, which it often can be. (*Rogena, 2011, interview*).

Mani Mitchell, who founded the Intersex Trust Aotearoa New Zealand (ITANZ), commented about the significance of *information* in relation to support:

Most parents are good, and want the best, but most parents are conservative. I think there's notions around the ideal that "my child is going to grow up and get married and have children and there'll be grandchildren". I think for many parents that's the fantasy. For any child, for any parent, how you accept that that may or may not happen. So I think one of the things with this intersex issue is that people go "Oh, how do we fix it?" There isn't a nice fixing, because I think this is one of our complicated social realities and really it's about difference and how we manage that, and how we move from this place of fear, shame, secrecy and silence into a new place. I think, if we're going to do anything, that's the starting process. And it's about different disciplines communicating and sharing information so the answer will come out of experts, the narratives of inter-sex people themselves, the narratives of parents with inter-sex children and out of that wealth of information the answers will emerge. The first step to that is visibility and doing what we're doing this afternoon [our interview], which is talking. (*Mitchell, 2010, interview*).

As well as her family, Anonymous 3 receives support from a friend with the same condition:

> ... we've pretty much been best friends ever since we found out we have the same condition [CAH]. ... it's been so long that we've been friends. I think we got in contact through our parents who ended up being friends, and then as we grew older and understood more we became good friends and helped each other out with questions. (*Anonymous 3, 2010, interview*).

This suggests that having a peer to talk to, hang out with and share experiences with can be a very uplifting and empowering experience. I also suggest that talking to someone who is *not* a clinician, psychologist or other 'professional' can eliminate feelings of stigmatisation—because that person (a friend or peer) has the same condition. Indeed, as Anonymous 3 stated previously, 'It's not as bad as people say it is.'

Conclusion

An implication of genital surgeries is not only practical considerations (vaginal dilation, for example) but its *emotional* considerations: a teenage girl can understandably feel embarrassed and hesitant about seeking advice about a very personal matter such as vaginal dilation. I therefore conclude that easily-accessible support for intersex adolescents, which Sarah's organisation in New Zealand offers, is particularly important. Support is also crucial for parents of intersex children. Because we live in a society with ingrained binary sex/gender assumptions, and because intersexuality is not a particularly well-known condition, parents of a newly-diagnosed newborn infant may be understandably bewildered and stressed that the classifications of 'son' or 'daughter' cannot be confirmed immediately.

Support groups are also important for intersex people and their families in terms of providing *legitimate* information. For example, parents of a newborn intersex baby—who may already be stressed—need to be careful when reading easily-accessible information on the inter-net. This is with regard to Portelli's (1991, p. 51) theoretical position: how do we know that a person's account posted on a website is true? This is particularly as some websites provide a 'stage' for some people who, for instance, like to boast about their 'uniqueness' for their own vanity. Some people therefore appear to romanticise lesser-known conditions for prurient appeal (akin to the 'shock' element in horror or art-house films).

Parents of a newborn intersex baby therefore need to be put in touch with other parents of intersex children, and indeed advocates such as Mani Mitchell (whose organisation's websites contain more legitimate information, as Lisa remarks). By contacting support organisations, instead of possibly becoming more stressed by sensationalist accounts on websites, parents can feel supported, comforted and empowered when listening to parents' first hand experiences—and possibly their children's too. Parents of a newborn intersex child may, I suggest, feel comforted by meeting a cheerful young woman like Anonymous 3, or a mother such as Anonymous 1 who appears to be proud of her child.

In closing, while living in New Zealand with a lesser-known condition can be problematic, support organisations can ensure that intersex New Zealanders and their families should not feel compelled to keep silent and feel isolated—despite follow-up medical care seeming far away in Australia, for instance. Having someone to exchange e-mails with, meeting another parent of an intersex child over a coffee, having someone of the same age to hang out with and talk to about a very personal matter: these activities can indeed alleviate feelings of isolation and silence amongst a small population.

GERALDINE CHRISTMAS was recently awarded a PhD from Victoria University in Wellington.

References

Anonymous 1. Interview with G. Christmas, 28 September 2010. Details of location in New Zealand withheld.

Anonymous 3. Interview with G. Christmas, 20 November 2010. Details of location in New Zealand withheld.

Anonymous clinician. Interview with G. Christmas, 5 July 2010. Details of hospital in New Zealand withheld.

Blackless, M., Charuvastra, A., Derryck, A., Fausto-Sterling, A., Lauzanne, K., Lee, E. (2000). How sexually dimorphic are we? Review and synthesis. *American Journal of Human Biology, 12,* 151-166.

Bronwyn (pseudonym). Interview with G. Christmas, 6 December 2010. Details of location in New Zealand withheld.

Chase, C. (1998). Affronting reason. In D. Atkins (Ed.), *Looking queer: Body image and identity in lesbian, bisexual, gay, and transgender communities.* Binghamton, NY, USA: Harrington Park Press.

Children's Hospital Boston (April 2007). *New clinic addresses intersex and gender issues.* Retrieved from http://www.childrenshospital.org/views/april07/new_clinic_addresses_intersex_and_gender_issues.html

Davies, B. & Gannon, S. (2005). Feminism/poststructuralism. In B. Somekh & C. Lewin (Eds.), *Research methods in the social sciences.* London, UK: Sage Publications Ltd.

Forest, M. G. (2001). Diagnosis and treatment of disorders of sexual development. In L. J. DeGroot & J. L. Jameson (Eds.), *Endocrinology.* Philadelphia, USA: W B Saunders Company.

Grumbach, M. M., Hughes, I. A., & Conte, F. A. (2003). Disorders of sex differentiation. In P. Reed Larsen, H. M. Kronenberg, S. Melmed & K. S. Polonsky (Eds.), *Williams textbook of endocrinology* (10th ed.). Philadelphia, USA: Saunders.

Hall, L. (2004). Confidentially speaking: Ethics in interviewing. In A. Green & M. Hutching (Eds.), *Remembering: Writing oral history.* Auckland, NZ: Auckland University Press.

Human Rights Commission. 5. *The rights of homosexual, transsexual and intersex people.* Retrieved from http://www.hrc.co.nz/report/chapters/chapter19/issues05.html

Jacqui (pseudonym). Interview with G. Christmas, 7 December 2010. Details of location in New Zealand withheld.

Jo. Interview with G. Christmas, 6 October 2010. Details of location in New Zealand withheld.

Kaiser, K. (2009, November). Protecting respondent confidentiality in qualitative research. *Qualitative Health Research, November 19*(11), 1632-1641. Retrieved from http://www.ncbi.nlm.nih.gov/pmc/articles/PMC2805454/pdf/nihms162528.pdf

Klempner, M. (2000). Narrating life review interviews with survivors of trauma, In R. Perks & A. Thomson (Eds.), *The oral history reader* (2nd ed. pub. 2006). London & New York: Routledge.

Laurie, A. J. (2004). Speaking the unspoken: Lesbian oral histories in Aotearoa New Zealand. In A. Green & M. Hutching (Eds.), *Remembering: Writing oral history.* Auckland, NZ: Auckland University Press.

Lisa (pseudonym). Interview with G. Christmas, 27 September and 6 December 2010. Details of location in New Zealand withheld.

Mayo Clinic. *Pediatric [sic] urology*. Retrieved from http://www.mayo.edu/research/departments-divisions/department-urology/pediatric-urology

McEwan, C. Interview with G. Christmas, 8 June 2010. Hamilton, New Zealand.

Ministry of Youth Development. *Sex distribution*. Retrieved from http://www.youthstats.myd.govt.nz/demographic/sex-distribution.html

Mitchell, M. Interview with G. Christmas, 7 April 2010. Wellington, New Zealand

Murray (pseudonym). Interview with G. Christmas, 6 December 2010. Details of location in New Zealand withheld.

Portelli, A. (1991). *The death of Luigi Trastulli and other stories: Form and meaning in oral history*. Albany, USA: State University of New York Press.

Quigley, C. A. (2009). *Disorders of sex development: When to tell the patient* [PowerPoint presentation]. Retrieved from http://www.accordalliance.org/images/stories/Quigley-LWPES_PAS_mini_course_may09_for_Accord.pdf

Rainbow Health Ontario (with assistance from Holmes, M. & Hunt, R.) (July 2011). *RHO fact sheet: Intersex health*. Ontario, Canada: Rainbow Health Ontario. Retrieved from http://www.rainbowhealthontario.ca/admin/contentEngine/contentDocuments/Intersex_final.pdf

Rogena. Interview with G. Christmas, 23 May 2011. Details of tertiary institute in New Zealand withheld.

Sarah (pseudonym). Interview with G. Christmas, 2 July 2010. Details of location in New Zealand withheld.

Spivak, G. C. (1988). Can the Subaltern speak? In B. Ashcroft, G. Griffiths & H. Tiffin (Eds.), *The post-colonial studies reader* (pub. 1995). London, UK & New York, USA: Routledge.

Statistics New Zealand (2008). *Considering sexual orientation as a potential official statistic: Discussion paper*. Wellington, NZ: Statistics New Zealand. Retrieved from http://www.stats.govt.nz/browse_for_stats/people_and_communities/marriages-civil-unions-and-divorces/considering-sexual-orientation.aspx

Thompson, P. (1988). The voice of the past: Oral history, In R. Perks & A. Thomson (Eds.), *The oral history reader* (2nd ed. pub. 2006). London & New York: Routledge.

The Work of Breastfeeding

Cindy A. Stearns

Breastfeeding Over Time and The Division of Labor in Families

The inherently embodied nature of breast-feeding has implications for how the work of caring for children is distributed in families. At the start, mothers breastfeed very frequently. In the first weeks this means a cycle of about two hours from the beginning of one feeding until the beginning of the next feeding. Frequent feeding is medically recommended and required to build up a mother's milk supply. In addition, other family members cannot provide supplemental bottles of formula or breast milk, because of concern about "nipple confusion." Artificial nipples provide liquid with less work for the baby and it is widely believed that when artificial nipples and bottles are provided too early in the breastfeeding relationship, babies will not develop the oral skills (and perhaps also the motivation) necessary to effectively breastfeed.

As long as a bottle is not possible fathers and others cannot participate in direct feeding. Typically a bottle is not introduced until six weeks or later in a child's life and even then, bottles are often supplementary rather than routine (see discussion below). Mothers in this study discussed the father's circumscribed role in baby care because of the exclusivity of breastfeeding as well as their beliefs about the short- and long-term consequences of this unequal division of labor. Two main themes emerge from the data concerning the father's role in caring for the breastfed baby: how men miss out because of breastfeeding and how men opt out of baby care and use breastfeeding as an excuse.

Men Miss Out

Mothers note that men "miss out" in not being able to breastfeed. Sam, a thirty-eight-year-old, white, married, part-time college teacher, notes her own sense of being special in an exclusive mother-baby dyad and her beliefs about her husband's less satisfying role:

> For the first six months especially there was something that I could do that no one else in the world could do and it was nice. I felt sort of special that way. And I think my husband who really loves children and was excited about having one, felt somewhat shut out of that and a little incapable. You know, he would pick her up and she would continue

crying and he would hand her to me and she would immediately be calmer. And I think that was probably a little hard on him.

Naomi, a married physician, suggests that breastfeeding was a mixed experience for her, but had a negative effect on her husband's relationship with the baby:

> That's one down side I think of breastfeeding, it, you know, if I have to be honest. I think it depends on the woman, I think it depends on the man, it depends on how you handle it, but with D [her baby] our relationship was so wrapped up in breastfeeding, he nursed so much, and he was colicky, he was a really difficult little infant. ... Nobody could take care of him except me. ... It was kind of overwhelming for me. On the other hand, it also in a weird way felt good that I was really the one who could do it all. And it really kind of turned into a not very good thing between B [her husband] and D. ... I think if I had not been nursing, he might have been able to be more involved earlier. (white, age forty-two)

According to mothers, the exclusiveness of early breastfeeding can lead fathers to wonder about whether their parenting efforts really matter or are noticed. As Alison notes, "I think definitely when Mark was a little younger, he would say, 'I wonder if he knows who I am?'" (twenty-seven-years-old, white, married, stay-at-home mother). Previous research, although

not extensive, also suggests a pattern of father involvement that is limited in the early stages of breastfeeding and less satisfying for fathers (Bar-Yam and Darby 1997).

Men Opt Out

Mothers also describe their partners as using breastfeeding as a defensible excuse to avoid or sidestep a large part of the work of having a baby. When these fathers expressed enjoyment and relief about their avoidance of that demanding work because of "natural" biological differences, mothers expressed irritation. As Sarah reports:

> The only bad thing about breastfeeding is feeling trapped like you, you know, like you're kind of stuck. Well, I have to breastfeed, so I can't go to this. It's all on me. [For her husband] it's kind of a joke, you know, he'll go, "Oh darn, hon, you have to breastfeed him," with a big smile on his face. And sometimes it does kind of make, you know, when I'm up at three in the morning and he's snoring, you kind of want to throw a little dagger over there, you know, 'cause, you know, you do feel like it's only you. (thirty-one years old, white, married, part-time sixth-grade teacher)

Often mothers complain that fathers stopped short in their duties because of a belief that breastfeeding and nothing else would solve the problem of an unhappy baby. Nadia notes, "He'll say sometimes, 'I've done everything. I've changed him. I've given him a bottle. He wants you, that's the only thing that's going to make a difference!'" Mothers may perceive that the exclusive mother-child dyad of the early weeks affects the father's role even when the child is no longer breastfeeding. For example, Bonnie describes the long-term impact of the "I can't breastfeed" rationale: "He'd say, 'There's nothing I can do for her. She wants you.' And now he'll still say it and I'm not breastfeeding!'" (twenty-seven years old, white, married, stay-at-home mother). Breastfeeding thus became a perceived excuse for longer-term lapses in father care. Mothers report frustration when they believe fathers are failing to help in ways other than breastfeeding (e.g., holding a baby, offering comfort, changing diapers).

Men also opt out by failing to recognize the maternal work involved in breastfeeding. Krista, a thirty-five-year-old, married, stay-at-home mother, describes her husband's lack of knowledge of the baby's sleeping habits: "When he was a week old, some of my mom's friends were asking, 'Does he sleep through the night?' And my husband said, 'Yes, he sleeps through the night!' And I said, 'No, honey, no—*you* are sleeping through the night! *Mom* is still getting up. And he is up every three hours, but you are sleeping through it!'" The exclusivity of the mother-baby relationship in the early weeks can make the body work of breastfeeding invisible to others in the family.

Breastfeeding the Older Baby

As babies get older they usually do not need to be fed as frequently. A typical six-month-old nurses far less frequently than a six-week-old baby. This reduces the amount of direct breastfeeding that mothers need to do and has the potential to change the distribution of child care duties. As breastfeeding continues with an older child, there is more opportunity for others to provide bottles of stored breast milk or infant formula, as well as solid foods. Yet as long as breastfeeding continues, the maternal body is the source of food and the mother has primary work responsibilities as the producer of that food.

The Breast Pump

Fifty-nine percent of the mothers in the study used a breast pump to extract and store milk at some point during breastfeeding. Mothers can extract milk by hand; however, it can be difficult to do, and all the mothers relied on a breast pump. Pumping, like breastfeeding, is learned body work and requires the development of skills and techniques, as well as access to a working and adequate breast pump.

Mothers pump their milk so that it will be available to their child when they do not want to feed them from the breast, for whatever reason. Some mothers do not want their child to have infant formula substitute because they view their breast milk as "liquid gold," an extremely valuable and irreplaceable form of nutrition.[3] Mothers who work outside the home are the most likely to pump. However, nonworking mothers pump as well. They may want an emergency supply of breast milk for safekeeping in their freezer. They may want breast milk available for the times when they are out shopping, going to the hairstylist, or undergoing medical treatments. Mothers also pump when they are away from their babies for an extended period (a day or more) so that their breast milk production will not lessen or disappear.

Pumping is often perceived as challenging by mothers. Similar to the working mothers in Avishai's (2007) study, most mothers found pumping to be time consuming and stressful:

> It takes longer for me to pump, even though I let down really easily with her nursing, it takes me long, it takes me twenty minutes, it only takes me ten minutes to nurse her. (Millie, age thirty-one, white, married, not working)

> It's not worth the time. I'd rather keep her close to me. So we just carried her everywhere. (Miranda, age thirty-two, white, married, part-time bookkeeper)

Pumping breast milk for future use must be fit in alongside the regular direct feeding of a child. When children nurse several times a day, it can be difficult to produce the extra milk necessary to pump. If a woman gets only an ounce when she pumps, she may not view the time and energy required from her as "worth it" and may decide to pump infrequently, as did Miranda (above). Glenda, a thirty-five-year-old, white, married mother who edits books from home, also describes her decision not to pump in terms of these costs:

> I also felt my time is so valuable. I mean every moment that she's asleep I'm working and so to take the time off to do that which was taking me, it took me half an hour to get like two ounces. This is not worth my time, that's billable time and I don't want to sit here and be doing this when I could be working, which is much more pleasurable to

me than this and earns money, so it was a decision I made because of my work situation.

If a woman chooses not to pump, she will continue to be responsible for the work of direct breastfeeding. Another consequence is less opportunity for others to bottle-feed their babies.

Fathers Bottle-Feeding

Pumping has the potential to allow more baby care to be shared. However, in this study, mothers who did not work outside the home typically pumped infrequently. Mothers who worked outside the home often reserved the pumped milk for the day care provider and breastfed the child directly when at home. This means that for mothers who breastfeed, whether they work outside the home or not, opportunities for father involvement in bottle-feeding are often not part of a daily routine.

Mothers often report that fathers enjoy being able to feed their child a bottle and that it was an important way that fathers could create a positive bond with the child. Christine, a thirty-six-year-old, white, married, stay-at-home mother, says, "That's their biggest need, is to be fed. And for the mother to be the only one to be able to do that, so I think it was really nice when I did start pumping that he was able to do that for him also. I think that for a woman who chose to formula feed right from the start than that might be nice for the father to be able to do that." As noted earlier, feeding may be perceived as one of the most nurturing and gratifying aspect of baby care and fathers may be perceived as "missing out" on a special bond.

In several cases, mothers described their partner's desire to have a more active role in infant feeding. Mary, a twenty-six-year-old, white, married student teacher, speculates: "Maybe part of the reason he really wanted Z [her baby] to be weaned was … he's very jealous of that bond, that closeness and he really wanted to be able to feed him and I didn't even try pumping my milk until Z was a couple of months old." Another mother describes how the father emulates breastfeeding when providing their daughter a bottle. Jackie describes a situation she found unusual: "When I pump milk he'll feed her a milk bottle, just because he wants that bond. He even takes off his shirt and will feed her a milk bottle that way, so she can smell him. I thought that was kind of interesting. I'd never heard of a man doing that. … And he'd say, 'Well you know, I want her to get used to me and to know me and my smell and I want that.' It's not just women who want the body-to-body contact." In this case, breastfeeding is the key reference for the style and form of this father's bottle-feeding.

Breastfeeding and Egalitarian Parenting

More than three-quarters of the mothers in the study expressed concern with issues of gender equality in child care. As indicated in several examples above, many mothers explicitly or implicitly also recognize that breastfeeding affected the balance of work and power in child care.

Some mothers indicate that breastfeeding gives them greater authority over child rearing and they enjoyed this role. Carrie describes how breastfeeding has given her dominance over not just how her child is fed, but also the entire house: "It's like I am the ultimate god of how this household is run because I am the life of B [her baby], you know what I mean? … It's another way of controlling, just by breastfeeding. It probably is, because if he were formula fed I could only be a 50/50 in that one. You know what I mean?" (age thirty, white, married, stay-at-home mother). While breastfeeding can increase a feeling of control or power over the home for the mother, it may come with a price of embodied and exclusive maternal labor. Some mothers imagine how equality in child rearing might be different if the baby were bottle-fed rather than breastfed. Sam describes her brother and his wife, who have always bottle-fed their child infant formula: "I always kind of look at it and think well, that is interesting, they didn't breastfeed and there seems to be more equality in the child and who she looks for."

While some mothers wonder or perhaps fantasize about whether bottle-feeding would have led to more help from the fathers, other mothers note that it is the characteristics and motivation of the father that matter, not the breast or bottle. Jasmine believes that her husband is highly involved and when asked whether bottle-feeding would have made a difference in his participation, responds, "Not with him. He's incredibly nurturing and, I mean, he's just great with kids. It's not like I breastfeed and held on to this kid all day. I can hand him right over and he will change the diapers, he does clothes, he does all of it. He walked around just as much at night as I did with a colicky baby."

The interview data suggests that egalitarian parenting from the maternal point of view requires fathers who are willing to find ways to fit into the embodied requirements of breastfeeding, actively helping the mother and baby in all the ways they could, depending in part on the age of the baby. In this study, mothers describe some fathers who were eager to help and were effective at doing so, fathers who were eager to be involved but less effective, fathers who became more involved as the child got older, and fathers who seemed content to be left out. The themes identified here suggest a need for additional empirical research focusing on both mothers' and their partners' ideas about and experiences of living and sharing child care work in a breastfeeding family over time.

Thinking about Breastfeeding as Work

As these mothers' accounts make clear, breastfeeding, especially in the early months, is time-consuming and labor-intensive maternal body work. Mothers report that breastfeeding can be both an enjoyable and demanding part of the work of being a mother. This work can sometimes seem overwhelming because it cannot be easily shared, while at other times it can provide an exclusive connection to the baby that is perceived as rewarding and also empowering in family relationships. Mothers portray the demands on their body and their time posed by the body work of breastfeeding as simultaneously amazing, miraculous, enjoyable, exhausting, and demanding.

In contrast to mothers' descriptions of the embodied labor involved in breastfeeding, in the popular press, breastfeeding seems to happen simply because women's bodies have that capacity. Breast milk is commonly understood as "nature's gift" to the infant rather than as the product of mothers' embodied labor.

Breastfeeding may lack public visibility as work in part because of the context for the performance of breastfeeding. In a previous article I argue that because breasts are sexualized in the larger culture, the performance of breastfeeding becomes tricky for mothers to manage (Stearns 1999). Some mothers breastfeed more at home or learn to breastfeed discreetly in public to avoid any possible awkward situations or negative feedback from onlookers. To the extent that breastfeeding is performed discreetly or is hidden, this maternal body work is invisible.

The body work of breastfeeding is not only hidden from popular view, it is also largely missing from feminist research and theory. The lived perspective of the embodied worker is lacking in empirical studies of breastfeeding and of early mothering. In a qualitative study of the physical challenges involved in early breastfeeding experiences, Kelleher argues, "For the most part, feminist discussion of breastfeeding offers very little explicit consideration of the physical challenges associated with breastfeeding—challenges that can only be fully understood by accounting for women's lived experiences" (2006, 2729). Similarly, Hausman reflects on the feminist politics of breastfeeding and urges an embodied perspective: "While we know that mothering as an activity is not limited to biological birth mothers and lactating women, when we ignore the specificity of these embodied activities of maternity we have difficulty seeing how maternity is, for most women, a profoundly embodied experience" (2004, 276).

The lack of focus on the embodied activities of motherhood may reflect a larger trend in feminist body theory that prioritizes reading the body as a cultural text and emphasizing the body not as fixed (especially in terms of gender) but as in flux. As Davis notes, "There seems to be an absence of bodies in contemporary feminist body theory that can be touched, smelled, tasted, or perceived. ... Ultimately, the focus seems to be upon the surface of the body and on how culture becomes imprinted upon it" (2007, 54). Davis offers a compelling argument that a theoretical focus on the surface of the body should not supplant phenomenological explorations of the experience of lived embodiment.

A focus on breastfeeding and other embodied labor performed by mothers (pregnancy, carework, and so on) is a necessary component of any larger analysis of contemporary mothering ideologies and practices, including the effects of maternal ideologies that equate "good" mothering with breastfeeding. This analytic focus seems especially relevant as medical and public health authorities promote increasingly longer periods of exclusive breastfeeding as essential for optimal infant health (American Academy of Pediatrics 2005). Without a clear focus on the actual lived and embodied work of breastfeeding in empirical research, we run the risk of allowing the intense and sometimes demanding physical and emotional labor performed by maternal body workers to remain invisible and unexamined. We also miss an opportunity to more closely focus on the unique and understudied implications of breastfeeding for sharing the work of child care with others in the family. Finally, failing to explore the body work of doing breastfeeding is to assume and encourage the notion that breastfeeding is effortless and occurs naturally from maternal bodies. Breastfeeding is work and the body workers who do the breastfeeding merit greater public and research attention.

Acknowledgments

The School of Social Sciences and the Research, Scholarship, and Creative Activity Program (RSCAP) at Sonoma State University provided important financial support for this project.

I am grateful to the mothers who participated in this study and to my student research assistants for help with this project: Sandi Davis, Ellen Heimann-Sullivan, Colleen Rodriguez, and Alicia Diaz Said.

CINDY A. STEARNS is professor of sociology at Sonoma State University. Previously she served as professor and chair of women's and gender studies at Sonoma State. She teaches courses about research methods, gender, the body, and the sociology of reproduction and has published articles on breastfeeding, medical work, and other topics.

Notes

1   It is possible to purchase breast milk from milk banks or through private arrangements, although it is expensive and uncommon to do so. It's also possible (with medical intervention and hard work) for nonbirth mothers to produce breast milk, although production is rarely large enough to provide complete infant nutrition. The most common situation is for the mother who gave birth to provide that child with breast milk, and I explore this situation here.

2   Additional points of potential difference in the interviews are sexuality and marital status. Although I only have a small sample of lesbians or single moms, I found no apparent differences among mothers in analyzing the data for the section "Breastfeeding as Maternal Body work." I explore heterosexual couples living together only in the section "Breastfeeding over Time and the Division of Labor in Families" because of the limitations of the sample. The division of labor in a wider variety of breastfeeding families merits future research attention.

3   See Stearns forthcoming for an extended discussion of the data concerning breast pumping and the value of breast milk.

Works Cited

American Academy of Pediatrics. 2005. "Policy Statement, Section on Breastfeeding: Breastfeeding and the Use of Human Milk." *Pediatrics* 115(2): 496–506.

Avishai, Orit. 2007. "Managing the Lactating Body: The Breastfeeding Project and Privileged Motherhood." *Qualitative Sociology* 30:135–52.

Bartlett, Alison. 2002. "Breastfeeding as Headwork: Corporeal Feminism and Meanings for Breastfeeding." *Women's Studies International Forum* 25(3):373–82.

Bar-Yam, Naomi Bromberg, and Lori Darby. 1997. "Fathers and Breastfeeding: A Review of the Literature." *Journal of Human Lactation* 13(1):45–50.

Blum, Linda. 1999. *At The Breast: Ideologies of Breastfeeding and Motherhood in the Contemporary United States.* Boston: Beacon Press.

Davis, Kathy. 2007. "Reclaiming Women's Bodies: Colonialist Trope or Critical Epistemology?" In *Embodying Sociology: Retrospect, Progress and Prospects,* ed. C. Shilling. Malden, Mass.: Blackwell Press.

Dykes, Fiona. 2005. "'Supply' and 'Demand': Breastfeeding as Labour." *Social Science & Medicine* 60:2283–93.

Gimlin, Debra. 2007. "What Is 'Body Work'? A Review of the Literature." *Sociology Compass* 1(1):353–70.

Hausman, Bernice L. 2004. "The Feminist Politics of Breastfeeding." *Australian Feminist Studies* 19(45):273–85.

Hays, Sharon. 1996. *The Cultural Contradictions of Motherhood.* New Haven: Yale University Press.

Kelleher, Christa M. 2006. "The Physical Challenges of Early Breastfeeding." *Social Science and Medicine* 63:2727–38.

Knaak, Stephanie. 2005. "Breast-Feeding, Bottle-Feeding, and Dr. Spock: The Shifting Context of Choice." *Canadian Review of Sociology and Anthropology* 42(2):197–216.

Kukla, Rebecca. 2006. "Ethics and Ideology in Breastfeeding Advocacy Campaigns." *Hypatia* 21(1):157–80.

Lee, Ellie. 2007. "Health, Morality, and Infant Feeding: British Mothers' Experiences of Formula Use in the Early Weeks." *Sociology of Health and Illness* 29:107–1090.

Murphy, Elizabeth. 1999. "'Breast Is Best': Infant Feeding Decisions and Maternal Deviance." *Sociology of Health and Illness* 21(2):187–208.

Shaw, Rhonda. 2004. "The Virtues of Cross-Nursing and the 'Yuk Factor.'" *Australian Feminist Studies* 19(45):287–99.

Stearns, Cindy A. 1999. "Breastfeeding and the Good Maternal Body." *Gender & Society* 13(3):308–25.

———. Forthcoming. "The Breast Pump." In *Giving Breast Milk,* ed. R. Shaw and A. Bartlett. Toronto, Ontario: Demeter Press.

USDA, Food and Nutrition Service. 2005. *USDA National Breastfeeding Promotion Campaign,* http://www.fns.usda.gov/wic/Breastfeeding/lovingsupport.htm.

Wolf, Joan B. 2007. "Is Breast Really Best? Risk and Total Motherhood in the National Breastfeeding Awareness Campaign." *Journal of Health Politics, Policy and Law* 32(4):595–636.

Wolkowitz, Carol. 2006. *Bodies at Work.* London: Sage.

Reflexive Questions

1. Why do you think baby clothes, toys, and belongings are gendered? What makes us uncomfortable about not being able to use color or objects to identify an infant's sex?

2. What limitations and constraints would be lifted if all children's clothes, bedrooms, games, and toys were gender neutral?

3. Do you agree that parents should be able to choose their child's sex?

4. What are your views about sex-selective abortion as a means to parent a boy?

5. What beliefs and values perpetuate the preference for males? Why is this preference prevalent across cultures? What would change if there were no gender preferences?

6. What are some implications for viewing sex and gender on a nonbinary continuum? What constraints would be lifted, and what complexities would be added?

7. Why are medical professionals and parents uncomfortable with intersex as a category? How do their biases reflect larger sociocultural attitudes and beliefs?

8. How would eliminating gender as a way to define ourselves affect identity and interpersonal relationships? What would be the advantages and possible disadvantages?

9. What are your views about breastfeeding? How are your views influenced by your gender, age, culture, and socioeconomic status?

10. Did your mother breastfeed you? Why or why not?

11. If people did not sexualize women's breasts, how would perceptions and accommodations regarding breastfeeding change? Why is this important?

CHAPTER 5

Early Childhood

Introduction

Early childhood is generally thought of as the ages occurring from 2 to 6 and often referred to as the preschool years. During this developmental period, children continue to develop biologically, cognitively, and psychosocially, which is positively associated with optimal adult health (Grantham-McGregor et al., 2007). Scholars often use a child's physical growth as a proxy indicator for current early childhood development in low- and middle-income countries (Grantham-McGregor et al., 2007). Physical growth often influences other developmental domains through brain and musculoskeletal development, and children with developmental delays may have compromised interactions with caregivers and others (Tran, Holton, Nguyen, & Fisher, 2019). Although these associations are noted, community and social factors strongly influence development as well.

Delays in physical growth and cognitive development often share individual-level risk factors; however, less is known about community-level risk factors (Heo et al., 2019). When family scholars control for individual-level variables, the association between community-level variables and development outcomes becomes more pronounced (Heo et al., 2019). Such findings indicate that the community in which a child grows and develops plays an imperative role in their well-being and outcomes. Communities with greater local healthcare resources and local programs run by the government were associated with physical growth and increased language skills. Additionally, communities with greater social problems are associated with lower math scores among children (Heo et al., 2019). Because the community affects early childhood development, many nations have some form of early childhood education program to reduce developmental disparities (Britto, Boller, & Yoshikawa, 2011).

A brief overview helps us better situate how US policies influenced early education programs. In the 1960s, President Johnson declared a "War on Poverty," and the government introduced the Head Start program as a means of breaking the cycle of poverty (Office of Head Start, 2019). It was theorized that greater education was a factor in reducing the rates of poverty. Early childhood education programs, like Head Start, have positive effects on children's cognitive abilities, pre-academic skills, and socio-emotional development (Magnuson et al., 2007; Ramey & Ramey, 2004; Yoshikawa et al., 2013). While these positive outcomes exist, systemic, institutional, and structural racism shaped early education policies in the United States (Johnson-Staub, 2017).

Despite best intentions, racism and sexism still affect young children's access to quality early childhood education and care. The Head Start program aims to take a culturally responsive stance (Office of Head Start, 2019); however, not all children have equal access to early childhood programs. For example, Mexican-origin families face complex ethnic and immigration-based barriers to enrollment in such programs (Ressler et al., 2020). Children of color who attend Head Start often experience systemic racism. African American male students who are characterized as "challenging" by teachers are more likely to have poor quality relationships with them, thereby affecting positive outcomes (Nunley, 2012). Moreover, at the earliest grade levels, African American males who are labeled "challenging" have similar disproportionate rates of school suspension and expulsion to older African American males (Lewis, Butler, Bonner, & Joubert, 2010). While racism and structural barriers to equity influence early education programs, so do the other forms of "isms," like sexism. Young children are taught to conform to rigid gender and sexual scripts that reinforce heterosexist and sexist ideologies (Duke & McCarthy, 2009). Additionally, early childhood educators often lack the knowledge, skills, and power to effectively challenge systems of oppression (Duke & McCarthy, 2009). Without attending to larger social structures, interventions aimed solely at the individual, community, or a co-action between the two are likely to remain limited in their effectiveness.

Other factors to consider related to childhood are the ways women are especially implicated when meeting the demands of raising children and providing for them. Much attention is given to the negative impact women's employment has on children, without attending to women's own needs, desires, and well-being (Walker, 2009). To compete with the demands of the provider role and the continuing responsibilities of other family members, many women have no other option but to earn a living, often with low-paying jobs (Walker, 2009). Family scholars often use the term "the second shift," coined by Hochschild in 1989, to describe how women hold two shifts: their job (i.e., paid labor) and household demands (i.e., unpaid labor). What scholars Blair-Loy, Hochschild, Pugh, Williams and Hartmann (2015) contend is that for the most part, women do the lion's share of domestic labor and childcare; however, they urge researchers to investigate how the widening social gap and social inequality influences work, caregiving, and intimacy for women and contemporary couples. They contend that issues such as job insecurity, tenuous job status, and working long hours all have an effect on overall well-being and home life. In the readings below, we will take a closer look at how socioeconomic status is conflated with gender and race for children in early childhood.

Summary of Readings

In the first reading, "**Unequal at the Start: Early Childhood Programs Pay Dividends for Life**" (2014), Ann O'Leary raises awareness about the harmful effects of social inequality at a young age and how it can have life-long effects. Early childhood is a sensitive stage for optimal cognitive, social, and emotional development. Having optimal learning support in quality childcare and preschool settings is important for all children. According to O'Leary, only half of the children in the United States receive early childhood education, mostly due to the high cost of childcare. O'Leary states that there are clear and attainable policy solutions that could expand early childhood education and offer enrichment opportunities to children for every socioeconomic class, not only for those who are middle or upper class. These policies would be important for everyone, not just directly for children and their families.

Given the negative social effects of socioeconomic disparity, quality childcare and early childhood education could potentially help level the playing field. For example, scholars found a clear connection between a child's social class and how many words they knew. This knowledge affected literacy rates, how well the child did in school, and ultimately, how much they earned in adulthood. In general, the author urges the United States to enact policies that focus on offering children access to high-quality, affordable early childhood education programs. These programs serve to not only prepare children for school and give them a head start in mathematics and other subjects but also socialize them to do well in school. Low-income families need additional support. Currently, the achievement gap in the United States is strongly correlated with the intersection of race and social class. O'Leary contends that if we invest in quality early childhood education for all children, we will be investing in all of our futures, regardless of a child's socioeconomic status or gender.

In the second reading, "**From Brilliant Baby to Child Placed at Risk: The Perilous Path of African American Boys in Early Childhood Education**" (2009), Hakim Rashid contends that although there are factors that strongly affect developmental trajectories of young African American children, there are a few that are especially salient to African American boys. Rashid asks the reader to consider why African American boys have the highest rate of expulsion in preschool. Factors identified will ultimately place young Black youth "at risk": on the track toward delinquency, school dropout, incarceration, less access to health insurance, and risk of dying from HIV and homicide. Often even enrollment in Head Start in early childhood did not facilitate quality education or emotional support and nurturance to African American boys. The author discusses the idea that African Americans become disadvantaged by the school system; the very thing that is supposed to give them an advantage. Rashid calls this the preschool-to-prison pipeline.

Protective factors such as quality classrooms and caring student-teacher relationships were associated with higher test scores. In general, teachers tend to have lower expectations for those from low income. The author suggests the following solutions to help ameliorate the disadvantages faced by African American boys in schools: 1) teachers willing to take responsibility for learning, 2) higher expectations for African American boys and highlighting their abilities and assets, 3) demonstrations of warmth and control, 4) proactive racial socialization, and 5) engagement of Black boys in more vigorous activities, especially those rooted in culture. Teacher responsiveness, quality programs, and developmental appropriateness must be carefully examined. Communities and policies must also prioritize offering truly high-quality early childhood education to African American boys. Overall, experiences in early childhood have direct effects on positive outcomes. Quality early childhood education lays an important foundation for all children, especially for children from economically disadvantaged and discriminated cultural groups.

In the third reading, "**Indigenous Children: Their Human Rights, Mortality, and the Millennium Development Goals**" (2010), author Jane Freemantle focuses on the needs of First Nations/Indigenous children. She contends that incomplete and often inaccurate data about Indigenous populations hinders the ability to effectively monitor the health of this population. Developed by the United Nations, the Millennium Development Goals (MDGs) aim to protect the rights of Indigenous children, especially their right to health. For example, the MDGs strive to reduce extreme poverty, child mortality, and disease epidemics, among other health concerns. Nevertheless, some Indigenous groups are under-registered in census data sets, and others are excluded entirely; therefore, their progress toward the MDGs cannot be measured. Without accurate data about Indigenous populations, including infant mortality rates, death rates, and children's health, the health of this community cannot be assessed, and healthcare cannot be improved. In other words, the lacking and inaccurate identification of Indigenous people bars them from their human right to health and optimal development. The remoteness of Indigenous communities, errors in census data collection, and historical and current discrimination against Indigenous people all contribute to the misrepresentation of indigenous people in census records.

In sum, it is my hope that these readings will help you reflect on how early childhood experiences are funneled through structural advantages and disadvantages based on race, gender, culture, and socioeconomic status. It is evident that more momentum is needed worldwide to disrupt and dismantle systemic injustice that continues to affect children and families. Without attending to how systems of privilege and oppression inform policies, we unknowingly continue to reinforce systemic and structural injustice.

References

Blair-Loy, M., Hochschild, A., Pugh, A. J., Williams, J. C., & Hartmann, H. (2015). Stability and transformation in gender, work, and family: insights from *the second shift* for the next quarter century. *Community, Work & Family, 18*(4), 435–454. doi:10.1080/13668803.2015.1080664

Britto, P. R., Boller, K., & Yoshikawa, H. (2011). Quality of early childhood development programs in global contexts: Rationale for investment, conceptual framework and implications for equity. *Social Policy Report, 25*(2), 1–31.

Duke, T. S., & McCarthy, K. W. (2009). Homophobia, sexism, and early childhood education: A review of the literature. *Journal of Early Childhood Teacher Education, 30*(4), 385–403. https://doi.org/10.1080/10901020903320320

Grantham-McGregor, S., Cheung, Y., Cueto, S., Glewwe, P., Richter, L., & Strupp, B. (2007). Development in the first 5 years for children in developing countries. *Lancet, 369*, 60–70.

Heo, J., Krishna, A., Perkins, J. M., Lee, H., Lee. J., Subramanian, S. V., & Oh, J. (2019). Community determinants of physical growth and cognitive development among Indian children in early childhood: A multivariate multilevel analysis. *International Journal of Environmental Research and Public Health, 17*(1), 182–194. https://doi.org/10.3390/ijerph17010182

Johnson-Staub, C. (2017). Equity starts early: Addressing racial inequities in child care and early education policy. *Center for Law and Social Policy, Inc. (CLASP).*

Lewis, C. W., Butler, B. R., Bonner III, F. A., & Joubert, M. (2010). African American male discipline patterns and school district responses resulting impact on academic achievement: Implications for urban educators and policy makers. *Journal of African American Males in Education, 1*(1), 7–25.

Magnuson, K. A., Ruhm, C., & Waldfogel, J. (2007). Does prekindergarten improve school preparation and performance? *Economics of Education Review, 26*(1), 33–51. doi:10.1016/j.econedurev.2005.09.008

Nunley, P. L. (2012). *Urban Head Start teachers' classroom interactions with Black male preschoolers identified as "challenging" or "externalizing": Opportunities for teaching self-regulation* (Doctoral dissertation, Mills College).

Office of Head Start. (June 4, 2019). *History of Head Start*. Retrieved from https://www.acf.hhs.gov/ohs/about/history-of-head-start

Ramey, C. T., & Ramey, S. L. (2004). Early learning and school readiness: Can early intervention make a difference? *Merrill-Palmer Quarterly, 50*(4), 471–491. doi:10.1353/mpq.2004.0034

Ressler, R. W., Ackert, E., Ansari, A., Crosnoe, R. (2020). Race/ethnicity, human capital, and the selection of young children into early childhood education. *Social Science Research, 85*, 102364. https://doi.org/10.1016/j.ssresearch.2019.102364

Tran, T. D., Holton, S., Nguyen, H., & Fisher, J. (2019). Physical growth: Is it a good indicator of development in early childhood in low- and middle-income countries? *BMC Pediatrics, 19*, 276–284. https://doi.org/10.1186/s12887-019-1654-9

Walker, A. J. (2009). A feminist critique of family science. In S. A. Lloyd, A. L. Few, & K. R. Allen (Eds.), *Handbook of feminist family studies* (pp. 18–27). Sage.

Yoshikawa, H., Weiland, C., Brooks-Gunn, J., Burchinal, M. R., Espinosa, L. M., Gormley, W. T., Ludwig, J., Magnuson, K., Phillips, D., & Zaslow, M. J. (2013). *Investing in our future: The evidence base on preschool education.* Society for Research in Child Development, Washington, D.C. https://www.fcd-us.org/the-evidence-base-on-preschool/

Unequal At the Start

Early Childhood Programs Pay Dividends for Life

Ann O'leary

No child wants to hear that they will receive a smaller share of pie. Yet, over the next decade, the share of government funding for children's programs and tax credits will shrink by about a quarter, from 10.2 percent to 7.8 percent, according to a recent report by the Urban Institute. Cutting back on investments during a child's youngest years can have serious long-term ripple effects well into adulthood; research finds that children's early language development, understanding of math concepts, and social-emotional stability at age five not only predict how well they will do in school but also largely determine their adult earnings.

One study, for example, finds that children's test scores in early elementary school largely explain the variation in their adult wages. Specifically, children who scored in the bottom 25 percent in these tests earned 20 percent less at age thirty-three than their counterparts who scored in the top 25 percent. The upshot is that on the day children arrive at kindergarten, one can already reasonably predict how much each will earn as an adult.

These findings have real implications for the investments we need to make to sustain a strong economy and to support today's youngest Americans—Generation Z, or those born in the twenty-first century. (This cohort is smaller than the Millennial generation but still growing, and it is even more racially and ethnically diverse.) Human capital—the level of education, skills, and talent in our workforce—is a main driver of economic growth, so in order to ensure that we have a healthy, productive workforce and a thriving economy in the decades to come, we must begin by developing human capital during early childhood through education and other enrichment activities.

Yet we already know that the older members of Generation Z in the United States are falling behind their teenage peers in other developed economies. The most recent data findings from the new Programme for International Student Assessment, the most-cited international educational ranking, finds that out of thirty-four developed countries, U.S. teenagers rank seventeenth in reading, twenty-first in science, and twenty-sixth in math.

Nothing is more important to the future of our nation than preparing our youngest generation to meet the unpredictable economic challenges of the 2020s and 2030s. Yet rising economic inequality and unstable economic growth define our society today, and this inequality and instability start from the very day a child is born. Many low- and middle-income families face extraordinary challenges to providing the care and education their children need to thrive in school and in the twenty-first-century workplace.

How can we better prepare our nation's youngest generation for success? Investments in K-12 schooling, college, and graduate education are important, but lasting investments need to be made earlier in a child's life. According to University of Chicago economist James J. Heckman, educational and enrichment investments during early childhood yield the highest return in human capital compared to other investments over time. Why? Because as the brain forms, children learn cognitive skills such as language and early math concepts, but also "soft" skills such as curiosity, self-control, and grit. These are critical for later academic success as well as valued traits in workers. By the time a child enters kindergarten, the difference in school readiness is already well established, and the gap widens by less than 10 percent between kindergarten and high school.

Early learning is enhanced by what happens in preschool, but the two factors that most explain the gaps in school readiness are parenting styles and home learning environments. Yet many parents are unaware of the importance of early brain development and of the tremendous impact they can have on their very young children's learning through simple actions such as

talking, reading, and singing to and with them. Even if parents are aware of the importance of these activities, they may have difficulty carving out time at home with their children as they juggle jobs and the family's other physical and emotional needs. Today, more children than ever are raised in single-parent families or in homes where both parents work. Parents today are constantly balancing work and family care, often without access to family-friendly workplace policies to support them.

If parents are unable to provide enriching home experiences, children can gain valuable developmental and learning support in quality child care and preschool settings. Unfortunately, about half of U.S. children receive no early childhood education, many because their parents simply cannot afford it. In 2011, the average cost for a four-year-old in full-time professional child care ranged from about $4,000 to $15,000 a year. This can put a major strain on the budgets of low- and middle-income families. Low-income families pay around $2,300 a year per child for care for children under age six—about 14 percent of their income. Families in the middle average $3,500 a year—6 percent to 9 percent of their income. Professional families pay about $4,800 a year—3 percent to 7 percent of their income.

Low-income families who are able to pay for child care often find that the care they can afford is merely a safe place for their child while they are at work, but offers poor or mediocre support to help their child in the critical stages of early childhood development. The limited spots in high-quality programs often go to more-affluent children, whose families can afford expensive care.

As a result, children have different enrichment experiences and are not starting from the same point early on in life. One famous study—often referred to as the "thirty million word gap" study, by professors Betty Hart and

Todd R. Risley—found that children living in poverty hear thirty million fewer words by age four than higher-income children. Hearing words directly translates into learning words. On average, a child from a low-income family knows 500 words by the age of three, compared with 700 words for a child from a working-class family and 1,100 for a child from a professional family. In recent years, not only has this study been replicated, but researchers have found that already by age two, there is a six-month gap in language proficiency between lower-income and higher-income children.

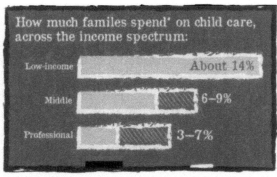

*March 2009 dollars

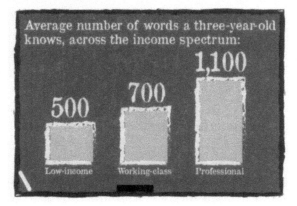

In order to have a productive workforce and thriving economy tomorrow, we need to invest in our children today. There are viable policy solutions that could expand early childhood education and enrichment opportunities to all children, rather than just a select few at the top. First, voluntary home visits by child development professionals could increase awareness among working-class parents of how they can foster their children's development at home, such as talking, reading, and singing to their children before bedtime. Home visiting programs are taking off under the Maternal, Infant and Early Childhood Home Visiting Program, established in 2010, and evaluations examining their effectiveness on parent and child outcomes are showing promising results.

Second, it is important to expand access to high-quality affordable early childhood education programs, which better prepare children for school, putting children more than a year ahead in mathematics and other subjects. Low-income families would greatly benefit from expanded access to quality child care, Early Head Start, and high-quality preschool programs.

Lastly, parents can only be better first teachers of their children if they have the time to be with them. Policies such as workplace flexibility, paid family and medical leave, and paid sick days could help all working parents better manage work and family obligations and spend more time with their children. Today, professional workers are the most likely to have access to these policies, often considered additional employee "perks" by employers.

The importance of investing in early childhood matters for our economic competitiveness. The United States should be making smart economic investments in early childhood to ensure that all children have an equitable start before their first day of school. All Americans need our youngest ones to succeed as adults, no matter their family background and income level, for the American Dream to continue in the twenty-first century and beyond.

From Brilliant Baby to Child Placed At Risk

The Perilous Path of African American Boys in Early Childhood Education

Hakim M. Rashid, Howard University

African American Boys and Early Childhood Education: The Current Context

A number of critical factors (outside of the family) affect the status of African American boys in early childhood education. Among these are quality of preschool setting; teacher beliefs, expectations, and behaviors; acquisition of early literacy and school readiness skills; and curriculum quality and relevance. Each of these factors is related to developmental trajectories of young African American children in general. However, they are particularly salient in the lives of young African American boys given the early consolidation of identities, roles, and behavioral patterns in school settings.

Quality of Preschool Setting

Issues related to quality continue to be at the forefront of research and policy debates related to early childhood programming. Definitions of quality are varied and multidimensional. Katz (1993) posited a "top-down perspective" that looks at quality by examining characteristics of the setting such as adult-child ratio, staff qualifications, quality of adult-child relationships,

and aspects of the physical environment (Katz, 1993). This approach is reflected by the majority of research studies that link quality to child outcomes (Locasale-Crouch et al., 2007).

Despite increased federal funding for Head Start and the proliferation of state funded early childhood programs (National Institute for Early Education Research, 2008) many low-income African American children are enrolled in preschool settings that are of questionable quality. Locasale-Crouch and colleagues (2007) found that children from higher poverty preschools, serving higher proportions of non-Caucasian children, were less likely to be exposed to practices associated with social, emotional, and academic gains. Generally, they describe preschool classrooms in terms of five "profiles" that identified characteristics ranging from the "highest quality" (Profile 1) to the "lowest quality" (Profile 5). Their descriptions of the five quality profiles are as follows:

> Profile 1 (14.5% of the sample)—
> "Classrooms in this profile attained scores more than 1 standard deviation above the sample mean on positive indicators of quality,

including positive climate, teacher sensitivity, behavior management, productivity, and quality of feedback ... These classrooms show consistent social, emotional and instructional support to children ... this profile contained classrooms with the lowest proportions of non-Caucasians ..." (p. 10)

Profile 2 (16.9% of the sample)—"... classrooms were near or above the mean on indicators of social and emotional climate ... fewer teachers with a B.A. and early childhood certification than expected ... lower proportions of non-Caucasian students than in Profile 5." (p. 11)

Profile 3 (31.4% of the sample)—"... above the mean on positive emotional indicators of quality including positive emotional climate, teacher sensitivity, and behavior management ... instructional support is considerably less than Profile 2. Classrooms in this profile contain a smaller proportion of non-Caucasian students ..." (p. 11)

Profile 4 (18.5% of the sample)— "Classrooms in this profile attained scores slightly below the mean on positive ... and negative indicators of social and emotional quality. ... These classrooms offer some social and emotional support but instructional support is very limited ... Additionally, this profile contained significantly more programs located in a public school, the longest program days, the highest number of children in the class and the highest adult/child ratio. ... Lastly, classrooms in this profile contained lower proportions of non-Caucasian students than Profile 5." (p. 12)

Profile 5 (18.8% of the sample)— "Classrooms in this cluster attained scores more than 1 standard deviation below the mean on positive social and emotional indicators of quality (positive climate, teacher sensitivity, and behavior management) and 1 standard above the mean on both negative indicators (negative climate and over control). ... instructional support indicators were nearly a full standard deviation below the mean ... **this profile contained classrooms with the highest proportion of non-Caucasians ...**" (p. 12 emphasis added)

The findings of LoCasale-Crouch and colleagues (2007) are consistent with previous studies (Pianta et al., 2005) that have documented the relationship between poverty and low-quality child care environments. In addition to an overall lower level of quality, many preschool settings serving low-income African American children are not equipped to deal with the broad range of social and emotional issues that often produce extremely challenging behaviors (McCabe & Frede, 2007). Those settings that are best able to respond to children's emotional needs and challenging behaviors are linked to support systems, such as teacher access to mental health consultation (Gilliam, 2008; Raver et al., 2008).

Peisner-Feinberg and colleagues (2001) examined the relationship between quality of the preschool experience and the cognitive and socioemotional development of children from four to eight years of age. They found a continuing influence of preschool quality on children's receptive language ability, math ability, cognitive and attention skills, problem behaviors and sociability through the end of the second grade. Peisner-Feinberg and colleagues examined two aspects of quality—observed classroom practices and the closeness of the teacher-child relationship. Among their findings were the following:

- Children who attended child care programs with higher quality classroom practices tended to have higher language scores, $F(1,165) = 10.69, p < .002$. (p. 1544)
- Children whose preschool teachers rated their relationships as closer tended to have higher language scores over time, $F(1,165) = 1.52, p < .007$. (p. 1544)
- Higher math scores were associated with better quality child care classroom practices, $F(2, 153) = 3.27, p < .04$. (p. 1548)
- Teachers reported fewer problem behaviors in second grade for children who had closer relationships with their preschool teachers, $F(3,152) = 3.50, p < .02$. (p. 1548)
- Closer kindergarten teacher-child relationships were also associated with higher ratings of sociability in second grade. (p. 1548)

Peisner-Feinberg and colleagues (2001) conclude that "It may be that children with positive early experiences with non-parental caregivers learn a pattern of interacting that facilitates their relationships with future caregivers, as well as their ability to utilize experiences provided in these environments to further their development" (p. 1551). Fostering "positive early experiences with non-parental caregivers" is clearly a challenge for young African American boys, a challenge that has a direct bearing on later life outcomes.

Teacher Beliefs, Expectations, and Behaviors

It is through the expectations and subsequent behavior of teachers that social class stratification in America is operationalized from one generation to the next. The literature shows that teachers have lower expectations for students who are from low-income backgrounds (Rist, 2000), and that these expectations are based on social class, race, and other student characteristics (Good & Brophy, 1994). The combination of race and gender has placed young African American boys at considerable risks in early childhood settings.

Barbarin and Crawford (2006) reported on the reflections of observers involved in a study of preschool program quality and outcomes. They noted that in many of the pre-K and kindergarten classrooms they visited, a single child was separated from the group and placed at a desk next to the teacher's desk. These children were the ones considered "difficult" and "disruptive." According to Barbarin and Crawford,

> The children who were separated and excluded 'were almost always boys of color', an observer reported. Another observer concurred: 'I observed it over and over again. And it wasn't [that it was only] boys. It was always, always Black boys.' The singling out of children in this way effectively assigned them to the stigmatized roles of *troublemaker* or *bad child* as clearly as if the words had been stamped on their foreheads. (p. 80)

Barbarin and Crawford (2006) noted the transformation of young African American boys from "compliant, happy, and productive" in one setting to reflecting "a downward spiral of the child's behavior in a second center or school with different teaching practices and a different emotional climate" (p. 81). They quoted one observer as follows:

> One boy had been doing really well in pre-K. He was engaged, motivated and on task in observations of him in pre-K. However, when I observed him in kindergarten he was wild and off task much of the time, but I think he was just bored. The teacher did not respond effectively to stimulate and engage him. Instead of finding a challenge that would interest him, she did the opposite and denied him opportunities. (p. 81)

The observations reported by Barbarin and Crawford (2006) are entirely consistent with numerous research studies that have shown the quality of the teacher-child relationship to be a major contributor to school success in the early childhood years (Birch & Ladd, 1998; Hamre & Pianta, 2001; Howes et al., 2008). Howes and colleagues (2008) found that the best predictor of gains in academic outcomes for preschoolers was high quality instruction and close teacher-child relationships. Hamre and Pianta (2001) found that children's relationships with their kindergarten teachers predicted academic and behavioral outcomes *through eighth grade.* Combining scores on conflict and dependency scales into a variable they called relational negativity, they found that, "Particularly for boys, kindergarten teachers' perceptions of conflict and overdependency were significantly correlated with academic

outcomes throughout elementary and middle school" (p. 634). Their results also suggested that the quality of teacher-child relationships may be more important for children at higher risk for later problems than those at lower risk. Relational negativity strongly predicted work habit marks (i.e., listening, participation, compliance, cooperation, study habits) in lower elementary school, $r (178) = -.52, p < .001$, and upper elementary school, $r (178) = .34, p < .01$, for students in the top third of teacher behavior problem ratings. Teacher-child conflicts are also related to school avoidance, declines in prosocial behavior, and higher levels of peer perceived aggression (Birch & Ladd, 1997).

Halvorsen, Lee, and Andrade (2009) examined teachers' attitudes toward teaching children from low-income backgrounds and their willingness to take responsibility for student learning. They described responsibility as "the willingness of teachers to take responsibility for all their students' learning and to accept that students' success or failure is attributable to the *quality of* teaching, rather than to outside determinants, including the students" (p. 183). Using a mixed method approach that combined both qualitative and quantitative data sources, Halvorsen and colleagues (2009) studied kindergarten and first grade teachers in low-income schools. The qualitative dimension was based on interviews with peers and supervisors. Teachers were considered "highly responsible" if they were ranked high on "enjoyment of teaching" and "making a difference in the lives of children" and low on "factors interfering with teaching." The quantitative dimension of their study used data from the Early Childhood Longitudinal Study-Kindergarten cohort (National Center for Educational Statistics, 2002). Teachers' feelings of high, medium, or low levels of responsibility were related to factors, such as sense of collective responsibility, teaching experience, teacher preparation, conference attendance, perception of administrative support, and teacher control over school policy and curriculum. Halvorsen and colleagues (2009) summarized their quantitative findings, which were entirely consistent with their qualitative data, as follows:

> Early elementary teachers with high levels of responsibility demonstrate the following characteristics of professional dedication: more preparation time, more frequent attendance at early childhood conferences, and a more general propensity for improving their own learning. Responsibility is also associated with teachers feeling empowered to influence both policy and curriculum. Highly responsible teachers also report they are supported by their principals. Our most important finding is that at low income, public schools, responsibility positively influences how much children progress in reading from the beginning of kindergarten to the end of first grade, both individually and collectively. (pp. 210–211)

Wentzel (2003) investigated the extent to which parent socialization models could be used to explain the impact of teachers on student attitudinal, behavioral, and academic outcomes. Looking at teaching through the parenting dimensions of control, maturity demands, democratic communication, and nurturance, Wentzel found high expectations (maturity demands) to consistently predict student goals and interests, while negative feedback (lack of nurturance) was a consistent negative predictor of academic achievement and social behavior. These findings suggest that good teachers may mirror the behavioral styles of good parents. The work of Mandara (2006), who reviewed research on effective strategies for the socialization of young African American boys, is worth noting here. He found that a uniquely African American authoritativeness (warmth and control) and a proactive racial socialization are clearly effective parenting practices for young African American boys, thus raising the potential of the socialization practices of effective African American parents as a source for effective teaching.

Acquisition of Early Literacy and School Readiness Skills

Both school readiness and early literacy are indicators of a "good start" for early school success (National Institute of Child Health and Human Development, 2000). Supporting, enriching, and enhancing school readiness and early literacy development are crucial to a child's long-term educational success. School readiness for four-year-olds is being able to stay on task, engage in acceptable behavior in the classroom, interact well with peers, and manifest emerging literacy skills. For children in high poverty areas, these skills have been linked to their attending high quality preschool programs. Educational environments that support early literacy and quality instruction are important for all children. Unfortunately, children from economically disadvantaged, primarily minority status groups comprise the larger proportion of those students placed at-risk for problems in the area of literacy success in today's mainstream schools. Low levels of literacy are associated with a range of long-term social problems, including unemployment and delinquency (ProLiteracy Worldwide, 2003).

For young African American males a major indicator of their acquisition of early literacy skills is their reading scores on the National Assessment of Educational Progress (NAEP). NAEP reading scores for African American male fourth graders are the lowest of any of the tested subgroups (Lee, Grigg & Donahue, 2007)). The literacy level of young African American boys has become a critical indicator of what is likely to transpire in the future. There is evidence that early elementary school literacy levels predict high school literacy (Cunningham & Stanovich, 1997). Research also suggests that reading problems are related to certain kinds of emotional problems in low income school age children (Ackerman, Izard, Kobak, Brown, & Smith, 2007). Gee (2001) suggested a sociocultural perspective on literacy acquisition that recommends situating the reading problems of young African American boys within their unique social, cultural, and historical contexts. This kind of approach would require that the issue of literacy for young African American boys be approached from broader political and economic perspectives. Former Assistant Secretary of Education Grover "Russ" Whitehurst, in response to a question about the relationship between reading scores and incarceration, reflects the need for this kind of broader perspective. Whitehurst said,

> ... if you look at the proportion of middle schoolers who are not at the basic level, who are really behind in reading, it is a very strong predictor of problems with the law and the need for jails down the line. Literacy for societies, literacy for states, literacy for individuals is a powerful determinate of success. The opposite of success is failure and clearly, being in jail is a sign of failure. ... What goes into law enforcement issues and jails, all the rest, underemployment, unemployment insurance, the need to support women and children who are not employed—all of these issues are connected to literacy and education. Presumably the cost for these programs would go down substantially in concert with increasing levels of literacy and education attainment. (Boulton, n.d., p. 1)

Curriculum Quality and Relevance

Curriculum quality and relevance in the context of early childhood education for young African American boys involves issues of developmental appropriateness, cultural relevance, and the ability of a program to meet a child's individual needs. More recently, the issue of developmental appropriateness has been extended to examinations of the level of physical activity experienced by preschoolers. Brown and colleagues (2009) examined physical activity levels for a sample of preschoolers (55% African American and 50% male) from a range of early childhood programs that included commercial child-care centers, church-affiliated preschools, and Head Start programs. They found that the preschool day is basically sedentary with 89% of coded behaviors being characterized as sit/squat, lie down, or stand. Only 8% of behaviors were coded as light physical activity and 3% as vigorous activity. Also, children in higher quality preschool programs have higher levels of vigorous physical activity than those considered lower quality (Dowda, Pate, Trost, Almeida, & Sirand, 2004).

The relationship between physical activity and program quality is particularly troubling with regard to the experiences of African American boys in preschool settings. The work of Bailey and Boykin (2001) suggested that African American children prefer learning environments characterized by "verve" or a preference for movement, stimulus variability, and physical stimulation. This is a preference that is rooted in an "Afro-cultural ethos" that characterizes most African American homes (Bailey & Boykin, 2001). For boys, the lack of vigorous physical activity may be more debilitating since preschool boys tend to have generally higher activity levels than girls (Finn, Johannsen, & Specker, 2002).

Connor and colleagues (2009) examined the role of individualizing instruction in the literacy development of first graders. They compared rates of literacy skill growth in children from high poverty schools taught by teachers specially trained to individualize literacy instruction with results from a control group. They were particularly interested in examining the impact of code-focused instruction (i.e., a focus on decoding, phonics, alphabet activities) versus meaning-focused activities designed to extract and construct meaning from text (i.e., reading aloud, independent reading, writing, vocabulary, comprehension activities). Their results showed that student growth in literacy is related to the nature of individualized prescriptions for specific kinds of instruction over the course of the year. Depending on their ability levels, students need varying amounts of teacher/child managed, child managed, and peer and child managed instructional activities. A main effect emerged from meaning-focused, teacher/child managed. Connor and colleagues (2009) noted that this finding "indicates that meaning-focused instructional activities, such as reading with children and explicitly teaching comprehension strategies,

had a positive effect on students' reading skill gains regardless of whether they had strong or weak reading skills" (p. 94).

Teaching young African American boys to be proficient in reading is one of the greatest challenges facing the early childhood education community. First grade traditionally is the setting where readiness skills are consolidated and more formal reading instruction begins. However, just as the quality of preschool programs has been found to be substandard in low-income areas, so also has the quality of first grade. Stuhlman and Pianta (2009) found a higher proportion of low-quality first grade classrooms serving low-income children and a corresponding higher proportion of high-quality first grade classrooms serving middle-income children. They posited "children who may be at greatest risk for difficulties in early grades, due to poor pre-academic skills or demographic factors, are the *least* likely to be enrolled in high opportunity classrooms and are more likely to be enrolled in classrooms with the lowest quality" (p. 339). As young African American boys transition from preschool to kindergarten to first grade, their struggles continue. While they should be establishing a firm foundation for later success, in reality they are moving further into the quagmire that is the preschool to prison pipeline.

Implications—Toward Refining the Quality dimension for Young African American Boys in Early Childhood Education

The perspectives on what constitutes quality in early childhood education are varied and multidimensional. However, these perspectives and attempts at definition focus on what is considered "high quality" for young children in general, rather than what may be "high quality" for any specific group of children. It is a "one size fits all" approach that suggests what is good for "most" is best for each and every subgroup of children. For young African American boys, however, the unique historical and sociocultural forces that continue to place them at risk for school failure (and its consequences) require a more refined and "group specific" definition of "high quality" early childhood education. Therefore, the following indicators of quality should be addressed when assessing early childhood programs (preschool and early elementary) for young African American boys:

- A willingness on the part of teachers to take responsibility for the learning of all young African American boys (Halvorsen el al., 2009)
- Expectations for the success of young African American boys (Halvorsen et al., 2009)
- A willingness to highlight the assets of young African American boys (Boykin, 2000, Halvorsen et al., 2009)
- A recognition that warmth *and* control are dimensions of effective socialization for young African American boys (Mandara, 2006)
- A willingness to engage in a proactive racial socialization of young African American boys (Mandara, 2006)
- A willingness to engage young African American boys in early literacy activities that includes individualization (Conner et al., 2009)
- A recognition that high levels of vigorous activity (Dowda et al., 2004), especially activities rooted in their culture (Bailey & Boykin, 2001), are good for young African American boys

Conclusion and Recommendations

Young African American boys are placed at risk by the very nature of preschool and early childhood settings that should promote their development. Issues of teacher responsiveness, program quality, and developmental appropriateness must be examined specifically as they relate to outcomes for young African American boys. Communities and the policymakers that represent them must prioritize the provision of truly high quality early childhood education to African American boys. Toward that objective the following recommendations are offered:

- The status of young African American boys in early childhood settings must become a priority for varied segments of the African American community. Community based organizations, parent groups, and religious communities will need to coalesce around the question "what is happening to young African American boys in preschools and the early elementary grades?" Policy forums and research-based seminars can serve as starting points for the development of action plans and programmatic initiatives.
- Policymakers and politicians must go beyond simply advocating the full funding of Head Start, and begin to advocate funding for a broad range of services in early childhood programs in high poverty communities. These services include expanding early literacy training for parents and preschool teachers, mental health consultation services for preschool and early elementary teachers, and professional development activities that focus on creating high quality

programs that address the needs of African American boys.

- Charter schools for African American boys (pre-K through third grade) focused on early literacy should be developed by nonprofit organizations and community groups. These schools should partner with culturally competent university researchers to evaluate their effectiveness in promoting early literacy acquisition. Concerted efforts should be made to recruit African American males to teach in these schools.

- Public schools must be encouraged to establish more all male classrooms in the early elementary grades. As part of this initiative, curriculum materials that reflect the interests (e.g., hip hop, sports) of young African American boys should be developed, field-tested, implemented, and evaluated.

- Professional development opportunities for ALL teachers of young African American boys should be developed with a focus on asset-based education, learning style preferences, and curriculum relevance. Organizations, such as the National Black Child Development Institute and the National Alliance of Black School Educators, should work closely with colleges and universities to develop distance learning opportunities that focus on African American child development.

- Public awareness campaigns should be initiated that highlight problems and offer solutions related to young African American boys in preschool and early elementary settings. These campaigns should utilize various forms of media (print, radio, television) and focus on issues, such as teacher expectations and behaviors, curriculum relevance, and the importance of parental involvement. African American celebrities and media personalities should be encouraged to participate in these campaigns.

- There should be continued advocacy for the development of programs to recruit African American males into teaching in early childhood settings, including scholarships, loan forgiveness, and alternative certification programs. The stigma around men teaching young children must be confronted and eradicated.

Critical issues, such as educational attainment, employment, incarceration, and parenting have their roots in the early experiences of young African American boys. Success for African American males is framed by the educational contexts in which they are immersed. We must lay the foundation for that success in the nation's preschool and early childhood classrooms.

References

Ackerman, B. P., Izard, C. E., Kobak, R., Brown, E. D., & Smith, C. (2007). Relation between reading problems and internalizing behavior in school for preadolescent children from economically disadvantaged families. *Child Development, 78*, 581–596.

Bailey, C. T. & Boykin. A. W. (2001). The role of task variability and home contextual factors in the academic performance and task motivation of African American elementary school children. *The Journal of Negro Education, 70*, 84–95.

Barbarin, O., & Crawford, G. (2006). Acknowledging and reducing stigmatization of African American boys. *Young Children, 61*, 79–86.

Barnett, W. S. (1996) *Lives in the balance: Age-27 benefit-cost analysis of the High/Scope Perry Preschool program.* Ypsilanti, MI: High/Scope Press.

Birch, S. H., & Ladd, G. W. (1997). The teacher-child relationship and children's early school adjustment. *Journal of School Psychology, 35,* 61–79.

Boulton, D. (n.d.) *Interview with Dr. Russ Whitehurst.* Children of the code. Retrieved from http://www.childrenofthecode.org/interviews/whitehurst.htm

Boykin, A. W. (2000). Foreword. In M. Sanders (Ed.), *Schooling students placed at risk: Research, policy and practice in the education of poor and minority adolescents* (pp. xi–xiv). Mahwah, NJ: Erlbaum.

Brown, W., Pfeiffer, K., McIver, K., Dowda, M., Addy, C., & Pate, R. (2009). Social and environmental factors associated with preschoolers' nonsedentary physical activity. *Child Development, 80,* 45–58.

Comer, J. (2004). *No child left behind. Preparing today's youth for tomorrow's world.* New Haven: Yale University Press.

Connor, C., Piasta, S., Fishman, B., Glasney, S., Schatschneider, C., Crowe, E., et al. (2009). Individualizing student instruction precisely: Effects of child x instruction interactions on first graders' literacy development. *Child Development, 80,* 77–100.

Cunningham, A. E., & Stanovich, K. E. (1997). Early reading acquisition and its relation to reading experience and ability 10 years later. *Developmental Psychology, 33,* 934–945.

Dowda, M., Pate, R., Trost, S., Almeida, M., & Sirand, J. (2004). Influences of preschool policies and practices on children's physical activity. *Journal of Community Health, 66,* 145–150.

Drakeford, W. (2004). Racial disproportionality in school disciplinary practices. Denver: National Center for Culturally Responsive Educational Systems.

Finn, K., Johannsen, N., & Specker, B. (2002) Factors associated with physical activity in preschool children. *The Journal of Pediatrics, 140,* 81–85.

Gee, J. (2001). A sociocultural perspective on early literacy development. In S. B. Neuman & D. K. Dickinson (Eds.), *Handbook of early literacy research* (pp. 30–42). New York: Guilford.

Gilliam, W. (2005). *Prekindergarteners left behind: Expulsion rates in state prekindergarten programs.* New York: Foundation for Child Development.

Gilliam, W. (2008). *Implementing policies to reduce the likelihood of preschool expulsion* (Policy Brief No. 7). New York: Foundation for Child Development.

Good, T., & Brophy, J. (1994). *Looking in classrooms.* (6th ed.). New York: Harper Collins.

Halvorsen, A., Lee, V., & Andrade, F. (2009). A mixed-method study of teachers' attitudes about teaching in urban and low-income schools. *Urban Education, 44,* 181–224.

Hamre, B. K., & Pianta, R C. (2001). Early teacher-child relationships and the trajectory of children's school outcomes through eighth grade. *Child Development, 72,* 625–638.

Holzer, H. Offner, P., & Sorensen, E. (2004). *Declining employment among young Black less-educated men: The role of incarceration and child support* (National Poverty Center Working Paper Series #04-5). Retrieved from http://www.npc.umich.edu/publications/working_papers/

Howes, C., Burchinal, M., Pianta, R., Bryant, D., Early, D., Clifford, R., & Barbarin, O. (2008). Ready to learn? Children's pre-academic achievement in pre-Kindergarten programs. *Early Childhood Research Quarterly, 23,* 27–50.

Kaiser Family Foundation. (2004). *Fad sheet: Young African American men in the United States* (Publication #7541). Menlo Park, CA: Kaiser Family Foundation.

Katz, L. (1993). *Five perspectives on quality in early childhood programs.* Clearinghouse on Early Learning and Parenting University of Illinois at Urbana-Champaign. Retrieved from http://ceep.crc.uiuc.edu/eecearchive/books/fivepers.html. Urbana IL: ERIC Clearinghouse on Elementary and Early Childhood Education ED355041

Lee, J., Grigg, W., & Donahue, P. (2007). *The nation's report card: Reading 2007* (NCES 2007-496). National Center for Education Statistics, Institute of Education Sciences, U.S. Department of Education, Washington, D.C.

Locasale-Crouch, J., Konold, T., Pianta, R., Howes, C., Burchinal, M., Bryant, D. et al. (2007). Observed classroom quality profiles in state-funded pre-kindergarten programs and associations with teacher, program, and classroom characteristics. *Early Childhood Research Quarterly, 22,* 3–17.

Mandara, J. (2006). The impact of family functioning on African American males academic achievement: A review and clarification of the empirical literature. *Teachers College Record, 108,* 206–223.

McCabe, L., & Frede, E. (2007, January). *Challenging behaviors: Preschool as a contributing or ameliorating factor?* National Institute for Early Education Research Policy Paper. Retrieved from www.nieer.org

National Center for Educational Statistics. (2002). *User's manual for the ECLS-K longitudinal kindergarten-first grade public-use data files and electronic codebook* (NCES 2002–149). Washington, DC: U. S. Department of Education.

National Institute of Child Health and Human Development. (2000). Report of the National Reading Panel. *Teaching children to read: An evidence-based assessment of the scientific research literature on reading and its implications for reading instruction* (NIH Publication No. 00–4769). Washington, DC: U. S. Government Printing Office.

National Institute for Early Education Research. (2008). *The state of preschool 2008.* Retrieved from http://nieer.org/yearbook/

Orfield, G., Losen, D.J., Wald, J., & Swanson, C. B. (2004). *Losing our future: How minority youth are being left behind by the graduation rate crisis.* Cambridge, MA: The Civil Rights Project at Harvard University.

Pianta, R. Howes, C., Burchinal, M., Bryant, D., Clifford, R., Early, D., & Barbarin, O. (2005). Features of pre-kindergarten programs, classrooms, and teachers: Do they predict observed classroom quality and child-teacher interactions? *Applied Developmental Science, 9, 3,* 144–159.

Peisner-Feinberg, E., Burchinal, M., Clifford, R., Culkin, M., Howes, C., Kagan, S., & Yazejian, N, (2001). The relation of preschool child-care quality to children's cognitive and social developmental trajectories through second grade. *Child Development, 72,* 1534–1553.

ProLiteracy Worldwide. (2003). *U.S. adult literacy programs making difference: A review of research on positive outcomes achieved by literacy programs and the people they serve.* Syracuse, NY: ProLiteracy America.

Raver, C., Jones, S., Li-Grining, C., Metzger, M., Champion, K., & Sardin, L. (2008). Improving preschool classroom processes: Preliminary findings from a randomized trial implemented in Head Start settings. *Early Childhood Research Quarterly, 23,* 10–26.

Reynolds, A., Temple, J., & White, B. (2009). *Cost-effective early childhood development programs: A synthesis of evidence in the first decade of life.* Retrieved from http://www.cehd.umn.edu/ICD/CLS/docs/cbasummary2009.pdf

Rist, R. (2000). Student social class and teacher expectations: The self-fulfilling prophecy in ghetto education. *Harvard Educational Review 70,* 257–301.

Schweinhart, L. J., Montie, J., Xiang, Z., Barnett, W. S., Belfield, C. R., & Nores, M. (2004). *Lifetime effects: the High/Scope Perry Preschool study through age 40.* Ypsilanti, MI: High/Scope.

Stuhlman, M., & Pianta, R. (2009). Profiles of educational quality in first grade. *The Elementary School Journal, 109,* 323–341.

Townsend, B.L. (2000). The disproportionate discipline of African American learners: Reducing school suspensions and expulsions. *Exceptional Children, 66,* 381–391.

Wald, J., & Losen, D. (Eds.). (2003). *Deconstructing the school-to-prison pipeline: New directions for youth development.* San Francisco: Jossey-Bass.

Wentzel, K. (2003). Are effective teachers like good parents? Teaching styles and student adjustment in early adolescence. *Child Development, 73,* 287–301.

Werner, E. (1972). Infants around the world: Cross-cultural studies of psychomotor development from birth to two years. *Journal of Cross-Cultural Psychology, 3,* 111–134.

Indigenous Children

Their Human Rights, Mortality, and the Millennium Development Goals

How will we know when we have achieved our target?

Jane Freemantle

The first effective attempt to promote children's rights was the Declaration of the Rights of the Child, drafted by Eglantyne Jebb in 1923 and adopted by the League of Nations in 1924.[1] On 20 November 1959, the United Nations General Assembly adopted a much expanded version as its own Declaration of the Rights of the Child, with ten principles in place of the original five.[2] The United Nations Convention on the Rights of the Child (UNCRC) was the first legally binding international instrument to incorporate the full range of human rights, describing child-specific needs and rights.[3] These human rights included civil, cultural, economic, political, and social rights, as well as aspects of humanitarian law.[3] The UNCRC was signed in 1989, and entered into force in 1990. As of May 2010, it had 193 parties which had ratified, accepted, or acceded with stated reservations or interpretations, including every member of the United Nations except Somalia and the United States, which have only signed.[3]

Nations that ratify this international convention are bound to it by international law. While all the rights contained in the Convention apply to all children, whether indigenous or not, the Convention on the Rights of the Child was the first core human rights treaty to include specific references to indigenous children in a number of provisions (namely, articles 17, 29, and 30). Despite an increased awareness of the rights of indigenous people within the international forum, indigenous children remain amongst the most marginalized groups within our society.[4] Further, in Australia, Canada, New Zealand, and the United States, the indigenous to non-indigenous infant mortality ratios range from 1.6 to 4.0.[5]

In 2000, the United Nations Millennium Declaration was adopted by the General Assembly.[6] Eight Millennium Development Goals (MDGs) were developed with each of the Goals having specific measurable indicators. Four of the MDGs concern reducing extreme poverty, reducing child mortality rates, fighting disease epidemics such as HIV/AIDS, and developing a global partnership for development. All 192 members of the United Nations and at least 23 international organizations have agreed to achieve these goals by 2015. MDG 4 aims to reduce child mortality, and the specific target is to reduce by two-thirds, between 1990 and 2015, the under-five mortality rate. The indicators for MDG 4 are under-five and infant mortality rates, and the proportion of one-year-old children immunized against measles.[7]

Pre-school children of the Indigenous Wayuu group line up to be vaccinated during a UNICEF-assisted immunization drive in Maracaibo City in the north-western state of Zulia, Venezuela. The drive is part of the Ministry of Health's Trio por la Vida (Trio for Life) programme, a UNICEF-supported initiative that promotes three components of child health: civil birth registration, breastfeeding, and immunization.

In this article I will consider the role (and limitations) of health statistics in monitoring the progress towards achieving the targets in reducing mortality rates in children under five and in infants (MDGs 4.1 and 4.2) among indigenous populations, and I will argue that in order to monitor and measure the impact of initiatives, strategies, policies, or practices aimed at achieving the targets, the human right to be counted must be universally exercised. The barriers to

obtaining accurate and complete identification of indigenous persons in vital statistics and administrative data will be considered.

Human rights have been described by the United Nations Children's Fund (UNICEF) as "those rights which are essential to live as human beings—basic standards without which people cannot survive and develop dignity: everyone, everywhere has the same rights as a result of our common humanity."[8] Human rights discourse argues that "governments have an international obligation to take proactive steps to improve the health and wellbeing of minority, disadvantaged and marginalized population groups".[9] These principles are expressed as a universal right to the opportunity to lead a healthy life, including equal access to quality care and the underlying social determinants of health.[9, 10, 11, 12] This "right" should not to be interpreted as an explicit right to good health, but rather as a right to the highest attainable standard of health.[13]

If we are to have an accurate understanding as to whether these principles have been upheld for indigenous infants and children worldwide, then we must be able to acknowledge the existence of indigenous people in population statistics and measure changing health status over time. We must not deny people the right to define themselves.[14] It is indeed a human right to be counted in population statistics in an accurate and timely manner and indigenous children should not be "invisible" in national and international statistics.[15]

Further, as infant and early childhood mortality statistics are important indicators of a population's health, an accurate picture of mortality informs a moral society of its social progress on a national and/or community level. This is particularly valid given that causes of infant and childhood mortality, such as infections, are potentially preventable. Others, such as low birth weight or preterm birth can be partially prevented with good health care and antenatal interventions.[16] Studies of the trends in mortality and related statistics demonstrate the changing health status of the population.

Measuring and monitoring indigenous rates and causes of morbidity and mortality as well as access to care is made possible through the identification of indigenous status (or ethnicity) in datasets, such as birth, hospital and death collections and registries, health surveys, and population censuses. These data are disaggregated by indigenous status to enable reporting on indigenous and non-indigenous populations and comparisons between the two. Health data disaggregated by indigenous status also provide an evidence base for the development of health policy and programmes, evaluating services and interventions, and monitoring public expenditure.[17, 18, 19] At a local level, these data enable assessment of the cultural appropriateness and responsiveness of health services to the needs of their clients. These data can be a valuable tool for communities in advocating for policy change and monitoring political accountability.[19] Internationally, these data are used to monitor and report on indigenous health in an international context, applying an additional degree of political accountability.[19]

Analysis of expenditure per capita, disaggregated by indigenous status also provides a baseline on which to assess the human right to an equal opportunity to good health.[19]

All too often in the post we have seen the effect of policies that reflect the principle of "no data, no problem, no change"

However, a statistical approach to measuring a population-level enjoyment of the right to health has its limitations due to issues of accuracy and completeness of identification of indigenous status.[14, 17, 19] Issues are generally due to a combination of differential classification of indigenous persons, the changing propensity to identify one's indigenous status, and/or inconsistencies in the routine asking of the question by census staff.[17, 18, 19]

Identifying indigenous peoples globally is also confounded by differences in classification across borders and according to use.[14] There are legal definitions, anthropological perspectives, and criteria used to identify persons in health records. In different circumstances, identification can rely on self-identification, require legal proof of identify, and/or proof from the community.[14]

In order to achieve the targets identified under MDG 4, we must be able to describe and monitor indigenous child health outcomes. This requires complete, accurate, reliable, and valid ethnicity data. However, despite wide acknowledgments of the significant disparities in the provision of healthcare and resulting health inequalities between indigenous and non-indigenous children, specific data describing indigenous children is lacking.[4]

Under-registration of indigenous births and deaths, and in some cases of entire groups of indigenous peoples, have been reported; they are being excluded from indigenous datasets.[20] Remoteness and accessibility issues for many indigenous communities, the role of self-identification and classification of "indigenousness", and the history of institutionalized discrimination against indigenous peoples by settler populations result in disjointed and incomplete data.[19] In Canada there are no infant mortality rates for non-status Indians and Metis despite the fact that when combined these two populations represent almost half of the Aboriginal-identified population in Canada.[20]

In Australia, it is estimated that only 59 per cent of Aboriginal and Torres Strait Islander children (0–14 years) are included in national infant and childhood mortality statistics due to incomplete and inaccurate identification in some states and territories.[21, 22] This being the case, the ability to measure progress in achieving improvements in indigenous infant and child mortality is significantly compromised at best, and at worst, completely impossible. One of the barriers to determining accurate indigenous infant mortality rates in Canada is the absence of a consistent identifier in provincial and territorial infant birth and death registrations that is inclusive of all major Aboriginal groups.[23] All too often in the past we have seen the effect of policies that reflect the principle of "no data, no problem, no change".

There is no doubt that attitudes are changing with regards to a genuine commitment of many federal and jurisdictional governments worldwide to reduce the unacceptably high inequalities in infant and child mortality being observed in indigenous populations and to improve the accuracy and coverage of indigenous identification. The accompanying policies, interventions, and health promotion education programmes are to be applauded.

The "Close the Gap" catch cry about indigenous infant and child mortality is being proclaimed in many indigenous communities, along the corridors of industry, and in the offices of federal and jurisdictional governments worldwide, and it is reflected in the intent of the MDGs. The transition from talking about "closing the gap" to action in achieving such closure will occur through the implementation of well-devised, evidence-based initiatives developed in close consultation with indigenous communities and those with specialist health knowledge and expertise.

However, we will also need to know how much impact such initiatives and policies have had on addressing the disparities in infant and child mortality and the social determinants of health that underpin these disparities. Thus, we need to be sure of the accuracy of the baseline from which we measure the changes in the current status. Improving the accuracy of indigenous identification in data collections must be achieved at the point of collection, through educating those who collect the information and those about whom the data are being collected as to the importance of collecting accurate information about indigenous status. Such education would include how these data are used to better inform policies, practices, and strategies. Assurances must be given and adhered to so that the data collected will not be used to discriminate against indigenous groups, and it becomes the responsibility of services to provide an environment where it is safe to identify one's cultural/ethnic origins without fear of discrimination.

The exclusion of indigenous persons or communities from basic public health surveillance based on their chosen place of residence, ethnic identity, or the use of government defined indigenous categories over indigenous determinations of identity and membership clearly violates the UN Declaration on the Rights of Indigenous Peoples.

Without accurate identification of indigenous persons in health datasets, we cannot accurately describe and monitor indigenous births, deaths, and child health outcomes. We cannot answer the questions: Who are our indigenous peoples? What is their current standard of health and how does it compare to other members of the population? Why is their health so poor and how can opportunities for better health care and health outcomes be supported and increased?

Accurate and complete indigenous status data will provide the evidence to answer such questions as: Are we there yet? Have we achieved the MDG 4 target to reduce child mortality? Has progress been made to ensure that the rights of the child are being promoted and that the opportunity for good health for indigenous and non-indigenous children is equal?

The author acknowledges Bree Heffernan, Research Assistant, Centre for Health and Society, University of Melbourne, in the preparation of this paper.

Notes

1   History of UNICEF: http://en.wikipedia.org/wiki/Declaration_of_the_Rights_of_the_Child

2   United Nations Declaration on the Rights of the Child: http://daccess-dds-ny.un.org/doc/RESOLUTION/GEN/NR0/142/09/IMG/NR014209.pdf?OpenElement

3   United Nations Convention on the Rights of the Child: http://www.un.org/documents/ga/res/44/a44r025.htm

4   S. Woolley, "The rights of indigenous children around the world-still far from a reality", *Arch Dis Child.* Vol. 94, Issue: 5, (2009): p. 397–400.

5   J. Smylie, J. Freemantle, D. McAullay, M. Taualli, S. Crengle, K. McShane, P. Adomako, G. Gilbert, "Health of Indigenous Children: Health Assessment In action", *Health Canada* (2009).

6   United Nations Millennium Declaration on 8 September 2000: http://www.un.org/millennium/declaration/ares552e.pdf

7   United Nations Development Program, Millennium Development Goals: http://www.undp.org/mdg/basics.shtml

8   UNICEF Convention on the Rights of the Child: http://www.unicef.org/crc/index_framework.html

9   N. Gray, "Can human rights discourse improve the health of Indigenous Australians?" *Australian and New Zealand Journal of Public Health,* Oct 2006, Vol.30 i5, p448 (5).

10 A. Hendriks, "Ethnic and Cultural Diversity: Challenges and Opportunities for Health Law", *European Journal of Health Law,* 15 (2008) p285–295.

11 United Nations Committee on Economic, Social and Cultural Rights, *General comment 14 (2000): The right to the highest attainable standard of health (article 12 of the International Covenant on Economic, Social and Cultural Rights),* UN Doc E/C.12/2000/4, 11 August 2000.

12 T. Evans, "A human right to health?" *Third World Quarterly,* Vol. 23, No. 2 (2002), *Global Health and Governance: HIV/AIDS* (Apr 2002), P197–215.

13 International Covenant on Economic, Social and Cultural Rights: http://www2.ohchr.org/english/law/pdf/cescr.pdf

14 J. G. Bartlett, I. Madarlaga-Vignudo, J.D. O'Neil, H.V. Kuhnlein, "Identifying indigenous peoples for health research in a global context: a review of perspectives and challenges", *International journal of circumpolar health,* Vol.66 (4) (2008) p287–307.

15 C.J. Freemantle, "Indicators of infant and childhood mortality for Indigenous and non-Indigenous infants and children born in Western Australia from 1980 to 1997 Inclusive" [Doctor of Philosophy]. (Perth: University of Western Australia; 2003).

16 C.J. Freemantle, A.W. Read, N.H. de Klerk, D.McAullay, I.P. S.Anderson, F.J. Stanley, "Infant mortality among Australian Aboriginals", *The Lancet* 368, Issue 9539 (2006): p916–917.

17 B. Heffernan, S. Sheridan, J. Freemantle, *An Overview of Statutory and Administrative Datasets: Describing the Health of Victoria's Aboriginal Infants, Children and Young People,* (Melbourne: Onemda VicHealth Koori Health Unit, The University of Melbourne, 2009).

http://www.vacms.net.au/files/vacms/VACMS%20Report.pdf

18 Human Rights and Equal Opportunity Commission, *Social Justice Report 2005*.

19 I. Barnsley, "The Right to Health of Indigenous Peoples in the Industrialized World: A Research Agenda", *Health and Human Rights,* Vol. 9, No. 1 (2006), p43–54.

20 J. Smylie, D. Fell, A. Ohlsson, Joint Working Group on First Nations, Indian, Inuit, and Métis Infant Mortality of the Canadian Perinatal Surveillance System, "A Review of Aboriginal infant mortality rates in Canada-Striking and persistent Aboriginal/ non-Aboriginal Inequities", *Canadian Journal of Public Health* (in press)

21 Australian Institute of Health and Welfare, *Health and wellbeing of Indigenous children* in *A picture of Australia's children.* (Canberra: Australian Institute of Health and Welfare, 2009). http://www.aihw.gov.au/publications/phe/phe-112-10704/phe-112-10704-c09.pdf

22 National Indigenous Health Equity Council, *Data sources and data quality* (Australian Government Department of Health and Aging), http://www.nihec.gov.au/internet/nihec/publishing.nsf/Content/datasource-quality

23 J. Smylie, S. Crengle, J. Freemantle, M. Taualii, "Indigenous Birth Outcomes In Australia, Canada, New Zealand and The United States-An Overview", *Open Journal of Women's Health,* (Accepted for publication May 2010).

Reflexive Questions

1. What type of community did you grow up in as a young child? How do you think it influenced your physical and cognitive development?

2. Were you enrolled in a childcare center or preschool? What memories do you have of it? How did early education shape your development?

3. Why is childcare in the US so costly, while at the same time, many of the childcare teachers are underpaid? What drives this contradiction?

4. What can be done to make early childhood education available to all children? What are some possible solutions to help give children from under-resourced families and communities the support they need? Why is this important?

5. Looking back at your early childhood, were you expected to act a certain way based on your race? Who was driving this expectation; parents, community, cultural beliefs, teachers, society, influence of social media, etc.?

6. How do you think racism affects children in early childhood? What messages do children need to receive from adults in order to buffer the effects of racism?

7. What are your thoughts about what influences the preschool-to-prison pipeline? What needs to change so that Black and Brown children are taken off this harmful trajectory? What will it take for everyone to care and to activate greater change?

8. What do you know about First Nations/Indigenous children and families? Where did you learn this information, or lack thereof?

9. What are your thoughts about the US Census? What happens if people from historically marginalized groups are not counted? Who benefits if they remain under-resourced?

10. Given that Indigenous people are a diverse "cultural group," how can early education and socialization of children be offered in a way that is culturally appropriate and responsive? Why is this important?

11. How do you think historical, systemic, and structural racism affect ethnic identity development and life trajectories among Native Americans?

12. Specifically, how can images, societal messages, programs, and attitudes change so that young children obtain a positive ethnic and cultural identity and resist internalizing racism? What changes need to be made so that these and all children thrive?

CHAPTER 6

Middle Childhood

Introduction

Middle childhood, from about age 6 to 11, is often thought of as "the school years" (Berger, 2019). Middle childhood is characterized by dramatic growth in the brain, psychomotor skills, skeletal muscles, and psychosocial development. It is a time when children need to feel productive and continue to form their sense of self. Not only is it a time of continued physical and cognitive development, but it is also a time when school-age children begin to have an increased awareness of their environment and their ability to influence it. How a child manages change and copes with challenges will depend strongly on their caregivers' ability to help them develop culturally appropriate prosocial behaviors (Callaghan & Corbit, 2018), a sense of morality, equality, fairness, justice (Killen, 2018), and a sense of the importance of civic engagement (Shubert et al., 2019). Positive family relationships and routines that are stable and reliable, yet flexible, are essential to a child's sense of predictability and consistency in their environment (Bridley & Sytsma-Jordan, 2012). These factors can be present, regardless of a child's family form, such as families led by a single parent, divorced or never-married parents, grandparents, or same-gender parents. Although family life and positive socialization remain essential to well-being, children's peers become increasingly important. Children at this age begin to make social comparisons, adhere to cultural and gendered social expectations, and make friends that are more like them.

Considering the above-mentioned factors that shape development during the middle childhood years, it is essential to examine how the intersecting effects of a child and their caregiver's gender, social class, culture, race, and abilities, situate them to experience life during these formative years. For example, we discussed this developmental stage as "the school years"; however, not every child in the world will receive a formal education. Girls and children with diverse physical abilities are still routinely denied access to school, especially as they advance in years. According to UNICEF (https://www.unicef.org/education/girls-education), despite strong evidence demonstrating the significance of education to a girl's development, gender disparities in education persist. Children who are economically disadvantaged are often denied access to a formal education, receive a poor-quality education, and/or are taken out of school prematurely to be wed or to provide income for their families. Worldwide, approximately 132 million girls do not attend school, with only 66% of countries granting equal access to girls and boys. In countries affected by war and conflict, girls are more than twice as likely to be out of school than girls living in non-affected countries. Additionally, many schools do not meet the safety, hygiene, or sanitation needs of girls.

In 1959, the United Nations General Assembly adopted the *Declaration of the Rights of the Child*, https://www.un.org/en/sections/issues-depth/children/, which marked international consensus and defined children's rights to include the right to protection, education, health care, shelter, and good nutrition. Although this was an important direction for children's rights, children all over the world are still dying of hunger and curable diseases, forced to fight wars, marry as children, live as sex workers, and live without food, shelter, and protection. According to the World Health Organization (https://www.who.int/life-course/news/women-and-girls-health-across-life-course-top-facts/en/), girls aged 5–9 have a relatively high risk of dying from preventable infectious diseases such as lower respiratory infections, diarrheal diseases, or malaria, and HIV/AIDS remains the second leading cause for this group of girls. Additionally, according to the World Health Organization, gender norms can place restrictions on girls' physical mobility and their access to information, which has lasting effects well into adulthood. Additionally, gender-based violence and femicide continue to be grave concerns, with approximately 18% of girls, compared to 8% of boys, experiencing sexual abuse during childhood. Approximately 120 million adolescent girls experience forced intercourse or other forced sexual acts. Furthermore, violating gender-based norms can also be stressful and dangerous for children and youth who have gender expansive or non-conforming expression, gender-variant behavior, or whose transgender identity emerges early (Nealy, 2017). It is vital that every child, irrespective of nationality, religious beliefs, race, gender, abilities, or socioeconomic status, has the right to be free from any form of violence, exploitation, humiliation, abuse, and neglect. It is every child's right to be protected by everyone and especially those entrusted with their care and guiding their development.

Lastly, it is well documented that children from privileged backgrounds will often continue on a path that affords them more privilege and vice versa (Nurius, Prince, & Rocha, 2015). Theories such as cumulative disadvantage theory (Merton, 1988) and life course theory, also known as life course perspective (Bengtson & Allen, 1993), have been helpful to scholars as they examine how people's socioeconomic position, sociohistorical and geographical location, and social context affect their life trajectories. Cumulative disadvantage theory and life course perspective have been applied to the study of race and SES in relation to delinquency (Sampson & Laub, 1997), health (Lynch, 2008; Seabrook & Avison, 2012), family SES-base inequalities in depressive symptoms in youth (Wickrama, Noh, & Elde, 2009), and educational disadvantage (Jackson, 2015; Walsemann, Geronimus, & Gee, 2008). Hudson (2016) discusses that understanding inequality due to race, class, and gender is important; however, it is merely a first step. He states that a longitudinal lens is vital for understanding how the cumulative effects of opportunities and constraints affect us over time and throughout the life course. If course corrections are not made, then disadvantage is likely to continue with a snowball effect. Masten (2014, 2018) states that innovative research on resilience can help increase an international knowledge base on resilience in children and youth, and offer guidance on how to help buffer their vulnerabilities and strengthen their ability to overcome adversity.

As you will learn from the readings below, children who belong to marginalized or oppressed groups or who have disadvantages due to diverse abilities will experience additional challenges that may impede their development and alter their trajectories throughout their lives. The readings selected in this chapter reflect some developmental challenges for specific groups of children, such as children with different abilities in challenging environments and intersex and transgender children.

Summary of Readings

"Childhood Disability in Turkana, Kenya: Understanding How Carers Cope in a Complex Humanitarian Setting" (2016) by Maria Zuurmond et al. presents the findings of a study conducted to explore the lived experiences of families with children with disabilities in the complex humanitarian environment of Turkana. In this study, 31 families caring for children with various disabilities were interviewed. Turkana is among the largest regions and the poorest, most marginalized and malnourished county in northwest Kenya. It has many barriers to health and well-being, such as famine, drought, flash flooding, weak infrastructure, and low education. Overall, having a child with a disability greatly affects a family; however, for the families in this study, women were especially affected and burdened, as most were the primary caregivers, and single mothers headed half of the households interviewed. Fathers were often absent due to the stigma associated with having a child with a disability; thus, caring for disabled children often interfered with a mother's ability to participate in income-generating activities. Additionally, there was often an absence of familial and communal support, posing serious negative consequences for the children. Overall, the authors discuss how humanitarian crises make people with disabilities more vulnerable. In Turkana, traveling long distances for basic needs further exacerbated challenges due to limited transportation and lost wages when seeking treatment or support for their child. Lastly, the fragmented medical system and social services posed grave challenges for families with special needs children.

The reading **"What Constitutes a Quality Program for Children Who Are Deaf?"** (2015) by J. Freeman King questions the current effectiveness of deaf education within public schools. The current interpretation of the law, the Individuals with Disabilities Education Act (IDEA), supports the inclusion/mainstreaming of students who are deaf or hard of hearing into public education and public schools. While the intention is benevolent, King asserts public schools are a restrictive and inappropriate environment for children who are deaf, often lacking opportunities for them to fully engage and communicate with their peers, teachers, and interpreters. To facilitate inclusive communication and socialization of deaf children, King proposes several remedies: 1) programs must include substantial numbers of deaf students, 2) teachers and interpreters should be highly knowledgeable about deaf culture, and 3) hearing students and faculty should have opportunities to learn American Sign Language (ASL).

The third reading, **"Safe Schools for Transgender and Gender Diverse Students"** (2014), written by an anonymous author, emphasizes the importance of familial and school acceptance for the well-being of transgender and gender diverse students. The author contends that parents should create safe, supportive spaces in the home and require others to accept their child's gender identity. The author states that several things can be especially supportive to transgender youth: 1) the presence of a Gay-Straight Alliance, 2) limiting gender segregation practices, and 3) addressing the needs of transgender students in written policies. All of these are ways schools can foster inclusion. School psychologists can also create a safe learning environment by helping schools develop anti-harassment procedures and providing education about LGBT issues to faculty and students.

References

Berger, K. S. (2019). *Invitation to the Life Span (4th ed.)*. Worth Publishers.

Bengtson, V. L., & Allen, K. R. (1993). The life course perspective applied to families over time. In P. Boss, W. Doherty, R. Larossa, W. Schumm, and S. Steinmetz (Eds.), *Sourcebook of family theories and methods: A contextual approach*. Plenum.

Bridley, A., & Sytsma-Jordan, S. (2012). Child routines moderate daily hassles and children's psychological adjustment, *Children's Health Care, 41*(2), 129–144. doi:10.1080/02739615.2012.657040

Callaghan, T., & Corbit, J. (2018). Early prosocial development across cultures. *Current Opinion in Psychology, 20*, 102–106. doi.org/10.1016/j.copsyc.2017.07.039

Hudson, R. B. (2016). Cumulative advantage and disadvantage: Across the life course, across generations. *Public Policy & Aging Report, 26*(2), 39–41 doi:10.1093/ppar/prw007

Jackson, M. I. (2015). Cumulative inequality in child health and academic achievement. *Journal of Health and Social Behavior, 56*(2), 262–280. doi:10.1177/0022146515581857

Killen, M. (2018). The origins of morality: Social equality, fairness, and justice. Philosophical Psychology, 31(5), 767–803. doi:10.1080/09515089.2018.1486612

Lynch, S. M. (2008). Race, socioeconomic status, and health in life-course perspective: Introduction to the special issue. *Research on Aging, 30*(2), 127–136. 10.1177/0164027507312086

Masten, A. S. (2018). Resilience theory and research on children and families: Past, present, and promise. *Journal of Family Theory and Review, 10*(1), 12–31. doi:10.1111/jftr.12255

Masten, A. S. (2014). Global perspectives on resilience in children and youth. *Child Development, 85*(1), 6–20. https://doi.org/10.1111/cdev.12205

Merton R. K. (1988). The Matthew effect in science, II: Cumulative advantage and the symbolism of intellectual property. *Isis, 79*, 606–623.

Nealy, E. C. (2017). *Transgender children and youth: Cultivating pride and joy with families in transition*. W. W. Norton & Company.

Nurius, P. S., Prince, D. M., & Rocha, A. (2015). Cumulative disadvantage and youth well-being: A multi-domain examination with life course implications. *Child and Adolescent Social Work Journal, 32*, 567–576. doi.org/10.1007/s10560-015-0396-2

Sampson, R. J., & Laub, J. H. (1997). A life-course theory of cumulative disadvantage and the stability of delinquency. In T. P. Thornberry (Ed.), *Developmental theories of crime and delinquency* (pp. 133–161). Transaction Publishers.

Seabrook, J. A., & Avison, W. R. (2012). Socioeconomic status and cumulative disadvantage processes across the life course: Implications for health outcomes. *Canadian Review of Sociology, 49*(1), 50–68. doi:10.1111/j.1755-618x.2011.01280.x

Shubert, J., Wray-Lake, L., Syvertsen, A. K., & Metzger, A. (2019). The role of family civic context in character development across childhood and adolescence. *Applied Developmental Science.* doi:10.1080/10888691.2019.1683452

Walsemann, K. M., Geronimus, A. T., & Gee, G. C. (2008). Accumulating disadvantage over the life course evidence from a longitudinal study investigating the relationship between educational advantage in youth and health in middle age. *Research on Aging, 30,* 169–199.

United Nations website- https://www.un.org/en/sections/issues-depth/children/

UNICEF- https://www.unicef.org/education/girls-education

Wickrama, K. A. S., Noh, S., & Elde Jr., G. H. (2009). An investigation of family SES-based inequalities in depressive symptoms from early adolescence to emerging adulthood. *Advances in Life Course Research, 14,* 147–161.

World Health Organization (https://www.who.int/life-course/news/women-and-girls-health-across-life-course-top-facts/en/)

Childhood Disability in Turkana, Kenya

Understanding How Carers Cope in a Complex Humanitarian Setting

Maria Zuurmond, Velma Nyapera, Victoria Mwenda, James Kisia,

Hilary Rono, Jennifer Palmer, and Maria Zuurmond

Authors
Maria Zuurmond[1]
Velma Nyapera[2]
Victoria Mwenda[2]
James Kisia[2]
Hilary Rono[3]
Jennifer Palmer[4,5]

Affiliations
[1]International Centre for Evidence in Disability, London School of Hygiene & Tropical Medicine (LSHTM), London, UK
[2]Kenya Red Cross Society, Nairobi, Kenya
[3]London School of Hygiene and Tropical Medicine, and Opthalmologist, Kitale, Kenya
[4]Department of Infectious Diseases Epidemiology, London School of Hygiene & Tropical Medicine, UK
[5]Centre of African Studies, School of Political & Social Sciences, University of Edinburgh, London, UK

Corresponding author
Maria Zuurmond,
maria.zuurmond@lshtm.ac.uk

Dates
Received: 21 Apr. 2016
Accepted: 01 July 2016
Published: 29 Sept. 2016

How to cite this article
Zuurmond, M., Nyapera, V., Mwenda, V., Kisia, J., Rono, H. & Palmer, J., 2016, 'Childhood disability in Turkana, Kenya: Understanding how caregivers carers cope in a complex humanitarian setting', *African Journal of Disability* 5(1), a277. http://dx.doi.org/10.4102/ajod.v5i1.277

Read online

Scan this QR code with your smart phone or mobile device to read online.

Background: Although the consequences of disability are magnified in humanitarian contexts, research into the difficulties of caring for children with a disability in such settings has received limited attention.

Methods: Based on in-depth interviews with 31 families, key informants and focus group discussions in Turkana, Kenya, this article explores the lives of families caring for children with a range of impairments (hearing, vision, physical and intellectual) in a complex humanitarian context characterised by drought, flooding, armed conflict, poverty and historical marginalisation.

Results: The challenging environmental and social conditions of Turkana magnified not only the impact of impairment on children, but also the burden of caregiving. The remoteness of Turkana, along with the paucity and fragmentation of health, rehabilitation and social services, posed major challenges and created opportunity costs for families. Disability-related stigma isolated mothers of children with disabilities, especially, increasing their burden of care and further limiting their access to services and humanitarian programmes. In a context where social systems are already stressed, the combination of these factors compounded the vulnerabilities faced by children with disabilities and their families.

Conclusion: The needs of children with disabilities and their carers in Turkana are not being met by either community social support systems or humanitarian aid programmes. There is an urgent need to mainstream disability into Turkana services and programmes.

Background

Disability in Humanitarian Crises

The World Report on Disability estimates that 15% of the world's population experience some form of disability, and an estimated 93 million children aged 0–14 years are living with a moderate or severe disability. The majority are in low- and middle-income countries (LMICs; World Health Organization 2011). The same report highlights that conflict and natural disasters can both cause disabilities and make people with existing disabilities even more vulnerable. Humanitarian crises are social and material environments which may exacerbate the vulnerability of people with disabilities because of a breakdown in social services (medical and education), a reduction in income support for food and other basic necessities, diminished mobility and opportunities for migration and the loss of carers (Kett & van Ommeren 2009; Reilly 2010). Article 11 of the Convention on the Rights of Persons with Disabilities emphasises measures to protect the safety of people with disabilities during armed conflict and natural disasters (UN 2006). Additionally, a number of guidelines exist to support the mainstreaming of disability in humanitarian interventions (Handicap International 2005; Sphere 2011). Within a low-resource context, community-based rehabilitation (CBR) is also an important recommended strategy for rehabilitation, poverty reduction and the social inclusion of people with disabilities that is relevant to humanitarian contexts. This approach recognises the central role of the family and their communities, as well as relevant government and non-governmental organisations, in reducing disability (World Health Organization 2010).

Humanitarian crises such as those caused by armed conflict and natural disaster inevitably create new social processes, not all of which lead to harm. Crises may reinforce a community's sense of identity and systems of coping (Hodgson 2000) or prompt exposure to global humanitarianism and associated liberal systems and concepts (Grabska 2014). Indeed, people with disabilities in some highly managed settings (such as refugee camps) experience access to humanitarian programming as liberating, not only because such programmes meet everyday accessibility needs such as by providing latrines that are easy to use, but also by helping transform displaced populations' attitudes towards disability (Mirza 2013). As in non-crisis affected contexts, disabled children and their families in humanitarian and post-humanitarian settings may face multiple barriers to social inclusion. These barriers include increased caregiving duties, which prevent participation in economic activities, and poor informational access to or discriminatory exclusion from services that mitigate vulnerabilities (Miles & Medi 1994; Ngo *et al.* 2012). The needs for informal care and CBR in crisis and post-crisis settings also likely impact women more than men (Berghs 2015). There is, however, a need for better understanding of the lived experiences of adults and children with disabilities during humanitarian crises; particularly, little is known about family coping strategies in such settings.

Coping in a Complex Humanitarian Context in Turkana

Turkana County, in north-west Kenya, has been classified at various points over the last several decades as suffering from a complex humanitarian crisis because of multiple causes of vulnerability which compound each other. The climate is arid and suited for livestock production, which supports 60% of the population (Boulton 2012), but is subject to periodic drought. Rains are not only erratic with frequent total failure, but they also produce flash flooding. Within Kenya, Turkana is the largest county geographically and one of the most historically under-developed; people who live there suffer from some of the poorest schools, roads and health services in the country, a situation which has been unable to reverse by long-standing (but often poorly funded) government and humanitarian interventions (Broch-Due & Sanders 1999). Health and rehabilitation services are limited to the county hospital and a small, fragmented network of faith-based clinics and hospitals.

Poverty levels are 20% above the national average with per capita livestock wealth declining and dependence on food aid increasing (Kenya National Bureau of Statistics 2014). The large majority (78–94%) of households in Turkana experience problems accessing food (Ochola 2011). In recent years, up to 15% of the population of Turkana has been served by United Nations 'food assistance for assets' programmes (food in return for work on projects that increase a community's resiliency), and the general acute malnutrition rate among children has hovered at around 15%, the threshold between a 'serious' and 'critical' nutritional emergency (Office for the Coordination of Humanitarian Affairs 2013). With the proliferation of small arms seen over the last several decades, livestock raiding also contributes to famine, inter-communal violence and displacement and harms social systems for coping (Hendrickson, Armon & Mearns 1998). Consequently, in Turkana, as in other pastoralist areas of Africa, low-level, chronic violence and the politics of marginalisation reproduce one another (Pike *et al.* 2010).

In such a setting, pastoral mobility, including crisis-induced displacement, largely configures Turkana people's access to food, social services and income (Pike *et al.* 2010). Turkana social institutions (such as the maintenance of land rights and systems of livestock redistribution during crisis) remain key for people to manage the environmental precarity of living here (McCabe 1990), but they tend to exclude families living in towns, making them more dependent on cash economies or aid (Broch-Due & Sanders 1999). As carers, women play a key role in upholding these social institutions which contribute to community resilience. A good example of the instrumentality of pastoralist women in northern Kenya is in the area of nutrition (Pike *et al.* 2010). Access to milk from livestock is a particularly important determinant of nutrition and therefore health. When crisis forces men to move with cattle, this puts women and children at a nutritional disadvantage. To counter such vulnerability, pastoralist women therefore practise nutritional buffering of children's diet in an age-related pattern of communal moral responsibility; older women buffer younger mothers and all women forego food when children are hungry. Women in the Turkana are also more likely to be in a polygamous union (21%) compared with the national average of 10.2% Kenyan average (Kenya National Bureau of statistics 2010), and crisis can put a particular strain on the resources of polygamous families, with family breakdown (Wawire 2003).

The results of a recent study of childhood disability and malnutrition in Turkana are therefore troubling, which found that children with disabilities are more likely to be malnourished than their neighbours and even their siblings (Kuper *et al.* 2015). This vulnerability could reflect difficulties that carers of children with disabilities have in accessing traditional social support systems and/or humanitarian interventions. As has been shown in post-conflict Mozambique (Miles & Medi 1994), for families already stressed from the effects of war, poverty and drought, having a disabled child can exacerbate an already desperate situation, with the family invariably becoming poorer.

In this study, we present a picture of the lived experiences of carers of children with disabilities living in an ongoing, complex humanitarian crisis in Turkana, Kenya. We use the World Health Organization's International Classification of Functioning, Disability and Health (ICF), a biopsychosocial model of disability that synthesises a medical and social model of disability. This framework outlines the dynamic relationship between the impairment or health condition with activity limitations and participation restrictions, and the mediating role that environmental and personal factors can play (World Health Organization 2001). We pay particular attention to carers' daily needs, priorities and coping strategies as well as the social processes which permit or limit opportunities for them to access services and participate in community life.

Methods

Study Setting and Sample

This research was conducted in September 2012 and May 2013 in Lodwar, the county's largest town, and surrounding areas of Turkana Central District (now a sub-county) in collaboration with the Kenya Red Cross Society (KRCS). An initial scoping visit was undertaken to map disability-related services and aid programmes in Turkana county (September 2012). Turkana Central District was selected for this study and for a later survey of childhood disability prevalence for several criteria: it supports a range of livelihood types (pastoralism, fishing, agriculture, small businesses), was relatively safe and KRCS was present in the district to facilitate access to families caring for children with disabilities. The survey, conducted Jul–Aug 2013, estimated a minimum prevalence of moderate-to-severe disability in children at 0.75% (0.66–0.83%), with the true prevalence likely to be much higher (Kuper *et al.* 2015). Physical impairment such as cerebral palsy, rickets and muscular dystrophy was the most prevalent form of disability followed by epilepsy, visual, hearing and intellectual impairment; congenital causes of the disability were most common. The majority of children (85%) had never received any form of rehabilitative service such as therapy/exercises, assistive devices, surgery or occupational advice.

For our qualitative interviews, a list of children with disabilities living in the Turkana district aged 10 years and younger was collated from existing KRCS disability project data; additional information on demographics and the type of impairment was provided by KRCS CBR workers and local community health workers. Children were purposively sampled to cover a range of ages (1–5 years and 6–10 years), genders and impairments (physical, visual, hearing and intellectual). As the research was conducted during the rainy season some adjustment had to be made to the final choice of villages to take into account accessibility for the survey team and resulted in the exclusion of the most isolated and inaccessible villages. Cattle-rustling and tribal conflicts also prevented access to some districts at this time.

Carers were interviewed from 31 households, providing information on a total of 36 children with disabilities, of which 25 were boys and 11 girls. Eight children were in school. Of the carers interviewed, 19 were mothers, 3 grandmothers, 3 grandmothers and mothers (combined), 2 siblings, 4 fathers and 1 mother and father (combined). Only the men did not self-identify as the primary carer. A quarter of the families interviewed had recently migrated: two were pastoralists who regularly moved with livestock, five were displaced by flooding, drought or cattle raiding. Families in the sample were drawn from 23 villages, in three divisions, four locations and seven sub-locations.

To contextualise information collected from carer interviews, interviews were conducted with 16 key informants including village elders, hospital- and clinic-based staff, community health workers and teachers. Furthermore, two focus groups were conducted in two sites (where unplanned groups of carers had congregated when they heard about the research), and individuals were selected from these groups for one-to-one interviews (Table 6.1.1).

Data Collection and Analysis

Interviews were semi-structured and conducted by two researchers (M.Z. and V.N.) through translation between Turkana or Kiswahili and English. At the end of each day the project team met to review all interviews, to discuss and agree on key emerging issues and to identify any gaps that necessitated further exploration and additional questions in follow-up interviews. Detailed notes were taken during all interviews, and all interviews were also recorded and transcribed into English.

Most interviews with carers took place at the child's home, unless roads were impassable, in which case interviews were undertaken at a nearby health centre. Given that most family dwellings were very small, it was often impossible to have privacy for the one-to-one interviews, and some interviews were inevitably conducted with other family members present. Interviews covered the following areas: beliefs and attitudes about the child's condition, the impact of caring for a child with a disability, nutrition and feeding practices and factors which impacted upon children's access to services (health, education and humanitarian programmes including nutrition programmes). Interviews with key informants and focus group discussions focused on the availability of services, referral procedures and barriers to inclusion of children with disabilities in social systems.

Both interviewers separately identified a list of key themes and sub-themes through an iterative process, and these were then discussed, refined and cross-checked for consistency to provide an overall thematic coding framework for systematic analysis by M.Z. after fieldwork, by using NVivo 10 software (Green & Thorogood 2009).

Ethical Consideration

This project received ethical approval from Moi Teaching Hospital in Kenya, and from the London School of Hygiene and Tropical Medicine in the UK. Families were contacted and visited by local KRCS volunteers in advance of the interviews to provide clear verbal and written information about the research, and signed consent was obtained for all interviews. One component of the ethics protocol was for referrals to be supported by the KRCS team following the interviews. Quotes from respondents have been anonymised to protect their privacy.

TABLE 6.1.1 **Sample of children (n = 36).**

Child disability	Male	Female	Total
Physical	8	5	13
Sensory (hearing or visual)	2	2	4
Intellectual	2	0	2
Multiple	13	4	17

Findings

The Gendered Impact of Caregiving and Livelihoods

In a context of widespread poverty, scarcity of services and poor infrastructure, it was evident from all interviews that having a child with a disability impacted the whole family, generating specific challenges related to caring, income generation and the psychosocial health of carers. Impacts were most notable on women, who are the primary carers in families in Turkana. Mothers, grandmothers and female siblings typically cared for the children in our sample. In the larger survey, children with disabilities were significantly more likely than neighbour controls to have a female head of household, and half of the households we interviewed were single parent, female-headed. Reasons given for a father's absence, or for spending a long period away from the home, commonly involved stigma related to the child's disability, with very little, if any, family support provided by the father following the birth of a child with a disability. These reactions compounded the gendered burden of caregiving and the poverty of the family.

Caregiving arrangements for 'P' are illustrative of the complexity of these issues. P is a 10-year-old boy who was intellectually impaired and had epilepsy; he lived with his mother and six siblings, and his oldest sister had been taken out of school to help care for P. His illness began when he was about 6 years old; his family sought treatment for him at the local health centre and spent a considerable amount of money on seeking a cure from a traditional healer. His father subsequently left the family and stopped providing any support. The family reported they were not in receipt of any community or humanitarian support and the psychosocial impact of this on P's mother was clear:

> 'I think someone bewitched the father of the chid, and then the spell went to the child. … They told me [at the health centre] to take the child home and seek the help of the traditional healer … my husband and I spent a lot of money. … When my son's condition worsened I felt desperate, I lost hope, and I know there is nothing I can do to heal my son.'

The impact of increased caregiving responsibilities on being able to pursue livelihood activities was a key issue for families, and particularly in, but not exclusive to, female-headed households. A mother from another single female-headed household described the frustration she felt of balancing her caregiving roles with income-generating activities:

> 'I am not able to do any work here all day. I have to carry the child all through the day. I am not able to make as many mats as other women make. I only make one mat every month while other women make even 5 mats. Sometimes I am not able to make any mats at all.' (Mother of 6-year-old boy with cerebral palsy)

The need to work often resulted in a child with a disability being left on their own for several hours during the day. One grandmother in a peri-urban context described how her grandson was often left on his own under a tree. The child had severe cerebral palsy and was immobile, without even an assistive device to sit on, and without support from close neighbours: 'When all the children have gone to school he is left alone. The mother might be in town and I might be collecting firewood or on the farm'.

For displaced families, the absence of support from extended family also accentuated the challenge of combining caregiving and livelihoods. One mother of an 8-year-old boy who had Down's Syndrome and was visually impaired described moving to a new village after her husband had been killed in a livestock raid. Although neighbours offered occasional support, working was difficult with no family nearby to help:

> 'He is with me throughout the day. It is so difficult … when I have to work I sometimes lock him in the compound, and sometimes I take him with me [*to collect firewood*]. When he is locked inside alone he runs around and he cries. Sometimes neighbours will come and comfort him and he will sleep.' (Mother of an 8-year-old boy with Down's Syndrome)

Beliefs About the Causes of Disability

Beliefs and attitudes linking disability and misfortune influenced parents' decisions to engage with services and seek treatment, as well as the type of treatment sought. Carers had very low levels of biomedical understanding about their child's impairment, and treatment was most commonly sought from traditional healers. In the small number of instances where families had visited a hospital or clinic, there was still considerable confusion about their child's condition, the cause and options for treatment.

While a very small group of parents provided a biomedical rationale for the disability, some carers suspected witchcraft as in the case of P above; 'God's will' and the intervention of ancestors were also common justifications. Moreover, many families held pluralistic views on the causes of the disability, whereby many possible reasons were considered simultaneously. Non-biomedical explanations cast disability as a misfortune typically interpreted in the context of problematic interpersonal relationships germane to the sociopolitics of the Turkana region, as in the following explanation:

> 'Some say that it is God who is annoyed with them. Others say that their forefathers were disabled, and it is a replica of that [*Interviewer: Can you explain more?*] In the past people went for raid and in the process of raiding they might have killed a disabled person, and so God now makes sure that they have got that disability.' (Mother of a 7-year-old girl with a hearing impairment)

As shown by others, intervention by ancestors, God and witches/wizards is a common rationale for childhood illness and disability in Turkana (Shelley 1985).

In communities close to Lake Turkana, poor natural environmental conditions such as salty water or soil were also commonly believed capable of causing disability. Yet, despite some carers' associations between health problems and the lake, the lake remained an essential source of livelihood. Disability therefore appeared to be interpreted as an unfortunate trade-off and

inevitability of living near the lake, and commonly no diagnosis or treatment was sought. As one single parent mother explained, in relation to her daughter's condition:

> 'People say the salty water from the lake and the sandy soil makes the bones weak, especially because it is difficult to walk in sand. Some people in the community call it 'agule' [*polio*], others call it 'lotoro'—a condition caused by the water in the environment and soil ... I have been considering taking her to the hospital but I have no faith that anything can be done medically about this disease; it is caused by the environment.' (Mother of a 5-year-old child with a physical impairment)

Stigma and the Absence of Support

Stigma and shame associated with having a child with a disability was pervasive and influenced how children were cared for, the wider support available from the community, and acted as a key barrier to accessing services and aid.

One mother, whose son of 8 years was completely blind and spent most of his day inside the house, illustrated this profoundly, saying 'I do not think 'S' is alive. I am just taking care of him until his final death'.

Children with disabilities were seen as a burden because they could not help with household chores or work with the livestock, all of which were important roles in this rural and pastoralist setting:

> 'I do not think that this child is of benefit to the family in any way. She just remains to be counted

as part of my household. She can't get married or help with household chores.' (Mother of a 6-year-old girl with a physical and intellectual impairment)

Stigma also prevented children from accessing services. One grandmother explained how she had never taken her 10-year old grandchild with multiple disabilities out of the compound to seek help or to register him for any type of aid project: 'My child has not been part of any food programme, but we haven't exposed him to any of these programmes. [*Interviewer: Why?*] I was ashamed to take him out'.

While some parents commented that their family or community did not overtly stigmatise their child, and some benefited from material support, they nevertheless felt shame in the absence of family or community social support. For instance, one single mother highlighted her pain from the fact that her sister refused to carry her child:

'I feel bad having to carry the child around by myself and no one is there to help me. My sister does not want to help me carry my child. She provides for us and helps me a lot with money and food. But she doesn't want to associate with my child because he is disabled. She does not carry him at all. That is not all; his father refused to take responsibility over his child because the child is disabled.' (Mother, with son of 3 years with cerebral palsy)

Key informants talked about the absence of children with disabilities in their services because the children are hidden. One village chief, discussing this point, argued that while disabled children in his village were not necessarily hidden, they were largely kept at home in the absence of clear support or knowledge of what treatment or rehabilitation might offer:

'I was surprised when Kenya Red Cross Society brought all the disabled together in one point. I was surprised how many I saw. They are not being hidden, but they are kept at home unless they know that something can be done with their situation.'

Caregiving in an Arid Rural Environment

The limited mobility of children was among the greatest challenges for carers in the arid Turkana environment where carers must carry disabled children while covering long distances to collect firewood and water. The absence of assistive devices as well as the difficult terrain for a wheelchair are additional challenges. Toileting and the personal care of children, particularly when they were incontinent, was also a major problem given the absence of latrines and huge difficulties around access to water. This challenge was highlighted by key informants and carers:

'I am confined to caring for him all day. ... You know, once somebody is lame or disabled and the family has no way to solve the problem, it becomes a desperate situation ... I am the one who cleans him up when he passes stool. I also take him out to pass his stool. This is very stressful but I have no way out.' (Mother of son of 10 years with epilepsy and intellectual impairment)

In one village, this problem was exacerbated when the communal pump was damaged following flash flooding, and the mother described needing to resort to a 4-h round trip to dig a shallow well at the nearest river bed, which is of course a challenge for all families, but it was magnified for her when carrying an older, heavy child with a disability. While some carers elected to leave children behind during water collection, others worried about the consequences of doing so, as one mother of a daughter with multiple disabilities explained:

> 'For me being with her most of the day is very difficult for me to bear. But I fear that if I leave her alone she may fall in the fire and this thought traumatises me, so I am forced to stay and care for her all day.'

Long distances to access healthcare was also a particular challenge for a mother recently displaced by flooding to a remote area. Although her 8-year-old daughter with epilepsy and an intellectual impairment was ill almost every month, it was rare that she could leave the rest of her duties to carry her daughter the 4 km to the nearest dispensary.

The difficult environmental conditions for all families in Turkana were furthermore raised by carers as a reason why other families may be reluctant to share the burden of caring. As described by this father of a boy with hydrocephalus and polio, 'Some community members support the children whenever they can. ... The majority, however, do not support them at all. In the community everyone fends for himself'.

The Challenges of Accessing Services

There were few projects in Turkana designed to serve people with disabilities (Office for the Coordination of Humanitarian Affairs 2013) and limited government or faith-based rehabilitation services even within the main county hospital, making it difficult for families to access assistive devices. The limited dedicated services is within a wider context of limited health service provision in Turkana, for example 19 nurses per 100 000 population compared to 55 nationally (Government of Kenya 2014). With the exception of eye health services, key informants highlighted that referral processes for treatment or rehabilitation of impairments were complex or absent in Turkana. There was a lack of information about the limited rehabilitation services which were available, and a wider lack of knowledge about disability amongst community-level healthcare professionals (Merlin 2012).

The large distances, the remoteness of villages and very limited transport meant there were very substantial opportunity costs, in the form of time lost away from work, for families who chose to seek out rehabilitation services.

> 'We had to stay in Lokichar for a month for the child to be assessed and given treatment ... we are business people; our long stay in Lokichar made our business not flourish. We also lost time and money in seeking treatment.' (Father of a girl with a physical disability)

Almost every carer identified costs as a barrier to accessing healthcare, and sometimes important assets such as livestock were sold off to pay for ongoing treatment or the constant quest for a 'cure' for the disability, which included use of traditional healers. The impact on families of paying for services could be substantial because in many cases the carers commonly described their child with a disability as being more frequently ill, compared with siblings:

'We are unable to save any money for the future because almost everything is spent on the treatment of our child. … You know when the child is well one can afford to save money for other things and for the children's education.' (Father of 3-year-old boy with a physical impairment)

In some families, the lack of income precluded seeking any health services, as explained by one single mother whose son was frequently ill: 'If he is ill, I boil water and bathe him in water, but I have no money to take him to the health centre'.

In terms of humanitarian aid programmes, there was also confusion and perceptions of unfairness around accessing nutrition programmes among parents—a key need given that most families reported difficulties in providing one meal a day for all family members. School feeding programmes are a common nutrition intervention in Turkana, for example, but most children with disabilities interviewed were not in school and were thus not able to benefit in the same way as their siblings. Others were too young for school and yet were also not accessing food supplementation programmes, as one mother explained:

'I have not received any help so far. We are still waiting for aid. My sister's children however … [receive] maize and beans in school.' (Mother of a 3-year-old boy with cerebral palsy)

Likewise, parents faced major practical challenges accessing 'food assistance for assets' programmes and food distributions, as the following quotes illustrate:

'There is a food-for-work programme within the area, but I'm not a beneficiary. There is no way I can leave the child and go to work.' (Mother of girl of 8 years with cerebral palsy)

'I used to carry my child across the lake … where distribution of food used to take place. I would pay for a bicycle to transport the food to the lake shore, then put it on a boat and cross over. It is much easier for parents without children with special needs. For instance, my sister used to carry the food by herself, she didn't need help [*requiring her to pay for additional transport*].' (Mother of boy of 5 years with a physical impairment)

Discussion

This research sought to explore the lived experiences of families who care for children with disabilities in the complex humanitarian environment of Turkana, with the overall aim of improving their inclusion in programming and policy. As described by the World Health Organization's model of disability (World Health Organization 2001), this study highlights how the multifaceted humanitarian context in Turkana magnifies the disabling impact of children's impairment on them, and also on the carer burden, through a variety of environmental, social and cultural factors which compound the vulnerability of the family. Our study also confirms many of the challenges faced by people with disabilities cited in the small but growing body of literature about disability in humanitarian contexts, which include the disruption of social support networks and dearth of supportive services (Lange 2015; Oosterhoff & Kett 2014; Scherrer 2015; Tomlinson & Abdi 2003).

Our study paints an often harrowing picture of the daily lives of children with disabilities and their families. Arguably many families in Turkana face extreme poverty, and access to basic healthcare for everyone is a challenge in pastoralist zones (Pike *et al.* 2010; Sheik-Mohamed & Velema 1999). Poor roads, large distances, few services and limited transport affect everyone's access to services; however, this problem is magnified for children with disabilities, who often need to be physically carried long distances, or complex transport arrangements need to be made. Our findings mirror those of an Australian study which describes the mobility restrictions of disability on top of the difficulties for dispersed populations to access services as a 'double disadvantage' (Gething 1997). In the drought-stricken environment of Turkana, water scarcity is a vital issue for everyone (London School of Hygiene and Tropical Medicine 2013), but the challenges are augmented in a household with a child with a disability who may need to be carried for water collection and may have additional self-care needs. Reviews of water and sanitation issues for persons with disabilities highlight the critical importance of these issues, yet they are often overlooked in programmes which are not disability inclusive (Danquah 2014; Groce *et al.* 2011).

It is well recognised that family and community support networks are essential in the care of children with disabilities in many low-resource settings, in particular where there is a paucity of services (World Health Organization 2011), and yet in emergency contexts, family and social networks are often weakened or destroyed (Oosterhoff & Kett 2014). Our findings emphasise the particular isolation of carers in this disability context and the limitations of community support mechanisms. Fathers were absent in more than half of families, for example, and the stigma of having a disabled child was offered as a common explanation. When even women's sisters would not touch a child with a disability to share the burden of carrying them during chores, this particularly heightened female carers' sense of social isolation. Although we could not investigate it in-depth, social isolation of women carers could also affect other crisis-related coping mechanisms, such as nutritional buffering. Stigma is a complex phenomenon often linked to the cultural context and associating disability with witchcraft or supernatural intervention is pervasive in many contexts, including in Turkana (Shelley 1985; Van Brakel 2014; World Health Organization 2011). In the specific region of Lake Turkana a recent environmental study highlighted reportedly high levels of skeletal 'deformities' linked to changing salinity levels, and a persistent local view that the deformation was a curse (Avery 2013). This behaviour which normalises a state of ill health and long-term suffering because of structural inequalities can also be common among marginalised groups in the region (Sundal 2009).

However, there are few studies which have also explored the specific impact of stigma on carers and caregiving. In our study, such stigma limited not only carers' access to support from extended families or communities, but also their access to government, NGO services and humanitarian programmes, which was because local social support is often needed to offset the opportunity costs involved in seeking formal services and programmes, such as providing care for children left behind whilst services are accessed or the costs of transportation when walking while carrying a heavy child is impossible.

This isolation of carers, in turn, impacts on children's access to healthcare and carers' access to livelihood opportunities. Several studies have indicated that children with disabilities in LMIC settings are more likely to have problems with serious illnesses or malnutrition (Groce *et al.* 2013; Tompsett, Yousafzai & Filteau 1999; Yousafzai, Filteau, & Wirz 2003). Our qualitative study corroborates the findings of the prevalence survey in Turkana which showed that children with disabilities were more malnourished but at the same time less likely to access feeding programmes (Kuper *et al.* 2015). Families in this setting also appear to face major challenges meeting the healthcare needs of their children with disabilities; limited service availability, a lack of information about rehabilitation service options and complex referral processes exacerbate this. The challenges of increased caregiving responsibilities on livelihoods in the context of HIV has been extensively described in the literature (Opiyo, Yamano, & Jayne 2008), but there is limited comparable evidence within the disability literature, and what little there is typically limited to studies of adults with disabilities. In humanitarian contexts, food-for-work programmes are intended to benefit the whole community and particularly attempt to target the most vulnerable, and yet our study indicates that carers of children with disabilities are often excluded from such programmes.

In conclusion, a multiplicity of factors compound the vulnerability of children with disabilities and their carers in the complex humanitarian context of Turkana. Our interviews illustrate that children and their carers in Turkana are falling through the safety nets of both community social support systems as well as humanitarian aid programmes established to assist the most vulnerable; this emphasises the urgent need for improved mainstreaming of disability, as well as targeted approaches for inclusion, for example, in terms of how these children can be included in nutrition and food assistance programmes. The intersectionality of gender and disability also needs some consideration given the gendered nature of caregiving. For example, livelihoods programmes need to be more gender-sensitive and more actively inclusive of families with children with a disability who may be 'invisible' to authorities, health and humanitarian workers in this setting. As called for by others, disability must be seen as a 'mobile cross-cutting issue' that can contribute to social injustice and should not be treated as a narrow 'specialist medical issue' (Berghs 2015).

Acknowledgements

We would like to thank the funders, CBM International, who commissioned the study, and for their support to undertake this study.

Competing Interests

The authors declare that they have no financial or personal relationships which may have inappropriately influenced them in writing this article.

Authors' Contributions

M.Z., project leader, was responsible for research design, conducted interviews and led on analysis and writing of the manuscript. V.N., field research coordinator, conducted interviews and commented on the manuscript. V.M. commented on manuscript and design. J.K. commented on manuscript. H.R. contributed to manuscript. J.P. contributed significantly to the writing of the manuscript.

References

Avery, S., 2013, *What future lies for Lake Turkana,* African Studies Centre, University of Oxford, Oxford, viewed n.d., from http://www.africanstudies.ox.ac.uk/what-future-lake-turkana

Berghs, M., 2015, 'Radicalising "disability" in conflict and post-conflict situations', *Disability & Society* 30, 743–758. http://dx.doi.org/10.1080/09687599.2015.1052044

Boulton, J., 2012, *Turkana through the Lens of Complexity, Final report for Oxfam GB Kenya,* Oxfam, Oxford.

Broch-Due, V. & Sanders, T., 1999, 'Rich man, poor man, administrator, beast: The politics of impoverishment in Turkana, Kenya, 1890–1990', *Nomadic Peoples* 3, 35–55. http://dx.doi.org/10.3167/082279499782409389

Danquah, L., 2014, *Undoing Inequity: Inclusive water, sanitation and hygiene programmes that deliver to all in Uganda and Zambia,* viewed n.d., from http://disabilitycentre.lshtm.ac.uk/undoing-inequity-inclusive-wash-programmes/

Gething, L., 1997, 'Sources of double disadvantage for people with disabilities living in remote and rural areas of new South Wales, Australia', *Disability & Society* 12, 513–531. http://dx.doi.org/10.1080/09687599727100

Government of Kenya, 2014, *Kenya Service Availability and Readiness Assessment Mapping (SARAM),* Ministry of Health, Nairobi.

Grabska, K., 2014, *Gender, home & identity: Nuer repatriation to Southern Sudan,* James Currey, Woodbridge.

Green, J. & Thorogood, N., 2009, *Qualitative methods for health research,* Sage, London.

Groce, N., Bailey, N., Lang, R., Trani, J. & Kett, M., 2011, 'Water and sanitation issues for persons with disabilities in low-and middle-income countries: A literature review and discussion of implications for global health and international development', *Journal of Water and Health* 9, 617–627, viewed n.d., from http://www.iwaponline.com/jwh/009/0617/0090617.pdf

Groce, N.E., Kerac, M., Farkas, A., Schultink, W. & Bieler, R.B., 2013, 'Inclusive nutrition for children and adults with disabilities', *The Lancet Global Health* 1, e180–e181. http://dx.doi.org/10.1016/S2214-109X(13)70056-1

Handicap International, 2005, *How to include disability issues in disaster managent: Following floods 2004 in Bangladesh,* Handicap International, Dhaka.

Hendrickson, D., Armon, J. & Mearns, R., 1998, 'The changing nature of conflict and famine vulnerability: The case of livestock raiding in Turkana District, Kenya', *Disasters* 22, 185–199. http://dx.doi.org/10.1111/1467-7717.00086

Hodgson, D., 2000, *Rethinking pastoralism in Africa: Gender, Culture and the myth of the patriarchal pastoralist,* James Currey, Oxford.

Kenya National Bureau of Statistics, 2010, *2009 Kenya Population and Housing Census: Marital Status by County and District,* Kenya Bureau of Statistics, Nairobi.

Kenya National Bureau of Statistics, 2014, *Kenya Demographic and Health Survey 2014 Key indicators,* Kenya National Bureau of Statitstics.

Kett, M. & Van Ommeren, M., 2009, 'Disability, conflict, and emergencies', *The Lancet* 374, 1801–1803. http://dx.doi.org/10.1016/S0140-6736(09)62024-9

Kuper, H., Nyapera, V., Evans, J., Munyendo, D., Zuurmond, M., Frison, S. et al., 2015, 'Malnutrition and childhood disability in Turkana, Kenya: Results from a case-control study', *PLoS One* 10, e0144926. http://dx.doi.org/10.1371/journal.pone.0144926

Lange, K., 2015, 'UNHCR's experience in strengthening protection of persons with disabilities in forced displacement', *Journal of Disability and International Development.*

London School of Hygiene and Tropical Medicine, 2013, *Research to inform the development of behaviour change interventions for the 'F' and 'E' of the SAFE strategy in Turkana and Marsabit, Kenya,* Final report, viewed n.d., from http://ehg.lshtm.ac.uk/trachoma/

Mccabe, J., 1990, 'Turkana pastoralism: A case against the tragedy of the commons', *Human Ecology* 18, 81–103. http://dx.doi.org/10.1007/BF00889073

Merlin, 2012, *Disability rapid assessment report Turkana County,* Merlin, Lodwar.

Miles, M. & Medi, E., 1994, 'Disabled children in post-war Mozambique: Developing community based support', *Disasters* 18, 284–291. http://dx.doi.org/10.1111/j.1467-7717.1994.tb00314.x

Mirza, M., 2013, 'Disability and cross-border mobility: Comparing resettlement experiences of Cambodian and Somalian refugees with disabilities', in M. Moore (ed.), *Moving beyond boundaries in disability studies: Rights, spaces and innovations,* Routledge.

Ngo, A., Brolan, C., Fitzgerald, L., Pham, V. & Phan, H., 2012, 'Voices from Vietnam: Experiences of children and youth with disabilities, and their families, from an Agent Orange affected rural region', *Disability & Society* 28, 955–969. http://dx.doi.org/10.1080/09687599.2012.741516

Ochola, S., 2011, *Turkana nutrition survey,* Final Report.

Office for the Coordination of Humanitarian Affairs, 2013, *Kenya: Turkana District who shat where (February 2013),* United Nations Office for the Coordination of Humanitarian Affairs.

Oosterhoff, P. & Kett, M., 2014, *Including people with disabilities in emergency relief efforts,* Institute of Development Studies.

Opiyo, P., Yamano, T. & Jayne, T., 2008, 'HIV/AIDS and home based care health care', *International Journal of Equity Health* 7. http://dx.doi.org/10.1186/1475-9276-7-8

Pike, I.L., Straight, B., Oesterle, M., Hilton, C. & Lanyasunya, A., 2010, 'Documenting the health consequences of endemic warfare in three pastoralist communities of northern Kenya: A conceptual framework', *Social Science & Medicine* 70, 45–52. http://dx.doi.org/10.1016/j.socscimed.2009.10.007

Reilly, R., 2010, 'Disabilities among refugees and conflict-affected populations', *Forced Migration Review* 35, 8–10.

Scherrer, V., 2015, 'Disability Inclusive Humanitarian Action and Disaster risk reduction: A story of successes and ongoing challenges', 4–8.

Sheik-Mohamed, A. & Velema, J.P., 1999, 'Where health care has no access: The nomadic populations of sub-Saharan Africa', *Tropical Medicine &*

International Health 4, 695–707. http://dx.doi.org/10.1046/j.1365-3156.1999.00473.x

Shelley, J.K., 1985, 'Medicines for Misfortune: Diagnosis and health care among Southern Turkana Pastoralists of Kenya', PhD thesis, The University of North Carolina.

Sphere, 2011, *The Sphere handbook: Humanitarian charter and minimum standards in humanitarian response,* viewed 29 June 2015, from http://www.sphereproject.org

Sundal, M.B., 2009, 'Difficult decisions: Karimojong healing in conflict', PhD thesis, University of Kansas.

Tomlinson, S. & Abdi, O.A., 2003, 'Disability in Somaliland', *Disability & Society* 18, 911–920. http://dx.doi.org/10.1080/0968759032000127326

Tompsett, J., Yousafzai, A. & Filteau, S., 1999, 'The nutritional status of disabled children in Nigeria: A cross-sectional survey', *European Journal of Clinical Nutrition* 53, 915. http://dx.doi.org/10.1038/sj.ejcn.1600850

UN, 2006, *Convention on the rights of persons with disabilities,* United Nations.

Van Brakel, W., 2014, 'Stigma in leprosy: Concepts, causes and determinants', *Leprosy Review* 85, 36–47.

Wawire, V.K., 2003, *Gender and the social and economic impact of drought on the residents of Turkana District in Kenya.*

World Health Organization, 2001, *World Health Organization. International classification of functioning, disability and health,* viewed 16 August 2013, from http://www.who.int/classifications/icf/en/

World Health Organization, 2010, *Community-based rehabilitation: CBR guidelines,* World Health Organization, Geneva.

World Health Organization, 2011, *World report on disability,* World Health Organisation, Geneva.

Yousafzai, A.K., Filteau, S. & Wirz, S., 2003, 'Feeding difficulties in disabled children leads to malnutrition: Experience in an Indian slum', *British Journal of Nutrition* 90, 1097–1106. http://dx.doi.org/10.1079/BJN2003991

What Constitutes a Quality Program for Children Who Are Deaf?

J. Freeman King

If parents decide a school district's inclusive/mainstreaming program is the optimum and appropriate educational program for deaf children, this should center around an approach that offers a quality education that prepares the deaf student to compete as an equal with hearing children in the school.

Education for the child who is deaf has historically gone through many changes related to educational ideology and placement decisions. Presently, for good or bad, in the United States, approximately 75 percent of deaf/hard of hearing children are educated in an inclusion/mainstreamed setting housed in the public schools. This educational placement decision can be directly attributed to the interpretation of PL 101-476, The Individuals with Disabilities

Education Act (IDEA) of 1990, which reinforced an earlier federal mandate, PL 94-142, The Education for All Handicapped Children Act of 1975 that stated: the child who has a disability will be educated in the most appropriate and least restrictive environment, and that this environment will lead to socialization of the child with his/her non-disabled peers.

On the interpretation of the law, the consensus has been that an inclusive/mainstreamed educational environment is best for the deaf/hard of hearing child. However, two important questions beg to be asked: (1) Should the deaf child be categorized as disabled? and, (2) Can socialization ever occur without deep and meaningful communication with peers and teachers? Answering these vital questions can often be difficult for the parents of a deaf/hard of hearing child, but arriving at the answers can assure that the child will have the optimum educational and social experience in the least restrictive and most appropriate environment.

The interpretation of the law as being inclusion/mainstreaming (into the local school district) has created a situation in which many deaf/hard of hearing children are being placed in the **most** restrictive and **inappropriate** environment. Often, this placement decision is made, disregarding the child's linguistic preferences, language development needs, identity, and sociocultural needs. Administrators, special education specialists, audiologists, and speech-language pathologists who do not understand the predisposition of the deaf child to acquire a natural, visual language with or without technological enhancements often make the decision.

Parents are also often led to believe that having an interpreter for their child will solve the "problem" of communication with his/her teacher and peers. The assumption is made that the interpreter will provide for equal language access and remediate the social and emotional needs of the child. This is not necessarily the case, in that many interpreters are not certified or qualified and do not possess the requisite skills to truly equalize communication in the classroom environment, especially if the child does not already possess a deep and meaningful visual language. It is also important to note that many inclusive/mainstreamed settings have only one or two deaf students in the entire program, thus circumventing the need for a critical mass of deaf/hard of hearing students that will foster identity and language development.

Therefore, if parents decide a local school district's inclusive/mainstreaming program is the optimum program for offering an appropriate educational program for deaf children, this program should center around an approach that will offer a quality education that prepares the deaf student to compete as an equal with hearing children in the school. Without a strong language and communication base and appropriate educational, social and emotional growth, the anticipated development for deaf students is not possible, and the prospects of deaf and hard of hearing students meeting high proficiency standards are diminished. Educational programming and the assessment of educational progress must reflect this reality.

OPEN TO INTERPRETATION: Arriving at the proper answers can assure that the child will have the optimum educational and social experience in the least restrictive and most appropriate environment.

If a local school district offers an appropriate inclusion/mainstreaming program for deaf/hard of hearing children, the foremost consideration should be focused on providing not only a quality academic education, but also a program that enables the student to be respected by his/her teachers and peers, well educated, and allowed to be Deaf, not an imitation of his/her hearing peers.

About the Author

J. Freeman King, Ed.D. is Director, Deaf Education at Utah State University, Logan, Utah.

THERE ARE CERTAIN CRITERIA THAT SHOULD BE CONSIDERED IN ORDER TO ASSURE APPROPRIATENESS, EFFECTIVENESS, AND A LEAST RESTRICTIVE ENVIRONMENT

1. The program should include a critical mass of deaf children (at least five per class) in order to provide for socialization, identity development, and language growth and enhancement;

2. Homogeneous grouping possibilities should exist that will facilitate grouping by age, IQ, and linguistic competence;

3. Only teachers who are qualified/certified and have a respect for and understanding of Deaf culture should have deaf students in their classes;

4. Only teachers who can communicate directly and appropriately with deaf students should be utilized in classes with deaf children;

5. Deaf adult role models should be present on a regular basis in the educational process, either as administrators, teachers, or aides;

6. Curriculum that includes Deaf history and Deaf culture should be available in classrooms that have deaf children;

7. Only intelligence, achievement, and other placement tests that have been normed on a deaf population and administered by personnel who can communicate fluently with the deaf child should be used;

8. Interpreters involved in the program should be highly certified and knowledgeable concerning the Deaf culture;

9. The hearing administrators, teachers, and students in the school should be offered continuing opportunities to learn and use American Sign Language, or whatever signing system is being employed.

NASP Position Statement Safe Schools for Transgender and Gender Diverse Students

The National Association of School Psychologists (NASP) supports efforts to ensure that schools are safe and inclusive learning environments for all students, family members, and school staff, including those who are transgender or gender diverse. NASP respects a person's right to express gender identity, and the right to modify gender expression when necessary for individual well-being. In addition, NASP supports all students' right to explore and question their gender identity. NASP is committed to a policy of nondiscrimination and the promotion of equal opportunity, fairness, justice, and respect for all persons (NASP, 2012).

NASP acknowledges that neither having a transgender identity nor being perceived as gender diverse is a disorder, and that efforts to change a person's gender identity are ineffective, harmful, and discriminatory. NASP works to ensure that settings in which school psychologists work are safe and welcoming and provide equal opportunity to all persons regardless of actual or perceived characteristics, including gender, gender identity, gender expression, sexual orientation, and any other personal identity or distinguishing characteristics (NASP, 2010). A glossary of terms may be found at the end of the statement.

Needs of Transgender Students

In many communities, it is dangerous to be gender nonconforming or to be known as transgender. Many children, youth, and adults blend with their chosen gender, and are safe to the extent that their transgender status is hidden. Data concerning school-age transgender youth are limited, but what data are available suggest that more action by school officials is needed to ensure schools are settings in which students can thrive.

Because transgender youth are so hidden, it would be easy to believe that these students are extremely rare. It is extremely difficult to estimate the prevalence of transgender students in school (Meier & Labuski, 2013). One of the few large districts to gather data is San Francisco. In 2011, 0.5% of San Francisco high school students self-identified as transgender on the annual Youth Risk Behavioral Survey (Timothy Kordic, personal communication, December 20, 2013). The prevalence of self-identified transgender adults has been estimated as 0.3% of the U.S. general population (Gates, 2011).

The experiences that transgender students have at school appear to have effects on their well-being as adults. Toomey, Ryan, Diaz, Card, and Russell (2010) showed that while gender nonconformity alone had no direct effect on these outcomes, the victimization experienced at school associated with gender nonconformity had a lasting impact and put these children at risk for negative mental health outcomes in adulthood. Harassment and assault lead to anxiety about school, leading to missing days of school. Nearly half (46%) of transgender students reported missing at least one school day in the previous month because they felt unsafe (Greytak, Kosciw, & Diaz, 2009).

Research suggests that gender diverse children are at higher risk of physical, emotional, and sexual abuse and are at higher risk of posttraumatic stress disorder (PTSD) in adulthood, with about a third of the higher risk of PTSD accounted for by being abused as a child (Roberts, Rosario, Corliss, Koenen, & Austin, 2012). Coming out to family members often results in physical assault and expulsion from the family home (Ray, 2006). In one study, more than half of transgender youth reported initial parental reaction to coming out as negative or very negative (Grossman, D'Augelli, & Frank, 2011). Young adults who experience low family acceptance of identity are more likely to be at risk for depressive symptoms, substance use, and suicidal ideation and attempts (Ryan, Russell, Huebner, Diaz, & Sanchez, 2010). In addition to longitudinal outcome risks, transgender youth face immediate challenges during their school-age years. Transgender youth are often desperate to transition. However, even if they have medical insurance, the healthcare procedures necessary to transition are explicitly excluded from most health insurance plans. Psychotherapy for gender dysphoria is often excluded. Transgender youth may take hormones obtained on the street or through the Internet without medical supervision, and take excessive doses. They may seek silicone injections at "pumping parties," resulting in severe disfigurement or death.

Despite these challenges, many transgender youth are resilient and there are a number of factors that may help them guard against the worst outcomes. Resilience in children and youth appears to depend on personal characteristics like being outgoing, resourceful, and having a positive self-concept. In addition, social relationships, such as having an emotional bond with at least one adult over a period of time, and having a supportive community are associated with resilience (Werner, 1995). Specifically for transgender and gender diverse children, attention has been focused on *family acceptance* and *school acceptance*. LGBT youth from families rated high in acceptance (e.g., they discuss their child's gender identity or sexual orientation openly, integrate their child's LGBT friends into family activities, express appreciation for their child's clothing choices even if the clothing was gender nonconforming) reported better self-esteem, better health, lower levels of depression, lower rates of substance abuse, lower rates of suicide attempts, and lower rates of risky sexual behavior (Ryan, Russell, Huebner, Diaz, & Sanchez, 2010). These findings suggest that similar acceptance in school environments is recommended.

Considerations for Parents, Physicians, and Schools

To adequately support their child's growth, parents must allow their child's personality to unfold while simultaneously protecting them from harm (Ehrensaft, 2011). Families go through a developmental process in accepting a transgender or gender diverse child. Much depends on a parent's beliefs and understanding of child development and of gender. Some children have unexpected gender behavior at an early age, which persists in spite of parent attempts to divert the child to gender conforming behavior. Parents may be embarrassed or ashamed of their child's behavior, depending on conformity pressures coming from extended family members, neighbors, clergy, daycare providers, and others. Parents may fear the future for their child, as well as their own future as they are judged by other adults. The parent who is the same sex as the child may question his or her own effectiveness as a role model. Children and youth are more likely to have successful outcomes if parents work to create safe and supportive spaces for their child within the home, require others to respect their child, and express love for their child (Brill & Pepper, 2008).

The World Professional Association for Transgender Health (WPATH) *Standards of Care* for the psychiatric, psychological, medical, and surgical management of gender transition notes that "Treatment aimed at trying to change a person's gender identity and expression to become more congruent with sex assigned at birth has been attempted in the past without success. Such treatment is no longer considered ethical" (Coleman et al., 2011, p. 175).

Some students arrive at kindergarten already living in their asserted gender, while others express a desire to make a gender transition later in elementary or in secondary school. The majority of gender diverse children under age 9 who assert that they are a different gender than assigned at birth do not persist in asserting that gender in adolescence and early adulthood. By comparison, the majority of youth age 11 and older asserting a gender different than assigned at birth persist in that identity throughout

adolescence and adulthood (Steensma, Biemond, de Boer, & Cohen-Kettenis, 2011). For children under age 9, only reversible social transitions are recommended (e.g., clothing, hair styles, activity preferences). For children age 11 or older, other treatments may be appropriate. A reversible medical treatment involving the administration of a gonadotropin-releasing hormone agonist (GnRH) in early puberty can put puberty on hold for several years, allowing the child time to mature and be ready for permanent changes. After puberty, youth can make more informed decisions regarding long-term treatment (Delemarre-van de Waal & Cohen-Kettenis, 2006; Spack, et al., 2012).

Educational persistence of transgender and gender diverse students may depend on their sense of safety and belonging in the school environment. Title IX of the Education Amendment Act of 1972 prohibits harassment of students on the basis of gender expression. Schools have a duty to ensure that gender diverse and transgender students are included in all school infrastructure. For example, providing gender-neutral bathroom options and avoiding the use of gender segregation in practices such as school uniforms, school dances, and extracurricular activities are structural ways to provide safer school environments (Toomey et al., 2010). The presence of a Gay–Straight Alliance (GSA) in school can lead to greater feelings of safety and belonging, better attendance, and lower rates of harassment (Toomey, Ryan, Diaz, & Russell, 2011). Comprehensive antiharassment policies that include protections for transgender and gender diverse students are helpful for all students. Adult intervention is helpful when homophobic or transphobic statements are heard (Case & Meier, 2014). Written policies and procedures addressing the needs of transgender and gender diverse students are helpful for staff and administrators and all students and families (e.g., Gay, Lesbian and Straight Education Network/National Center for Transgender Equality, 2011; Massachusetts DOESE, 2012).

Role of the School Psychologist

The school psychologist should be in tune with the needs of students and staff, and can provide evidence-based information about transgender issues. The school psychologist should be welcoming and supportive of transgender and gender diverse staff and parents, and be able to foster a climate of acceptance and security for all (Case & Meier, 2014). A student's transgender status or history must be kept confidential and within the student's control. In all cases, school psychologists must be sensitive to the needs and welfare of all individuals at their school sites, including transgender and gender diverse students and staff. School psychologists must advocate for the civil rights of all students, including those who are transgender or gender diverse. This can be accomplished by:

Advocating for gender-neutral spaces and helping establish safe zones for trans-gender students

Seeking additional training or supervision as needed regarding issues affecting transgender and gender diverse people

Modeling acceptance and respect

Providing staff training to increase awareness regarding transgender issues in the schools

Responding to bullying, intimidation, and other forms of harassment whether perpetrated by students or staff

Minimizing bias by using phrasing and pronouns that are not gender specific and by avoiding gender stereotypes

Providing counseling and attending to the social–emotional needs of transgender and gender diverse students in school

Acquiring and providing information on community agencies that provide services and supports to the transgender community

Supporting or contributing to research regarding best practices for integrating transgender and gender diverse students in school

Gender diverse and transgender students might be referred to a school psychologist due to school victimization or bullying, suicidal ideation or attempts, nonsuicidal self-injury, sexual orientation instead of gender issues, social anxiety, and/or autism spectrum symptoms. School psychologists should be aware of resources for these children and their families. Transgender and gender-diverse students may benefit from learning healthy coping skills and building resilience, but interventions for associated social–emotional problems should not attempt to enforce gender stereotypical behavior.

NASP's *Principles for Professional Ethics* (NASP, 2010) include provisions that pertain to gender diverse and transgender individuals, including the following:

Standard 1.2.6: School psychologists respect the right of privacy of students, parents, and colleagues with regard to sexual orientation, gender identity, or transgender status. They do not share information about the sexual orientation, gender identity, or transgender status of a student (including minors), parent, or school employee with anyone without that individual's permission.

Standard II.1.2: Practitioners are obligated to pursue knowledge and understanding of the diverse cultural, linguistic, and experiential backgrounds of students, families, and other clients. When knowledge and understanding of diversity characteristics are essential to ensure competent assessment, intervention, or consultation, school psychologists have or obtain the training or supervision necessary to provide effective services, or they make appropriate referrals.

Principle I.3: In their words and actions, school psychologists promote fairness and justice. They use their expertise to cultivate school climates that are safe and welcoming to all persons regardless of actual or perceived characteristics, including race, ethnicity, color, religion, ancestry, national origin, immigration status, socioeconomic status, primary language, gender, sexual orientation, gender identity, gender expression, disability, or any other distinguishing characteristic.

School psychologists should encourage schools to develop and implement policies and procedures to prevent harassment of gender diverse and transgender students in order to promote safe schools for all students. School psychologists can provide education about gender expression and LGBT issues to teachers, administrators, students, and staff (Toomey et al., 2010). School psychologists should encourage the formation of support or social groups for gender diverse and transgender students (Goodenow, Szalacha, & Westheimer, 2006; Toomey et al., 2010). School psychologists can work with teachers and administrators to serve as mentors for these students. Being accepted by even just one coach, teacher, or administrator can serve as a protective factor against negative psychosocial outcomes for these youth.

Glossary

Language is evolving rapidly. Some terms that were considered acceptable in the past may be offensive in the present. Some previously offensive terms have been reclaimed by newer generations. We have attempted to use currently acceptable terms in this glossary. A glossary that is frequently updated is the *Media Reference Guide* available online from the Gay and Lesbian Alliance Against Defamation (GLAAD, 2010).

Asserted Gender. The gender a person declares to be, verbally, nonverbally, covertly, or overtly. A transgender person's gender is usually affirmed insistently, consistently, and persistently over years. In transgender people, there is a difference between birth-assigned gender and affirmed gender. In *cisgender* people, affirmed gender aligns with birth-assigned gender. Depending on ecological safety, gender affirmation may be nonverbal and covert, or it may be a verbal declaration ("coming out") in a safe place.

Cisgender. A person whose sex assigned at birth matches current gender identity. The opposite of *transgender*. "Nontransgender" is sometimes used, but implies that being transgender is not a normal variant of human difference.

Gender. *Gender* implies the psychological, behavioral, social, and cultural aspects of being male or female (VandenBos, 2007). Gender refers to the socially constructed roles, behaviors, activities, and attributes that a given society considers appropriate for boys and men or for girls and women (APA, 2011). While sex is a biological construct, gender is a social construct. As most people's sex and gender align, the two terms are sometimes used interchangeably.

Gender Assignment. *Gender assignment* is the classification of an infant at birth as either male or female (VandenBos, 2007); this assignment of a legal gender (sex) to a child triggers a variety of social events and developmental tasks related to gender role.

Gender Constancy. *Gender constancy* is a child's emerging sense of the permanence of being a boy or a girl (VandenBos, 2007), an understanding that occurs in stages but is mostly complete by age 7. School entry presents greater pressure to conform to gender expectations. At this age, some children with a gender identity incongruent with their birth-assigned sex may experience distress if they are not permitted to express and be witnessed as their gender. At clinically significant levels, this is called *gender dysphoria* (VandenBos, 2007).

Gender Dysphoria. Discontent with the physical or social aspects of one's own sex (VandenBos, 2007). The degree of distress can vary from mild to severe, and can be life long, although not all transgender people experience gender dysphoria. The child with gender dysphoria may demonstrate symptoms of depression, anxiety, self-harm, or oppositionality (APA, 2013).

Gender Diverse. Someone is *gender diverse* if his or her *gender expression* does not match what is culturally expected for the sex assigned at birth (Gender Equity Resource Center, n.d.). Individuals may dress or act in ways that others believe are not feminine enough or not masculine enough. Gender expression has become one aspect of diversity in human resource practice and in civil rights law, including nondiscrimination laws. Gender diverse implies that all humans express gender, and that no gender expression is inherently better than another. Gender diverse is an alternative term for *gender nonconformity*, which implies that gender diverse people are violating rules for gender expression; it is also an alternative for *gender variant*, which implies difference from a norm. Other respectful terms for gender diversity include *gender creative* and *gender expansive*.

Gender Expression. *Gender expression* refers to how a person represents or expresses gender identity to others, often through behavior, clothing, hairstyles, voice, or body characteristics (NCTE, May 2009). Gender expression is visible, while gender identity is not. Being gender diverse means having an unexpected gender expression; being transgender means having an unexpected gender identity. Some transgender people do not appear gender diverse. Some people with diverse gender expression are happy with their sex assigned at birth and have no desire or intention to transition genders.

Gender Identity. *Gender identity* is a person's internal sense of being male, female, both, or neither (APA 2011). This sense of maleness or femaleness typically develops from a combination of biological and psychic influences (VandenBos, 2007). Shortly after children begin to speak, most are able to state whether they are a boy or a girl, and this identity is stable and resistant to change. Gender identity typically forms between 2 and 5 years of age. For most people, gender identity is consistent with sex assigned at birth.

Genderqueer. A person who defies or does not accept stereotypical gender roles and may choose to live outside expected gender norms may self-identify as genderqueer. (Center for Excellence in Transgender Health, April, 2011). Gender-queer people may or may not avail themselves of hormonal or surgical treatments.

Sex. The term sex refers to a person's biological characteristics, including chromosomes, hormones, and anatomy (VandenBos, 2007).

Sexual Orientation. A person's gender identity is distinct from sexual orientation. *Sexual orientation* refers to an enduring pattern of emotional, romantic, and/or sexual attractions to men, women, both sexes, transgender people, no one, or all genders (APA, 2008; VandenBos, 2007). A transgender adult may be attracted to women, to men, to both women and men (bisexual), to no one (asexual), and/or to other transgender people. One's sexual orientation identity label is typically derived from gender identity, and not birth assigned sex. For example, a female-to-male transgender man who is primarily attracted to other men is likely to self-identify as gay. A male-to-female transgender woman who is primarily attracted to men is likely to identify as straight. Transgender people are more likely to also identify as LGBQ than cisgender people.

Trans. Shorthand term for a variety of transgender identities. Also, trans people or transpeople (Center for Excellence in Transgender Health, April 2011). Because there are a variety of disputes about the terms *transgender* and *transsexual*, *trans* is seen as a more widely accepted and respectful term than transgender. There are other terms which are more universally perceived as offensive, such as "tranny." See the GLAAD *Media Reference Guide* (2010) for terms that are universally offensive.

Transgender. *Transgender* refers to having a gender identity that differs from culturally determined gender roles and biological sex (VandenBos, 2007). It is an umbrella term that includes diverse identities and includes persons identifying as female-to-male, male-to-female, two-spirit, genderqueer, and other terms (APA, 2011). The transgender umbrella includes those assigned female at birth who are or who wish to be living as men (*transgender men*), and those assigned male at birth who are or who wish to be living as women (*transgender women*). Many transgender people appear indistinguishable from *cisgender* people. They may or may not desire body modifications to express their asserted gender. Body modifications may be temporary (e.g., shaving, changing hair style, binding, using hormone blockers) or permanent (e.g., hormones, electrolysis, surgeries; APA, 2011). Medical assistance can help transgender people live more comfortable lives as they may be better able to blend in as their affirmed gender. Transgender women typically identify as *women*, and transgender men typically identify as *men*.

Transition. The process of changing gender expression from that of one gender to another is called *transition* (APA, 2011). *Social transition* may include changes in clothing, grooming, pronouns, names, and identity documents. Children, adolescents, and adults may undergo social transition at any time. Medical transition may include hormones and surgeries. Surgeries are only available after age 18, after at least one year of living persistently and consistently as the desired gender. Youth who have lived persistently in their preferred gender and who have reached Tanner Stage 2 for their birth sex (around age 12 for female-born youth and about 14 for male-born youth) may be eligible for medication that can suppress puberty until they reach age 16 or older when they may be eligible to be treated with hormones appropriate to their desired gender, saving much of the expense, pain, and cost of medical transition for adults.

References

American Psychiatric Association. (2013). *Diagnostic and statistical manual of mental disorders.* (5th Edition). Arlington, VA: American Psychiatric Publishing.

American Psychological Association. (2008). *Answers to your questions: For a better understanding of sexual orientation and homosexuality.* Washington, DC: Author. Retrieved from www.apa.org/topics/sorientation.pdf

American Psychological Association. (2011). *Answers to your questions about transgender people, gender identity, and gender expression.* Washington, DC: Author. Retrieved from http://www.apa.org/topics/sexuality/transgender.pdf

Brill, S., & Pepper, R. (2008). *The transgender child: A handbook for families and professionals.* San Francisco, CA: Cleis Press.

Case, K., & Meier, C. (2014). Developing allies to transgender and gender-nonconforming youth: Training for counselors and educators. *Journal of LGBT Youth, 11:1,* 62–82. doi:10.1080/193653.2014.840764

Center for Excellence in Transgender Health. (2011, April). *Primary care protocol for trans-gender patient care.* San Francisco, CA: University of California at San Francisco, Department of Family and Community Medicine. Retrieved from http://www.transhealth.ucsf.edu/trans?page=protocol-terminology

Coleman, E., Bockting, W., Botzer, M., Cohen-Kettenis, P., DeCuypere, G., Feldman, J., & Zucker, K. (2011). Standards of care for the health of transsexual, transgender, and gender-nonconforming people, Version 7. *International Journal of Transgenderism, 13,* 165–232. doi:10.1080/15532739.2011.700873

Delemarre-van de Waal, H. A., & Cohen-Kettenis, P. T. (2006). Clinical management of gender identity disorder in adolescents: A protocol on psychological and paediatric endocrinology aspects. *European Journal of Endocrinology, 155,* S131–S137. doi:10.1530/eje.1.02231

Ehrensaft, D. (2011). *Gender born, gender made.* New York, NY: The Experiment.

Gates, G. (2011, April). *How many people are lesbian, gay, bisexual, and transgender?* Los Angeles, CA: The Williams Institute, UCLA. Retrieved from http://williamsinstitute.law.ucla.edu/wp-content/uploads/Gates-How-Many-People-LGBT-Apr-2011.pdf

Gender Equity Resource Center. (n.d.). Gender diverse. *Definition of terms.* Berkeley, CA: University of California at Berkeley. Retrieved from http://geneq.berkeley.edu/lgbt_resources_definiton_of_terms#genderdiverse

GLAAD. (2001). *Media Reference Guide, 8th Edition.* Gay and Lesbian Alliance Against Defamation. Retrieved from http://www.glaad.org/files/MediaReference-Guide2010.pdf

GLSEN/NCTE. (2011). *Model district policy for transgender and gender nonconforming students.* New York, NY: Gay, Lesbian and Straight Educators Network/National Center for Transgender Equality. Retrieved from http://www.glsen.org/binary-data/GLSEN_ATTACHMENTS/file/000/001/1977-1.pdf

Goodenow, C., Szalacha, L. A., & Westheimer, K. (2006). School support groups, other school factors, and the safety of sexual minority adolescents. *Psychology in the Schools, 43,* 573–589. doi:10.1002/pits.20173

Grant, J. M., Mottet, L. A., Tanis, J., Harrison, J., Herman, J. I., & Keisling, M. (2011). I*njustice at every turn: A report of the national transgender discrimination survey.* Washington, DC: National Center for Transgender Equality and National Gay and Lesbian Task

Force. Retrieved from http://www.thetaskforce.org/reports_and_research/ntds

Greytak, E. A., Kosciw, J. G., & Diaz, E. M. (2009). *Harsh realities: The experiences of transgender youth in our nation's schools.* New York, NY: Gay, Lesbian and Straight Education Network. Retrieved from http://www.glsen.org

Grossman, A. H., D'Augelli, A. R., & Frank, J. A. (2011). Aspects of psychological resilience among transgender youth. *Journal of LGBT Youth, 8,* 103–115.

Massachusetts Department of Elementary and Secondary Education. (2012). *Guidance for Massachusetts public schools creating a safe and supportive school environment: Nondiscrimination on the basis of gender identity.* Malden, MA: Author. Retrieved from http://www.doe.mass.edu/ssce/GenderIdentity.pdf

Meier, C., Pardo, S., Olson, J., & Sharp, C. (2014). *Demographics of gender non-conforming children in the United States.* Submitted for presentation at the biennial symposium of the World Professional Association for Transgender Health in Bangkok, Thailand, February 2014.

Meier, S. C., & Labuski, C. M. (2013). The demographics of the transgender population. In A. K. Baumle (Ed.), *International handbook on the demography of sexuality* (pp. 289–327). New York, NY: Springer.

National Association of School Psychologists. (2010). *Principles for professional ethics.* Retrieved from http://www.nasponline.org/standards

National Association of School Psychologists. (2012). *Nondiscrimination and equal opportunity policy.* Retrieved from http://www.nasponline.org/leadership/nondiscrimination_equal_opportunity.pdf

NCTE. (2009, May). *Transgender terminology.* Washington, DC: National Center for Trans-gender Equality. Retrieved from http://transequality.org/Resources/NCTE_TransTerminology.pdf

Ray, N. (2006). *Lesbian, gay, bisexual and trans-gender youth: An epidemic of homelessness.* New York, NY: National Gay and Lesbian Task Force Policy Institute and National Coalition for the Homeless. Retrieved from http://www.thetaskforce.org

Roberts, A. L., Rosario, M., Corliss, H. L., Koenen, K. C., & Austin, S. B. (2012). Childhood gender nonconformity: A risk indicator for childhood abuse and posttraumatic stress in youth. *Pediatrics, 129,* 410–417. doi:10.1542/peds.2011-180

Ryan, C., Russell, S. T., Huebner, D., Diaz, R., & Sanchez, J. (2011). Family acceptance in adolescence and the health of LGBT young adults. *Journal of Child and Adolescent Psychiatric Nursing, 23,* 205–213. doi:10.1111/j.1744-6171.2010.00246.x

Spack, N. P., Edwards-Leeper, L., Feldman, H. A., Leibowitz, S., Mandel, F., Diamond, D., & Vance, S. R. (2012). Children and adolescents with gender identity disorder referred to a pediatric medical center. *Pediatrics, 129,* 418–425. doi:10.1542/peds.2011-0907

Steensma, T. D., Biemond, R., de Boer, F., & Cohen-Kettenis, P. T. (2011). Desisting and persisting gender dysphoria after childhood: A qualitative follow-up study. *Clinical Child Psychology and Psychiatry, 16,* 498–516. doi:10.1177/1359104510378303

Toomey, R. B., Ryan, C., Diaz, R. M., Card, N. A., & Russell, S. T. (2010). Gender-nonconforming lesbian, gay, bisexual, and transgender youth: School victimization and young adult psychosocial adjustment. *Developmental Psychology, 46,* 1580-1589. doi:10.1037/a0020705

Toomey, R. B., Ryan, C., Diaz, R. M., & Russell, S. T. (2011). High school Gay–Straight Alliances (GSAs) and young adult well-being: An examination of GSA presence, participation, and perceived effectiveness. *Applied Developmental Science, 15,* 175–185. doi:10.1080/10888691.2011.607378

Travers, R. (2012). Mental Health. In *Improving the health of trans communities: Findings from the Trans PULSE project.* Ottawa, Canada: Rainbow Health Ontario Conference.

VandenBos, G. R. (Ed.). (2007). *APA dictionary of psychology.* Washington, DC: American Psychological Association.

Werner, E. E. (1995). Resilience in development. *Current Directions in Psychological Science, 4,* 81–85.

Reflexive Questions

1. What memories do you have of middle childhood during your elementary school years?

2. What were your greatest joys? What were your greatest challenges and stressors?

3. What traditions, routines, celebrations, and events do you most remember? How did they shape who you are today?

4. As routine and uneventful as your childhood may have been, no childhood is "normal." How were your experiences influenced by your identity and context—gender, family, culture, race, religion, socioeconomic status, immigration status and place where you lived?

5. How do you think a child's ability status affects their trajectories in life? How did aspects of your abilities affect your trajectory or that of your siblings?

6. How can public schools foster the inclusion of deaf students while also being more responsive to their needs? How do hearing children benefit from integrated classrooms?

7. How does a family's financial status and social class affect their ability to care for a child or sibling with a disability? How could a parent's disability affect a child's development, both in positive and negative ways?

8. How do care, kindness, and acceptance positively affect the mental and physical health of transgender children? Conversely, what are the harmful effects of rejection, discrimination, and harassment?

9. How can schools do a better job at mitigating harassment and transphobia? What steps can they take to ensure everyone learns in a safe and inclusive environment? Why is this important?

10. In general, what do children need in order to thrive, regardless of their abilities, culture, ethnicity, country of origin, immigration status, religion, race, gender identity, or social class? What seems foundational and essential to their care?

CHAPTER 7

The Adolescent Years

Introduction

Adolescence is the transitional developmental stage between childhood and adulthood. It is often marked by the onset of puberty, which can start as early as middle childhood or as late as the late teens (Berger, 2019). Although puberty is marked by an increase in sex hormones that triggers physical maturation in the body, psychoemotional/social maturity often lasts years after the onset of menarche and spermarche. Accompanying rapid changes to the body are rapid changes in the mind (Steinberg & Morris, 2001). Adolescents' brains are still developing while their sense of self is forming, and their egocentrism, susceptibility to influences, and invincibility fable place them at risk (Wickman et al., 2008). Children and teens who physically mature early have added risks of mental health problems related to early exposure to substances, unwanted sexual advances and content, and pregnancy (Kaltiala-Heinoa et al., 2003). Additionally, there are countless psychosocial issues currently facing teens that were not present in the past. The role of technology, the internet, and social media (Pascoe, 2011), the hypersexualization of children and teens (Zurbriggen & Roberts, 2013), and geographic distance from extended family (Jaeger, 2012) have created unique challenges for teens today. Given these contextual realities, teens are increasingly in need of stronger societal and familial messages about body positivity (Roberts & Waters, 2004) and acceptance of diverse identities as well as clear and unbiased information, such as comprehensive sex education (Kohler, Manhart, & Lafferty, 2008). Additionally, there is a great need for culturally relevant prevention and intervention programs aimed at reducing the harmful effects of traumatic experiences (e.g., substance abuse, addiction, bullying, incarceration, violence, gangs, sexual abuse/rape, suicidality) that can impede a teenager's development into adulthood.

The complexity of our understanding of this developmental life stage is also intensified when we consider how a teen's identity and understanding of self is influenced by their culture, gender identity, religion, abilities, nationality and socioeconomic and immigration status. Furthermore, the added stressors of structural and systemic oppression are strong social forces that youth internalize and often impose on each other—to everyone's detriment (Phinney, 1989). By the time a child reaches adolescence, their sense of self is strongly shaped by familial and societal messages that prescribe who they are, who they should become, and what they can and cannot do based on their identity and social location.

These messages are particularly strong when it comes to the culturally ascribed performance of gender. Scholars such Tony Porter (2016), Jackson Katz (2006), and Michael Kimmel (1996, 2008) have long talked about the socialization of boys and men and the dangers and constraints of the "man box," "tough guise," "guyland," and "the macho paradox." They discuss how cultural scripts embedded in misogyny, sexism, and homophobia dictate a singular form of masculinity that is toxic and dangerous for everyone, but especially for girls and women, with gender-based violence and murder/femicide at catastrophic levels (Johnson, Eriksson, Mazerolle, & Wortley, 2019). According to the World Health Association (2012), femicide involves "intentional murder of women because they are women," but broader definitions include any killings of women or girls. Femicide is most often committed by men and most often partners or ex-partners, who have a history of violence and intimate partner terrorism, and among women who have less individual and social power or fewer resources than their partner (United Nations, 2019). When the larger sociopolitical climate supports male dominance, girls and women are especially vulnerable to abuse, violence, and murder, most often at the hands of the men in their lives.

In the end, we are all constrained and harmed by prejudicial beliefs and norms. White supremacy harms people of color, heteronormativity harms LGBTQ and non-gender conforming people, xenophobia harms immigrants, ableism harms people with different abilities, and male superiority harms girls and women. Furthermore, given their stage of development, teens are especially susceptible to internalizing harmful cultural and societal scripts, leading to internalized "isms" (Tatum, 1997). The following readings were chosen with the hope that they will provide a glimpse at how teens are affected by the intersections of their identity, cultural and religious values, and immigration status.

Summary of Readings

In the first reading, "**Schools and the Social Control of Sexuality**" (2006), Melinda S. Miceli explores how public schools influence American sexual culture by promoting heterosexuality and gender roles as ideals while ostracizing students who challenge these norms. Because public schools are "neutral" informants of valuable knowledge, their perpetuation of inequalities and culture especially favors the dominant social group, which is historically white, upper- and middle-class, heterosexual, Christian, and male. This knowledge is perceived as *neutral* and *objective*; however, heteronormativity is one behavior that is so prevalent in schools that it is practically invisible for those who are heterosexual and gender conforming. The participants in Miceli's study stated that displays of heterosexual attraction in the halls, classroom, and at dances are normalized and accepted, as is the harassment of LGBT students. Non-gender-conforming and LGBT students are particularly at risk for being rejected and bullied, and their schools are often places of fear and hostility. The very curriculum schools use to teach, often simultaneously ostracizes LGBT students by perpetuating heteronormative values and omitting gay and lesbian experiences.

Miceli's findings show that school curriculums erase LGBT experiences, and sex education programs, like abstinence-only education, deny students factual information about sexuality. Proponents of comprehensive sex education argue that public health problems are linked to misinformation or lacking information. Silence often exacerbates ignorance, shame, and the prevalence of unplanned teen pregnancies and sexually transmitted infections. The conflict over what type of sex education should be implemented ultimately reflects values defining sexuality and what is deemed appropriate.

The reading "**Lost in the Shuffle: Culture of Homeless Adolescents**" (2009) by Joanne O'Sullivan Oliveira and Pamela Burke investigates the culture of homeless youth. Oliveira's and Burke's study collected data by observing and interviewing 19 teens over an 18-month period. They were between 16 and 21 years of age, displaced from their homes, and from a major urban area in the northeastern United States. The authors identified risk factors for adolescent homelessness: family conflict, running away, physical or sexual abuse, leaving foster care, and coming out to parents as an LGBTQ individual. Living on the periphery of society, homeless adolescents are often "lost in the shuffle" because they are not in child welfare, juvenile justice, or mental health systems. While mainstream culture often frames homeless adolescents as "victims" lacking autonomy or choice, many youths in this study revealed living on the streets was a rational alternative to staying in a dangerous home environment. In contrast to their previous homes, many study participants felt cared for on the streets, where they found camaraderie and nurturing through music, religion, and drug use. Although they came from diverse backgrounds and identities, many formed subgroups to bond and survive living on the streets together.

The reading "**Female Genital Cutting: Crossing Borders**" (2014) by Hazel Barrett examines the widespread practice of female genital cutting (FGC), also known as female genital mutilation (FGM). In her reading, Barret discusses the four types of FGC and their varying degrees of detriment to girls' and women's health. She also discusses the factors that continue to perpetuate this practice, which include controlling female sexual desire, ensuring virginity, upholding a family's honor, and equating female "circumcision" with male circumcision, which emphasizes religious and hygienic reasons for the practice. Female genital cutting/mutilation is concentrated in 29 African and Middle Eastern countries; however, it is spreading to other parts of the world, including Europe and the U.K. Over *140 million* girls and women worldwide have been subjected to genital mutilation.

To eradicate this practice, FGC was conceptualized as a violation of human rights during the 1990s. As a result of the reconceptualization of FGC as a violation, most countries in Europe created legislation that defines FGC as a criminal offense, and 26 African and Middle Eastern nations have prohibited the practice by law or constitutional decree. Although this practice is painful, dangerous, and causes life-long complications, life-threatening and nonconsensual FGC persists. *Sunna*, a term for FGC that translates as "blessings," is related to societal gender and sexual scripts for girls and women and is often justified on religious grounds. Failure to practice FGC can lead to social exclusion and ostracism in some communities. As a result, even when parents understand FGC can cause serious harm and lifelong consequences and be life-threatening, they continue to practice it to avoid moral judgment.

References

Berger, K. S. (2019). *Invitation to the life span (4th Ed.)*. Worth Publishers.

Jaeger, M. (2012). The extended family and children's educational success. *American Sociological Review, 77*(6), 903–922. doi.org/10.1177/0003122412464040

Katz, J. (2006). *The macho paradox: Why some men hurt women and how all men can help*. Sourcebooks.

Kaltiala-Heinoa, R., Marttunen, M., Rantanen, P., & Rimpelä, M. (2003). Early puberty is associated with mental health problems in middle adolescence. *Social Science & Medicine, 57*(6), 1055–1064.

Kimmel, M. S. (2008). *Guyland: The perilous world where boys become men*. Harper.

Kohler, P. K., Manhart, L. E., & Lafferty, W. E. (2008). Abstinence-only and comprehensive sex education and the initiation of sexual activity and teen pregnancy. Journal of Adolescent Health, 42(4), 344–351. doi:10.1016/j.jadohealth.2007.08.026

Johnson, H., Eriksson, L., Mazerolle, P., & Wortley, R. (2019). Intimate femicide: The role of coercive control. *Feminist Criminology, 14*(1), 3–23. doi:10.1177/1557085117701574

Pascoe, C. J. (2011). Resource and risk: Youth sexuality and new media use. *Sexuality Research and Social Policy, 8*, 5–17. doi.org/10.1007/s13178-011-0042-5

Phinney, J. S. (1989). Stages of ethnic identity development in minority group adolescents. *The Journal of Early Adolescence, 9*(1–2), 34–49. doi:10.1177/0272431689091004

Porter, A. (2016). *Breaking out of the man box: The next generation of manhood*. Skyhorse.

Roberts, T., & Waters, P. L. (2004). Self-objectification and that "not so fresh feeling": Feminist therapeutic interventions for healthy female embodiment. *Woman & Therapy, 27*(3–4), 5–21. doi.org/10.1300/J015v27n03_02

Steinberg, L., & Morris, A. S. (2001). Adolescent development. *Annual Review of Psychology, 52*, 83–110. doi.org/10.1146/annurev.psych.52.1.83

Tatum, B. D. (1997). *Why are all the Black kids sitting together in the cafeteria? And other conversations about race*. Basic Books.

United Nations Office on Drugs and Crime: Global study on homicide 2019 (Vienna, 2019). https://www.unodc.org/unodc/en/data-and-analysis/global-study-on-homicide.html

Wickman, M. E., Anderson, N. L. R., & Smith Greenberg, C. (2008). The adolescent perception of invincibility and its influence on teen acceptance of health promotion strategies. *Journal of Pediatric Nursing, 23*(6), 460–468. doi.org/10.1016/j.pedn.2008.02.003

World Health Organization (2012). WHO reference number: WHO/RHR/12.38 https://apps.who.int/iris/bitstream/handle/10665/77421/WHO_RHR_12.38_eng.pdf;jsessi onid=071B19B2A1A533320B0DD391DDC8DDE9?sequence=1

Zurbriggen, E. L., & Roberts, T. -A. (Eds.). (2013). *The sexualization of girls and girlhood: Causes, consequences, and resistance*. Oxford University Press.

Schools and the Social Control of Sexuality

Melinda S. Miceli

The question of whether or not schools should teach students about sexuality has been one of heated debate since the early twentieth century. The simple fact remains that schools do teach students countless lessons about sexuality, in a variety of ways, every single day. As social institutions through which every citizen passes, schools have an enormous amount of power to influence the beliefs and values of young people. In this chapter, I analyze some of the ways that public schools shape America's sexual culture by looking at their informal and formal curriculum, culture, and their sex education policies. My chief claim is that schools have tried to promote what is considered a "normal" and "respectable" sexuality, that is, heterosexuality, conventionally gendered norms governing sexual behavior, and an ideal of marriage and family.

Michel Foucault argued persuasively "Western societies simultaneously repress and obsess over sexuality. Sexual speech is both amplified and silenced. The patterns of what about sex is spoken about and what is silenced is not random, but rather both are part of the weave of power relations and social control." According to Foucault, it is a mistake to conclude that, as Western cultures increased the amount of sexual speech and the number of arenas where sex is discussed, the less sexuality is repressed and controlled. Conversely, it is incorrect to conclude that, in spaces where sexual speech is forbidden or regulated, it is successfully repressed or absent.

Foucault argued that a concerted effort to control the sexuality of youth began in the eighteenth century, with schools being a logical target of rules and regulations. However, he argued:

> It would be less than exact to say that the pedagogical institution has imposed a ponderous silence on the sex of children and adolescents. On the contrary since the eighteenth century it has multiplied the forms of discourse on the subject; it has established various points of implantation for sex; it has coded contents and qualified speakers. Speaking about children's sex, inducing educators, physicians, administrators, and parents to speak of it, or speaking to them about it, causing children themselves to talk about it, and enclosing them in a web of discourses which sometimes address them, sometimes speak about them, or impose canonical bits of knowledge about them, or use them as a basis for constructing a science that is beyond their

grasp—all this together enables us to link an intensification of the interventions of power to a multiplication of discourse. The sex of children and adolescents has become, since the eighteenth century, an important area of contention around which innumerable institutional devices and institutional strategies have been deployed. (Foucault 1976: 29–30)

Sex education classes introduce direct and purposeful sexual discourse into the regulated space of the school. Janice Irvine (2002) argues that "[s]ince the sixties, as openness about sexuality in popular culture has intensified, U.S. communities have fought over whether to allow discussions about sexual topics in the classroom. At stake is what is in the best interest of young people. The history of sex education in America is part of long-standing efforts to regulate sexual morality through the control of sexual speech" (2002: 4). In her book, *Talk About Sex: the Battle over Sex Education in the United States*, Irvine provides a detailed historical account and a sophisticated sociological analysis of these battles and how they fit into larger power struggles to control cultural norms, beliefs, and values.

The idea of formal sexual education classes in schools was first proposed in the early twentieth-century by a collection of moral reformers, which included suffragists, clergy, temperance workers, and physicians dedicated to eliminating venereal disease. From the beginning there was disagreement about the specific content and aim of sex education classes, and yet agreement that accurate information about sexuality needed to be taught for the good of public health. This group also felt that the

restrictive measures of the Comstock laws that sought state restriction of virtually all public discussion of sexuality, including sex education and contraception information, had to be combated (Irvine 2002). Contemporary conflicts between advocates of abstinence-only and proponents of comprehensive sex education are situated in this long-standing tension between those who feel that the public is best served by limiting children's access to information about sexuality and those groups who feel that public health problems are caused by a lack of such information.

Comprehensive sexuality education stresses abstinence for youth, and it also provides information on contraception and abortion. The Sex Information and Education Council of the United States (SIECUS) was founded in 1964, and has become the leading advocate of comprehensive sexuality education programs being integrated into schools at all levels. SIECUS and its supporters argue that students should receive age-appropriate information on subjects like human reproduction, anatomy, physiology, sexually transmitted diseases, masturbation, and homosexuality, and engage in discussion of sexual values. "Advocates of comprehensive sex education endorse what they consider to be the therapeutic potential of open and informative sexual discussion in the classroom. They believe that silence has fostered ignorance, shame and social problems like teen pregnancy and sexually transmitted diseases. They view sexuality as positive and healthy and they generally support gender equality and acceptance of sexual diversity" (Irvine 2002).

Opponents criticize SIECUS's model of sexual education as irresponsible and misinformed. These groups argue that providing students with information about sexual practices, such as the use of contraceptives, has contributed to rising levels of adolescent sexual activity, sexually transmitted diseases, and teenage pregnancy. Since the 1960s conservative Catholics and Christian fundamentalists have founded a variety of political organizations in order to fight for regulation of sex education. These groups are affiliated with the religious right, and opposition to sex education has bolstered their social movement to restore traditional sexual and gender values and norms to American culture (Irvine 2002). One of many strategies for achieving this goal is restricting the sexual discourses to which young people are exposed. Carefully controlling or eliminating sexual discussion from school, they argue, is essential to efforts to protect children and adolescents from the "dangers" of sexuality and to reinstating sexual morality to the culture (Irvine 2002).

All schools promote what Bourdieu and others (e.g. Sears 1992; Giroux and McLaren 1989) have called a hegemonic curriculum, a curriculum which simultaneously legitimizes the dominant culture and marginalizes or rejects other cultures and forms of knowledge. The concept of the hegemonic curriculum, and the closely related concept of the hidden curriculum, have been well documented in research into educational institutions and practices since the 1960s. Early studies examined the ways in which upper- and middle-class, white and male culture, history, morals, behaviors, norms and values are taught and enforced in schools through the power of a hegemonic process where they are also naturalized, neutralized, and made invisible. Over the past decade and a half several studies of school culture have included an examination of a hidden sexuality curriculum in schools (Sears 1992; Epstein 1994; Miceli 1998; Best 2000; Irvine 2002; Kehily 2002). Michelle Fine (1988) and others have argued that the struggles over sex education

are not only about broadly whether "talk about sex" in schools is appropriate or not, but also, through what is said and what is unsaid, to specifically define appropriate sexuality for males and females. Fine's (1988) investigation into the content of the prevalent sex education programs in the United States concluded that "within today's standard sex education curricula and many public school classrooms, we find:

1. the authorized suppression of a discourse of female sexual desire;
2. the promotion of a discourse of female sexual victimization; and
3. the explicit privileging of married heterosexuality over other practices of sexuality. (1988:30)

The sex education programs to which Fine refers emerged in the early 1980s as a result of the Adolescent Family Life Act (AFLA), the first federal law specifically passed to fund sex education. The AFLA, which is still in use and has become increasingly funded and expanded since, was written by conservative Republican senators with the goal of ending premarital teen sex and therefore teen pregnancy and teen abortion (Levine 2002). Because it is girls who get pregnant and have abortions, they became the target of the abstinence education programs. These programs, Fine (1988) and others have argued, teach girls to fear their own sexuality, to view sex as dangerous and harmful, and to guard themselves from becoming the victims of their own or males' uncontrolled sexuality. In this discourse of abstinence education, young women are held responsible not only for controlling their own sexuality but also for preventing their own victimization.

This approach to sex education in the United States contrasts sharply with that taken by many other countries. In countries like Sweden,

France, Germany, and The Netherlands the approach is to educate students about sexuality in all of its aspects so that they can develop healthy and responsible sexual attitudes and behavior. Judith Levine argues that studies of sex education in other countries prove that their more comprehensive approach has been successful.

> In many European countries, where teens have as much sex as in America, sex ed starts in the earliest grades. It is informed by a no-nonsense, even enthusiastic, attitude toward the sexual; it is explicit and doesn't teach abstinence. Rates of unwanted teen pregnancy, abortion, and AIDS in every "Western European country are a fraction of our own; the average age of first intercourse is about the same as in the United States. (Levine 2002: 98)

Interestingly, surveys on public opinion about sex education constantly find that the majority of Americans support a more comprehensive model. "In fact, the degree of consensus reported in national surveys about sex education is striking. A 1998 national survey found that 87 percent of Americans favor sex education and of those 89 percent believe that, along with abstinence, young people should also have information about contraception and STD prevention" (Irvine 2002). Despite public opinion, the issue of expanding current sex education curricula more often than not sparks intense local controversies and makes national headlines. In addition, despite the opinion polls, the federal government has continued to increase its funding of abstinence-only programs and

the religious right has continued to have a loud voice in the discourse of sexuality.

In 1997, the U.S. Congress committed a quarter billion dollars over five years to finance more education in … abstinence. As part of the omnibus "welfare reform bill," the government's Maternal and Child Health Bureau extended grants to the states for programs whose exclusive purpose is teaching the social, psychological, and health gains to be realized by abstaining from sexual activity In a country where only one in ten school-children receives more than forty hours of sex ed in any year, the regulations prohibit funded organizations from instructing kids about contraception or condoms except in terms of their failures. In a country where 90 percent of adults have sex before marriage and as many as 10 percent are gay or lesbian, the law underwrites one message and one message only: that "a mutually faithful monogamous relationship in the context of marriage is the expected standard of human sexual activity." Nonmarital sex, educators are required to tell children, "is likely to have harmful psychological effects." (Levine 2002: 91)

These debates over sex education curricula are a prime example of the efforts to regulate sexual discourse, knowledge, and behavior, and of the fact that schools are central arenas in this power struggle. The amount of energy, resources, and passion expended by all sides to control what schools teach about sexuality indicates the impact schools have on the broader social control of sexuality.

Discussion Questions

1. Do you think it is appropriate for a sexual education classes to promote abstinence for teenagers or young adults? Why or why not?

2. Do you think it is appropriate for a sexual education classes to promote particular kinds of sexual practices and relationships as "healthy"? Why or why not?

3. Who are the interest groups standing behind abstinence-only sex education programs and why do they support these programs?

4. Why is it that the typical sexual education curriculum singles out girls and their sexual behavior as problematic and in need of control more so than boys and their sexual behavior?

References

Best, Amy L. 2000. *Prom Night: Youth Schools and Popular Culture*. New York: Routledge.

———. 2005. "The Production of Heterosexuality at the High School Prom", in Chrys Ingraham (ed.), *Thinking Straight: The Power, the Promise, and the Paradox of Heterosexuality*. New York: Routledge.

Epstein, Debbie (ed.). 1994. *Challenging Lesbian and Gay Inequalities in Education*. Buckingham, UK: Open University Press.

Fine, Michelle. 1988. "Sexuality, Schooling, and Adolescent Females: The Missing Discourse of Desire." *Harvard Educational Review 58*: 29–53.

Foucault, Michel 1990. *The History of Sexuality: An Introduction, Volume 1*. New York: Vintage Books.

Giroux, Henry A. and Peter McClaren. 1989. *Critical Pedagogy: The State and Culture Struggle*. Albany: SUNY Press.

GLSEN. 2003. The 2003 National School Climate Survey. New York: GLSEN.

Irvine, Janice M. 2002. *Talk About Sex: The Battles over Sex Education in the United States*. Berkeley, CA: University of California Press.

Kehily, Mary Jane. 2002. *Sexuality, Gender and Schooling: Shifting Agendas in Social Learning*. New York: Routledge.

Levine, Judith. 2002. *Harmful to Minors*. Minneapolis: University of Minnesota Press.

Miceli, Melinda S. 2005. *Standing Out, Standing Together: The Social and Political Impact of Gay-Straight Alliances*. New York: Routledge.

Pascoe, C. J. 2007. *Dude, You're a Fag: Masculinity and Sexuality in High School*. Berkeley, CA: University of California Press.

Sears, James T. 1992. *Sexuality and the Curriculum: The Politics and Practices of Sex Education*. New York: Teachers College Press.

Lost in the Shuffle

Culture of Homeless Adolescents

Joanne O'Sullivan Oliveira and Pamela J. Burke

Joanne O'Sullivan Oliveira, PhD, RN, FNP, BC, is Director, Nurse Scientist/Researcher, Surgical Programs, Children's Hospital, Boston, MA.

Pamela J. Burke, PhD, RN, FNP, PNP-BC, is Nurse Practitioner, Division of Adolescent Medicine, Co-Director for Nurse Training, Children's Hospital, LEAH Interdisciplinary Fellowship Program, and Assistant Professor of Pediatrics, Harvard Medical School, Boston, MA.

Statement of Disclosure: The authors reported no actual or potential conflict of interest in relation to this continuing nursing education article.

Estimates indicate that approximately 1.7 million youth are homeless in the United States. Many associated risk factors have been identified for adolescent homelessness, including family conflict, leaving foster care, running away or being thrown away, physical or sexual abuse, and coming out to parents as gay, lesbian, bisexual, transgender, or questioning one's sexual identity (GLBTQ). The purpose of this ethnographic study was to explore the culture of homelessness for adolescents. Nineteen homeless adolescents from a major urban area in the northeast U.S. were observed and interviewed over an 18-month period. The elements of the street culture of homeless adolescents were identified by study participants' stories. For many study participants, the decision to live on the streets was a logical and rational alternative to remaining in possibly dangerous and unstable home environments. It provided a means to their generating social capital. Nevertheless, it can be concluded that existing programs and policies relative to adolescents who are at risk for homelessness or already living on the streets should be re-examined and redesigned to meet the unique needs of vulnerable youth so they do not get lost in the shuffle.

Note: The names of the youth cited in this study have been changed.

Every culture has a schema, which can be expressed as family structure; dietary habits; religious practices; the development of art, music, and drama; ways of communicating; dress; and health behavior. Literature on runaway adolescents dates back to the 1920s, but very little research focuses on the culture of homeless adolescents. Homeless adolescents exist literally on the periphery of society, often leading to exclusion and marginalization, as these youth gravitate toward isolated locations, such as abandoned areas of the city, hidden spaces in public buildings, and remote or inaccessible sites. Ultimately, they find themselves prohibited from participating in society and limited in their use of societal powers and resources (Raleigh-DuRoff, 2004; Rice, Milburn, Rotheram-Borus, Mallett, & Rosenthal, 2005). This study explores the culture and life experiences of homeless adolescents in a major urban area.

Life on the streets has the potential to erode the emotional and physical welfare of the abandoned child (Milburn et al., 2007; Robertson, 1998). To survive, many of these adolescents resort to drug dealing and a myriad of high-risk activities that render their life issues different from those of the general adolescent population (Auerswald & Eyre, 2002; Barry, Ensign, & Lippek 2002; Ginzler, Garret, Baer, & Peterson, 2007). These youth are at increased risk for a host of physical, psychosocial, and psychological problems (Alexander & Schrauben, 2006; Slesnick, Prestopnik, Meyers, & Glassman, 2007; Taylor-Seehafer, Jacobvitz, & Steiker, 2008).

Homeless Adolescents

Homeless adolescents, also referred to as street youth, tend to roam the streets at night in search of safe shelter and/or to avoid victimization. Because of their fear of victimization, these homeless youth try to avoid contact and interactions with the adult homeless population (Rew, 2008). Fear and the need to survive may evolve into participation in alternative behaviors, such as selling and/or using drugs, prostitution, and other crimes that elicit disdain from mainstream society and perpetuate isolation and marginalization (Auerswald & Eyre, 2002; Peterson, Baer, Wells, Ginzler, & Garrett, 2006).

Adolescence is a period of profound biopsychosocial development. Identity formation, the quest for autonomy and independence, and transformations in family and peer relationships, emerging cognitive abilities, and socioeconomic factors interact and affect the adolescent's thoughts, feelings, and behavior. Adolescents who no longer think they belong or feel safe at home may run to the streets in a seemingly fruitless attempt to find another place they can call home (Armaline, 2005; Whitbeck, Hoyt, Johnson, & Chen, 2007). In effect, street youth no longer fit within main stream social networks, and thus, tend to shy away from institutions designed to help them, including shelters and soup kitchens. For many, this hiding out behavior stems from a mistrust of the adult population, as well as the lack of privacy and personal space within institutional environments (Armaline, 2005; Auerswald & Eyre, 2002).

Homeless youth's transient, invisible, and/or illegal status make it difficult, if not impossible, to obtain an accurate count (Kidd & Scrimenti, 2004; Knopf, Park, Brindis, Mulye, & Irwin, 2007; Raleigh-DuRoff, 2004). According to the Youth Services for the Child Welfare League, most of these youth are not in the child welfare, juvenile justice, or mental health systems, and therefore, get "lost in the shuffle" (Slavin, 2001). Estimates indicate that 1.7 million youth are homeless in the U.S. (National Network for Youth, 2009). According to a report from the 2007 U.S. Conference of Mayors, unaccompanied (homeless) youth account for 1% of the urban homeless population (National Coalition for the Homeless, 2008). However, such a low prevalence rate is most likely an under-re presentation of the actual population. The number of homeless youth is equally divided among males and females, and most are between the ages of 15 to 17 years (Molino, 2007). Ten percent of homeless youth were reported as pregnant. It is estimated that nationally, at least 6% to 10% of homeless youth are gay, lesbian, bisexual, or transgender (GLBT) (Alexander & Schrauben, 2006; Milburn et al., 2007; Robertson & Toro, 1998).

The term *homeless youth* is used as an over-arching term connoting the many pathways through which youth find their way to the streets. (Hammer, Finkelhor, & Sedlak, 2002; Raleigh-DuRoff, 2004). Thousands of youth are thrown out of their homes each year (Milburn et al., 2007; Robertson & Toro, 1998). There is no official definition of a throwaway/castaway/pushed-out youth. The parents or legal guardians have ejected the youth from their living environment, making it clear that he or she is no longer welcome back home. These youth have literally been abandoned or deserted (Armaline, 2005; Hammer et al., 2002). Some are homeless because they have simply lost track of their families, or their families are homeless and unable to care for them. Immigrant adolescents who become homeless face additional challenges, such as language-barriers, cultural conflicts, and legal obstacles to seeking help or readily integrating into the culture of the street (Van Wormer, 2003). System youth are individuals who have been, at one time or another, in the custody of the state due to familial conflicts, neglect, or abuse. Some of these youth have been repeatedly placed in foster homes and/or group homes, but eventually run away from this care (Smith, 2008). Brannigan and Caputo (1993) referred to youth who left the system prematurely as absconders from care.

Homeless adolescents have few options for services available to them because they are on the fringe of society. Vulnerable, lost, alone, and often victimized, they no longer fit society's definition of children. The official U.S. government definition for street youth is those who are indefinitely or intermittently homeless and at high risk for sexual abuse, sexual exploitation, prostitution, or drug abuse (National Center for Missing and Exploited Children, 2000). Street youth are often chronically homeless, long-term runaways, or throwaway youth. According to Hagan and McCarthy (1997), street youth sleep in locations such as doorways, heating vents, ATM enclosures, bus terminals, and railroad tunnels or platforms, and often engage in illegal survival strategies. These youth spend most of their time on the streets unsupervised and may seek shelter in abandoned buildings or makeshift camp sites in outdoor parks, under bridges, or on rooftops. Some may have intermittent contact with family, but they are usually left to their own devices for survival (Milburn et al., 2007).

Many associated risk factors have been identified for adolescent homelessness, including family conflict, leaving foster care, running away or being thrown away, physical or sexual abuse, and coming out to parents as gay, lesbian, bisexual, transgender, or questioning one's sexual identity (GLBTQ). Much of the existing research on homeless adolescents has focused on the epidemiology of homelessness, precipitating factors, and perspectives of service providers. However, what is not well understood is the youth's perspective of life on the streets and the dynamic relationships that homeless youth form for survival. Previous research has focused intently on the problems and deficits of homeless adolescents, with little or no attention to the strengths and competencies these youth possess. Research is needed to explore the subculture of homelessness as experienced by the adolescents and described from their own perspective.

The aims of this doctoral dissertation study were to 1) explore the meaning of life for homeless adolescents, 2) examine how these youth structure their lives and how society has helped create that structure, 3) describe the cultural norms and mores of street life, and 4) understand how social, economic, and political forces within mainstream culture may influence the formation of a homeless adolescent subculture. The most appropriate study design to meet this study's aims was ethnography.

Method

The principal investigator (O'Sullivan-Oliveira) used ethnographic data collection methods (participant observation and tape recorded interviews) to study homeless adolescents. Spradley's (1979) 12-Step Developmental Sequence Method guided data collection and analysis. The intent of the observations and interviews was to see the world through adolescents' eyes, discover what life on the streets was actually like, and understand what activities and relationships structure held in their unique street subculture. Observations by the principal investigator provided a context or background for the adolescents' stories and enriched the descriptions of their experiences (Spradley, 1980). The principal investigator conducted observations in a variety of settings, including a medical outreach van, a homeless youth drop-in center, and outdoors at two sites where street youth gathered—a metropolitan urban subway center and a public park. These observations were made in various settings over an 18-month

period in 2001 and 2002 during an average of 10 to 20 hours per week, and at various times of day and days of the week. One setting, the medical van, was an outreach program staffed by volunteer social service providers, nurses, and physicians to provide first aid or basic medical care and social support to homeless individuals. The medical van traveled around the city to high-risk areas, and typically logged visits with adults and adolescents, yielding encounters with approximately 8 to 10 street youth per night.

The principal investigator noted homeless street youth's interactions with each other as well as with people from the mainstream culture, such as pedestrians, students from the surrounding universities, tourists, and other health care professionals. She observed their physical appearance, moneymaking endeavors such as panhandling (also known as *s'panging*—asking people for spare change), and recreational activities. Observation dates, duration, and detailed descriptions of the social environment were documented. Field notes were written during observations, including the dates and duration of observations as well as detailed descriptions of the environment, atmosphere, mood, and interactions that occurred. Reflective journaling was also incorporated into field notes.

Sample

Sampling for formal interviews was not predetermined, but rather, it occurred after entry into the field. Purposive sampling was used to recruit adolescents, ages 16 to 21 years, who reported they were homeless and living/sleeping on the street or some other location not intended for human habitation. In the process of recruiting participants, it became apparent that not all homeless youth lived exclusively on the street. Some reported they were "couch surfing" (staying with friends) or alternated between living in their homes of origin during the week and living on the streets on the weekends. Although obviously at-risk, these youth were essentially flirting with homelessness, and thus, were excluded from this study.

Parents of homeless adolescents are generally unavailable. Furthermore, obtaining parental permission for the adolescent to participate in research would potentially compromise the adolescent's need for privacy a round sensitive areas, and in turn, could provoke parental reprisal—emotional, physical, or economic. Researchers who have studied homeless adolescents cite precedent from state statutes that allow emancipated or mature minors to obtain health care without parental notification if such notification would be contrary to the adolescent's best interest (Rew, Taylor-Seehafer, & Thomas, 2000).

This study was approved by the Institutional Review Boards (IRB) of the university where the investigator was a doctoral student at the time, as well as the health care agency that had oversight for the youth drop in center. Participation in the study was voluntary and involved minimal risk. Particular attention was paid to the need to maintain privacy. In keeping with the study aims, and the recommendations cited in the Office for Protection from Research Risks, Code for Federal Regulations (1996) Article 46.407, as well as the Society for Adolescent Medicine's position paper on adolescent health research (Santelli et al., 2003), the investigator requested and was granted an IRB waiver of parental consent. Informed consent was obtained from the adolescent participants who selected a pseudonym for their interview. In appreciation for their time, participants were given a $20 gift card.

Nineteen street youth (15 males and 4 females) were interviewed. The sample included 1 Latino, 2 bi-racial (Caucasian and African American), 1 African-American, and 15 Caucasian participants. Caucasian youth were more likely to be sleeping on the streets. According to anecdotal reports from homeless youth and from service providers, this may be attributed to a lack of extended family members for Caucasians as compared with minority youth. Although most African-American and Latino youth who "hung around" on the streets may not have been living with their family of origin, they did not sleep on the street. They were couch surfers, staying with extended family members or friends, and therefore, were excluded from the study. Although the 4 female participants said they considered themselves bisexual, at the time of the study, they were all in heterosexual relationships. Fourteen of the 15 males described themselves as heterosexual. One male identified himself as bisexual.

Interview questions explored the experiences of informants and elicited information about emerging themes. There were no preconceived notions about the outcome of the research. Some questions were formulated before the actual fieldwork to help guide the research (Morse, 1991). However, the youth were very informative without the use of these guided questions. Audio taped interviews conducted by the researcher began with this introductory probe: "I am a Martian, a being from another planet, and I do not know anything about your civilization. I landed here. Tell me about your life on the streets." This usually led to the youth's talking about their daily lives, and then the researcher's following up with questions as needed. Immediately after each interview, the researcher recorded field notes as well as observations pertaining to the appearance of the participants and their environment.

Analysis

Although the process of data collection and analysis was intertwined, Spradley's (1979) 12-Step Developmental Sequence Method was followed. These steps were 1) entering the field and locating informants, 2) doing participant observation, 3) making a record, 4) asking descriptive questions, 5) analyzing the interviews, 6) creating domain analysis, 7) asking structural questions, 8) performing taxonomic analysis, 9) asking contrasting questions, 10) performing componential analysis, 11) doing a theme analysis, and 12) writing the findings.

The domain analysis identified the rich and thick descriptions that were central components of the homeless culture. In the domain of the "Pit rat," homeless street youth used labels that signified the clique with which they identified. These groupings were akin to tribal names of a larger group. Within the larger culture of homeless adolescents, a variety of self-identified subgroups were based on qualifications these youth deemed important, such as aesthetic style (Goth), spiritual or religious belief (Wiccan), mode of travel (hitchhiker), or residential identification (squatter kids). Domains found in this study included the aesthetic styles worn and coveted by youth and their accompanying symbols, rituals and behaviors, codes/law and ethics, drugs, ways to earn money, place/location—home away from home, and daily

routines. A major theme within these domains was the importance of relationships for survival. Ironically, it was because they did not fit in so well elsewhere that these youth felt they fit in with each other. No matter how disparate their backgrounds, their desperate and immediate need for survival bound them together. This need transcended differences that can cause serious social problems in mainstream society. Their strategy for survival was the formation of a subculture that lived on the margins of mainstream culture.

Taxonomic analysis was used to examine the relationships among terms within a domain. In the process, relationships among certain domains became apparent. Taxonomies were developed as these domains were placed under a larger umbrella of organizing domains.

Componential analysis focused on identifying the unique characteristics of terms within a domain (Spradley, 1979). For example, within the domain of supportive techniques for surviving life on the streets, most participants were ambivalent about their relationships with systems, including helping professional agencies. Instead they related to individual outreach clinicians outside the agency proper. A thematic analysis integrated the domains and components of the sub-culture of homeless adolescents.

Credibility or internal validity was a strong point of this study because the participants and the researcher developed relationships. According to Lincoln and Guba (1985), three activities can increase the probability of credible findings: 1) prolonged engagement, 2) persistent observations, and 3) triangulation. Prolonged engagement with study participants sensitized the principal investigator to multiple contextual factors influencing the phenomenon being studied. Persistent observation allowed the most salient features of the adolescents' culture to emerge. Triangulation of methods (such as participant observations, interviews, and reflexive journaling) was designed to ensure credibility. Other strategies used for credibility as suggested by Lincoln and Guba (1985) were peer debriefing, referential adequacy, and member checking.

On-going data analysis was shared with a peer-debriefer, who was a fellow doctoral student. In addition, interview transcripts and field notes were shared with the first author's (O'Sullivan Oliveira) dissertation committee chair (Burke) and her two dissertation committee members, who all had extensive experience working with vulnerable and marginalized populations. Referential adequacy was used to keep some raw data aside, unanalyzed, until after themes emerged. This was done with one follow-up interview for each teen. The data were then brought back into analysis for comparison and confirmation of the emerged hypothesis. Member checking was accomplished by checking the accuracy of statements and conclusions with the participants in the study. Three participants, Casper, Chains, and Elizabeth, were interviewed as member checkers, and they confirmed the findings.

Confirmabiltiy was assessed to ascertain whether the findings were grounded in the data. This was done through the audit trail, by examining a sample of findings and tracing them back to the raw data (such as interview and journal/field notes).

Findings

Culture can be defined as a set of guidelines that individuals inherit as members of a particular society (Helman, 2000). According to Spradley (1980), when ethnographers study other cultures, they must deal with what people do (cultural behavior), what people know (cultural knowledge), and what people make (cultural artifacts). The elements of the street culture of homeless adolescents were identified by the study participants' stories.

Environment

Typically, homeless youth found one another at the *Pit*, a Mecca to homeless youth. This sunken plaza was adjacent to the subway stop across from a major university. A variety of individuals could be found at the Pit, including musicians, rebellious teens (with and without homes), students, and tourists. The environment provided a cultural center and a place to belong.

Religion and Rules

Cultures are made up of customs, mores, and ethos that are based on a belief system. The roots of these youth were grounded in the practice of Wicca. The ritualistic religion of Wicca emerged in almost every participant's interview. Religion, particularly Wicca (a pre-Christian pagan religion), was one of the strongest threads holding these street youth together. Wicca's major influence was on the rules of conduct and ethics of their culture. These youth felt a connection with pagan rituals that were inclusive and provided a sense of family and community. Experienced members tutored those who were new to the streets in the ways of Wicca. This became an important bonding process and a factor in whether the new member would be accepted into the street family.

For Bam-Bam, as for many others living on the street, religion (whether main stream or alternative) played a significant role in homeless "family" ties. Bam-Bam stated he had been practicing Wicca for over 8 years. In presenting a portrait of Bam-Bam, the practice of Wicca was reported as a central component to the structure of the subculture of these homeless adolescents. Divorced from families of origin and mainstream society, these youth have foraged for a sense of structure and organization.

Bam-Bam's religious beliefs in Wicca, as with many of his fellow homeless adolescents, provide a mirror into this culture. Quoting Bam-Bam:

> There is a large community around the "Pit," and many of the members in the "Pit" are part of one joint community family. Our family is Wicca/Pagan. We have our parents. We have kids. We have aunts and uncles. Being Pagan, our family is definitely different from most other families. Most of us in the family believe that we have been around for many centuries on earth or whatever people want to call it, this planet, this rock. You have to be part of our energy circle where we transfer energy between one another. Then we will fill you in on some history of our family
>
> Wicca is an old Celtic religion, which took on New Age philosophies in the 1980s. We all have been around for a long time. We have a high council of members of the family that have been in the family the longest, that know all the functions around the family, the rules of the family. How things are supposed to be done the right way and on council, where I'm the eldest son. So I am next in line to help protect my family. We all like to protect each other, make sure everybody is safe at all times. There are always other members in the family around at all times if there's ever an emergency or something like that.
>
> On the street, most come to Wicca because it means family, community, and commitment. Wicca beliefs and practices arose from a sense of community just like the street family, within the early clans. To "go it alone" was not a traditional Wicca value. We believe in following our own intuition and own personal code of ethics and morality. Wiccas look within, perceiving themselves to be both student and teacher at the same time. A lot of it is street family, but we tie in Wicca. Most of the family members are Wicca.
>
> We have one member, the newest member of the family; she's fairly new to the Wicca and Pagan religion ... we are slowly bringing her in and letting her know what is going on. We are doing it so it is not overwhelming or scary. We are just slowly showing her this is what happens. I feel that in some way, everybody is Wicca or Pagan because there is always energy transferred no matter what, human or inhuman. (2/02)

Street Families

Although these youth had run from or been abandoned by their families of origin, they had not, in fact, abandoned the cultural ideal of a family unit. To survive on the streets, they formed new street families complete with pseudo parents, siblings, and other extended family relationships. A street Mom and Dad in their 30s and former homeless youth helped scout out squats for sleeping and were instrumental in resolving conflicts. In this street family unit, there were two family factions headed by elder sons who were designated because of their length of time living on the streets. Bam-Bam and Casper were regarded as elders and initiated new homeless youth into the family. These street families provided the homeless youth with the resources and social support needed to survive the danger, boredom, poverty, challenges, and frustrations inherent in their transient and fragile existence.

"The best thing that has happened to me since I began life on the streets is the making of my street family" (Jade, female, 1/02). During each interview, a repetitive theme surfaced about life on the streets and the formation of "street families." What most professionals would regard as a negative experience was described positively by many of these youth. The adolescents had either run from or been abandoned by their original families. This left a void in their need for family ties. Their street families took alternate forms, as evidenced by both Bam-Bam's and Jade's accounts, and for these vulnerable youngsters, such ties were as important as food and water. These youth felt they finally belonged because they had established a family bond and found unconditional acceptance. They now had a family upon which they could depend, and this generated feelings of security. Some of these youth stated this was the first time in their lives they could "act like a kid," while others said they were discovering their lost childhood and finally felt part of a family, a community, a society, and a culture.

Street Brands

Language is the primary symbol of each social group and is fully understood by its members. In this group, the language was hip-hop or street-slang. The study participants were a diverse group of adolescents who identified themselves as freaks, grunge, taggers, Goths, punks, skinheads, hippies, wannabe thugs, vampires, hitchhikers, or squatters. They congregated in relative peace and harmony. There was an unspoken pact of live and let live, despite their use of different clothing, hairstyles, hair color, tattoos, and other accessories to distinguish themselves.

Thugs, for example, tended to wear big, baggy clothing, while Freaks donned chains, leather coats, spikes, patches, black boots with white laces, and long hair. Within the larger group of Punks were subgroups, such as Skank Punks, Skin Punks, and Nazi Punks. Punks wore every color of hair and proclaimed their unity through their common interest in punk music. They viewed themselves as a social group, accepting and welcoming peer obligations with a sense of family and respect for the elders. Vampire Wannabes dressed in full-length black clothing, distinguishing them from others as they listened to heavy metal rock music.

Music

Music was reported by participants as an important, if not *the* most important, component of their culture. Though they owned very few material goods, they owned their music. Most youngsters possessed a portable compact disc (CD), Walkman, or a musical instrument. For adolescents in general, music and musical artists are a big part of their lives, and this was especially true for these homeless youth. Music was a way to bond with peers.

Various categories of music, with specific themes and symbolic meanings, provided each a place within the street family. Punks saw their music as a cry for social change. Hip-hop music represented freedom of choice and a form of permission to smoke drugs or have casual sex. Music also helped maintain strong bonds within street families. Specific lyrics and compositions bonded these youth together for physical, emotional, and economic safety and comfort. The lyrics of a popular rap song was a particular favorite and represented the violent maternal abuse that a youth had endured through Munchausen's Syndrome by Proxy.

Street Economy

Within this group, drug dealing was regarded as a sporadic occupation used to supplement panhandling/spare changing (s'panging). Bam-Bam said:

> Drug transactions, that's where people can make a lot of serious money ... I live on the streets, making my money and doing it honestly. Selling drugs may be illegal, but I'm working. I'm earning what I'm making."

Individuals who sold drugs sporadically said that although the main purpose of selling drugs was to earn enough money to eat, it also helped support their own drug use.

There is a familiar hierarchy within the street culture. Leaders usually set up the business, take care of the big deals, and hire other homeless youth to distribute and sell smaller amounts. Most admitted they sold small amounts of marijuana to their inner circles or to others wanting to buy drugs.

Several individuals who smoked marijuana did not consider it to be a drug. Many said they had been smoking "weed" since they were 8 or 9 years old. Marijuana was a common substance used in their homes and communities of origin. When asked if they believed they had a drug problem, they insisted they did not, even though they smoked pot all day long. Marijuana use was considered a cultural norm among homeless youth in this study. It played a significant role in their communal life. It was something they used recreationally, as well as for self-medication for anxiety, depression, fear, hunger, and sleep.

The code "420" is a euphemism for smoking marijuana and is widely known by adolescents. There are differing renditions of oral history that relate to the origin of the term 420, but these youth agreed that the term originated in California. Some believed it was a California police code for marijuana smoking or that it was a criminal code number. There is no evidence to support these claims. Anecdotes were offered in support of an urban legend that the term 420 had originated on the West Coast in 1971 with some California high school students. The youth often met after school to smoke marijuana at 4:20 p.m. each day. Whatever the origin, the term was entrenched in this homeless youth society. A blunt, an inexpensive large marijuana cigarette, would serve the entire group during a smoke-out session every day at 4:20 p.m. This activity was reminiscent of a peace pipe smoking ritual in the Native American tribal culture. The smoke-out session was an incentive to attend street community meetings. Several Internet sites had developed as part of the 420 culture, and they were popular among these homeless adolescents. One participant, Bat, described the use of marijuana in this way:

> I smoke pot because it's fun. I've done it for years, and it's a way to relax and kind of ... like how the college professor goes home at night and has himself a brandy and a cigar. That's just my way of ... chilling out.

All participants reported using some drug or alcohol. Individuals who reported having previously been diagnosed with attention deficit hyperactivity disorder (ADHD) said cocaine-based drugs calmed them down, similar to methylphenidate (Ritalin®) prescribed when they were younger. Heroin was affordable and readily available on the streets for as little as $4.00 per bag. They reported they had begun by using opiates with more expensive prescription pain medications, such as oxycodone (OxyContin®) (8 mg pill—street value $80.00 per pill). Within a few months, they advanced to snorting heroin and rapidly progressed to intravenous (IV) use. Heroin was the least expensive and purest drug used on the street. The average daily dose of heroin was 10 to 20 bags per day. However, the end result of this spiraling addiction was often death by overdose.

Participants reported witnessing the ravages of IV drug addiction earlier in their lives when their parents died of AIDS or hepatitis C. Several were orphaned to the streets as a result of their parents' drug-related deaths. Poly-substance abuse was common among the youth, all of whom reported some form of substance use prior to living on the streets. In fact, some reported using more substances when they lived at home because parental/guardian substance use allowed easier access to both money and drugs. The most sought after drugs on the street were benzodiazepines, such as clonazepam (Klonopin®) (street name "pins"), which were taken to alleviate anxiety. Youth reported obtaining prescriptions from psychiatrists at hospital emergency rooms. Participants also reported overdoses and hospitalizations due to mixing different types of drugs.

Another drug fad reported by these street youth was abuse of over-the-counter Robitussin® cold tablets (DXL), referred to as "robo tripping." One participant reported that ingesting 18 Robitussin cold tablets "made you feel like you were acid tripping." These over-the-counter medications were somewhat costly, and thus, shoplifting was often the means of obtaining them. These youth were not only endangering their health by abusing this medication, but were also breaking the law by shoplifting, and thus, risking an arrest.

Summary

Findings revealed that homeless adolescents fashioned a defined culture of unprecedented freedom and baffling complexity that is neither seen nor imagined by mainstream society. It is a culture with rules but little structure, with values but questionable morality, and with codes but not much consistency. Although street life may generate social capital, it can also be dangerous because of youth's engagement in multiple risk activities, such as drug use and survival sex.

Limitations

The limitations of this study involve the areas of self-report and generalization. The risk of bias is always present in self-reporting. People sometimes tend to romanticize answers to questions while telling life stories. As previously described in the "Methods" section, the principal investigator conducted observations in a variety of settings over an 18-month period during 2001-2002. This study was conducted among a small group of homeless youth ($n = 19$) in a particular city during a particular time frame. Although these youth travel, there is no evidence to support that this study's findings reflect populations of homeless youth in other cities, and therefore, should not be generalized to them. Nevertheless, recent national reports about homeless adolescents describe similar characteristics and issues (National Coalition for the Homeless, 2008; National Runaway Switchboard, 2008). As an ethnographer, the principal investigator's (O'Sullivan Oliveira) active participant observation was limited because of personal safety issues. There had been a rash of violent crimes and victimization against the target group during her study, and the youth expressed concern for her safety if visiting outdoor campsites or squats. Drug-related activities were also off limits. Although the principal investigator spent a considerable amount of time with the youth, she was not present during drug dealings or drug use, and relied upon participant information through informal and formal interviews.

Discussion

By understanding how homeless youth fit into the broader picture of society and their subculture, one can begin to understand some of the ways in which their situation differs from those of other adolescents. Much of the current literature on street youth focuses on them as victims who lack any agency or choice. In this study, however, many of the homeless youth revealed that their decision to live on the streets was a logical and rational alternative to remaining in a dangerous and unstable home environment. This study sample of homeless adolescents ages 16 to 21 years is probably more typical of today's street youth as compared to Coleman-Lundy's (1995) study that focused on transvestites and prostitutes over age 18.

The youth in this study felt better cared for on the streets than at home because of the camaraderie and nurturing within their subculture. Therefore, they were not necessarily opting to be homeless perse, but were selecting a safer and more welcoming environment. The street community offered tangible support through shared resources, such as food, shelter, money, and other basic necessities.

These homeless adolescents also formed nationwide networks that they referred to as a community or family, and whose members were cultivated through Internet communication. They accessed the Internet via computers at public libraries or social service centers, exchanging email addresses and communicating with each other as they traveled across the country. They sought out companionship and acceptance from other youth who came from similar backgrounds, and this spawned a sense of belonging to this street family culture. The more these youth felt embraced by their street family, the longer they remained on the streets.

Homelessness among adolescents is recognized as a social problem of increasing magnitude. Social capital theory provides a useful way to understand the pathways taken by communities to survive and flourish. Social capital refers to positions and relationships in groupings and social networks, including memberships, network ties, and social relations that enhance an individual's access to opportunities, information, material resources, and social status (Ebaugh & Curry, 2000). In the lives of people who are not homeless, personal contacts and networks are sources of social capital used to find jobs, get apartments, locate daycare, and find reliable medical care. The homeless adolescents in this study displayed relationships that emphasized survival and resilience through trustworthiness and exchange of social capital.

Social capital was one of the many resources or types of capital used by these homeless adolescents in daily life. Mobilization of social and human capital occurred most often in the informal economy that operated as part of their street life. Informal economic activities (such as s'panging) were essential to the survival achieved by youth and their street families. Their relationships included street family members who provided social and economic capital, replenishing the capital that had been absent or lost from their mainstream culture. These findings are consistent with what Ferrell and Hamm (1998) described as the phenomenon of street youth capitalizing on a street culture to generate social capital, even though the means to that end entailed illicit activities.

As Taylor-Seefer et al. (2008) noted, "Youth who wind up on the streets are, at times, the strength of the families, as demonstrated by their visions of a better life, conviction that they do not deserve maltreatment and abuse, and ability to pursue and achieve a life with resources, connections, and dreams" (p. S86). Successful coping promotes positive self-esteem that in turn strengthens resilience in homeless youth (Kidd & Shahar, 2008).

Findings from this study indicated that well before their exodus to the streets, these homeless adolescents were engaged in multiple risk activities that were harmful to their health and well being. Clearly, every clinician's encounter with an adolescent is an opportunity for teaching risk/harm reduction. Because homeless youth rarely seek assistance, use of outreach-street workers has been shown to be the most effective way to access these high-risk adolescents. Reaching out to street youth is not an easy task. Many mainstream social service agencies encourage youth to leave the street families/culture and enter into traditional programs. However, some of these youth reported that street life was less menacing than remaining in their homes, where they tended to be more fearful. The street may have been the only positive family unit they trusted, and thus, they were reluctant to leave.

Interdisciplinary collaboration is needed to form networks of care that stimulate positive changes through access to health care, housing, education, and recreation. For some of these youth, survival sex was a means of revenue, which carried a number of physical and mental health risks. Nonjudgmental reproductive health services should be available to these youth, including screening for sexually transmitted diseases (STDs) and easy access to condoms and birthcontrol. In regard to substance use and other risk factors, there is a need to explore the effectiveness of harm reduction/ harm minimization programs rather than focusing exclusively on zero tolerance programs for homeless adolescents (Osgood, Foster, Flanagan, & Ruth, 2005; Single, 1996; Stimson, 1998; Wodack, 1999). Motivational enhancement techniques can be used to help homeless adolescents explore their ambivalence about change (Baer, Garrett, Beadnell, Wells, & Peterson, 2007; Miller & Rollnick, 2002; Peterson et al., 2006).

Homelessness interferes with healthy youth development. Adolescents in general are negotiating new roles to become socially competent. Without appropriate adult guidance, they are at increased risk for engaging in life-threatening behaviors. Homeless youth face multiple risks, including mental health disorders, violence, self mutilation, suicide, homicide, substance abuse, and sexually transmitted diseases (Rew, Chambers, & Kulkarni, 2002; Rew, Grady, Whittaker, & Bowman, 2008; Solorio, Milburn, Andersen, Trifskin, & Rodriguez, 2006; Van Leeuwen, Rietmeijer, LeRoux, White, & Petersen, 2002; Whitbeck et al., 2007).

Health care providers need to be able to recognize and use social capital in the community to help support families and youth in turmoil. Pediatric nurses play a key role in prevention and outreach. Disenfranchised youth who drop out of school lose their primary connection to mainstream society. Thus, truancy is a red flag for possible behavioral or social issues, and may be the first place to intervene in preventing homelessness in the adolescent population. There is a critical need for alternatives for adolescents who run away, are thrown away, or simply age out of the public system of care.

If an adolescent is on the street s, especially during winter months, then it is a good indication that something is wrong at home. Family problems can include physical, emotional, and sexual abuse, as well as neglect.

Homelessness exacerbates common pediatric health conditions, such as asthma, seizure disorders, anemia, skin problems, and obesity, to name a few. However, nurses and helping professionals must keep in mind that high-risk adolescents may initially resist overtures for help and outreach interventions because they are coping with fears from unsuccessful past experiences. Adolescents who leave home because of rigid family rules or harsh parenting practices may avoid structured programs that they perceive as exerting authority and expecting conformity. However, youth living on the streets need ready access to health care and services, such as housing/shelter (options for those under 18 years of age as well as youth-friendly environments), educational opportunities (for acquiring high school diplomas or a GED), job training, food, and facilities for personal hygiene (showers and laundry).

Some youth in this study verbalized plans to eventually leave the streets. Although many of their goals for career and property acquisition seemed unrealistic, they were similar to the goals of domiciled adolescents who live in mainstream society. Adolescents in general tend to be optimistic or somewhat naïve about achieving their goals, and homeless youth were no exception. Of note, however, is the fact that these homeless youth did have personal goals, including a desire to leave the street. Considering their difficult circumstances, the level of optimism that many homeless adolescents had about life was both surprising and impressive.

Conclusion

Assisting homeless adolescents in successfully managing the transition to adulthood is both a challenge and an opportunity for professionals (Osgood et al., 2005). There is no one right approach and no absolute intervention that guarantees success. There are, however, many possibilities. These must be grounded in an authentic human connection focused on genuine caring, mutual respect, enduring patience, and a willingness to work together to create a safe environment in which to learn from life experiences.

References

Alexander, B., & Schrauben, S. (2006). Outside the margins: Youth who are different and their special health care needs. *Primary Care, 33*(2), 285–303.

Armaline, W. (2005). Kids need structure: Negotiating rules, power, and social control in an emergency youth shelter. *American Behavioral Scientist, 48*(8), 1124–1148.

Auerswald, C.L., & Eyre, S.L. (2002). Youth homeless in San Francisco: A life cycle approach. *Social Science & Medicine, 54*, 1497–1512.

Baer, J.S., Garrett, S.B., Beadnell, B., Wells, E.A., & Peterson, P.L. (2007). Brief motivational intervention with homeless adolescents: Evaluating effects on substance use and service utilization. *Psychology of Addictive Behavior s, 21*(4), 582–586.

Barry, P., Ensign, J., & Lippek, S. (2002). Embracing street culture: Fitting health care into the lives of street youth. *Journal of Transcultural Nursing, 13*(2), 145–152.

Brannigan, A., & Caputo, T. (1993). *Runaways and street youth in Canada in the 90s—Revised final report*. Canada: Social Science Consulting.

Coleman-Lundy, K. (1995). *Sidewalk talk—A naturalistic study of street kids*. New York: Garland Publishing, Inc.

Ebaugh, H., & Curry, M. (2000). Fictive kin as social capital in new immigrant communities. *Sociological Perspectives, 43*(2), 189–209.

Ferrell, J., & Hamm, M. (1998). *Ethnography at the edge: Crime, deviance, and field research*. Boston: Northeastern University Press.

Ginzler, J.A., Garrett, S.B., Baer, J. S., & Peterson, P.L. (2007). Measurement of negative consequences of substance use in street youth: An expanded use of the Rutgers Alcohol Problem Index. *Addictive Behaviors, 32*(7), 1519–1525.

Hagan, J., & McCarthy, B. (1997). *Meansteets: Youth crime and homelessness*. New York: Cambridge Press.

Hammer, H., Finkelhor, D., & Sedlak, A. (2002). *Runaways/thrown away children: National estimates and characteristics. National incidence studies of missing, abducted, run away and thrown away children (NIS-MART bulletin series)*. Washington, D. C.: U.S. Department of Justice, Office of Justice Programs, Office of Juvenile and Delinquency Prevention. Retrieved April 13, 2008, from www.ncjrs.org/pdffiles1/ojjdp/196469.pdf

Helman, C. (2000). *Culture, health and illness*. New York: Oxford University Press

Kidd, S., & Scrimenti, K. (2004). Evaluating child and youth homelessness. *Evaluation Review, 28*(4), 325–341.

Kidd, S., & Shahar, G. (2008). Resilience in homeless youth: The key role of self-esteem. *American Journal of Orthopsychiatry, 78*(2), 163–172.

Knopf, D.K., Park, M.J., Brindis, C. D., Mulye, T.P., & Irwin, C.E., Jr. (2007). What gets measured gets done: Assessing data availability for adolescent populations. *Maternal and Child Health Journal, 11*(4), 335–345.

Lincoln, Y.S. & Guba, E.G. (1985). *Naturalistic inquiry*. Newbury Park, CA: Sage.

Milburn, N., Rosenthal, D., Rotherum-Borus, M. J., Mallett, S., Batterham, P., Rice, E., et al. (2007). Newly homeless youth typically return home. *The Journal of Adolescent Health, 40*(6), 574–576.

Miller, W., & Rollnick, S. (2002). *Motivational interviewing: Preparing people for change* (2nd ed). New York: Guilford Press.

Molino, A.C. (2007). *Characteristics of help-seeking street youth and non-street youth*. Retrieved April 16, 2009, from http://www.huduser.org/publications/pdf/p7.pdf

Morse, J.M. (1991). Strategies for sampling. In J.M. Morse (Ed.), *Qualitative nursing research: A contemporary dialogue*. Newbury Park, CA: Sage.

National Center for Missing and Exploited Children. (2000). *Missing, Exploited, and Runaway Children Protection Act, P. L. 106-71, Section 387*. Retrieved April 16, 2009, from http://www.oscn.net/applications/oscn/DeliverDocument.asp?CiteID=406670

National Coalition for the Homeless. (2008). *Homeless youth*. Retrieved April 16, 2009, from http://www.nationalhomeless.org/publications/facts/youth.html

National Network for Youth. (2009). *Who are run away and homeless youth?* Retrieved April 16, 2009, from http://www.nn4youth.org/about-us/faqs-and-other-resourcesNational Runaway Switchboard. (2008).

National Runaway Switchboard 2008 reporter's source book on run away and homeless youth. Retrieved April 16, 2009, from http://www.1800runaway.org/news_events/documents/2008MediaSourcebook_000.pdf

Office for Protection from Research Risks. (1996). *Code of Federal Regulations, Title 45, Part 46*. Retrieved April 16, 2009, from http://www.hhs.gov/ohrp/humansubjects/guidance/45cfr46.htm

Osgood, D.W., Foster, E.M., Flanagan, C., & Ruth, G.R. (2005). *On our own without a net: The transition to adulthood for vulnerable populations*. Chicago: University of Chicago Press.

Peterson, P., Baer, J.S., Wells, E., Ginzler, J.A., & Garrett, S.B. (2006). Short term effects of a brief motivational intervention to reduce alcohol and drug risk among homeless adolescents. *Psychology of Addictive Behaviors:*

Journal of the Society of Psychologist in Addictive Behaviors, 20(3), 254–264.

Raleigh-DuRoff, C. (2004). Factors that influence adolescents to leave or stay living on the street. *Child and Adolescent Social Work Journal, 21*(6), 561–572.

Rew, L. (2008). Caring for and connecting with homeless adolescents. *Family and Community Health, 31*(Suppl. 1), S42–S51.

Rew, L., Chambers, K., & Kulkarni, S. (2002). Planning a sexual health promotion intervention with homeless adolescents. *Nursing Research, 51*(3), 168–174.

Rew, L., Grady, M., Whittaker, T.A., & Bowman, K. (2008). Interaction of duration of homelessness and gender on adolescent sexual health indicators. *Journal of Nursing Scholarship, 40*(2), 109–115.

Rew, L., Taylor-Seehafer, M., & Thomas, N.Y. (2000). Without parental consent: Conducting research with homeless adolescents. *Journal of the Society of Pediatric Nurses, 5*(3), 131–138.

Rice, E., Milburn, N.G., Rotheram-Borus, M.J., Mallett, S., & Rosenthal, D. (2005). The effects of peer group network properties on drug use among homeless youth. *American Behavioral Scientist, 48*(8), 1102–1123.

Robertson, M.J. (1998). *Homeless youth in Hollywood: Patterns of alcohol use.* A Report to the National Institute on Alcohol Abuse and Alcoholism (Report No. C51). Berkeley, CA: University of California, Berkeley.

Robertson, M.J., & Toro, P. (1998). *Homeless youth: Research, intervention, and policy.* Washington, DC: U.S. Department of Housing and Urban Development and U.S. Department of Human Services.

Santelli, J.S., Rogers, A.S., Rosenfeld, W.D., DuRant, R.H., Dubler, N., Morreale, M., et al. (2003). Guidelines for adolescent health research: A position paper of the Society for Adolescent Medicine. *Journal of Adolescent Health Care, 33*(5), 396–409.

Single, E. (1996). Harm reduction as an alcohol prevention strategy. *Alcohol Health Research World, 20*(4), 239–243.

Slesnick, N., Prestopnik, L., Meyers, R., & Glassman, M. (2007). Treatment outcome for street-living, homeless youth. *Addictive Behavior, 32*(6), 1237–1251.

Slavin, P. (2001). *Life on the run, life on the streets.* Retrieved April 16, 2009, from http://www.cwla.org/articles/cv0107life.htm

Smith, H. (2008). Searching for kinship: The creation of street families among homeless youth. *American Behavioral Scientist, 51*(6), 756–771.

Solorio, M., Milburn, N., Andersen, R., Trifskin, S., & Rodriguez, M. (2006). Emotional distress and mental health service use among urban homeless adolescents. *The Journal of Behavioral Health Services & Research, 33*(4), 381–393.

Spradley, J.P. (1979). *The ethnographic interview.* Orlando, FL: Harcourt Brace College.

Spradley, J.P. (1980). *Participant observation.* New York: Holt, Rinehart and Winston.

Stimson, G. (1998). Harm reduction in action: Putting theory into practice. *International Journal of Drug Policy, 9*(6), 401–409.

Taylor-Seehafer, M., Jacobvitz, D., & Steiker, LH. (2008). Patterns of attachment organization, social connectedness, and substance use in a sample of older homeless adolescents. *Family and Community Health, 31*(Suppl. 1), S81–S88.

Van Wormer, R. (2003). Homeless youth seeking assistance: A research-based study from Duluth, Minnesota. *Child & Youth Care Forum, 32*(2), 89–104.

Van Leeuwen, J., Rietmeijer, C., LeRoux, T., White, R., & Petersen, J. (2002). Reaching homeless youths for Chlamydia trachomatis and Neisseria gonorrhea screening in Denver, Colorado. *Sexual Transmitted Infections, 78*(5), 357–359.

Whitbeck, L.B., Hoyt, D.R., Johnson, K.D., & Chen, X. (2007). Victimization and post-traumatic stress disorder among run away and homeless adolescents. *Violence and Victim s, 22*(6), 721–734.

Wodack, A. (1999). What is this thing called harm reduction? *International Journal of Drug Policy, 10*(3), 169–171.

Female Genital Cutting

Crossing Borders

Hazel Barrett

Abstract: Over 140 million girls and women globally have been subjected to the harmful practice of female genital cutting (FGC). While FGC is concentrated in 29 countries in Africa and the Middle East, the practice is spreading to other parts of the world –including Europe and the UK –as international migration continues to increase. It is estimated that 66,000 women living in the UK are affected by FGC, with up to 98,000 girls under the age of 15 being 'at risk' of the procedure, and more than 30,000 of these girls being at 'very high risk'. This article explores the 'Mental Map' of FGC using examples from research undertaken with Somali and Sudanese communities in the UK and Netherlands as part of a Daphne III EC-funded project.[1,2] The article explains how the continuation of FGC is motivated by a complex mix of inter-related socio-cultural factors and how beliefs associated with religion, hygiene and female sexuality combine with social norms and community enforcement mechanisms to perpetuate the practice, despite negative health implications and the fact that the practice is illegal in the EU (including the UK).

Introduction

Female genital cutting (FGC), sometimes labelled female genital mutilation (FGM) or female circumcision, is a deep-rooted traditional practice that adversely affects the health and well-being of millions of girls and women worldwide. It is estimated that 140 million females worldwide have been subjected to FGC, with three million girls at risk each year (UNFPA, 2007; WHO, 2008, 2011; Population Reference Bureau, 2010; Unicef, 2010, 2013; Royal College of Midwives (RCM), 2013).

The practice of FGC is concentrated in 29 countries in Africa and the Middle East, where it is estimated 125 million girls and women have been subjected to FGC (Unicef, 2013). Two-thirds of these girls and women (83 million) live in four countries: Egypt (27.2 million), Ethiopia (23.8 million), Nigeria (19.9 million) and Sudan (12.1 million) (Unicef, 2013). Unicef (2013) states that an additional 30 million girls and women are at risk of FGC in these 29 countries over the next decade. Prevalence rates of FGC vary between these 29 countries –ranging from 98% in Somalia to 1% in Cameroon and Uganda. Unicef has placed these countries into five groups according to FGC prevalence levels amongst females aged 15 to 49 (see Table 7.3.1).

Due to increases in international migration, the practice of FGC is no longer restricted to the 29 countries of Africa and the Middle East where

TABLE 7.3.1 **Groupings of the 29 countries where female genital cutting is concentrated, by FGC prevalence levels amongst females aged 15 to 49. Adapted from: Unicef, 2013, p. 27.**

Groupings by FGC prevalence level (15–49 year-old females)	FGC prevalence rate	Number and name of countries in this group
Group 1: Very high	>80%	8: Djibouti, Egypt, Eritrea, Guinea, Mali, Sierra Leone, Somalia, Sudan
Group 2: Moderately high	51–80%	5: Burkina Faso, Ethiopia, Gambia, Liberia, Mauritania
Group 3: Moderately low	26–50%	6: Chad, Guinea-Bissau, Ivory Coast, Kenya, Nigeria, Senegal
Group 4: Low	10–25%	4: Benin, Central African Republic, Tanzania, Yemen
Group 5: Very low	<10%	6: Cameroon, Ghana, Iraq, Niger, Togo, Uganda

FGC is concentrated (Equality Now, 2012). FGC is occurring in other parts of the world, including Asia (particularly Malaysia and Indonesia), North America, Australasia and Europe (see Figure 7.3.1). Although there are no reliable statistics for the prevalence of FGC in Europe, the European Parliament believes the practice is a serious issue in those EU Member States (including the UK) that are home to significant numbers of migrants from high-prevalence countries. In 2009, the European Parliament estimated that up to half a million women living in the European Union had been subjected to

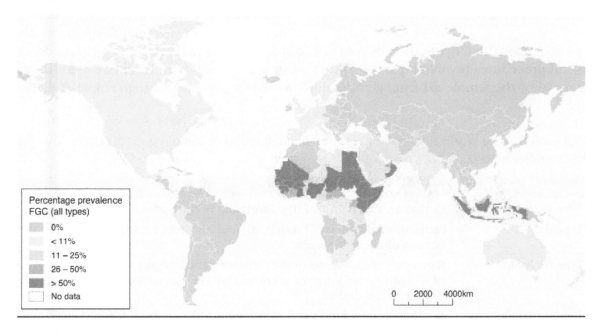

Percentage prevalence FGC (all types)

- 0%
- < 11%
- 11 – 25%
- 26 – 50%
- > 50%
- No data

0   2000   4000km

FIGURE 7.3.1 World-wide prevalence of female genital cutting, 2011.
SOURCE: Women's Database, 2011.

FGC, with a further 180,000 at risk (European Parliament, 2009).

It is known that FGC is practised in the UK (RCM, 2013). A study published in 2007, based on the UK 2001 Census, estimated that 66,000 women in England and Wales had undergone FGC, and 23,000 girls under the age of 15 were at risk (Dorkenoo *et al.*, 2007). Another study, again using the UK 2001 Census but together with birth registration data from 1993 to 2004, suggests that over 98,376 girls under the age of 15 living in the UK have been subject to or are at risk of FGC (Equality Now, 2012). These figures are, according to the Royal College of Midwives, 'alarming' (2013, p. 10). The number of girls at risk of FGC in the UK is growing as the births to women affected by FGC have increased –from 1.04% in 2001 to 1.67% in 2008 (Equality Now, 2012; RCM, 2013). According to the Royal College of Midwives, FGC is a 'hidden phenomenon' in the UK.

FGC: Definition and Classification

The World Health Organisation defines FGC as: 'all procedures involving partial or total removal of the female external genitalia or other injury to the female genital organs for non-medical reasons' (2008, p. 4). WHO recognise four types of FGC (described in Table 7.3.2). Types I to III reflect increasing invasiveness of the cutting, while Type IV includes unclassified genital injuries where flesh is not removed but bleeding occurs. EndFGM (2010) estimates that globally, of females who have been affected by FGC, 90% have been subjected to Types I, II and IV, with 10% subjected to the more serious Type III which predominates in Sudan and Somalia.

Table 3 indicates the diversity of FGC performed within a selection of countries. For example, despite having an FGC prevalence in excess of 90%, in Somalia 63% of girls under 15 years old have been subjected to FGC Type III; whereas in Djibouti the proportion is 30%. This illustrates the difficulties of using a single term, female genital cutting, to refer to the range of FGC practices.

In the UK a recent study estimating the numbers of girls under 15 with or at risk of FGC indicates that all types of FGC are present in the UK (Equality Now, 2012). Furthermore, this study suggests that over 24,000 girls under the age of 15 have or are at risk of FGC Type III, with a further 9000 girls at high risk of FGC Type

TABLE 7.3.2 **The World Health Organisation classification of female genital cutting by type. Adapted from: WHO, 2008; Unicef, 2013.**

FGC classification	Procedure may include
Type I: Clitoridectomy	Partial or total removal of the clitoris and/or the prepuce
Type II: Excision	Partial or total removal of the clitoris and labia minora, with or without excision of the labia majora
Type III: Infibulation	Narrowing of the vaginal orifice by cutting and bringing together the labia minora and/or labia majora to create a type of seal, with or without the excision of the clitoris
Type IV: Symbolic circumcision	All other harmful procedures to the female genitals for non-medical purposes, for example, pricking, piercing, incising, scraping, cauterising

TABLE 7.3.3 Percentage of girls who have undergone FGC, by type (see Table 7.3.2), as reported by their mother. After: Unicef, 2013.

Country	Type as a percentage of total FGC			FGC prevalence rate (15–49 years)
	Type IV	Types I and II	Type III	
Benin	2	95	2	13
Djibouti	15	53	30	93
Eritrea	52	6	38	89
Mali	16	71	3	89
Nigeria	16	69	6	27
Somalia	5	25	63	98
Tanzania	1	98	2	15

TABLE 7.3.4 Estimated numbers of girls aged under 15 living in England and Wales with or at risk of FGC by type of FGC. Adapted from: Equality Now, 2012, p. 25.

Countries of heritage by Unicef FGC grouping	Level of risk	Number of girls under 15 affected by FGC		
		born in country	born in England and Wales	Total
Group 1	High risk of FGC Type III	6800	17,212	24,012
Group 1 and 2	High risk of FGC Type I or II	1972	6941	8913
Group 3 and 4	Medium risk FGC Type I or II	2346	13,488	15,834
Group 4 and 5	Low risk FGC Type I or II	7622	41,995	49,617
Total		**18,740**	**79,636**	**98,376**

I or II, and in excess of 65,000 girls at low or medium risk of FGC (Table 7.3.4). This study also highlights that over 80% of girls under 15 years old with or at risk of FGC have been born in England or Wales, and almost 72% of girls with or at risk of Type III having been born in England or Wales. British citizens and permanent residents are continuing to be victims of FGC, despite the procedure being made illegal in the UK in 1985, and with an extra-territoriality clause (added in 2003) making it illegal for a British citizen or permanent resident to have the procedure performed overseas.

FGC: A Traditional Harmful Practice

Health Impacts

There are many studies which demonstrate a significant association between FGC and various gynaecological and pregnancy complications (Okonofua, 2006). Succeeding WHO Reports (2000, 2006, 2011) conclude that FGC has negative implications for women's health –with women who have undergone FGC being more likely than others to have adverse obstetric outcomes. FGC has no health benefits and, as Figure 7.3.2 shows, it harms girls and women in many ways, both physically and mentally (WHO, 2008).

The health impacts on girls and women subjected to FGC occurs at the time of the procedure as well as later into adulthood, particularly motherhood (UNFPA 2007). The effects are both physical as well as mental: all types of FGC have immediate health risks such as excessive bleeding, septicaemia, death and HIV transmission (Cook *et al.*, 2002). There are, however, differing long-term health impacts between FGC types. Types I and IV, whilst presenting risks, do allow a speedy recovery, unimpaired urination, menstruation and sexual intercourse in later years. However, Types II and III are likely to have the most serious health implications. These may include urinary tract infections, chronic pelvic infections resulting in infertility, scar and tissue cysts, painful intercourse, complications in pregnancy and childbirth, post-partum haemorrhage, foetal distress and death and obstetric fistulae (a hole between the bladder and/or rectum and the vagina). Indeed, Type III FGC

is a significant causal factor in maternal death where delivery is unattended or obstructed labour is not appropriately treated (WHO, 2000). Studies suggest that the vulval scarring associated with FGC is a significant contributory factor in many foetal deaths (WHO, 2000). All forms of FGC can have psychological affects, particularly related to female sexuality and sexual relationships. Figure 7.3.2 shows the possible impacts of Types I, II and III FGC on female health, infant and maternal mortality. There is little doubt that FGC has a negative effect on female health as well as being a violation of female human rights.

In 1979 the World Health Organisation held its first conference on FGC, which recommended that the practice be totally eliminated. The Conference participants advocated the official involvement of the international health and development assistance communities in supporting programmes to stop FGC (Toubia and Sharief, 2003). In the 15 years that followed, programmes aimed at reducing FGC emphasised the health risks of the practice, because this was

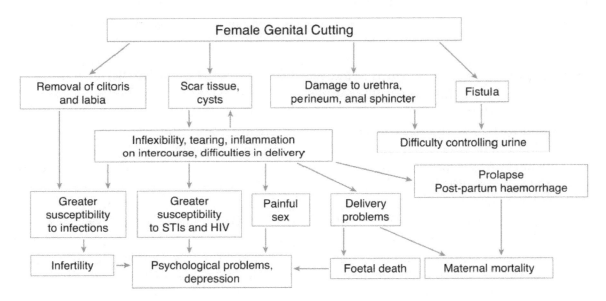

FIGURE 7.3.2 The health impacts of FGM Types I, II and III. Adapted from: Morison et al., 2001, p. 645; Cook et al., 2002; WHO, 2008.

felt to be the most acceptable and sensitive way to approach the problem. However, by the 1990s the emphasis on the health consequences of the practice had begun to decrease –partly because the campaigns had not resulted in significant reductions in FGC prevalence, but also because the focus on health had inadvertently promoted the medicalisation of the practice, with FGC increasingly being carried out by medical professionals (Unicef, 2013).

A Violation of Human Rights

During the early 1990s, FGC was reconceptualised as a human rights issue. At the World Conference on Human Rights held in Vienna in 1993, gender-based violence (including FGC) was accepted as a violation of human rights. The United Nations classify the practice of FGC as a violation of human rights, in particular as a violation of female reproductive health rights (UNFPA, 2007; WHO, 2008). Unicef, UNFPA, UNIFEM and WHO all recognise FGC as a form of violence against girls and women (Toubia and Sharief, 2003; Unicef, 2010). Figure 7.3.3 lists the main elements of the human rights approach to FGC.

- Right to physical and mental integrity
- Right to the highest attainable standard of health
- Freedom from discrimination on the basis of sex including violence against women
- Rights of the child
- Freedom from torture, cruel, inhuman and degrading treatment
- Right to life (when the procedure results in death)

FIGURE 7.3.3 Internationally accepted list of human rights abuses associated with female genital cutting. Adapted from: EndFGM, 2010.

The human rights approach emphasises the criminalisation of FGC, with Unicef regarding legislation and enforcement as a crucial component in the ending of FGC. As a result of this reconcept ualisation of FGC, 26 countries in Africa and the Middle East have prohibited FGC by law or constitutional decree. The list includes South Africa and Zambia, neither of which are among the 29 countries where FGC is concentrated. Five of the countries where FGC is concentrated have not enacted legislation related to FGC, these are: Cameroon, Gambia, Liberia, Mali and Sierra Leone. Even in those countries where legislation has been enacted, challenges remain with enforcement of the law with, in 2012, only seven of these countries having reported cases of FGC, and resulting in only four prosecutions (Unicef, 2013). The most aggressive application of the law in 2012 occurred in Eritrea where 155 cutters and parents were convicted and fined. In Burkina Faso in 2012, seven cases of FGC involving 33 girls under 15 years of age –four of whom died –were recorded. To date, only eight cutters have been convicted. In addition, legislation prohibiting FGC has been adopted in 33 other countries, its principal aim is to protect children with cultural links to practising countries (UNFPA-Unicef, 2012). This includes the Member States of the EU.

The European Union frames FGC as domestic violence against females, a violation of human rights and a form of discrimination against females. Most EU Member States have criminal legislation which defines the practice of FGC as an offence; and Austria, Belgium, Cyprus, Denmark, Italy, Portugal, Spain, Sweden and the UK all have specific provisions associated with FGC. Other Member States address FGC under general criminal law, such as grievous bodily harm. Most also have an extra-territoriality clause. However, there have been few convictions in the EU, thus indicating that the law is not being enforced.

Female genital cutting has been a criminal offence in the UK since 1985, when the Prohibition of Female Circumcision Act came into force. This was replaced in 2003 by the Female Genital Mutilation Act (updated to address FGC performed on UK citizens and permanent residents outside the UK), with a maximum 14 years imprisonment penalty. To date there have been no prosecutions in the UK, although three doctors have been found to have committed serious professional misconduct by the General and the Dental Medical Council in relation to FGC and have been struck off the GDMC Register (RCM, 2013).

UK law treats FGC as child abuse and as such frontline professionals, including doctors, nurses, teachers, social workers and others have a legal duty to protect girls from FGC. It is the Local Safeguarding Children's Boards that have the responsibility for developing inter-agency policies and procedures for safeguarding and promoting the welfare of children, which covers FGC. There is evidence that child-protection guidelines are not being followed when girls affected by FGC are identified (RCM, 2013). In 2013 the NSPCC launched a national FGM helpline for children at risk and as a point of reference for the public and professionals to report concerns. In the first three months of the setting up of the helpline, 102 enquiries were received and 38 referrals made to the police (RCM, 2013). This indicates a serious under-reporting of FGC in the UK by those who have undergone or are at risk of the procedure, as well as those who encounter FGC professionally.

FGC: Why Does It Persist?

The origins of FGC are unknown; it does not appear to be connected to any particular religion or culture and is performed by both Christian and Muslim communities. According to Unicef, 'female genital mutilation/cutting has been perpetuated over generations by social dynamics' (2007, p. 2). All communities where it is common are highly patriarchal, with FGC often defended as a rite of passage from girlhood into womanhood and preparation for marriage (Unicef, 2007; 2010). The practice is used to curb female sexual desire and protect virginity. In some communities it is justified for health and hygiene reasons, 'purity' being a word often used.

Female genital cutting is a practice which occurs among all socio-economic groups with widespread support from women (Cook et al., 2002). The procedure is usually performed on girls from infancy to 15 years, but in some communities takes place at an older age (WHO, 2008). This depends on local rituals and customs. The ritual is usually performed by traditional practitioners who have no formal medical training and who perform the operation in non-sterile conditions using blades and razors (UNFPA, 2007; Unicef, 2013). It is often performed on groups of girls at the same time, with a risk of cross-infection. Support for the practice comes from mothers, mothers-in-law, fathers, and religious and community leaders (Shaaban and Harbison, 2005).

As FGC decisions are made within and influenced by the broader social and political context, which WHO have conceptualised as an FGC 'Mental Map'. The 'map' in Figure 7.3.4 demonstrates how beliefs (sometimes false, or myths) surrounding religion, hygiene, aesthetics and social acceptance combine to support

FIGURE 7.3.4 The FGC 'Mental Map'. Source: WHO, 1999, p. 7.

decision-making in communities that practice FGC. Figure 7.3.4 further illustrates that even when such beliefs are changed, overarching beliefs relating to the protection of chastity and family honour through FGC continue to influence decision-making in favour of FGC. These are referred to as 'community enforcement mechanisms'. This FGC 'Mental Map'

acknowledges that FGC is not the decision of an individual, but an act done to an individual (with or without consent) as a result of community convention or pressure, which will vary in different communities.

The FGC 'Mental Map' is illustrated by research undertaken with Somali and Sudanese communities in the UK, and the Netherlands

TABLE 7.3.5 **Terms used by UK and Dutch Somali and Sudanese communities when referring to FGC.**

SOURCE *BARRETT* et al., 2011, p. 56.

Term used by participants	English translation	WHO FGC classification (see Table 7.3.2)
Gudnin/Gudniinka (Somali)	Female or male circumcision	—
Gudniinka gabdhaha	Female circumcision	—
Gudniika Pharaonica (Somali) *Kutairi*	Pharaonic circumcision Usually refers to male circumcision, but is also used to refer to female circumcision	Type III —
Kukeketwa	Female circumcision	—
Khitan (Sudanese)	Circumcision (can be used to refer to female or male circumcision)	—
Khitan al-rejaal (Sudanese)	Male circumcision	
Khitan al enaath	Female circumcision	—
Halaalayn (Sudanese)	From the Arabic word 'halal'. Purification (can refer to female and male circumcision)	—
Aladdia (Sudanese)	Re-infibulation	Type III. Women are closed after childbirth
Pharanoi tahoor (Sudanese)	Pharaonic circumcision/infibulation	Type III
Tahoor (Sudanese)	Female and male circumcision	—
Tahara (Sudanese) 'Extreme', 'heavy' or 'bad one' (Somali)	Cleanliness/purification Pharaonic circumcision/infibulation	— Type III
'Old one' (Somali)	Pharaonic circumcision/infibulation	Type III
'Big' *sunna* (Somali)	Blessings	Type II or III
'Small' *sunna*	Blessings	Type I or II
'Light', 'small', 'soft' or 'half' *sunna* (Somali and Sudanese)	Blessings	Type I
Sunna (Somali and Sudanese) Female genital mutilation	Blessings (can refer to female and male circumcision) Pharaonic circumcision/infibulation	Type I or II Type III

(Barrett *et al.*, 2011). The psycho-sexual and social reasons for the practice are clearly illustrated by the diverse terms these communities used to refer to different types of FGC.[3] The research identified 19 different terms used by members of these communities. These terms are listed in Table 7.3.5 together with their English translation and WHO FGC type. Terms which translate to 'circumcision' were most frequently used; and terms such as *gudnin, kutari, khitan* and *tahoor* may be used to refer to both male and female circumcision. This suggests that some communities equate female circumcision with male circumcision and thus emphasise the religious and hygiene aspects of the practice –as this Somali man living in the UK explains:

> *'Physical practice … for a woman … she's … you know … cutting a bit of foreskin off her vagina … a little bit, not, not, not a lot'* (18–23 year old participant).

The second most commonly-used term, *sunna*, translates as 'blessings', which has very strong religious links. A Sudanese woman living in the UK stated:

> *'Sunna it's the same thing as the man, like in Islam we do, we cut the begin things of the man, and the woman as well, just a tiny bit just to clean it that's all, which is, it is something alright'* (18–23 year old participant).

Other terms, such as *halaalayn* and *tahara*, stress the link between FGC and 'purification'. One UK Sudanese woman explains that she believes FGC is benefical: 'for keeping women clean and eliminating bad smells' (60–65 year old participant). The terms used for FGC Type III (infibulation) include *pharanai tahoor* and *big sunna*. A Dutch-Somali woman described this practice:

> *'In the pharonic one, the whole clitoral hood and both labias have been removed then they pour malmal [a traditional herb] and other flora in order to attach it together'* (60–65 year old participant).

This type of FGC is clearly linked to societal expectations of female sexuality and is often justified on religious grounds. It is interesting to note that this type of FGC was also referred to as the 'extreme', 'heavy' or 'bad' one and the 'old one', indicating that many members of these communities do not agree with the practice of infibulation (FGC Type III). However, *sunna* was viewed positively –with women who have undergone *sunna* often regarded as 'a good Muslim woman' –as this Dutch-Somali man comments:

> *'if she follows [has sunna] that, it just shows that she's more religious, she's practising, she's not fake… I see the one [that has sunna] as having a higher degree of faith to the one who doesn't'* (18–24 year old participant).

This last statement illustrates that support for FGC is a matter of social convention, which is, in turn, reinforced by real or perceived community enforcement mechanisms.

As the community enforcement mechanisms associated with the continuation of FGC are often religious as well as social, individuals find it very difficult to refuse to conform. FGC is thus a procedure undertaken on an individual, and which is condoned by families in order to conform to social norms and community enforcement mechanisms. These may include ones that allow their daughters to access social networks and resources, such as marriage partners. Family honour and social expectations play a powerful role in perpetuating FGC, which makes it very difficult for individuals or their families to stop the practice. Failure to conform to FGC norms can lead to social exclusion, ostracism or even violence, and it inevitably affects the standing of the family within the community. Conformity on the other hand meets with social approval, brings respect and admiration and maintains social standing in the community. The situation is well summarised by Unicef:

> *'Even when parents recognise that FGM/C can cause serious harm, the*

practice persists because they fear moral judgements and social sanctions should they decide to break with society's expectations. Parents often believe that continuing FGM/C is a lesser harm than dealing with these negative repercussions' (2010, p. 3).

Conclusion

The elimination of FGC has proven very difficult. This deep-rooted cultural tradition is very resistant to change. Despite campaigns designed to explain to communities the health implications of the rite, and the criminalisation of the practice in many countries, FGC has continued. As international migration increases, the practice has crossed borders and now is on the rise in many European countries, including the UK. Ending FGC is not going to be easy, simply because, as this article has shown, its continuation is motivated by a complex mix of socio-cultural factors, *viz* a combination of beliefs associated with religion, hygiene, female sexuality, social acceptance and community enforcement. As Toubia and Sharief state, FGC is: 'located in the realm of social structures and gender power relations in relation to sexuality' (2003, p. 260).

In December 2012 the United Nations General Assembly unanimously passed a resolution: 'Intensifying global efforts for the elimination of female genital mutilation'. This resolution urged all UN Member States to:

> *'take measures to accelerate the ending of FGC, to pass and enforce legislation banning the practice, to raise awareness about the effects of FGC and to allocate adequate resources to protecting girls*

and women from this form of violence' (UNFPA-Unicef, 2012, resolution 67/146).

This resolution is regarded as 'a milestone in global efforts to end the practice' (Unicef, 2013, p. 4); the target is to end FGC within one generation (UNFPA-Unicef, 2012).

Notes

1   The research reported here formed part of REPLACE1 EC-funded project through Daphne III (see website for further information).
2   This article reports on the author's research which formed the focus of a session at the GA's Annual Conference in Derby in April 2013.
3   The identity of all participants in the research reported here has been anonymised.

References

Barrett, H.R., Brown, K., Beecham, D., Otoo-Oyortey, N. and Naleie, S. (2011) *Pilot toolkit for replacing approaches to ending FGM in the EU: implementing behaviour change with practising communities.* Coventry: REPLACE, Coventry University.

Cook, R.J., Dickens, B.M. and Fathalla, M.F. (2002) 'Female genital cutting (mutilation/circumcision): ethical and legal dimensions', *International Journal of Gynaecology and Obstetrics*, 79, pp. 281–7.

Daphne III: *http://ec.europa.eu/justice/grants/programmes/daphne/* (last accessed 26 November 2013).

Dorkenoo, E., Morison, L. and Macfarlane, A. (2007) *A Statistical Study to Estimate the Prevalence of FGM in England and Wales.* London: FORWARD.

EndFGM (2010) *Ending Female Mutilation: a strategy for the European Union Institutions.* Brussels: EndFGM.

Equality Now (2012) *Female Genital Mutilation: Report of a research methodology workshop on estimating prevalence of FGM in England and Wales (22–23 March 2012)*. London: Equality Now.

European Parliament (EP) (2009) *European Parliament Resolution on Combating FGM in the EU*. 24 March 2009 (2008/2071(INI)). Brussels: EU.

Morison, L., Scherf, C., Ekpo, G., Paine, K., West, B., Coleman, R. and Walraven, G. (2001) 'The long-term reproductive health consequences of Female Genital Cutting in rural Gambia: a community-based survey', *Tropical Medicine and International Health*, 6, 8, pp. 643–53.

Okonofua, F. (2006) 'FGM and reproductive health in Africa', *African Journal of Reproductive Health*, 10, 2, pp. 7–9.

Population Reference Bureau (PRB) (2010) *Female Genital mutilation/Cutting: data and trends*. Available online at *www.prb.org/pdf10/fgm-wallchart2010.pdf* (last accessed 3 February 2011).

Royal College of Midwives (RCM) (2013) *Tackling FGM in the UK*. London: Royal College of Midwives.

Shaaban, L.M. and Harbison, S. (2005) 'Reaching the tipping point against FGM', *The Lancet*, 366, pp. 347–9.

Toubia, N.F. and Sharief, E.H. (2003) 'FGM: have we made progress?', *International Journal of Gynaecology and Obstetrics*, 82, pp. 251–61.

Unicef (2007) *Coordinated Strategy to Abandon Female Genital Mutilation/Cutting in One Generation*. New York, NY: Unicef.

Unicef (2010) *FGM/C Prevalence Among Women 15-49 as of 1st October 2010: Unicef global databases based on data from MICS, DHS and other national surveys, 1997–2009*. New York, NY: Unicef.

Unicef (2013) *Female Genital Mutilation/Cutting: a statistical overview and exploration of the dynamics of change*. New York, NY: Unicef.

UNFPA (2007) *A Holistic Approach to the Abandonment of FGM/cutting*. New York, NY: UNFPA.

UNFPA-Unicef (2012) *Joint Programme on Female Genital Mutilation/Cutting: accelerating change. Annual Report 2012*. New York, NY: UNFPA-Unicef.

World Health Organisation (WHO) (1999) *Female Genital Mutilation: Programmes to date. What works and what doesn't*. Geneva: Department of Women's Health, WHO.

WHO (2000) *A Systematic Review of the Health Complications of FGM*. Geneva: Department of Women's Health, Family and Community Health, WHO.

WHO (2006) 'FGM and obstetric outcome: WHO collaborative study in six African countries', *The Lancet*, 367, pp. 1799–1800.

WHO (2008) *FGM WHO Fact Sheet 241*. Available online at *www.who.int/mediacentre/factsheets/fs241/en/print.html* (last accessed 12 September 2011).

WHO (2011) *An update on WHO's work on FGM: Progress Report*. Geneva: WHO.

Reflexive Questions

1. Looking back on your teen years, what factors strengthened you and which ones created vulnerability?

2. To what extent did your high school perpetuate heteronormativity and hetero-romanticism? How did these hegemonic (imposed ideology of the dominant group) norms affect straight and LGBT students differently?

3. How were LGBT students treate[...] [...]ss to a Gay-Straight Alliance (GSA)? If so[...]

4. What are the values, fears, and w[...]ensive sex education in schools? How wo[...]cation mitigate sexual problems for teens[...]

5. How does a culture and climate of [...] mar-ginalization affect a teen and young[...]

6. What social and familial factors put [...]ng homeless?

7. How do you think living on the stre[...] [...]e development, sense of self, and life outcomes for teens? What resources [...]uld they need to get out of that way of life?

8. What are some reasons why girls and women do not have say over what happens to their bodies?

9. When considering the practice of FGC, what values, beliefs, and ideologies create and perpetuate this practice?

10. How are organizations and governments trying to eliminate FGC? What else can be done to eliminate it?

11. Overall, why are harmful or life-threatening things done to girls and women and their bodies?

12. What are driving forces for gender-based violence like intimate partner terrorism, femi-cide, and genital mutilation, as well as queer-based violence such as targeted murders of trans women and trans teens of color?

CHAPTER 8

Emerging and Young Adulthood

Introduction

Young adulthood is commonly thought of as a time between the ages of 18 and 25 (some say 30). During this time of life, most adults enjoy the benefits of optimal physical, cognitive, and psychosocial development. This is a time when most adults begin to have a stronger sense of self, explore possibilities, and gain a clearer understanding of their place within the contexts of their lives. Jeffrey Arnett was the first to coin the term emerging adulthood (2000, 2001). Based on his empirical studies, he began to theorize this age period as a distinct developmental period in which a person feels like they are in an in-between stage (Arnett, Kloep, Hendry, & Tanner, 2011), no longer feeling like a teen, but not fully feeling like an adult. Arnett examined adolescence and emerging adulthood from a cultural approach (2004), applying the theory across social classes in the United States (2016). His work has been applied internationally and has generated countless studies over the last two decades.

This work has been important to the area of adult development, and there is evidence to suggest that this life stage is mitigated by culture (Schwartz & Pantin, 2006). Similar to the young adults in the United States, Sirsch et al. (2009) found that young adults in Austria also identified young adulthood as an in-between stage; however, in a study conducted by Nelson, Badger, & Wu (2004) with college students in China, the majority stated that they did, in fact, reach adult status in their early twenties. Their adult status was influenced by cultural values and actions that were different from young adults in Western cultures. Similarly, Fierro Arias & Moreno Hernández (2007) conducted a study with a Mexican and Spanish sample and found mixed findings. Young adults from Mexico and Spain were sure about when adolescence ended for them, but less sure about when adulthood began. Overall, researchers caution scholars not to generalize this life stage to all cultures, given that there are vast differences in educational and work opportunities and that emerging adulthood descriptors are particular to certain conditions and social groups, as Arnett (2004) suggests. They state that perhaps there might be more emerging adulthood qualities across cultures for those who live in urban areas and are highly educated and exposed to globalization and new technologies. Nevertheless, regardless of how young adults define or perceive adulthood and navigate material realities, most young adults will experience optimal cognitive and physical abilities compared to their earlier and later years. What most of us cannot predict are the countless factors that will mitigate our development into middle adulthood and far into our futures.

While many young adults have hopes and dreams for their futures, structural and systemic oppression are strong social forces that youth internalize to their own detriment. By the time a person has reached young adulthood, they have unknowingly internalized and accepted societal messages that further oppress and limit possibilities for their lives. Internalized oppression is the toxic process by which we accept discriminatory and stereotypical sociocultural beliefs about who we are and what we can and cannot do based on our intersecting identities (David, 2014). The effects of this process are harmful to everyone, but especially to young people who are still developing their sense of self.

Perhaps the most studied externalized and internalized forms of oppression are racism (James, 2017), sexism (Bearman, Korobov, & Thorne, 2009), homo/trans/biphobia (Nadal & Mendoza, 2014; Williamson, 2000), and ableism (Campbell, 2008). Scholars have studied the legacy of slavery (O'Connell, 2020) and how it is still felt today as attitudes of White supremacy infiltrate every domain of life. McIntosh (2015) states that because many White people are unaware of the legacy of slavery and systemic racism, they often do not recognize the privilege and power they hold because of their skin color. Consequently, as young people from ethnic and racial minoritized groups increase social comparisons, they often blame themselves (i.e., internalized racism) for not "measuring up" to their peers, who successfully launch into adulthood according to White, middle-class standards and accumulate countless structural and systemic advantages for the unearned privilege of being White. The negative effects of these unfair social comparisons most strongly affect people with less social status, such as women, LGBTQ+ people, people of color, and people of other marginalized identities. On a broader level, sexism and misogyny continue to be strong social forces that negatively affect girls and women worldwide—of every race, culture, nationality, age, sexual orientation, and social status.

Sexism and misogyny are universal oppressive forces that harm girls and women. According to the World Health Organization (2020), gender inequality is pervasive worldwide and negatively affects girls and women in every realm of life. Ambivalent sexism theory helps us unravel the confusing and complex nature of gender inequality and sexism (Glick & Fiske, 1996). This theory posits that sexism is composed of two seemingly opposite domains, benevolent and hostile sexism. Benevolent sexism captures seemingly positive attitudes toward women in traditional roles (e.g., women are nice, warm, and nurturing), and hostile sexism/misogyny captures negative attitudes toward women (e.g., women are weak, deceptive, manipulative, and cannot be leaders). Glick and Fiske contend that hostile and benevolent sexism operate together to sustain masculine control/dominance and feminine submissiveness and serve to keep women in subordinate positions. Although women may appear to "win" with benevolent sexism, like when men are chivalrous and treat women like "a lady," these attitudes keep women in a one-down position and prevent them from being treated as equal to men. This minority status is evident in romantic and familial relationships, the workforce, politics, corporations, the military, and other professional places where women are blocked from having individual, interpersonal, institutional, and structurally reinforced power. Because sexism is socially and structurally created and maintained, women internalize these attitudes for themselves and often unknowingly impose them onto other women (Ellis & Bermudez, 2020).

Another topic important to note for emerging adults is embodiment. The term embodiment was first coined by French philosopher Merleau-Ponty (1962), who wrote about the body as a social agent. He stated that all of our perceptions and experience of the world are embodied. People of all genders and body types are affected by societal norms, beliefs, and expectations about our bodies and the amount of space, and the spaces and places we occupy. For example, many spaces are still separated by gender (e.g., binary bathrooms and places of worship), and women are still relegated to inferior spaces or restricted from men's spaces. Additionally, men and women take up space differently, as men are taught to take up space (e.g., "manspreading") and women to take up less space. Furthermore, in terms of women's bodies, feminist scholars such as Chrisler and Johnston-Robledo (2018) review the current theories and literature on female embodiment and discuss how girls and women can resist negative embodiment and the never-ending and impossible standards of beauty that objectify, harm, and oppress them. Body positivity is an important stance for everyone, regardless of their gender, age, or life stage.

Lastly, many women and their personhood are still considered the property of men. For many living today, fathers and husbands are still afforded legal authority over their daughters and wives and their bodies. Women's bodies are often used as commodities to be trafficked, sold, traded, purchased, and consumed for personal use and profit. Women's bodies continue to be sites of control and contention—materially, legally, and symbolically. In a collection of essays, Fischer and Delezal (2018) and Conboy, Medina, and Stanbury (1997) offer critical reflections about issues that continue to strongly effect women's lives—pregnancy, reproductive technologies, commercial surrogacy, sexual violence, eating disorders, body shaming, dowries, the beauty industry, the pornography industry, sexual objectification, body politics, transsexuality, transnationality, motherhood, and sex trafficking, among others. They contend that neoliberalism exacerbates and fuels these problems in which women's bodies are used as sites of control and human capital. My hope is that the readings in this chapter will offer insights into the effects of embodiment, space, and place by taking a closer look at emerging adults' sexual decision-making, disability status, and unauthorized immigration status.

Summary of Readings

In the reading "**Agency and Error in Young Adults' Stories of Sexual Decision Making**" (2008), Allen, Husser, Stone, and Jordal explore how young adults perceive their sexual decision-making and histories. Given our current realities, youth are primarily informed about sex through electronic media. Media such as advertising, the internet, films, social media, and pornography often perpetuate contradictory messages and promote and challenge gendered expectations. To study the complex territory of sexual attitudes and behaviors, the authors collected data from 148 young adults in college who answered written, open-ended questions about their sexual behavior and identified four main attitudes about their sexual decision-making. Findings in this study show that college students consider their adolescent experiences important building blocks for constructing their current ideas about sexual agency; however, their sexual contexts adhered to gendered and heteronormative expectations for women and men. The authors contend that if young adults begin exploring their sexuality without adequate, accurate information about sex, the sexual double standard will continue, and young adults will be ill-equipped to navigate risks and responsibilities, such as unwanted pregnancy and sexually transmitted infections.

In the reading "**Emerging Adults With Disabilities: Theory, Trends, and Implications**" (2015), Jill Meyer and colleagues examine the principles and expectations of emerging adulthood and how disabled young adults face unique challenges when navigating these expectations. First, the reading details how the journey of young adults today, disabled and otherwise, differs from past generations. The milestones of adulthood, such as graduating from high school, going to college or getting a job, finding a partner, and starting a family, now occur in an extended, more complicated period, often at a later age than past generations. Meyer and colleagues outline the five principles of emerging adulthood and explore how these principles manifest themselves in the lives of young adults with differing abilities. For example, uncertainty is particularly salient in a disabled adult's decision, or ability, to leave home, and they are twice as likely to be living with their parents. The authors contend that people who demonstrate self-determination are more likely to live outside the family home, have greater independence, and report a higher quality of life. Additionally, despite the uncertainty of emerging adulthood, optimism and understanding how emerging adults cope with and manage stress may lead to improved services that facilitate and support youth with disabilities to manage developmental challenges. The authors offer important recommendations for counselors that apply to everyone, regardless of their abilities.

In the reading "**My Life as a DREAMer who ACTed Beyond the Barriers: From Growing Up 'Undocumented' in Arizona to a Master's Degree From Harvard**" (2010), Silvia P. Rodríguez Vega shares her journey through university education as a DREAM Act student. The DREAM Act, or the Development, Relief, and Education for Alien Minors Act, aimed to establish a path to citizenship for children of undocumented immigrants. This reading is the story of a woman who was the child of undocumented immigrants. As a child, she had a similar life to her friends, but as she got older, she was confronted with obstacles that affected her future opportunities. Due to Proposition 300, she lost her college scholarship but went on to earn her bachelor's and master's degrees. Even after graduating from Harvard, she faced more obstacles but persevered. Despite feelings of uncertainty about her future and frustration with these barriers, Vega persisted in achieving her goals. Ultimately, Vega sees her success as something bigger than herself and proof that undocumented people can achieve their dreams despite the arduous challenges they face.

References

Arnett, J. J. (2000). Emerging adulthood: A theory of development from the late teens through the twenties. *American Psychologist, 55*(5), 469–480.

Arnett, J. J. (2001). Conceptions of the transition to adulthood: Perspectives from adolescence through midlife. *Journal of Adult Development, 8*(2), 133–143.

Arnett, J. J. (2004). *Adolescence and emerging adulthood: A cultural approach.* Prentice-Hall.

Arnett, J. J., Kloep, M., Hendry, L. A., & Tanner, J. L. (2011). *Debating emerging adulthood: Stage or process?* Oxford University Press.

Arnett, J. J. (2016). Does emerging adulthood theory apply across social classes? National data on a persistent question. *Emerging Adulthood, 4*(4), 227–235. doi:10.1177/2167696815613000

Bearman, S., Korobov, N., Thorne, A. (2009). The fabric of internalized sexism. *Journal of Integrated Social Sciences, 1*(1), 10–47.

Campbell, F. A. K. (2008). Exploring internalized ableism using critical race theory. *Disability & Society, 23*(2), 151–162. doi:10.1080/09687590701841190

Chrisler, J. C., & Johnston-Robledo, I. (2018). *Woman's embodied self: Feminist perspectives on identity and image.* American Psychological Association.

Conboy, K., Medina, N., & Stanbury, S. (Eds.) (1997). *Writing on the body: Female embodiment and feminist theory (7th ed.).* Columbia University Press.

David, E. J. R. (Ed.) (2014). *Internalized Oppression: The psychology of marginalized groups.* Springer Publishing Co.

Ellis, E., & Bermúdez, J. M. (2020). Funhouse mirror reflections: Resisting internalized sexism in family therapy and building a women-affirming practice. *Journal of Feminist Family Therapy.* doi:10.1080/08952833.2020.1717903

Fierro Arias, D., & Moreno Hernández, A. (2007). Emerging adulthood in Mexican and Spanish youth: Theories and realities. *Journal of Adolescent Research, 22*(5), 476–503. doi:10.1177/0743558407305774

Fischer, C., & Dolezal, L. (Eds.) (2018). *New feminist perspectives on embodiment: Breaking feminist waves.*

Glick, P., & Fiske, S. T. (1996). The ambivalent sexism inventory: Differentiating hostile and benevolent sexism. *Journal of Personality and Social Psychology, 70*(3), 491–512. doi:10.1037/0022-3514.70.3.491

James, D. (2017). Internalized racism and past-year major depressive disorder among African Americans: The role of ethnic identity and self-esteem. *Journal of Racial and Ethnic Health Disparities, 4,* 659–670. doi:10.1007/s40615-016-0269-1

McIntosh, P. (2015). Extending the knapsack: Using the white privilege analysis to examine conferred advantage and disadvantage. *Women & Therapy, 38*(3–4), 232–245. doi:10.1080/02703149.2015.1059195

Merleau-Ponty, M. (1962). *Phenomenology of perception.* Routledge and Kegan Paul.

Nelson, L., Badger, S., & Wu, B. (2004). The influence of culture in emerging adulthood: Perspectives of Chinese college students, *International Journal of Behavioral Development, 28*(1), 26–36. doi:10.1080/01650250344000244

Nadal, K. L., & Mendoza, R. J. (2014). Internalized oppression and the lesbian, gay, bisexual, and transgender community. In E. J. R. David (Ed.), *Internalized oppression: The psychology of marginalized groups* (p. 227–252). Springer Publishing Co.

O'Connell, H. A. (2020). Monuments outlive history: Confederate monuments, the legacy of slavery, and black-white inequality. *Ethnic and Racial Studies, 43*(3), 460–478. doi:10.1080/01419870.2019.1635259

Schwartz, S. J., & Pantin, H. (2006). Identity development in adolescence and emerging adulthood: The interface of self, context, and culture. In A. Columbus (Ed.), *Advances in psychology research,* 45, 1–40. Nova Science Publishers.

Sirsch, U., Dreher, E., Mayr, E., & Willinger, U. (2009). What does it take to be an adult in Austria?: Views of adulthood in Austrian adolescents, emerging adults, and adults. *Journal of Adolescent Research, 24*(3), 275–292. doi:10.1177/0743558408331184

Williamson, I. R. (2000). Internalized homophobia and health issues affecting lesbians and gay men. *Health Education Research, 15*(1), 97–107. doi:10.1093/her/15.1.97

World Health Organization. (2020). https://www.who.int/health-topics/gender

Agency and Error in Young Adults' Stories of Sexual Decision Making

Katherine R. Allen, Erica K. Husser, Dana J. Stone,

and Christian E. Jordal*

Abstract: We conducted a qualitative analysis of 148 college students' written comments about themselves as sexual decision makers. Most participants described experiences in which they were actively engaged in decision-making processes of "waiting it out" to "working it out." The four patterns were (a) I am in control, (b) I am experimenting and learning, (c) I am struggling but growing, and (d) I have been irresponsible. The diverse ways in which young adults perceive themselves as sexual decision makers and actors reveals multiple contexts for promoting healthy sexual development through parental socialization, education, and research.

Key Words: adolescent sexuality, gender relations, narratives, premarital sex, sexual risk behaviors.

The sexual revolution of the 1960s and 1970s has been successful in separating sex and reproduction from marriage (Coontz, 2005). Premarital, unmarried, and postdivorce sex are now conceptualized as individual choices for *both* men and women (Risman & Schwartz, 2002). The liberation of individual choice regarding sexual decision making is reflected in Western media, which is saturated with contradictory messages and images that alternately exploit and repress sexuality. Teenagers, growing up in this era of highly sexualized media, are sexual actors, with the vast majority having initiated their sexual practices by the time they reach age 20 (Irvine, 2004). Understanding how young people have constructed and currently perceive their sense of agency as sexual decision makers is of critical importance for parents, educators, and policymakers who have the potential to guide and support them in making wise choices for agentic sexuality (Baber, 2000).

Learning to Make Sexual Decisions

Family, Peer, and Social Contexts

Families are the primary context in which messages about sexuality are first communicated. Children's earliest learning occurs as they observe and make meaning from their parents' actions. Parents who provide a stable and secure home environment facilitate their children's ability to form stronger sexual and emotional

Katherine R. Allen, et al., "Agency and Error in Young Adults' Stories of Sexual Decision Making," *Family Relations*, vol. 57, no. 4, pp. 517–529. Copyright © 2008 by National Council on Family Relations. Reprinted with permission. Provided by ProQuest LLC. All rights reserved.

relationships as they develop (DeLamater & Friedrich, 2002). A positive socialization context for children allows them to experience more connection and emotional bonds with significant others, learn to regulate their behavior through the imposition of consistent limits, and develop a stable sense of self and personal autonomy (Barber & Olsen, 1997).

Socialization is complex, and multiple contexts, such as peers, schools, and social institutions interact, particularly as children transition to early then later adolescence (Peterson & Hann, 1999). Although families provide the foundation for children's socialization, not all parents are interested in or are adept at providing for children's positive sexual socialization. For example, as DeLamater and Friedrich (2002) pointed out, some parents instruct their children not to touch their bodies or they forbid talk about sex. Furthermore, as children become adolescents, peer influences rival or replace parenting influences as sources of knowledge and support. Richardson (2004) surveyed middle school students (ages 10–15) about the kinds of topics they would like to talk about with their parents. The most important issues they preferred to talk about with parents centered around the parent-child relationship, including autonomy and privileges, love, support, conflict, and trust. Far less important to these young adolescents was seeking out their parents for information about sensitive issues such as drugs, alcohol, sex, and pregnancy. Rosenthal and Feldman (1999) also found that adolescents did not approach their parents directly for sexual information.

Parents are often perceived as lacking the will and knowledge to openly discuss sexual topics with their sons and daughters, as Brock and Jennings (1993) found in their retrospective study of adult daughters' reflections on their mothers' sexual communication, and Fingerson's (2005) study of adolescent experiences

with masturbation. Instead, Pistella and Bonati (1998) found that adolescents relied on a complex network of kin and nonkin sources for information about reproductive health and family-planning services. Siblings and peers are strong influences on adolescents as sources of knowledge and role models (Reinisch & Beasley, 1990). From a life course perspective, the period from childhood to adulthood is no longer easily demarcated as a distinct developmental phase. Young people are more aptly seen as emerging adults—no longer adolescents but not quite independent adults. Many are still financially and emotionally dependent on parents, but as emerging adults, they are experimenting with a variety of romantic and sexual roles (Arnett, 2000).

Sexual and romantic experiences among peers interact in multiple ways and often differ by gender (Christopher & Sprecher, 2000; Wood, Koch, & Mansfield, 2006). Young men and women confront complex choices and make decisions about initiating sexual contact and giving consent (Regan, 1998). As Risman and Schwartz (2002) observed, although the sexual revolution has been successful in disentangling sex from restrictive behavioral norms, double standards still play out in gendered relationships. Although young women have acknowledged their desire for sex, their behavior is constricted by the condition that sexual expression occur only within their romantic relationships (Thompson, 1995; Tolman, 2002). Female sexual desire is still regulated through the tool of sexual reputation, with women carrying the burden of protecting their reputation *and* ensuring safer sex and contraceptive responsibility, perhaps more so than ever (Baber, 2000; Jackson & Cram, 2003). Casual sex remains a male prerogative (Risman & Schwartz).

The new social construction of heterosexuality, in which women are expected to be both responsive to the wants and desires of their male partner *and* responsible for the care and maintenance of their intimate sexual relationship, acknowledges the triumph of the sexual revolution but also the stalled gender revolution (Risman & Schwartz, 2002). Men's needs and desires are privileged, and women's are muted (Fine, 1988). Holland, Ramazanoglu, Sharpe, and Thomson (1998) found that young women's expressions of desire were not about their own experiences but represent their internalization (e.g., "the male in the head") of male needs, bodies, and desires. This incomplete gender revolution puts women, more so than men, at risk of being labeled promiscuous and feeling disempowered about their sexuality. Women's margin for error in sexual decision making is much narrower than their male counterparts.

Competing with the idea that families, parents, and peers are the main socializers of adolescent sexuality, Brown, Halpern, and L'Engle (2005) claimed that in the 21st century, private electronic media has become the primary sexuality educator of youth. Summarizing data from the Kaiser Family Foundation Report of 1997, DeLamater and Friedrich (2002) stated that young teens (ages 10–15) consider the mass media (e.g., movies, TV, magazines, music), as more important sources of information about sex and intimacy than parents, peers, and sexuality education programs. Mass media helps construct, reflect, challenge, and exploit human sexuality and gender relations. Sex is used to sell everything from household products to luxury vehicles and fast food; explicit sex acts are shown on prime-time television; and pornography is easily available on the Internet. Children and adolescents are increasingly exposed, often unintentionally, to pornographic or violent images, or both, at younger ages through aggressive advertising, personal Internet use, and various entertainment outlets (Greenfield,

2004; Valkenburg & Soeters, 2001). These media depict contradictory messages about sexuality that alternatively perpetuate and challenge gendered expectations.

Contradictory gendered discourses are also found in popular magazines that promote female sexuality, even sexual prowess, yet also push for the perfect romance or love story (Tolman, 2000). Women are encouraged to be readily available for sex without any relational context but are simultaneously encouraged to be in a romantic loving relationship before engaging in sexual behaviors. Furthermore, Jackson's (2005) analysis of advice columns dealing with sexual health and identity from *Girlfriend*, an Australasian teen magazine, found that the majority of articles constructed sex as painful or dangerous. A discourse about safe sex or sex as a technique for self-exploration was rare, and few articles positioned young women as active, aware, or desiring sexual agents.

Although sex saturates both private and public discourse and is used to persuade and sell, Americans, both historically and today, are queasy about acknowledging the sexual desire of children and youth (Irvine, 2004). If adults are reticent to proactively and fairly address sexuality issues, such as the tension between sexual exploitation and repression, then, young people will remain vulnerable to misinformation from the very institutions (e.g., families, school, faith communities, and the media) that are charged with providing sex education. Young people will be left to generate their own ideas about what constitutes healthy sexual development and positive sexual decisions (Baber, 2000; Russell, 2005).

If young people begin their sexual careers with an inadequate knowledge about what constitutes sex, they are unprepared for the risks and responsibilities, including unwanted pregnancy, sexually transmitted infections, and participation in sexually coercive behavior. They are also unprepared to act with agency on behalf of their own sense of sexual desire. Lacking the knowledge to be empowered, their threshold for error—and the possibility of making mistakes—is lowered. Understanding the variety of ways in which sexual behavior can occur, such as sexual touching and kissing, vaginal intercourse, oral-genital stimulation, anal intercourse, and self-pleasuring through masturbation (Baber, 2000), as well as the variety of relational contexts in which sexual desire is felt and expressed, such as romantic relationships, dating, and casual sex (Tolman & Diamond, 2001), can demystify some of the misinformation promoted by inaccurate and multidetermined sources (Christopher & Sprecher, 2000). How young adults develop a sense of sexual agency given fragmented and contradictory knowledge, uncertain sexuality educators at home, school, and in the community, an overall exploitive culture of sexuality, and inequitable gender schemes is critical because young people *are* clearly being sexual in their everyday lives (Bearman & Bruckner, 2001; Irvine, 2004; Manlove, Franzetta, Ryan, & Moore, 2006; Russell, 2005).

Critical Feminist Framework on Developing Sexual Agency

To examine these issues, a critical feminist perspective guided the current study on sexuality. Our goal was to examine sexuality and power relations in society as manifested in the divergent sexual scripts that confront young people in the process of becoming sexual agents. The concept of sexual scripts from a feminist perspective focuses on structural intersections with personal biographies and views participants as active agents in their own

lives (Baber, 2000). A feminist perspective is critical of the exclusive focus on the normative model of male sexual desire and behavior (Wood et al., 2006).

Feminism critiques traditional sexual scripts as cultural scenarios that reflect gender inequalities, heterosexism, and racism (Baber, 2000). Traditional gender scripts presume that young women are passive, compliant, and responsive to male needs and sexual prowess, and young men are assertive and knowledgeable about sexuality. Young women, of course, are not simply victims; they are agents who can negotiate affirming and empowering sexual meanings in their lives (Wood et al., 2006). A feminist perspective also considers the possibility that young men are not simply sexual leaders in relationships. They, too, can desire affirming and mutually empowering relationships (Regan, 1998). Traditional scripts contain both harmful and inaccurate messages. Viewed from a critical feminist perspective, the reality faced by emerging young adults is far more complex.

Method

Research Approach and Guiding Questions

The growing literature on emerging adults reveals that contemporary young people are dealing with sexuality as a central developmental issue, despite the lack of affirmative discourse on adolescent sexuality in the research literature or in public institutions (Russell, 2005). Qualitative, narrative approaches provide in-depth information about the ways in which young people give voice and ascribe meaning to their own sexual behavior (Jackson & Cram, 2003; Russell; Thompson, 1995; Tolman, 2002; Wood et al., 2006). Given the promises of a narrative approach, we asked young people to reflect on their emergent experiences as sexual agents. We framed this reflexive opportunity in the context of sexual learning in their home environments and its possible connections to making mistakes and learning from those mistakes. We wanted to know how young people made sense of their own sexual histories, how they connected their sexual experiences to family and other important relationships, and how they perceived their earlier sexual experiences now that they were transitioning to young adulthood.

Three research questions guided this study: (a) How do young adults conceptualize their learning process about responsible sexual behavior? (b) In what ways, if any, do they perceive that making mistakes has helped or hindered them in developing sexual agency? (c) How do they account for family influences in their stories of making mistakes and developing sexual agency?

Sample Description and Data Collection Procedures

Data consisted of 148 undergraduate students' written responses to three questions from an open-ended survey. Students were enrolled in an upper division human sexuality course at a public university. Students from every college on campus (e.g., architecture, agriculture, arts and sciences, education, engineering, human development) were enrolled in the class, which had a particular focus on global issues in human sexuality. All four authors have instructed the course. Permission to conduct the study was granted by the university Institutional Review Board.

The procedure used to collect data was to first show a 45-min film, *Teen Sex* (Discovery Channel University, 2004). The video is a documentary that follows the lives of several male and female adolescents from diverse socioeconomic and racial backgrounds as they explore their sexuality. For example, in one story, a 14-year-old girl is acting out sexually in the midst of her peers. The video captures her conversations and actions, along with several of her male and female friends. Both she and her mother are interviewed about how much knowledge each thinks the mother has about her daughter's sexual behavior. A second story involves a 19-year-old couple who have decided to wait until marriage before engaging in sexual activity. The video portrays both partners' perspectives of sexual decision making as well as that of the young woman's parents. The video captures the struggles inherent in the decision they have made and chronicles their relationship over time.

We selected the video as a prompt for the current study because of its attention to the family, peer, and social contexts associated with teen sexuality. Reasoning that this film provided a common context for students to focus their written reflections, we showed the video following a unit with instructor lectures on childhood and adolescent sexuality. As feminist researchers, we made use of the "situation at hand" (Fonow & Cook, 1991) to collect qualitative data on a topic relevant and critical to the lives of the young people we teach.

To compose the questions for the students' responses, we viewed the film together as a group of researchers, discussed the content of the film following the first viewing, and then reflected individually on the salient themes. We each composed a written reflection, then met as a group to discuss the themes, questions, and concerns about teenage sexuality that emerged from our individual narratives. Many of the comments shared among the researchers included reflections of our own experiences with sexuality in adolescence and early adulthood. As human sexuality teachers, using our reflexive processing of the content of the film (e.g., do teenagers perceive their behavior as mistakes; are parents informed of their children's behavior) and our knowledge of the literature, we crafted three open-ended questions to focus students' reflection upon their own experiences with sexual decision making as teens and emerging adults.

The film was shown to students attending the first author's human sexuality class, in which 163 students were enrolled. Immediately following the film, students were given a form consisting of requests for their gender and age, as well as the three open-ended questions. They were asked to write a narrative response to each question:

1. Were there any experiences in your home life when you were growing up that influenced your sexual behavior or sexual decision making? Please describe.

2. Sometimes the best learning experiences come from a mistake. Did you make any mistakes in regard to your sexual decision-making when you were a teen that you learned from? If so, please describe the experience, and who or what helped you through it.

3. If the filmmakers had interviewed the people who raised you, what would they have said about you, and how accurate would they have been?

After the participant responses were collected, their names and any identifying information were removed. The narratives were photocopied, and a research team member typed student responses into a Word document. The data were subsequently entered in a qualitative software program, MAXqda, for data management and coding purposes.

A total of 148 responses were collected (100 female [67.6%] and 48 male [32.4%]). The average age of the participants was 20 years, with a range of 18–24. Although students were not explicitly asked other demographic information, we were able to ascertain the following: The course is a university core requirement, with students from diverse majors enrolled; therefore, course enrollment reflects the demographics of the university as a whole. That is, 70% of the students were from in-state. Two thirds were from suburban areas and one third from rural areas. Regarding undergraduate enrollment patterns by race, 72% of students were White, 7% Asian, 4% African American, 2% Hispanic, 2% International, less than 1% Native American, and 12% unknown.

Data Analysis Process

The data analysis was guided by our theoretical framework, research questions, literature review, and insiders' experiences as teachers of human sexuality (Bogdan & Biklen, 1998). We conducted a constructivist grounded theory analysis (Charmaz, 2006), where the categories that emerge from our analysis are a function of our collective interactions with and questions about the data. We completed an initial phase of open coding, first independently reading the student narratives multiple times, noting nouns, verbs, themes, trends, and storylines that informed the initial open-coding process. For the second phase of data analysis, we again read the cases independently. Over a period of several months, we met together to read each case aloud to discuss and reflect on emerging themes and contradictions as we developed a fully elaborated coding scheme. This process involved independent coding, which we then reviewed together, one person sharing codes, often reading the data aloud, to consider nuances and interpretations. Through constant comparison and reflective analysis, we discussed coding disagreements in the context of the entire narrative until we reached 100% consensus on a final coding scheme that was applied to the data.

Our first coding scheme consisted of 10 major categories but after 12 iterations and revisions, we arrived at 6 major categories: (a) social contexts for sexual learning, (b) students' perceptions of their parents as sources of knowledge about sex, (c) how my parents perceive me as a sexual being, (d) sexual mistakes college students said they made, (e) the discourse of mistakes, and (f) students' stories of self as sexual decision makers and actors.

growing, and I have been irresponsible about my sexual behavior (see Table 8.1.1). Because of insufficient information, seven student narratives could not be coded. For example, a 19-year-old female said that her parents did not really talk to her about sex, she did not make any mistakes, and her parents do not know anything about her sexual experiences. Thus, we did not code this case (and 6 others) because of such limited information.

As we explain below, we define students' self-perceptions of sexual agency within the context of making mistakes and consider how students situate their narratives in relationship to their family environment. Collectively, we tell a story of sexual decision making within the context of individual and family development, as young people struggle with the tensions of developing agency and dealing with error.

Results

The analysis for this study is focused primarily on students' stories of self as sexual decision makers and actors. We generated four substantive codes regarding students' self-perceptions of sexual agency: I am in control, I am experimenting and learning, I am struggling but

I Am in Control

Nearly half of the sample (45%) expressed a view that they were in control of their sexual decision-making process. They had not made mistakes, either because they had not yet had any, or many, sexual experiences, or they saw themselves as making good decisions. The message in their narratives was, "I am exercising

TABLE 8.1.1 **Young Adults' Self-Perceptions of Agency in Sexual Decision Making**

Group	Self-Perception of Sexual Agency	Males	Females	Subgroup Subtotals	Total
A	I am in control	24 (50%)	42 (42%)		66 (45%)
	1. Waiting it out	3 (6%)	13 (13%)	16 (11%)	
	2. Taking it slow	21 (44%)	29 (29%)	50 (34%)	
B	I am experimenting and learning	13 (27%)	36 (36%)		49 (33%)
C	I am struggling but growing	5 (11%)	16 (16%)		21 (14%)
D	I have been irresponsible	2 (4%)	3 (3%)		5 (3%)
	Could not be coded	4 (8%)	3 (3%)		7 (5%)
Total		48	100	148	

agency by following my own values and/or morals, and I learned them from my family." These individuals perceived that their behaviors and decision making were congruent with their values. Only a few said they arrived at their values and morals independently of their parents' influences.

We found two subgroups in the "I am in control" category: (a) those who were sexually inactive ("waiting it out") and (b) those who were acting in a responsible or relational manner, or both ("taking it slow"). Although the two subgroups differed in terms of degree of sexual activity they reported, they were alike in their self-perception of not having made any mistakes. Students in this group had learned to "protect" themselves—in the broadest sense of the word—by waiting out the decision to act sexually or by resisting peer pressure and taking their time to make sexual decisions that were right for them. They were not ready or willing to take risks, or both, beyond their family's teaching or beyond their own comfort level.

Waiting it out. In this first subgroup of 16 students (3 males and 13 females) who felt in control of their sexual decision making, the prominent storyline was "I am inactive." These students, 11% of the sample, explicitly indicated that they are not sexually active. Mostly, they said they are waiting to have sex until marriage or they are abstaining from sex altogether. In responding to questions about their experiences growing up, mistakes they have made, and what their parents would say about their sexual behavior, inactive students referred to their parents' values, religious convictions, and childrearing strategies as having strong influences on their decisions to "wait it out." Two female students, aged 21 and 19, respectively, said,

The way I was raised affects my sexual decision-making. I was taught to wait till I get married and that has had a huge impact on my decisions about sex. I have never been put in a sex related situation. ... I am a virgin.

I grew up Christian with the idea that no sex before marriage was the right way to go. I became involved with a Christian organization on campus and that strengthened my feelings even more. ... My parents would say that they were sure I was not sexually active and they would have been right.

A 23-year-old male echoed these sentiments about parental influence, religiosity, and sexual abstinence:

I grew up in a very religious family. My parents never had a discussion about sex with me or my older brother. They expected us to wait until marriage. The conservative nature of my family has definitely influenced me to not commit to any sexual activity until marriage. Considering the fact that I am still a virgin and have never had a girlfriend, I've never had to make a decision about my sexual activity.

A 19-year-old male indicated that although he was able to act on his own behalf, he also credited his parents for their educational guidance:

My parents talked to me about sex and made it very clear that when I do it, it would be my decision. They even offered me condoms when I went on a trip to the beach with my friends, in case that I decided to,

I would be safer about it. That all helped me feel more comfortable about making a decision for myself, which is as of now to abstain until marriage. I have never made any mistakes; I came close, but always found the strength to overcome.

Taking it slow. In the second subgroup of students who felt in control of their sexual decision making, 50 narratives from 21 males and 29 females, consisting of three storylines, emerged: "I am responsible," "I am relational," and "I am relational and responsible." Unlike the "waiting it out" group, all the "taking it slow" students indicated that they had been or currently were sexually active. One third of the sample (34%) fell into the "taking it slow" subgroup. Males were overrepresented here (44% of males in the sample), with the majority of them telling the "I am responsible" storyline (33% of males in the sample). Clearly, a gendered script of male responsibility was prominent in this group.

The first storyline involves *responsible* students (16 males and 14 females) who did not perceive that their learning about sex came from making mistakes. They credited their sense of responsible decision making to (a) the lessons learned from their families, (b) observing and learning from others' mistakes, or (c) having a good head on their shoulders. Two 20-year-old males, who indicated a degree of influence from their parents, stated:

> My parents allowed me to be responsible for my own decisions and tried to make sure I used good judgment.

I usually think about my actions and consequences and many things come into play in my mind ... [My parents] would say that I am responsible, make wise decisions, and think before I act, yes.

Responsible students tended to share specific stories about the people around them. Again, several males commented on seeing the unplanned or unexpected pregnancies of others as influencing their responsible decision making. A 21-year-old explained:

> When I was 10 my brother got his [girlfriend pregnant]. I felt like sex was the direct cause (not their wrecklessness [sic]).

A 19-year-old male shared:

> There was one situation in my house that influenced me. My stepsister became pregnant and went along and had the baby. This showed me how easily your life can change [with] one decision.

Other responsible students credited their behavior to having a good head on their shoulders. They did not question their decisions because they did not feel they had made mistakes. They were matter-of-fact, as if it went without saying that they would be responsible and make the right choices because they were informed. A 21-year-old male simply stated:

> I haven't really made mistakes. I've never regretted any of my sexual decisions. I didn't have any sexual mistakes; I'm a very responsible person.

In the second storyline, *relational* students (three males and six females) explained that their sexual decision making was tied to being in a relationship with the right person. These students were choosy about the people they had sex with. Their decision-making process was based on a commitment to their sexual partner. This commitment was used synonymously with, or as a substitute for, love. Two 21-year-old females demonstrate the importance of love as a precursor for having a sexual relationship.

> I have not made any mistakes regarding sexual decision-making. I am proud of my choice to wait until I was in love.

> I, personally, have never made a sexual mistake. I'm engaged and being with him (and only him) is the best decision I've ever made.

The third storyline in this subgroup consisted of 11 students (2 males and 9 females) who *blended* responsible and relational narratives. These students learned from other people's choices and mistakes and then applied those lessons to their own lives. A 21-year-old female said:

> Actually, I had a few friends who were extremely sexually active with multiple partners. By watching them go through the regret [and] the bad reputation made me realize that I want my first time to be with someone special.

A 19-year-old female concurred:

> Everyone was having sex and such in high school, and I didn't want to be like everyone else, so I didn't. I waited until I was almost 17 and in a serious relationship before having sex. I don't regret it at all. I just learned from everyone else's mistakes and didn't want to make the same ones.

Some of these students said they arrived at that decision on the basis of their own experiences or their sense of personal preference rather than someone else's influence, as this 19-year-old female explained:

> I wanted to wait till I felt mature enough and was in a loving, mature relationship. No, I did not make any mistakes. I think all of my decisions were right for me.

I Am Experimenting and Learning

The next group consisted of 49 students (27 male and 36 female) comprising 33% of the sample. They were actively engaged in learning about themselves as sexual actors and decision makers. Although the *Taking it slow* (relational/responsible) subgroup in the previous example of the *I am in Control* group said they learned from *others'* mistakes or behaved in congruence with their own ideals about sexuality, the *Experimenting and Learning* group was learning to exercise agency by incorporating their *own* sexual experiences into their personal sense of self as a decision maker. They were in process: reflecting on their past experiences and, in reaction to their experiences, they were *working it out*, by constructing their own ideas about what sexual behaviors were appropriate for them. They were actively shaping their own sense of personal agency, telling stories that were less congruent or less concerned with parental values. Typically, the active shaping of their sense of agency led them to expand their horizons beyond the expectations of their family.

The majority of young people in this group (38) *resisted* the researchers' language of mistakes and instead talked about regret, which only a few students felt (3 females). Five students (4 female and 1 male) suggested they would do things differently if they could, but the rest of the respondents downplayed or resisted the idea of making a "mistake." Instead, they said that they had learned valuable life lessons from their behaviors.

This 18-year-old female, who went to a private Catholic school, explained that sex was a "forbidden" word in her house. She described herself as precocious and said she had fewer regrets than her friends:

> I've learned a lot from sex. It's helped me decide that waiting for marriage is not necessarily a good idea. Sex can change a relationship drastically. I've also learned that it's ok to say no and that sleeping with someone doesn't guarantee closeness to that person.... I've only been with 2 people that I deeply cared about.

The following 21-year-old female, who resisted the language of mistakes, said she acted "like a guy" in high school and explained that it was good preparation for college life.

> I made so many "irrational" decisions pertaining to my sexual awakening but I wouldn't call them mistakes. Many of my sexual experiences I feel equipped me for life out on my own. ... I lost my virginity at an early age and experienced many ups and downs

with the opposite sex while I was in the confines of my parents house and their rules. ... Now that I am in college I am so appreciative that I have gone through those stages, this way I don't take advantage of my freedom. I've known many females who were "sexual angels" in their parents' house then came to [school] and end up heart-broken and ready to drop out.

Yet, over half of the young women (19 of 36) in the *Experimenting and Learning* group also spoke about sex in the context of love and relationships. As the following 19- and 20-year-old females explained, their mistakes involved the absence of love or commitment in their first relationships:

> I had a few sexual experiences that I wish I didn't participate in, now that I look back as I take it from a point of view of being in a serious monogamous relationship. At the time it was fine—but now I kind of regret it.

> I "hooked up" with a guy at 16 who I was not in a relationship with, and because there was no emotional feelings I thought it was horrible and it made me want to wait to have sex even more so that it would be special when I was with someone I loved.

Conversely, 4 of the 13 males in this group explained that love and commitment were not desired prerequisites for sex. The following 21- and 22-year-old males rejected emotional attachments with females:

> Sure, I hooked up with girls that had a tendency to get attached. I

learned to try and stay away from those kinds.

I had oral sex with a female and she became too attached afterwards. Calling all times of the day. I learned that women take things a lot more serious than men.

A 20-year-old male, who struggled with family loyalty issues, explained how he had managed to distance his emotions from sex:

My first sexual encounter I think was affected by attachment more than other guys. ... I've learned to take sex less seriously in the past few years.

I Am Struggling But Growing

In the third group, we found 21 students (5 males and 16 females) comprising 14% of the sample. These students were also in the process of working out their own sense of sexual agency, but they were facing difficult challenges about their earlier decisions. As with the previous group, *Experimenting and Learning*, the students in the *Struggling but Growing* group also believed their experiences have provided valuable lessons for them as sexual actors and decision makers.

What differentiates these students from the previous group is the echo of pain that resulted from past experiences. They are actively engaged in exercising agency by acknowledging, often with great sadness, humility, and pain, that their mistakes had serious consequences. The language of burden permeated their sexual narratives, suggesting that they were grappling with how to assimilate past behaviors into their current sense of self. More students in this group than the previous two groups expressed ambivalent views about their families. Few of

the struggling students cited their parents as sources of support in working out lessons that could be learned from making mistakes. As indicated below, they were more likely to cite helpful friends.

This *in process with pain* group was sadder but wiser, as the following reflective statements reveal. A 19-year-old female said:

I was at a party and ended up hooking up with a guy. After this I felt obligated to continue to do this with every guy I was with. But I talked with my friend and she made me realize that just because I made a mistake once, I didn't need to keep on making it.

A 20-year-old male described an experience he continues to rue:

I have one regret that changed my life forever; although I would prefer to refer to it strictly as a learning experience as I may not have been the person I am today had it not occurred. But we decided to abort— although at least I know I work.

The students in this group were struggling typically to come to grips with their past decisions and experiences. The residual pain from past mistakes challenged them as they negotiated their path forward as sexual decision makers and actors. A 19-year-old female described how her friends supported her when she decided to make more agentic choices following an earlier time of regret:

I definitely made mistakes—having sex too early, having unprotected sex, having sex with people I had no business sleeping with. I've been lucky to escape unharmed. Friends always helped me through this learning process.

I Have Been Irresponsible

Irresponsible students, two males and three females, comprised the smallest portion (7%) of the sample. These five students did not overtly acknowledge remorse for their sexual behavior nor did they engage in a reflective process as sexual decision makers. Irresponsible students stated or implied that they had made risky sexual decisions. Their narratives suggested they are not exercising agency. All but one student expressed ambivalent views about their families.

The two males were coded solely as "I have been irresponsible," in contrast to the females who were also coded as irresponsible and relational/responsible. As a 22-year-old male stated:

> I never really had any mistakes that cost me more than buying a few pregnancy tests. ... In hindsight, the anxiety sucked and the risk was great, but I would and still do it today.

The following 20-year-old female indicated her extra burden in dealing with reputation issues in relationships:

> Oral sex at too young an age with basically a stranger—I knew after that it was dumb—it never happened again for years, especially because a lot of guys at school knew and would joke around—I didn't want to be known as 'that girl' and get around.

A 20-year-old female described her behavior as irresponsible and recognized it as not smart:

> I was in a long-term relationship with a boy. I decided I didn't want to be in a relationship like that anymore and I went crazy. I started dating another guy and right off the bat we were sexually active and not smart about it.

Discussion

In this study, we conducted a qualitative analysis of 148 college students' written comments about their views of themselves as sexual decision makers. We found four patterns in which students described themselves as sexual actors: (a) I am in control (either waiting it out or taking it slow), (b) I am experimenting and learning, (c) I am struggling but growing, and (d) I have been irresponsible. Taken together, participants described several kinds of experiences in which most were proactively engaged in decision-making processes ranging from "waiting it out" to "working it out."

In the first group, students expressed agency as a sense of self-control. They were choosing to follow prescriptions they had learned at home and from their parents' values, to wait until marriage before initiating sexual activity. For a few, they had relaxed the marital proscription and were choosing to wait until they were in a significant relationship characterized by love. A few more were waiting it out because they simply had not had an opportunity to be sexual, and perhaps in that sense, they were not yet exercising agency, but like their cohorts in this group, they had not yet made mistakes.

A subgroup of students in the self-control group revealed that they were already sexual, but they had not made mistakes. Their sexual learning, for the most part, had occurred in the context of and in congruence with their parents' teachings. Their narratives, though following mostly a gendered script of men as responsible and women as relational/responsible, revealed agency in the sense that these young people were "taking it slow." By following cultural narratives of responsible and/or relational decision making, they perceived themselves as exercising sexual agency in ways that were self-protective *and* validating. They were very clear that their decision-making process had kept them from making mistakes.

These qualitative data revealed a new understanding of young people's sense of agency in which making mistakes was not an issue. The women, in particular, said they were waiting to begin having sex until the time was right *for them*. This finding can be interpreted in light of Sprecher and Regan's (1996) survey of college students who remain virgins. The primary reasons that college females cite for remaining abstinent are (a) not feeling love; (b) being fearful of AIDS, sexually transmitted infections, and pregnancy; or (c) having beliefs supportive of virginity. Although our findings support Sprecher and Regan's information about college females, we also found a small subset of college *males* who had beliefs supportive of virginity and/or waiting to have sex until they were ready. Overall, our finding is consistent with recent trends in the literature about the complex relationship among young people's self-judgments, sexual expression, and experiences in close relationships (Christopher & Sprecher, 2000).

In the *in process* groups, students who perceived their past behaviors in the context of their own mistakes and who were working out their sexual agency beyond parental influence revealed narratives that seemed to reflect society's dominant views about gender and sexuality (Holland et al., 1998; Risman & Schwartz, 2002).

Males were more likely to excuse themselves for their own sexual choices and disregard a partner's desire for intimacy and emotionality, even when they were being reflective about their past experiences. Females were more likely to describe how they had to deal with the sexual double standard when handling and recovering from mistakes. On the surface, these differences can be explained in gendered terms: More young women than men described themselves as sexual actors within the context of a relationship, whereas more young men than women described themselves as responsible sexual actors independent of a relational context.

At a deeper level, however, the data revealed that more females than males were critically reflective about the process of *becoming* sexually agentic. The females were more effusive about the process of *claiming* their sexuality, albeit for some, in the context of their relationships. The males, on the other hand, seemed to presume they were automatically responsible as sexual agents without the critical reflection evident in females' narratives. The dominant discourse still ascribes sexual agency to men, but women must struggle to achieve it. Women used language that indicated they were working harder at becoming sexually agentic (e.g., it helped me decide; I feel equipped, I don't take advantage) because sexual agency was not something they took for granted. Women's work in claiming their sexuality is evidence of new sources of agency *and* responsibility in sexual relationships, as explained by a feminist perspective (Baber, 2000).

The students in the process of working it out, whether *Experimenting and Learning* or *Struggling but Growing*, were actively engaged in exploring their sexuality and learning about themselves as sexual agents. The outcome of their early explorations involved varying degrees of regret. Some students had no regrets at all; others resisted the idea of making mistakes and claimed life lessons from their experiences; and others who felt regret, or carried the burden of pain, were in the process of assimilating, understanding, and reconciling their behaviors. Sexually active students who were in process told stories about growth, change, and discovery of new ways to be a responsible sexual person in today's world. Student mistakes included (a) jumping in too fast, (b) being coerced into sexual relations, (c) experimenting without understanding the consequences, (d) experiencing faulty contraceptives, or (e) making bad decisions on the basis of incorrect relational assumptions. Despite their level of regret, these students also described themselves as agentic sexual decision makers: experimenting, learning, and constructing their own beliefs about what healthy sexuality is for them. The only students who seemed to lack any form of agency in this study were the ones who claimed to be irresponsible. Specifically, they did not indicate a desire to learn from or change their irresponsible behavior.

Our data reveal an important connection between students as agentic sexual decision makers and (non) actors and the context of their family environments. The groups who see themselves as having made mistakes, from which they are now learning, some more painful than others, suggest that they had more challenging home environments. Only in the *I am in Control* group, where students did not see themselves as making mistakes, did students express congruence between their own views of themselves as sexual decision makers and how they perceived their parents would see them (Barber & Olsen, 1997; Peterson & Hann, 1999).

In the groups where students acknowledged experimentation and subsequent struggle, that is, where mistakes were made and lessons learned, students expressed more self-reliance and support from peers. Their more complex and at times contradictory stories suggested ambivalent or distant family relationships. The lack of connection to family and home environment was prevalent only in the narratives of students who reported a learning experience in spite of painful mistakes. They were more free or willing to experiment and take risks and thus to make mistakes. The ambivalent stories about their family environment inspired this group of students to take sexual learning into their own hands and as a result to learn, often with difficulty, from their experiences.

Implications

The variety of ways in which young adults perceived themselves as sexual decision makers and agentic actors reveal multiple opportunities and contexts to promote healthy sexual development through research and practice. The findings, however, are limited by a volunteer sample of primarily White, middle class college students enrolled in a human sexuality class at a public university. Future research should examine more diverse and representative samples. A second limitation involves the data collection process. Although qualitative research on young adult sexuality is among the most illuminating to date (Christopher & Sprecher, 2000), the use of an open-ended written survey prevented us from asking follow-up questions that would have enabled deeper levels of understanding about each participant. Although students were encouraged to share their stories and be reflective about their past experiences, not all students provided rich information. This limitation may speak to some students' lack of careful process or simply to their unwillingness to provide a thoughtful response. Despite this limitation, our qualitative approach allowed for the exploration of new pathways into how young people perceive and reflect upon their past and present sexual experiences (Russell, 2005).

These data reveal that college students consider their adolescent experiences important building blocks for constructing their current ideas about sexual agency and behavior. The sexual revolution may have liberated women and men from the institution of marriage, but the appropriate context within which they are socialized to engage in sexual activity is still gendered. Even though young women are empowered to make sexual decisions, the road is not smooth; many students in our sample revealed they jumped in too fast. In the face of a pervasive, sexually saturated, and exploitive media environment, the narratives of emerging adults provide ample evidence of opportunities where parents, teachers, and community leaders can be proactive about ensuring that children and teens are well supported, socially connected, and accurately informed as they begin to make independent choices that have consequences for their personal and relational development.

One result of this study that bears further investigation is the small yet cautionary number of students who stated, without regret or reflection, that they were irresponsible sexual decision makers. Most students in the sample who had made mistakes contextualized them as "learning from the past," but the candidness of the five irresponsible students who simply "admitted" mistakes bears follow up. In what ways is error or irresponsibility linked to student isolation from peers, inadequate parental support, or not receiving accurate information about human sexuality and intimate relationships? Perhaps students who lacked responsibility for their past behaviors were disconnected from others. This possibility has implications for both family socialization practices and sexuality education programs where the focus should be on the nexus of developing communication skills and knowledge (DeLamater & Friedrich, 2002).

Finally, sexuality education programs must be of high quality in order to prepare young persons for the complex world in which healthy sexual choices can be made (Russell, 2005). Students who indicated they had engaged in the most risky behavior, at the youngest ages, and that they regretted the most, were least likely to cite parents as influential sources of knowledge and support. Students who were or had waited until they felt ready for a mature sexual experience felt congruent with parental values and support from family—both signs of positive parent-child socialization (Barber & Olsen, 1997; Peterson & Hann, 1999). The mass media is making incursions into young lives at earlier ages, with greater frequency, and more explicit content, but parents and peers can serve as positive socializing forces as young people learn to make agentic sexual choices.

References

Arnett, J. J. (2000). Emerging adulthood: A theory of development from the late teens through the twenties. *American Psychologist, 55,* 469–480.

Baber, K. M. (2000). Women's sexualities. In M. Biaggio & M. Hersen (Eds.), *Issues in the psychology of women* (pp. 145–171). New York: Kluwer.

Barber, B. K., & Olsen, J. A. (1997). Socialization in context: Connection, regulation, and autonomy in the family, school, and neighborhood, and with peers. *Journal of Adolescent Research, 12*, 287–315.

Bearman, P. S., & Bruckner, H. (2001). Promising the future: Virginity pledges and first intercourse. *American Journal of Sociology, 106*, 859–912.

Bogdan, R., & Biklen, S. (1998). *Qualitative research in education* (3rd ed.). Needham Heights, MA: Allyn and Bacon.

Brock, L. J., & Jennings, G. H. (1993). What daughters in their 30s wish their mothers had told them. *Family Relations, 42*, 61–65.

Brown, J. D., Halpern, C. T., & L'Engle, K. L. (2005). Mass media as a sexual super peer for early maturing girls. *Journal of Adolescent Health, 36*, 420–427.

Charmaz, K. (2006). *Constructing grounded theory: A practical guide through qualitative analysis.* London: Sage.

Christopher, F. S., & Sprecher, S. (2000). Sexuality in marriage, dating, and other relationships: A decade review. *Journal of Marriage and the Family, 62*, 999–1017.

Coontz, S. (2005). *Marriage, a history: From obedience to intimacy or how love conquered marriage.* New York: Viking.

DeLamater, J. D., & Friedrich, W. N. (2002). Human sexual development. *Journal of Sex Research, 39*, 10–14.

Discovery Channel University (Producer). (2004). *Teen sex.* [DVD Video]. Retrieved from Films for the Humanities & Sciences.

Fine, M. (1988). Sexuality, schooling, and adolescent females: The missing discourse of desire. *Harvard Educational Review, 58*, 29–53.

Fingerson, L. (2005). Agency and the body in adolescent menstrual talk. *Childhood, 12*, 91–110.

Fonow, M. M., & Cook, J. A. (1991). Back to the future: A look at the second wave of feminist epistemology. In M. M. Fonow & J. A. Cook (Eds.), *Beyond methodology: Feminist scholarship as lived research methodology* (pp. 1–15). Bloomington: Indiana University Press.

Greenfield, P. M. (2004). Inadvertent exposure to pornography on the Internet: Implications of peer-to-peer file-sharing networks for child development

and families. *Applied Developmental Psychology, 25*, 741–750.

Holland, J., Ramazanoglu, C., Sharpe, S., & Thomson, R. (1998). *The male in the head: Young people, heterosexuality and power.* London: Tufnell Press.

Irvine, J. M. (2004). *Talk about sex: Battles over sex education in the United States.* Berkeley: University of California Press.

Jackson, S. (2005). 'Dear *Girlfriend*...': Constructions of sexual health problems and sexual identities in letters to a teenage magazine. *Sexualities, 8*, 282–305.

Jackson, S. M., & Cram, F. (2003). Disrupting the sexual double standard: Young women's talk about heterosexuality. *British Journal of Social Psychology, 42*, 113–127.

Manlove, J., Franzetta, K., Ryan, S., & Moore, K. (2006). Adolescent sexual relationships, contraceptive consistency, and pregnancy prevention approaches. In A. C. Crouter & A. Booth (Eds.), *Romance and sex in adolescence and emerging adulthood: Risks and opportunities* (pp. 181–212). Mahwah, NJ: Lawrence Erlbaum Associates.

Peterson, G. W., & Hann, D. (1999). Socializing children and parents in families. In M. Sussman, S. K. Steinmetz, & G. W. Peterson (Eds.), *Handbook of marriage and the family* (2nd ed., pp. 327–370). New York: Plenum Press.

Pistella, C. L. Y., & Bonati, F. A. (1998). Communication about sexual behavior among adolescent women, their family, and peers. *Families in Society: The Journal of Contemporary Human Services, 79*, 206–211.

Regan, P. C. (1998). Of lust and love: Beliefs about the role of sexual desire in romantic relationships. *Personal Relationships, 5*, 139–157.

Reinisch, J. M., & Beasley, R. (1990). *The Kinsey Institute new report on sex: What you must know to be sexually literate.* New York: St. Martin's Press.

Richardson, R. A. (2004). Early adolescence talking points: Questions that middle school students want to ask their parents. *Family Relations, 53*, 87–94.

Risman, B., & Schwartz, P. (2002). After the sexual revolution: Gender politics in teen dating. *Contexts, 1,* 16–24.

Rosenthal, D. A., & Feldman, S. S. (1999). The importance of importance: Adolescents' perceptions of parental communication about sexuality. *Journal of Adolescence, 22,* 835–851.

Russell, S. T. (2005). Conceptualizing positive adolescent sexuality development. *Sexuality Research and Social Policy: Journal of NSRC, 2*(3), 4–12.

Sprecher, S., & Regan, P. C. (1996). College virgins: How men and women perceive their sexual status. *Journal of Sex Research, 33,* 3–15.

Thompson, S. (1995). *Going all the way: Teenage girls' tales of sex, romance, and pregnancy.* New York: Hill and Wang.

Tolman, D. L. (2000). Object lessons: Romance, violation, and female adolescent sexual desire. *Journal of Sex Education and Therapy, 25*(1), 70–79.

Tolman, D. L. (2002). *Dilemmas of desire: Teenage girls talk about sexuality.* Cambridge, MA: Harvard University Press.

Tolman, D. L., & Diamond, L. M. (2001). Desegregating sexuality research: Cultural and biological perspectives on gender and desire. *Annual Review of Sex Research, 12,* 33–74.

Valkenburg, P. M., & Soeters, K. E. (2001). Children's positive and negative experiences with the Internet. *Communication Research, 28,* 652–675.

Wood, J. M., Koch, P. B., & Mansfield, P. K. (2006). Women's sexual desire: A feminist critique. *Journal of Sex Research, 43,* 236–244.

Emerging Adults with Disabilities

Theory, Trends, and Implications

Jill M. Meyer, Vanessa M. Hinton, and Nicholas Derzis

Abstract—Emerging adulthood, a relatively new and promising developmental period coined by Arnett (2000), has come to the forefront of the developmental psychology literature. Emerging adulthood is defined as the developmental period between late adolescence and young adulthood that includes individuals between 18-29 years old. As a developmental period, emerging adulthood applies to all individuals, including those with disabilities. Although there have been numerous studies on youth with disabilities, this population has not been studied from the vantage point of Arnett's concept of "emerging adulthood. "The purpose of this manuscript is to explore the primary theoretical constructs of emerging adulthood: (a) self-exploration (e.g., identity development); (b) uncertainty; (c) self-focus; (d) transition; and (e) optimism, as well as the social trends and implications. Emerging adulthood provides insight that has implications for the educational and rehabilitation services for young adults, including transition services.

Keywords: emerging adulthood, disabilities, rehabilitation, social trends

Emerging Adults with Disabilities

Emerging Adulthood is a developmental period established by Arnett (2000) in the field of developmental psychology which recognizes the social and economic trends affecting young adults ages 18-29. This manuscript is topical in that it provides a select exploration of theoretical and empirical literature on the developmental period of emerging adulthood (EA). Articles published between 1990 and 2013 were included because EA came about in the early 1990's (Arnett, 2006). Articles that were used for this manuscript involved the defining characteristics, psychological constructs, developmental milestones, social trends, and transition issues affecting individuals with disabilities age 18–29. The commonalities of these constructs will be explored in terms of the considerations for vocational rehabilitation counseling and youth with disabilities. This manuscript is a broad exploration of the primary constructs, trends, and implications of emerging adulthood and seeks to highlight factors of EA that influence the practice of rehabilitation counseling. Exploration of the actual

Jill M. Meyer, Vanessa M. Hinton, and Nicholas Derzis, "Emerging Adults with Disabilities: Theory, Trends, and Implications," *Journal of Applied Rehabilitation Counseling*, vol. 46, no. 4, pp. 3-10. Copyright © 2015 by National Rehabilitation Counseling Association. Reprinted with permission. Provided by ProQuest LLC. All rights reserved.

impact of EA however, will need to be examined in future empirical studies.

Emerging Adulthood

Emerging adulthood (EA) is a developmental period during which individuals experience delays in attainment of adult roles and social expectations (Arnett, 2000). The emerging adulthood phenomenon offers insight that can enhance the educational and rehabilitation services for young adults. The theory of EA is based on five distinct principles: 1) self-exploration (e.g., identity development); 2) uncertainty; 3) self-focus; 4) optimism; and 5) transition. Although this developmental stage was accounted for in past works by Erickson (1968) and Keniston (1971), it was not defined to the extent that it could be identified by name, nor was it postulated as a specific developmental period until recently (Tanner & Arnett, 2011).

EA is a time of great self-exploration (Arnett, 2000). During emerging adulthood older adolescents pull away from nuclear families, and the process of exploring identity in terms of intimate relationships, independent living, and working become the central focus. There are greater opportunities for emerging adults in comparison to past generations, which has encouraged extended exploration of the self, career opportunities, and life goals, prior to making adult commitments (Tanner & Arnett, 2011).

America has undergone a dramatic change since the late 1800's and shifted from an agricultural focus to an industrial and production based economy which has now become a very technologically involved workforce (Martin & Oehler, 2001). Today, the traditional expectations that a new employee could begin in the workplace, work hard, perform well, display loyalty and commitment, and expect career security has been replaced by new requirements such as an expectation to continuously learn new skills and have an evolving vocational identity (Russell, 2005). This makes vocational counseling more difficult as employment expectations are shifting and job developers must adjust to keep up with the trends (Bissonnette, 1994; Blustein, 2008). Rehabilitation counselors have to be aware of the great demands employees must possess in future jobs and careers.

In addition to economic changes, there are changes in beliefs and values, social perceptions and expectations of today's youth that create very different experiences in their journey toward adulthood compared to previous generations. Young adults expect and experience vast changes in relationships, occupations, residential locations, and living arrangements that otherwise would not have been viewed beneficial in the past (Arnett, 2000). In comparison to 60 years ago, the experiences of emerging adults paint a distinctly different picture from past beliefs about the transition to adulthood (Arnett, 2006). Not only have these changes affected the somewhat linear trajectory from adolescence to adulthood, but also the time-frame in which this transition occurs. Therefore, commonly held beliefs about adolescents becoming adults by finishing school, going to college or getting a job, leaving home, finding a partner, and establishing families are now things of the past (Tanner & Arnett, 2011). These milestones still exist, but the prioritization, trajectory, and time-frame in which they occur is extended and more complicated than the past. Not only are adult milestones occurring at a later age, the value of such accomplishments held by emerging adults has also changed creating a distinct departure from previous expectations of young adults, as they are not reaching adulthood at the same rate or time compared to previous generations (Arnett, 2006). By gaining a better understanding of the younger generation of people that may receive rehabilitation services, we can better prepare practitioners with strategies that are effective for the consumer and the counselor. Of primary importance during this phase of maturation are the five distinguishing principles of emerging adulthood (i.e., self-exploration tied to identity development, uncertainty, self-focus, transition, and optimism: Arnett, 2000; 2006). Each principle is discussed along with implications for rehabilitation counseling services.

Self-Exploration as Identity Development

The first principle of EA is self-exploration as identity development (Arnett, 2000; 2006). It is important for rehabilitation counselors to have a vast knowledge base of how young adults with disabilities currently explore various possibilities for their future, prior to making choices that set the foundation for their adult lives. During self-exploration young adults learn more about who they are and what they want out of life (Arnett, 2006). Hanjorgiris, Rath, and O'Neill (2004) explained that identity development for an individual with a disability is a process that permits self-acceptance and allows the person to integrate identified differences into their self-concept. Therefore, an important aspect of rehabilitation counseling for youth with disabilities is assistance in exploring various options for their future that also includes the process of embracing individual and social perceptions about their disability. Counselors support emerging adult clients in the process of integrating their disability into a positive self-concept. Thus, practitioners should be aware of research that conceptualizes identity

development and individuals with disabilities (Grant, 1996).

Grant (1996) investigated the development of a "disability identity," that is based upon the Minority Identity Development model (Atkinson, Morten, & Sue, 1993). Within this process there are four distinct phases of disability identity: (a) Dissociation, (b) Diffusion/Dysphoria, (c) Immersion/Solidarity, and (d) Introspective Acceptance. In phase one people with disabilities protect their self-identity by not associating with others who have disabilities. This avoidance may be based on negative attitudes towards the population of people with disabilities in general, discomfort regarding these negative thoughts, or negative contact with others regarding disability issues. In phase two people with disabilities can experience considerable emotional distress and conflict. Individuals in this phase maintain self-identity through certain defense mechanisms (e.g., projection, denial, displacement, and identification with dominate nondisabled community). In phase three, individuals with disabilities begin to resolve their identity conflict by trying to understand and bond with the disability community and culture. During this phase, individuals with disabilities begin distancing themselves from the dominant, typical community. Finally, in phase four, individuals with disabilities can integrate positive and negative experiences with both communities of individuals with and without disabilities. During this phase, individuals with disabilities make reality-based judgments regarding their relationships to others in the disabled community and the nondisabled community.

In conclusion, identity development is a process where young adults explore who they are and what they want out of life. Through this process individuals with disabilities integrate identified differences into their self-concept.

During EA youth spend a great deal of time in self-exploration and understanding processes of identity development can contribute to providing effective services for young adults with disabilities (Arnett, 2000). In particular, identity development for youth with disabilities concerns the incorporation of minority identity as well, making identity development for those who have a disability a more involved process compared to peers. Identity development for youth with disabilities may take more time and exploration than is currently expected or provided by educators and rehabilitation professionals. This research demonstrates that identity development for young adults with disabilities includes self-acceptance, advocacy, and integration into a social network. Best practices in rehabilitation counseling include empowerment and customer self-concept and services which reflects continuous learning and identity change (Fleming, Dev Valle, Muwoong, & Leahy, 2012; Russell, 2005). Future research in identity development for emerging adults with disabilities could include studies on family and community dynamics within the process of identity exploration, or the effects of self-perceived significance of disability on identity development, as well as ways practitioners can assist with self-acceptance for youth with disabilities.

Construct of Uncertainty

The second principle of emerging adulthood is uncertainty (Arnett, 2000; 2006). Specifically, EA is a time of uncertainty about one's present life and future pathways because there are high rates of change regarding important aspects of life. Arnett explains in EA there are high rates of occupational experiences, residential locations, and living arrangements all contributing to experiences of uncertainty. For example, consider the improvements in

the residential living arrangements for people with disabilities. In the early 20th century children and youth with disabilities left home at a very early age to live in residential facilities, where they were isolated from their families and society (Martin & Oehler, 2001). From the 1960s to present, caregivers and individuals with disabilities have pushed to change policies to protect individuals' 14th Amendment rights, which support independence, productivity, and inclusion for people with disabilities. These policies have improved various aspects of life for individuals with disabilities, including education, employment, housing, transportation, health care, and community living (Martin & Oehler 2001; Ward, 2005). Therefore, today, individuals with disabilities have more opportunity to acquire similar living arrangements and leave home within a similar time-frame as their typical peers (Leiter & Waugh, 2009).

Leiter and Waugh (2009) reviewed and synthesized the literature on young adults with and without disabilities and their living situations. The authors reported that four years after high school, for those young adults between ages 17-22 with disabilities, 67.6% were still living with their parents. This rate was comparable to the 69.8% of young adults between the ages of 18 to 22 in the general population who were living with their parents. By age 30 the likelihood of adults with disabilities living away from home differs by disability status, and adults with disabilities are twice as likely to be living with their parents at that age. Leiter and Waugh explained there are four factors that influence the contemporary living arrangements of young adults with disabilities: (a) educational and economic opportunities; (b) associated changes in norms regarding co-residence with parents; (c) family resources and supports in the transition to adulthood; and (d) requirements for care assistance. Rehabilitation Counselors manage supports and services to assist youth with disabilities in employment and areas surrounding the world of work. Counselors are consciously aware of these four factors when providing services.

Due to the vast amount of changes that take place during the EA period, it is critical that rehabilitation counselors see uncertainty as an expected developmental process (Tanner & Arnett, 2011). Rehabilitation counselors should not view uncertainty as a negative occurrence, but as something that is expected and healthy in an industrialized society. Research conducted by Trainor (2007) on young women with specific learning disabilities illustrates the uncertainty that exists among young adults in the emerging adulthood stage. Trainor examined self-perceptions of self-determination in adolescent females with specific learning disabilities while they were receiving special education transition services. Within the lens of emerging adulthood however, this uncertainty is considered developmentally appropriate, as women (and men) at this age are expected to ruminate over their identities, future career aspirations, and interpersonal relationships (Arnett, 2000). In viewing uncertainty as a developmental process, rehabilitation services could place more emphasis on job shadowing, internships, or rotate community based learning sites to observe different types of work (Johnstone et al., 2003).

The rehabilitation system has historically measured a counselor's effectiveness with consumers based on the number of consumers a counselor places into successful employment outcomes (Martin, 2007). This is an area that the Rehabilitation Services System administration needs to address on a national level to assist state agencies in exploring additional ways to measure counselor effectiveness. Consumers may be in a rehabilitation counselor's case load for a number of years gaining training and exploring potential careers while utilizing a counselor's expertise throughout the rehabilitation program.

Self-Focus

The third principle of EA is self-focus which refers to the process that allows a young adult to seek opportunities in interpersonal relationships, work, and education that promote self-knowledge and eventually self-sufficiency (Arnett 2000; 2006). The purpose of self-focus is to attain self-sufficiency. Self-determination is a broadly used term in disability literature that encompasses knowing oneself and self-advocacy, which is tied to the attainment of self-sufficiency. Specifically, Wehmeyer (2005) defined self-determination as self-initiated actions that enable an individual to act as their primary causal agent in life and to maintain or improve quality of life. Characteristics of self-determination include: (a) choice making; (b) decision making; (c) problem solving; (d) goal setting and attainment skills; (e) self-management; (f) self-advocacy; (g) self-efficacy; (h) self-awareness; and (l) self-knowledge (Wehmeyer & Schwartz, 1997). Much of the research on self-determination for youth and adults with disabilities has focused on cognitive, social, environmental, and behavioral variables that lead to the development of self-determined behavior (Nota, Soresi, Ferrari, & Wehmeyer, 2011; Wehmeyer et al., 2011). Specifically, research in this area has examined skills that promote autonomy, self-awareness, and self-regulation that lead to improved adult outcomes in life.

Teaching rehabilitation counselors best practices in building self-determination could improve client's quality of life and enhance services. Researchers demonstrate that the development of interpersonal skills, self-development, and problem solving facilitate greater independence and better quality of life. Additionally, people who demonstrate self-determination are more likely to live outside the family home, have greater independence, gain employment with better pay and benefits, and report a higher quality of life (McDougall, Evans, Baldwin, 2010; Nota, Ferrari, & Wehmeyer, 2007; Wehmeyer & Palmer, 2003; Wehmeyer & Schwartz, 1997). It is also very important for counselors to be aware that self-determination is known to be influenced by one's culture, family environment, and educational experiences (Dunn, Chambers, & Rabren, 2004; Field & Hoffman, 1999; Shogren et al., 2007; Wehmeyer et al., 2011; Zhang & Benz, 2006). Therefore best practices involving self-determination in rehabilitation should be client centered in that service provision is to be tailored to each client's unique culture, family environment, and educational experiences.

Optimism

The next construct of the EA period is optimism (Arnett, 2000; 2006). Even though emerging adulthood is filled with uncertainty, change, and the feeling of not yet being an adult, this stage of development is marked by optimism (Arnett, 2006). Most young adults express positive views about their future. Morningstar, Turnbull and Turnbull (1995) conducted a study that researched optimism experienced by young adults with disabilities. Specifically, the authors examined the importance of family involvement in the transition to adulthood, highlighting the optimism experienced during early adulthood for individuals with disabilities. Morningstar et al. explained that young adults had definite dreams for their future and saw their future as bright. Very few students viewed their future negatively. When negative expectations were expressed these thoughts and experiences were not often shared by other participants. This research demonstrates that emerging adults with and without disabilities express optimism and positive perceptions of their future, regardless of challenges.

Despite the multitude of changes accompanied by feelings of uncertainty, emerging adults remain optimistic (Arnett, 2000). Even though these young adults have positive views about their future, there is little known about how they navigate such conflicting feelings, and extensive fluctuations and changes. Future research may explore how emerging adults are coping with these challenges, specifically the chosen styles of coping used to manage the associated stress of this time period. Understanding how emerging adults cope with, and manage stress may lead to improved services that facilitate and support youth with disabilities to traverse such developmental challenges.

Transition as Feeling In-Between

The last principle of EA is transition (Arnett 2000; 2006). For most youth, there is a substantial amount of time in which they feel "in-between" during the emerging adulthood period (Arnett, 2006). That is, they are just beginning to feel as if they are adults, but have not completely attained adulthood. To feel fully adult one must accomplish the following: (a) accept responsibility for oneself, (b) make independent decisions, and (c) become finically independent (Arnett, 2006). Conceptualizing transition through the lens of EA can provide insight into how transition services could be implemented for emerging adults with disabilities.

Transition as it pertains to rehabilitation and special education is different than the "feeling in-between" concept that Arnett described about emerging adults (Individuals with Disabilities Education Improvement Act,

2004). Transition in rehabilitation and special education literature is defined as a change in status from behaving primarily as a student to assuming emergent adult roles in the community (Halpern, 1994). Transition research examines individual characteristics such as socio-economic status, work experiences, and type of disability along with employment and educational outcomes that impact one's ability to live independently. Work experiences are among the most prominent and well-documented predictors of favorable post-school employment outcomes in the transition literature (Benz, Lindstrom, & Yovanoff, 2000; Benz, Yovanoff, & Doren, 1997; Carter, Trainor, Ditchman, Sweden, Sun, & Ownes, 2010; Rabren, Dunn, & Chambers, 2002). Also, work experiences impact vocational identity by shaping career awareness and aspirations; developing workplace values, skills, and knowledge; and promoting collateral skill development (Hartung, Porfeli, & Vonderacek, 2008). Lindstrom, Doren, and Miesch (2011) found common themes that influenced employment (with a living wage) for young adults with disabilities. Key themes that influenced initial post-school placements were: (a) work experiences, (b) transition services and supports, and (c) family support and expectations. Key themes that emerged as influences in career advancement were: (a) participation in postsecondary education or training, (b) stability of employment over time, and (c) personal attributes. Together these themes provide a list of important resources and opportunities leading towards future vocational success for youth with disabilities.

Understanding transition through the theory of emerging adulthood as a developmental process, as well as a service and time period pushes practitioners to make changes in how transition services are viewed. Instead it brings to light that youth with and without disabilities have similar aspirations and there seem to be a number of commonalities for all youth in the transition to adulthood, such as the need for social supports and vocational experiences (Stewart et al., 2013). One can see this in practice through the multi-tiered framework of instruction now implemented at the secondary level, blurring the distinction between specialized and general education (Reed & Vaughn, 2010). In fact some argue services provided solely for youth with disabilities (i.e., transition services) should be given to youth without disabilities (Morningstar, Bassett, Kochlar-Bryant, Gasman, & Wehmeyer, 2012).

Some research has been done on emerging adults and transition services post high school. Izzo, Cartledge, Miller, Growicki, and Rutkowski (2000) examined transition services for individuals with disabilities, provided after high school. The authors conducted a three-year experimental study with random assignment to explore the effects of extended transition services on post-graduate outcomes. Individualized transition services were provided to recent graduates (by job training coordinators), post-graduation. The results of the study demonstrated that participants who received the intervention (i.e., transition support beyond high school) in comparison to the control group earned significantly higher wages over a two-year period, had higher employment rates, and were more likely to be socially active, demonstrated by having a savings account and credit cards. At follow up, between four to six-years post-services participants still demonstrated higher rates of employment. The emerging adults (with disabilities) in this study realized significant increases in terms of employment and social independence, two important markers of adulthood. The authors recommended providing two-years of post-secondary transition services, or extend vocational programs for youth with disabilities, as it is expected to have an exponentially positive impact on students' post-graduate, adult outcomes. It is possible that knowledge of emerging adulthood could assist in the creation of unifying transition practices, giving all youth the much needed social supports and vocational experiences enabling emerging adults to reach their potential as adults.

In another study, Kirby, Edwards, and Sugden (2011) examined the difficulties and related factors of developmental coordination disorder (DCD) otherwise known as Dyspraxia, for emerging adults with disabilities. Dyspraxia is a motor coordination condition affecting motor skill development, especially fine motor activity. This condition is often accompanied by additional difficulties with planning and prioritizing. Youth with various disabilities often experience difficulty with social connections and understanding social norms, leading to fewer opportunities to develop these skills. Yet, it is these social opportunities that are needed to develop internal factors such as self-esteem, autonomy and overall confidence. An absence or diminished presence of these factors can delay or even lengthen the period of emerging adulthood (Kirby et al., 2011). The results of this study demonstrated that emerging adults with DCD continued to experience the expected physical limitations, but additionally experienced difficulties with social isolation, executive functioning, coping and well-being. Although few studies have been conducted on "emerging adults" with disabilities since the advent of EA, themes such as increased social supports, family, adaptation, resilience, and opportunities that affect psychosocial outcomes have been identified as important factors. Central to

success appears to be the time-frame in which support and services are provided, indicating a need for an extension of transition services over a greater period of time, as we see emerging adults accomplishing adult roles into the mid to late 20's (Arnett, 2006).

Implications for Rehabilitation Counselors

Service providers recognize the importance of preparing youth for the adult roles they will assume in the future. According to EA, young adults continue to develop mentally, physically, and emotionally, well beyond high school years, during which time students' segue from entitlement of services, to eligibility based rehabilitation programs and services. Furthermore, medical studies have demonstrated that the brain of a young adult does not completely mature until the early 20's (U.S. Department of Health and Human Services, 2011). Proof that emerging adults undergo significant development at a point when services and supports are often reduced. This evidence indicates that rehabilitation counselors are assuming services for individuals who may have more developmental (specifically, cognitive and emotional) needs than historically assumed. It is essential that rehabilitation counselors understanding the role of family in the life of the consumer, and the external feelings that can impact the world of work for consumers. The burden of social changes for emerging adults with disabilities is falling squarely on the shoulders of the rehabilitation system. Factors that need to be considered are professional development that builds awareness of the different beliefs that influence the success of emerging adults, ways of extending transition services that lead to successful rehabilitation, and a reexamination of rehabilitation counseling practices in general.

One strategy that rehabilitation counselors can utilize to foster adaptation and coping when providing direct services to consumers is motivational interviewing. Motivational interviewing (MI; Miller & Rollnick, 2002) is a person centered direct approach to communication, aimed at facilitating change through techniques such as empathy, unconditional positive regard, and genuineness. In particular, this technique focuses on discrepancies between what an individual has and what he or she wants, and motivates change based on individual needs and desires. Allowing individuals to explore issues and discrepancies, while determining internal motivation to change allows counselors to partner with clients to reduce and normalize ambivalence, and facilitate change. Emerging adults experience an inordinate number of changes, which naturally includes ambivalence and uncertainty. Different from other therapeutic approaches, MI is directive in eliciting motivation for change and change talk, but is not directive through suggestions or solutions created by the counselor, which benefits emerging adults' inherent need for extensive exploration (Iarussi, 2013).

Awareness of Different Values

An important aspect of practitioner or counselor preparation is understanding the influence of different cultural values and identity development for today's youth, as these values and beliefs impact transition to adulthood. A value is an enduring belief that manifests itself into actions (Browning, 1997). Specifically, rehabilitation counselors need to be aware that emerging adults hold different beliefs and place different values on adult roles, as well as the time-period in which transformation into those roles should take place. Understanding of EA as a developmental period builds knowledge of the changes in social values held by youth today and normalizes experiences of youth in terms of numerous occupational experiences and living arrangements, in addition to general expressions of uncertainty during this time period. Given the economic instability of our time, and the advent of emerging adulthood (which is likely no coincidence) it is probable that all students are feeling the effects of these changes. Students with and without disabilities alike will transition from high school to adult roles, which is a commonly shared experience among all high school students regardless of ability status. Therefore, emerging adulthood is a unifying construct that professionals with various backgrounds can use to shape and improve services (e.g., rehabilitation counselors, special educators, general educators, and administrators).

Professional development for counselors should highlight the importance and influence of values within the lens of emerging adulthood. Trainor and colleagues (2008) explained it is possible that conflict of values and beliefs between diverse youth with disabilities and service professionals create barriers to successful services for youth with disabilities. Youth today express differences in the prioritization, trajectory, and time-frame in which they expect to finish high school, go to college, get a job, find a partner, and leave home, in comparison to the generations that have come before them (Arnett, 2006). Thus, there is a substantial need to pay more attention to values and beliefs of youth with disabilities and their transformation into adulthood. If approached from a developmental perspective, services should incorporate the beliefs, values, and developmental constructs of EA, in addition to services and supports that meet the needs of emerging adults.

Transition Services

Conventional approaches to transition policies for students with disabilities stress expedited time-frames, and adult goal achievement shortly after high school (i.e., employment and independent living). The need to begin services at an early age is clear, but the expedition of attaining adult goals prior to the mid to late 20s may be premature according to the theory of EA. Expecting students with disabilities, especially those with intellectual or cognitive conditions to compress and consolidate adult goals into such a condensed time-frame may not only be developmentally unrealistic, but also is not fitting with the prevailing social phenomenon of EA. The average high school student is likely not discussing independent living or career decisions at such an age, and by all accounts from the literature on EA, is not successful in these areas until the mid 20s. As of yet, little exploration has been ventured in terms of the impact of these social trends on students with disabilities, or the transition process.

Viewed as a developmental period, emerging adulthood can bring new meaning to the term transition. This means extended time-frames and services that address the need for further exploration in living, working and socializing. Findings on EA coupled with the results from Izzo et al. (2000) have demonstrated a poignant need for additional services during this transitional period, which extends into the mid 20s of a young adult's life.

Emerging adults spend significantly more time exploring different career and living options than previous generations. As mentioned earlier, emerging adults may experience a multitude of jobs prior to settling on a career.

A career that is likely to change more often than past generations (Arnett, 2000). This inherent need of identity development through exploration will likely translate into extended exploration of vocational options. Currently, the United States is transitioning high school students to college at a higher rate than ever before. According to the National Center for Education Statistics, 70% of high school students transition to college the fall semester after high school graduation. Of the transitioning college students, 11% of these students are students with a disability. The National Center for Education Statistics also reports that 57% of first time college students beginning college in fall semester 2002 completed their Bachelor's degree within six years. With a greater number of college students completing their degree and the unemployment rate high, there is greater competition among those searching for jobs. With 11% of the college freshmen class being an individual with a disability we must better identify ways to transition students with the knowledge they need to be successful in the post-secondary environment, or reexamine the current model being used in transition rehabilitation services.

Rehabilitation counselors should be prepared for the need for extended exploration, incorporating a diversity of experience prior to an emerging adult settling on an occupational choice. Although tenure on the job has been viewed as an asset for an employee, this paradigm shift may emphasize the importance of diversity in experience over length of employment in one occupation. With emerging adults securing multiple occupational experiences during the 20s, youth with disabilities may appear to lack experience, comparatively, if they have had only one or two jobs. Consideration should be given to a new service or program (i.e., rehabilitation service status/code) that addresses the extended time-period emerging adults need to make career decisions. A new service framework with extended time-frames would provide the services and support that emerging adults need. Thus affording counselors the necessary time it takes to appropriately serve emerging adults, and accurately reflecting the progress of the emerging adult within the rehabilitation context. One commonly accepted mode of vocational exploration and a means of extending services is the internship experience through which vocational services would allow consumers to have greater career experiences prior to more permanent job placements.

Conclusion

The social phenomenon of becoming an adult has changed, and with it comes an impact on youth with disabilities, and by extension an impact on the system and services that support emerging adults who have disabilities. Service providers and support systems (i.e., the rehabilitation system) are obligated to keep current with social and economic trends affecting the individuals they serve. Incorporation of the differences in values, beliefs, trends and developmental challenges is important to the future success of services created for emerging adults.

Finally, it is important to realize that emerging adulthood normalizes some experiences that youth with disabilities live with today. Specifically, EA normalizes individuals with disabilities having numerous occupational experiences and living arrangements, and the general expressions of uncertainty during this time period. Therefore, it is important service providers understand emerging adulthood and

in turn shape and improve rehabilitation services to meet these needs.

In conclusion, during the EA stage, young adults begin to feel as if they are adults, but have not yet reached adulthood (Arnett, 2006). Career exploration, decisions, and outcomes are indicators of successful transition. Emerging adulthood presents the idea that decisions young adults make between the ages of 18 to 29 are not static and the expectation should be that they could have very different opinions and desires by their late 20's. According to Arnett, Kloep, Hendry and Tanner (2011), emerging adults experience at least seven job changes between ages 20-29, yet we do not know how youth with disabilities are negotiating these changes, and often we view this type of occupational fluctuation as an internal problem or behavioral issue for youth with disabilities. Conflicting feelings, extensive fluctuation and changes are considered normal and developmentally appropriate for EA, which applies to youth with disabilities ages 18-29 as well. Future research may explore how to provide services that address navigating the general social and economic conditions and opportunities faced by emerging adults with disabilities.

References

Arnett, J. J. (2000). Emerging adulthood: A theory of development from the late teens through the twenties. *American Psychologist, 55,* 469–480. doi: 10.1037//0003-066X.55.5.469

Arnett, J. J. (2006). The psychology of emerging adulthood: What is known, and what remains to be known? In J. J. Arnett & J. L. Tanner (Eds.), *Emerging adults in America: Coming of age in the 21st century* (pp. 303–330). Washington, DC: APA. doi: 10.1037/11381-013

Arnett, J. J., Kloep, M., Hendry, L. B., Tanner, J., L (2011). Debating Emerging Adulthood Stage or Process? New York: Oxford University Press.

Atkinson, D. R., Morten, G., & Sue, D. W. (Eds.). (1993). *Counseling American minorities: A cross-cultural perspective* (4th ed.). Madison, WI: W.C. Brown & Benchmark.

Benz, M. R., Lindstrom, L. E., & Yovanoff, P. (2000). Improving graduation and employment outcomes of students with disabilities: Predictive factors and student perspectives. *Exceptional Children, 66,* 509–529.

Benz, M., Yovanoff, P., & Doren, B. (1997). School to work components that predict post school success for students with and without disabilities. *Exceptional Children, 63,* 152–165.

Bissonnette, D. (1994). *Beyond traditional job development.* Granada Hills, CA: Milt Wright and Associates.

Blustein, D. L, (2008). The role of work in psychological health and well-being: A conceptual, historical, and public policy perspective. *American Psychologist, 63,* 228–240.

Browning, P, (1997). Transition in Action for Youth and Young Adults with Disabilities. Montgomery, AL: Wells Printing

Carter, E., W., Trainor, A., A., Ditchman, N., Swedeen, B., Sun, Y., & Owens, L. (2010). Summer employment and community experiences of transition-age youth with severe disabilities. *Exceptional Children, 76,* 194–212.

Halpern, A. S. (1994). The transition of youth with disabilities to adult life: A position statement of the Division on Career Development in Transition, The Council for Exceptional Children. *Career Development for Exceptional Individuals, 77*(2), 115–124.

Dunn, C., Chambers, D., & Rabren, K. (2004). Predictive factors in dropping out of school for students with disabilities. *Remedial and Special Education, 25,* 314–323.

Erikson, E. H. (1968). *Identity: Youth and crisis.* New York: Norton.

Field, S., & Hoffman, A. (1999). The importance of family involvement for promoting self-determination in adolescents with autism and other developmental disabilities. *Focus on Autism and Other Developmental Disabilities, 14,* 36–41. doi: 10.1177/108835769901400105

Fleming, A. R., Del Valle, R., Kim, M., & Leahy, M. J. (2013). Best practice models of effective vocational rehabilitation service delivery in the public rehabilitation program: A review and synthesis of the empirical literature. *Rehabilitation Counseling Bulletin. 56,* 146–159. doi: 10.1177/0034355212459661

Grant, S. K. (1996). Disability identity development: An exploratory investigation. *Dissertation Abstracts International, 57* (09), 5918B (UMI No. 9704201).

Hanjorgiris, W., F., Rath, J., F., & O'Neill, J., Fl. (2004). Gay men living with chronic disability: A sociocultural, minority group perspective on mental health. *Journal of Gay & Lesbian Social Services, 17,* 25–41.

Hartung, P. J., Porfeli, E., J., Vondracek, F., W. (2008). Career adaptability, *Career Development Quarterly, 57,* 63–74.

Individuals with Disabilities Education Improvement Acts of 2004, Pub. L. No. 108–446, 118 Stat. 2647 (2004) (amending 20 U.S.C. §§ 1440 et seq.).

Iarussi, M. S. (2013). Examining how motivational interviewing may foster college student development. *Journal of College Counseling, 16.* 158–175. http://dx.doi.org/10.1002/j.2161-1882. 2013.00034.x

Izzo, M. V., Cartledge, G., Miller, L., Growicki, B., & Rutkowski, S. (2000). Increasing employment earnings: Extended transition services that make a difference. *Career Development for Exceptional Individuals, 23,* 139–156. doi: 10.1177/08857288 0002300203

Johnstone, B., Mount, D., Gaines, T., Goldfaders, P., Bounds, T., & Pitts, O. (2003). Race differences in a sample of vocational rehabilitation clients with traumatic brain injury. *Brain Injury, 17,* 95–104. doi: 10.1080/0269905021000010212

Keniston, K, (1971). *Youth and dissent: The rise of a new opposition.* New York: Harcourt Brace Jovanovich.

Kirby, A., Edwards, L. & Sugden, D. A. (2011). Emerging Adulthood and Developmental Co-ordination

Disorder. *Journal of Adult Development, 18,* 107–113. doi: 10.1007/sl0804-011-9123-1

Leiter, V., & Waugh, A. (2009): Moving out: Residential independence among young adults with disabilities and the role of families. *Marriage & Family Review, 45,* 519–537. doi: 10.1080/01494920903050847

Lindstrom, L., Doren, B., & Miesch, J. (2011). Waging a living: Career development and long-term employment outcomes for young adults with disabilities. *Exceptional Children, 77,* 423–434.

Martin, D., E. & Oehler, J., S. (2001) Significant Disability: Issues Affecting People with Significant Disabilities from a Historical, Policy, Leadership, and Systems Perspective. Thomas, Charles C. Publisher, Ltd.

Martin, Jr. E. D. (Ed). (2007). *Principles and practices of case management for rehabilitation counselors.* Springfield, IL: Charles C. Thomas.

McDougall, J., Evans, J., & Baldwin, P. (2010). The importance of self-determination to perceived quality of life for youth and young adults with chronic conditions and disabilities. *Remedial and Special Education, 31,* 252–260.

National Center for Education Statistics. (2013, January). Retrieved from http://nces.ed.gov/.

Miller, W. R., & Rollnick, S. (2002). Motivational interviewing: Preparing people for change (2nd ed). New York: Guilford Press.

Morningstar, M., E., Bassett, D., S., Kochlar-Bryant, C., Casman, J., & Wehmeyer, M., L. (2012). Aligning transition services with secondary education reform: A position statement of the Division on Career development and Transition. *Career Development and Transition for Exceptional Individuals, 35,* 132–142.

Morningstar, M., E., Turnbull, A., P., & Trumbull, R., E. (1995). What do students with disabilities tell us about the importance of family involvement in the transition from school to adult life? *Exceptional Children, 62,* 249–260.

Nota, L., Ferrari L., & Wehmeyer, M., L. (2007). Self-determination, social abilities and the quality of life of people with intellectual disability. *Journal of Intellectual Disability Research, 51,* 850–865.

Nota, L., Soresi, S., Ferrari, L., & Wehmeyer, M., L. (2011). A multivariate analysis of the self-determination of adolescents. *Journal of Happiness Studies, 12,* 245–266.

Rabren, K., Dunn, C., & Chambers D. (2002). Predictors of post high school employment among young adults with disabilities. *Journal of Career Development for Exceptional Individuals, 25*(1), 25–40.

Reed, D., & Vaughn, S. (2010). Reading interventions for older students. In T. A. Glover & S. Vaughn (Eds.), *The promise of response to intervention: Evaluating current science and practice* (pp. 143–186). New York, NY: Guilford.

Russell, J. E. (2005). Work performance and careers. In S. Brown & R. Lent (Eds.), in *Career development and counseling* (pp. 203–224). Hoboken, NJ: John Wiley and Sons, Inc.

Shogren, K., A., Wehmeyer, M., L., Palmer, S., Soukup, J., H., Little, T., D., Gamer, N., & Lawrence, M. (2007). Examining individual and ecological predictors of the self-determination of students with disabilities. *Exceptional Children, 73,* 488–509.

Stewart, D., Freeman, M., Law, M., Healy, H., Burke-Gaffney, J., Forhan, M., Young, N., & Guenther, S. (2013). Transition to adulthood for youth with disabilities: Evidence from the literature. In: JH Stone, M., Blouin, editors. International Encyclopedia of Rehabilitation. Available online:http://cirrie.buffalo.edu/encyclopedia/en/article/110/

Tanner, J. L. & Arnett, J. J. (2011). Presenting emerging adulthood: What makes it developmentally distinctive? In J. J. Arnett, M. Kloep, L. B. Hendry, & J. L. Tanner (Eds.), *Debating emerging adulthood: Stage or process?* (pp. 13–31). New York: NY: Oxford University, doi: 10.1093/acprof:oso/9780199757176.003.0002

Trainor, A., A. (2007). Perceptions of adolescent girls with Id regarding self-determination and postsecondary transition planning. *Learning Disability Quarterly, 30,* 31–45.

Trainor, A., A., Lindstrom, L., Simon-Burroughs, M., Martin, J., E., & Sorrells, A., M. (2008). From marginalized to maximized opportunities for diverse youths with disabilities: A position paper of the division on career development and transition. *Career Development and Transition for Exceptional Individuals, 31,* 56–64.

U.S. Department of Health and Human Services. (2011). *The teen brain: Still under construction.* National Institute of Mental Health, NIH Publication No. 11–4929. http://www.nimh.nih.gov/health/publications/the-teen-brain-still-under-construction/complete-index.shtrnl

Ward, M., J. (2005). An historical perspective of self-determination in special education: Accomplishments and challenges. *Research & Practice for Persons with Severe Disabilities, 30,* 108–112.

Wehmeyer, M., L., (2005). Self-determination and individuals with severe disabilities: Re-examining meanings and misinterpretations. *Research and Practice for Persons with Severe Disabilities, 30,* 113–120.

Wehmeyer, M., L., Abery. B., H., Zhang, D., Ward, K., Willis, D., Hossain, W., A., Balcazar, F., Ball, A., Bacon, A., Calkins, C., Heller, T., Goode, T., Dias, R., Jesien, G., S., McVeigh, T., Nygren. M., A., Palmer. S., B., & Walker, H., M. (2011). Personal self-determination and moderating variables that impact efforts to promote self-determination. *Exceptionality, 19,* 19–30.

Wehmeyer, M. L., & Palmer, S. B. (2003). Adult outcomes for students with cognitive disabilities three years after high school: The impact of self-determination. Education and Training in Developmental Disabilities. 38, 131-144.

Wehmeyer, M. L., & Schwartz, M. (1997). Self-determination and positive adult outcomes: A follow-up study of youth with mental retardation or learning disabilities. Exceptional Children, 63, 245–255.

Zhang, D., & Benz, M., R. (2006). Enhancing self-determination of culturally diverse students with disabilities: Current status and future directions. *Focus on Exceptional Children, 38,* 1–12.

My Life as a Dreamer Who Acted Beyond the Barriers

From Growing Up "Undocumented" in Arizona to a Master's Degree from Harvard

Silvia P. Rodríguez Vega

Silvia P. Rodríguez Vega is a 2011 master of arts in education candidate at the Harvard University Graduate School of Education.

> *"Like a candle braving the wind, I refused to burn out."*
>
> —Samuel Diaz Morales, friend of the author, 2010

My life as a DREAM Act student has never been easy. The DREAM Act, defined as the Development, Relief, and Education for Alien Minors Act, is an effort to establish a path to citizenship for some children of illegal immigrants. Most of my peers in this situation face endless stress, experience discrimination, and walk on paths with dead ends. My story begins like the thousands of other students who are in my shoes. My parents brought me into the United States when I was too young to remember. In my case, I was two years old and came to the United States with a tourist visa that expired years later. My mother and father were dreaming of a future for me filled with education and opportunity. They could never have foreseen the events that would happen as I grew into an adult and the suffering our family would endure because of our legal status.

As a child, I never saw myself as any different from my peers. I learned English while watching *Barney & Friends* and loved sleepovers and pizza parties. I grew up with many mentors and role models who demonstrated that women like me could go on and earn a postsecondary education. Much of my inspiration came from the community service projects I joined when I was ten. I was a peer health leader and became very active in theater and other arts for social change. I wanted to help people, and I knew that to do so effectively and at the highest level would require an education.

However, trying to obtain a driving permit and looking into scholarships for college brought the realization that I was not normal. Unlike my friends, I was unable to get a driver's license or apply for many scholarships because my undocumented status did not permit me to do so. But I decided not to give up. I applied and was accepted to Arizona State University (ASU), receiving the Maroon and Gold Scholarship.

In 2006, in the middle of my sophomore year, however, Arizona voters passed Proposition 300, which forced undocumented students to pay out-of-state tuition and further made them ineligible for state, federal, and university-based scholarships. I was devastated and thought my dreams were over. Students affected by this proposition—undocumented students and allies—protested, embarked on seven-day hunger strikes, and lobbied members of Congress including then Speaker of the House Nancy Pelosi, but Prop 300 passed and the DREAM Act was nowhere in sight.

Collaboration between student groups and the university's administration allowed us to continue for another year, but our scholarships were taken away again due to harassment from the state legislature. I attended a Chicano Latino faculty meeting and told them what was happening to students like me. The following week ASU President Michael Crow met with Chicanos Por La Causa (CPLC), a community development corporation in Phoenix, and CPLC launched the American Dream Fund to help us finance our education. However, students who were freshmen when I was graduating are now without the funds to continue their education because CPLC wasn't able to meet its fund-raising goals. Going through these events felt like

being seasick, caught in the ups and downs of a political storm.

When I was in my senior year in college and it looked like I was going to make it, my family decided to leave Arizona. The daily harassment and community raids, due both to my efforts to challenge the proposition as well as a general sentiment against undocumented individuals, were threatening my family, so they moved to the Midwest. This was a very difficult situation for my family. In just one week, my younger brother and sister were pulled from school, and my family had to sell or give away everything for which we had worked so hard over the past eighteen years to acquire. I sold my car and everything but my paintings, some clothes, pictures, and books. I told my mom that I had a place to live and not to worry about me. She did not know that I actually had no place to go. I hid in my friend's dorm room and then lived with nine different people over the following two years while I finished college as I lacked the funds for room and board.

My family members returned to Arizona for my graduation. While many of my classmates were thrilled and celebratory, I was in a strange stage of emotions. Part of me was happy because I had made it. Yet most of me was sad and frustrated at the uncertainty of my future. I was not sure what I would do after graduation, I had no opportunities for employment due to my status, and I was not even sure where I would live.

After graduation, I continued my community organizing, making art, and working with youth. Yet, I felt like a big part of me was missing. I went to visit Professor Carlos Velez-Ibañez who had been my mentor at ASU. When I told him that I was interested in graduate school and why, he said, "*Muchacha*, you want six Ph.Ds!" He encouraged me to do some research and come back in a week. When I returned to his office he pointed me to his computer where he described a program that incorporated many of my areas of interest. When I realized it was at the Harvard University Graduate School of Education, I looked at him with eyes so wide open they threatened to fall out of my head. So many questions were running through my mind: You really think I can make it? How will I get in? He looked at me with believing eyes and said, "That's where you need to go."

The process to apply was long and exhausting. I focused all my attention, mind, heart, time, and resources on the application. My mentors sponsored my application fees and GRE preparation. I had never worked so hard and prayed so hard. In March 2010 I was accepted. It was just like I had dreamed, pictured, and visualized. It began with a letter saying, "Congratulations." It took me days to believe it. When I finally did, I truly thought I was going to die because I thought being accepted was the best thing that could ever happen to me. I could not fathom anything better happening to someone like me—pushed out, criminalized, and undocumented—than being offered an education from Harvard.

I moved forward and submitted my application for financial aid. The cost of tuition alone was $40,000; including room, board, and very conservative living expenses, it would be much closer to $70,000 for the one-year program. Harvard could only offer me a $10,000 grant. Without the opportunity to receive financial aid or loans, my worries increased. I would need to raise $60,000 from other sources. However, I was not going to give up that easily. With a group of good-hearted people who called themselves Friends of Harvard, I began a campaign called Harvard Sí Se Puede!—"Harvard, yes I can!"—to raise money to help fund my education.

It has been a miraculous process. People from the most humble walks of life have stepped up to help me get to where I am now—at Harvard. Working with community groups and churches, we've held bake sales, art shows, and other fund-raising events. I applied for every scholarship I could find and received a few. Despite all my efforts, I kept having moments where I could not understand how this could be possible. Nonetheless, I woke up everyday determined to do it not just for myself, but for all the other students who knew my pain. I was determined to prove that my legal status did not validate or invalidate my humanity. I was simultaneously angry and inspired. But most importantly, I wanted to prove to all undocumented students that any dream could be achieved.

I made it to Harvard, despite a funding deficit. I simply had faith that I would make it. I was not sure how I'd manage to get the rest of the money; I only knew that this was bigger than me.

Right when finals began in the fall semester, I got a call from my sister telling me to pray for our mother. I thought my mother had been injured. I called back right away and found out that my sister's high school was calling U.S. Immigration and Customs Enforcement (ICE) on our mother. I was in complete disbelief; I could not understand why or how this was happening.

I dropped everything and flew to be with my mother and sister. My mother was not in custody so when I arrived we decided to leave the house. We drove to a town where we had a relative. As soon as we arrived my mother had a stroke, and we took her to the hospital. She was there a week, and the doctors told me she needed medical treatment and medication, which she had no access to because she could not legally obtain health insurance. As a family we decided that it would be best for my mother to return to Mexico to be with the rest of our family there so she could receive the medical care she needed. She will not be allowed to return to the United States for ten years. Though still in the United States, because my father is sick and my brother is in prison, only my sister will be able to see me graduate from Harvard in the spring of 2011.

Rewinding back to the day my mother and father brought me to the United States, I do not think this is what they pictured when they thought of the "American Dream." To be honest, our lives have at times felt almost like the American Nightmare.

In December 2010, the DREAM Act failed to pass the U.S. Senate, leaving its future uncertain. Consequently, undocumented youth are dropping out of school in record numbers, and families are being torn apart by xenophobic immigration policy in Arizona. But I keep fighting. I fight for the youth who are not ready to give up. I fight for the children who cannot defend themselves, and I scream for the millions who remain voiceless.

My goals are to help my sister attend college and to be her mentor and role model like the ones I've had in my life; to publish a book from a child's perspective on immigration and Sheriff Joe Arpaio in Arizona and the effect his raids have had on children whose parents have been detained and/or deported; to obtain a Ph.D.; to help as many students as possible follow their dreams; and to seek justice and create change for future generations and the people of Arizona. One day I hope to run my own school and start my own nonprofit with a focus on community empowerment through the arts and educational advancement for underserved people.

The same fire that burned inside me when I was a child continues to burn today. My mission is to help people, and that is why I refuse to let the flame even flicker. I brave the wind, and nothing can stand in my way.

Reflexive Questions

1. As a young adult, what most strongly influenced your knowledge about sex, intimacy, and sexuality?

2. What were your strongest influences in terms of your decisions about sexual interactions?

3. How do you think your gender, culture, race, religion, and nationality, among others, influence your attitudes and actions about sexual decision-making?

4. What does dating mean to you, and how do you think your culture, familial messages, and media messages affect your outlook on dating?

5. When thinking about sexism, what social forces maintain sexism and misogyny as oppressive forces in girls' and women's lives? What are the consequences?

6. How do traditional dating scripts and gendered expectations in romantic relationships undermine gender equality?

7. From your perspective, is emerging adulthood a universal life stage? Explain.

8. How do the expectations of young adults differ from previous generations? How are these expectations influenced by social class, culture, and gender?

9. What stereotypes do you have about young adults with differing cognitive or physical abilities? How do you think societal beliefs shape our prejudice and actions?

10. When considering emerging adulthood, how do you think young adults with different abilities experience this life stage similarly or differently?

11. When considering undocumented young adults, how can legal barriers block teens and young adults from fulfilling their full potential?

12. What liberties and advantages do you take for granted that undocumented young adults do not have? Were these advantages earned or unearned?

CHAPTER 9

Middle Adulthood

Introduction

I have taught undergraduate courses on human development, gender roles, cultural diversity, human sexuality, and family dynamics for over 20 years. For most of these years, I have asked my students what it means to be an adult and if they consider themselves to be an adult. Similar to the participants of Arnett's study (2001), consistently, year and after, most of them have hesitated to claim this identity. They most often feel comfortable with identifying as an emerging adult—not quite an adolescent and not quite an adult. When I ask them what factors they would consider as "adulting," they often mention financial independence, graduating from college, being married or in a long-term relationship, having children, a career, and owning a car and home. When I ask them to pause and contemplate the cultural and socioeconomic values reflected in their beliefs, they begin to understand the biases that inform their perspectives. Worldwide, we know that many women will never be financially independent nor have careers, and many adults will never go to college, own their own home, marry, or have children. These markers of adulthood are by no means universal. Then I probe further. What if a significant life-altering event takes a person off the social clock? For example, what if a teenager has a child or gets married? Are they suddenly catapulted into adulthood? After considering their biases and perspectives, they will often say, "Well, regardless of these factors, I will be an adult, for sure, after the age of 30." For many of my students who are young adults, being an adult often means being an older adult. So then, what does it mean to be an adult, especially at midlife?

Midlife is roughly considered the ages between 40 and 55, often beginning between the ages of 35 and 40 and ending between 60 and 65 (Etaugh, 2018). Although personality traits remain stable into adulthood (Morizot & LeBlanc, 2003), especially with mood and conscientiousness (Harris, Brett, Johnson, & Deary, 2016), menopause and andropause (androgen decline in the aging male) brings forth hormonal changes that affect changes in our bodies and a decline in our senses, organs, circulatory and muscular systems, physical and reproductive health and abilities, among others (Armeni et al., 2016; Morales, Heaton, & Carson, 2000). From a psychosocial perspective, midlife also represents a crossroad in which we often evaluate what we want to continue and what we want to change (Lomranz, et al., 1994; Stewart & Vandewater, 1999). We look back to where we have been and reflect on what we want to do with the time we have left. Many will focus on continuity of what is going well, enjoying the benefits of good health; an established work, family and spiritual life, a sense of community, and lifelong friends. For others, this time will also represent a wake-up call to make important changes (Lachman, 2004). Oftentimes, struggles related to health, finances, romantic and familial relationships will alert an individual to make necessary changes. Some will divorce, cut off from certain family members and friends, relocate, change careers, and change health behaviors. Some will initiate important shifts in gender or sexual identity (Rickards & Wuest, 2006). Others may not be in a position of power to initiate change (Lachman & Weaver, 1998; Sakraida, 2005).

The readers of this text will know by now that a person's experience of advantages and disadvantages at midlife will largely depend on a lifetime of experience with structural inequalities that were in place at one's birth (Cashin, 2014). These factors are often based on the place of one's birth, physical abilities, appearance, race, ethnic group, gender assignment at birth, socioeconomic status of one's parents, sexual orientation, and immigration status, among many others. These factors will often determine where and how we live, how much and what type of food we eat, the quality of the air we breathe and the water we drink, the quality of our education, and access to healthcare and a livable wage. By midlife, these socioeconomic determinants of health will have important effects on the ways we age in our bodies and minds (Braveman & Gottlieb, 2014).

How we define age also adds to this complexity. There are different types of aging, such as chronological, psychological, and biological (Dziechciaz & Filip, 2014). These interconnected ways of aging (senescence) will often have significant effects on our self-perceptions, levels of activity, and how we care for ourselves and interact with others (Degges-White & Myers, 2006). Although we cannot change our chronological age (our actual age in years and months), many of us can affect change in our biological age (based on biomarkers such as the age your body looks, acts, and works at the cellular level) (Jylhävä, Pedersen, & Hägg, 2017). Our psychological or subjective age (subjective description based on experience, logic, attitude, mental abilities, and emotions) is the age you act and feel based on your thoughts, feelings, actions, and reactions to your biological age. Those adults at midlife who are physically active, challenge themselves with new learning and experiences, are adaptive to change, and see themselves as younger in their bodies and minds (subjective age) can effect changes at the cellular level (Spuling, Miche, Wurm, & Wahl, 2013). This is truly remarkable! Remaining strong, optimistic, and healthy is truly preventative and life-affirming.

The extent to which we are able to have overall health and wellbeing will largely determine one's quality of life. Studies in epigenetics and neurogenesis indicate that lifestyle factors are vital to helping prevent certain illnesses and positively affect quality of life (Block & El-Osta, 2017). The influence of epigenetics is further influenced by socioeconomic adversity, with greater adversity leading to accelerated epigenetic aging, linking socioeconomic status to age-related diseases and a person's lifespan. (Fiorito et al., 2017; Meloni, 2015). Additionally, Meloni (2015) suggests that socio-contextual factors are also at play, with the body being deeply dependent on its materially and socially shaped context, He refers to this as embodied constructivism. As noted above, many adults at midlife will continue to enjoy the benefits of cumulative advantage, while others will suffer the consequences of cumulative disadvantage (DiPrete & Eirich, 2006; Rigney, 2010). The interaction effects of individual, interpersonal, structural, and contextual factors have profound effects on one's quality of life during midlife and the extent to which we are able to experience intimacy versus isolation or generativity versus stagnation, as Erikson suggests.

There are endless topics to review for the midlife stage. For this chapter, I selected readings that offer a glimpse at how the effects of one's race (i.e., racism, white privilege) and gender (sexism, male privilege) create the wage gap, as well as how the effects of age (ageism) and gender (sexism, internalized sexism, and misogyny) intersect to affect health and self-esteem. Lastly, the final reading in this chapter offers a first-person account of the challenging and liberating effects of transitioning from male to female during middle adulthood.

Summary of Readings

The reading "**Gender Pay Equity in Advanced Countries: The Role of Parenthood and Policies**" (2013) by Joya Misra and Eiko Strader explores potential causes of and solutions for the gender wage gap. Although the wage gap varies across countries and ethnicities, men consistently earn more than women, oftentimes for the same jobs, and even when women are more qualified. Additionally, fathers earn more than men without children (fatherhood bonus), and mothers receive penalties in pay (motherhood penalty), whereas women without children tend to receive more pay, promotions, and accolades. The researchers note that there are differences in these gender penalties and bonuses based on racial stereotypes and prejudice. They also note that gender socialization in the home is likely to lead to the gender wage gap. Laws aimed at decreasing gender-based wage gaps are helpful, whereas protective labor laws, which exclude women from types of dangerous and hazardous work, often increase gender wage gaps.

Laws and policies are important for mitigating gender-based discrimination. For example, in the United States, the Civil Rights Act of 1964 and the Family and Medical Leave Act of 1993 were created to work toward gender equity. In Europe, many countries provide public, subsidized childcare to lessen the burden of childcare that disproportionately negatively affects women. Authors Misra and Strader posit two types of policies that can help mediate income inequality: gender-neutral paid-leave policies and publicly funded childcare. In sum, the authors argue that policies should be designed with an understanding of the differences in cultural contexts and attitudes toward the care of children. As long as childcare is relegated to women, and women are less valued in society, gender-based income inequality in the workplace will continue. The authors contend that if the appropriate childcare and family policies are in place, gender-based equity in the workplace can be achieved.

The reading "**Is Anti-Aging Medicine the New Ageism?**" (2010) by Arlene Weintraub focuses on how the anti-aging industry preys on older people and their insecurities based on living in an ageist society. Anti-aging medicine advertisements often depict a negative and debilitated image of older adults. Even the term anti-aging is ageist! The anti-aging industry preys on insecurities about the "symptoms" of aging, such as hot flashes or a decrease in sexual drive as if aging were an illness. Moreover, Weintraub contends that anti-aging medicine may have numerous unknown consequences on health, and there are no studies that have proven their effectiveness. Hormones are often the focal point of anti-aging medicine's credo, despite the fact that "there are no long-term, placebo-controlled studies proving that hormones extend life." The author contends that anti-aging doctors are ageist and have negative attitudes toward aging. By pathologizing and problematizing aging, they sell the idea that being old should be avoided at all costs, without warning patients of potentially deadly risks. In sum, the author states that the anti-aging industry preys on the vulnerabilities of middle-aged adults living in a discriminatory and youth-obsessed culture.

In the reading, "**A Midlife Transition**" (2001) by Heather Lamborn, she shares her journey toward self-acceptance as a transgender woman. Lamborn begins the reading by discussing her feelings of grief over spending years and years of her early life trying to live up to others' expectations by trying to act like a boy and a man. From grade school to high school, she felt different and isolated from her male peers. After high school, she struggled to hide her desire to be a woman. All aspects of her life were performative, even her marriage and sex life. Later in life, she came out to her friends and family and sought therapy to help her finally feel free to be herself. Lamborn laments the time she lost longing to be female. Moving forward, however, she no longer grieves over "what has been lost." She now chooses to take the good from her past into her future, feeling happier than ever before.

References

Armeni, E., Lambrinoudaki, I., Ceausu, I., Depypere, H., Mueck, A., Pérez-López, F., van der Schouw, Y., Senturk, L., Simoncini, T., Stevenson, J., Stute, P., & Rees, M. (2016). Maintaining postreproductive health: A care pathway from the European Menopause and Andropause Society (EMAS). *Maturitas, 89,* 63–72. doi:10.1016/j.maturitas.2016.04.013

Arnett, J. J. (2001). Conceptions of the transition to adulthood: Perspectives from adolescence through midlife. *Journal of Adult Development, 8,* 133–143. doi:10.1023/A:1026450103225

Block, T., & El-Osta, A. (2017). Epigenetic programming, early life nutrition and the risk of metabolic disease. *Atherosclerosis, 266,* 31–40. doi:10.1016/j.atherosclerosis.2017.09.003

Braveman, P., & Gottlieb, L. (2014). The social determinants of health: It's time to consider the causes of the causes. *Public Health Reports, 129*(suppl 2), 19–31. https://doi.org/10.1177/00333549141291S206

Cashin, S. (2014). *Place, not race: A new vision of opportunity in America.* Beacon Press.

Degges-White, S., & Myers, J. E. (2006). Women at midlife: An exploration of chronological age, subjective age, wellness, and life satisfaction. *Adultspan Journal, 5,* 67–80. doi:10.1002/j.2161-0029.2006.tb00018.x

DiPrete, T. A., & Eirich, G. M. (2006). Cumulative advantage as a mechanism for inequality: A review of theoretical and empirical developments. *Annual Review of Sociology, 32*(1), 271–297.

Etaugh, C. (2018). *Midlife transitions.* In C. B. Travis, J. W. White, A. Rutherford, W. S. Williams, S. L. Cook, & K. F. Wyche (Eds.), *APA handbooks in psychology. APA handbook of the psychology of women: History, theory, and battle-grounds* (p. 489–503). American Psychological Association. https://doi.org/10.1037/0000059-025

Dziechciaz, M., & Filip, R. (2014). Biological psychological and social determinants of old age: Bio-psycho-social aspects of human aging. *Annals of Agricultural and Environmental Medicine, 21*(4), 835–838.

Fiorito, G., Polidoro, S., Dugué, P., Kivimaki, M., Ponzi, E., Matullo, G., Guarrera, S., Assumma, M., Georgiadis, P., Kyrtopoulos, S., Krogh, V., Palli, D., Panico, S., Sacerdote, C., Tumino, R., Chadeau-Hyam, M., Stringhini, S., Severi, G., Hodge, A., ... Vineis, P. (2017). Social adversity and epigenetic aging: A multi-cohort study on socioeconomic differences in peripheral blood DNA methylation. *Scientific Reports, 7*(16266). doi.org/10.1038/s41598-017-16391-5

Harris, M. A., Brett, C. E., Johnson, W., & Deary, I. J. (2016). Personality stability from age 14 to age 77 years. *Psychology and Aging, 31*(8), 862–874. doi:10.1037/pag0000133

Jylhävä, J., Pedersen, N. L., & Hägg, S. (2017). Biological age predictors. *EBioMedicine, 21,* 29–36. doi:10.1016/j.ebiom.2017.03.046.

Lachman, M. E. (2004). Development in midlife. *Annual Review of Psychology, 55*(1), 305–331.

Lachman, M. E., & Weaver, S. L. (1998). Sociodemographic variations in the sense of control by domain: Findings from the MacArthur studies of midlife. *Psychology and Aging, 13*(4), 553–562. https://doi.org/10.1037/0882-7974.13.4.553.

Lomranz, J., Shmotkin, D., Eyal, N., Friedman, A. (1994). Expectations for changes in midlife men. *Social Behavior and Personality: An International Journal, 22*(20), 111–121. doi:10.2224/sbp.1994.22.2.111

Morizot, J., & Le Blanc, M. (2003). Continuity and change in personality traits from adolescence to midlife: A 25-year longitudinal study comparing representative and adjudicated men. *Journal of Personality, 71*(5), 705–755. https://doi.org/10.1111/1467-6494.7105002

Meloni, M. (2015). Epigenetics for the social sciences: justice, embodiment, and inheritance in the postgenomic age. *New Genetics and Society, 34*(2), 125–151. doi:10.1080/14636778.2015.1034850

Morales, A., Heaton J. P., & Carson, C. C. (2000). Andropause: a misnomer for a true clinical entity. *The Journal of Urology, 163*(3), 705–712. doi:10.1016/s0022-5347(05)67788-9

Rickards, T., & Wuest, J. (2006). The process of losing and regaining credibility when coming-out at midlife. *Health Care for Women International, 27*(6), 530–547. doi:10.1080/07399330600770254

Rigney, D. (2010). *The Matthew effect: How advantage begets further advantage.* Columbia University Press. doi:10.7312/rign14948

Spuling, S. M., Miche, M., Wurm, S., & Wahl, H. (2013). Exploring the causal interplay of subjective age and health dimensions in the second half of life: A cross-lagged panel analysis. *Zeitschrift für Gesundheitspsychologie. 21,* 5–15. doi:10.1026/0943- 8149/a000084

Sakraida, T. J. (2005) Divorce transition differences of midlife women. *Issues in Mental Health Nursing, 26*(2), 225–249. doi:10.1080/01612840590901699

Stewart, A. J., & Vandewater, E. A. (1999). "If I had it to do over again ...": Midlife review, midcourse corrections, and women's wellbeing in midlife. *Journal of Personality and Social Psychology, 76*(2), 270–283. doi:10.1037/0022-3514.76.2.270

Gender Pay Equity in Advanced Countries

The Role of Parenthood and Policies

Joya Misra and Eiko Strader

Parenthood & Earnings

In most advanced economies, mothers earn substantially less than childless women, while fathers earn somewhat more than childless men.[1] These phenomena have been termed the motherhood penalty and fatherhood bonus, respectively. In the United States, while researchers identify a 7 percent wage penalty per child, only one-third of this penalty can be attributed to the loss of work experience.[2] There are two major explanations that have been advanced to account for these outcomes. Some scholars theorize that gendered specialization in the household is a key driver of wage differentials.[3] Consider a household composed of a married man and woman. If each focuses on different household roles—with the man emphasizing paid employment and the woman emphasizing caregiving responsibilities—this might affect workplace productivity. The man may work harder and longer while the woman may work less due to her engagement in caregiving responsibilities outside of the work environment. Research finds that time spent on household tasks that are typed as "female," such as meal preparation and housekeeping, reduces the wages of both men and women.

Women tend to engage in those tasks more on average. This suggests that those tasks may drive the gender wage gap.[4] A longitudinal study examining changes in women's wages over time found that the motherhood penalty is primarily realized when mothers interrupt their employment due to childcare responsibilities.[5] However, findings do not always support this specialization theory. For example, motherhood penalties in the United States vary by race and ethnicity, with white women paying the largest penalties. Yet this does not explain why Latinas do not see a motherhood penalty, despite more traditional divisions of labor among men and women in Latino households.[6]

Researchers also explore the effect of specialization on wage bonuses for men. Drawing upon some of the research mentioned above, one can theorize that only men who benefit from a partner who "specializes" in unpaid work would earn a wage bonus. For each additional hour an American wife works, her husband's wage gains reduce, which may support the idea that a heterosexual married man's higher wages are due to higher productivity.[7] Research also suggests that white and Latino men, whose families have more traditional breadwinner or caregiver divisions, do appear to earn larger fatherhood bonuses—4 percent and 8 percent, respectively.[8] Yet these effects do not hold for African-American men.[9] Employer perceptions, rather than differences in productivity, may play a role. The employers "may be less likely to view black fathers as committed breadwinners, and black men may experience less of a labor market bonus for fatherhood."[10]

Other research considers the role of employer discrimination. One study looks at a worker's race and gender and compares their employer's productivity descriptions with the employee's actual work records. The results demonstrate that some employers discriminate against women—particularly African-American women—stereotyping them as less committed or productive, even when their work records do not indicate any basis for such characterization.[11] Experimental research similarly suggests that employers stereotype mothers as less competent and committed. In a laboratory experiment carried out with undergraduate volunteers, the students assessed application materials for a mid-level marketing position; the materials established that candidates had the same credentials, experience, and productivity, but varied resumes by the first name of the worker, indicating race and gender, and listed that they volunteered in a community organization or for a parent-teacher organization. The researchers found that those who were believed to be mothers were less likely to get positions, and of those who were, they were offered lower salaries—7.9 percent less than perceived childless women and 8.6 percent less than fathers.[12]

The same study carried out an audit of actual employers advertising employment vacancies to see how they responded to applications. Some of the employee applications included a cover letter mentioning that the potential employee was relocating to the city, while others noted that they were specifically relocating with their families to the city. Women who mentioned families were half as likely to be interviewed than women who did not mention families, while men who mentioned families were slightly more likely to be interviewed than men who did not.[13] Therefore, employers' assumptions about mothers' productivity may help account for some of the gender wage gap.

There remain important gendered distinctions behind wage penalties and bonuses, rather than productivity differences due to specialization.

Well-designed studies based on survey data may also challenge the specialization argument. One study compares partnered and single men and women, both childless and parents, and argues that if specialization explains wage differences, both partnered women and mothers would see penalties. Instead, both partnered men and women see wage premiums, relative to single men and women, though the gain is larger for men.[14] In addition, if the specialization theory holds true, both men and women who have full-time working partners should experience penalties. Yet men's wages are higher when their partners work less than full-time, while the same is not true for partnered women. Moreover, while mothers appear to alter employment hours, job traits, and tenure in ways similar to fathers, whose wages increase, mothers experience a substantial wage penalty.[15] In conclusion, there remain important gendered distinctions behind wage penalties and bonuses, rather than productivity differences due to specialization.

Both motherhood penalties and fatherhood bonuses vary cross-nationally. Considering this may allow us to analyze the factors driving these penalties and bonuses, since these reflect different patterns in employment, caregiving, and policies aimed at addressing work-family conflict. More research considers how motherhood wage penalties differ across countries, while considerably less examines the fatherhood bonus across countries.[16] Wage premiums exist for fathers in all countries. However, these premiums are only robust in a few countries after controlling for variables such as human capital, marital status, and work hours. This bonus also links to their partners' employment status. Men with a caregiving partner are more likely to earn the premium in a number of countries.[17] Motherhood penalties are more consistent across a wide range of countries, controlling for human capital, marital status, and work hours, though they vary dramatically in degree.[18] Previous cross-national studies suggest that work-family policies, such as paid leaves and state-subsidized childcare, may help explain this variation, a point we will examine below. [...].

Policies Aimed at Reducing the Gender Gap

There are many policies that aim at reducing the gender gap, such as the U.S. Civil Rights Act of 1964.[19] In a meta-analysis, researchers find that equal treatment laws are associated with lower gender wage gaps cross-nationally, although protective labor legislation targeted at women, usually excluding them from particular types of dangerous or hazardous work, tends to increase gender wage gaps.[20] Hence, equal opportunity policies may lose power over time if enforcement mechanisms are not in place.[21] In the U.S., for example, the Equal Pay Act of 1963 has a number of loopholes that make it less effective at fighting gender wage discrimination.[22]

Much of the gender wage gap can also be attributed to occupational gender segregation, with women earning less in occupations traditionally staffed by women.[23] This leads to a range of policy approaches, such as comparable worth and other policies aimed at integrating occupations.[24] These policies, if designed effectively, also have the potential of making strong inroads regarding gender inequality.

In addition to these approaches, however, we believe that there are other policies that can address the gender wage gap, and particularly the gaps that reflect parenthood, including motherhood penalties and fatherhood bonuses. We argue for two major sets of policies that can effectively mediate these inequalities. The first are moderate-length, gender-neutral, paid-leave policies, which allow both parents to share care for infants and toddlers. A second policy set includes publicly-funded childcare that aims at providing employment support for the parents, as well as caring for and educating toddlers and preschoolers and providing afterschool and vacation care.

Leave Policies

Leave policies include maternity and paternity leaves—aimed at supporting mothers and fathers after the immediate birth or adoption of a child—as well as parental leaves, which are often longer and meant to enable parents to care for infants and young toddlers. These leaves may be paid or unpaid. In most countries, maternity and paternity leaves are well-paid, while parental leaves vary more in compensation. Parental leaves are often gender-neutral by design, but are generally taken by mothers, particularly if they earn less, and leaves are paid as a proportion of usual income. The most effective gender-neutral parental leave policies have relatively high compensation rates and include "use it or lose it" periods of leave that can only be taken by fathers.[25]

Maternity leave policies are integral to maintaining women's continuing labor force participation, especially when children are first born or adopted.[26] Mothers who reside in countries with short unpaid or non-mandatory leave policies often must leave the labor force to care for infants. They then face the prospect of reentering the work force with less experience.[27] Paid maternity leaves are common across wealthy countries, although the U.S. and, until recently, Australia, have been outliers.[28] In the U.S., while some workers qualify for twelve weeks of unpaid leave as provided by the Family and Medical Leave Act (FMLA), this leave is an unaffordable right for many working-class and poor families.[29]

Scholars have long argued that lost tenure from labor force withdrawal may explain a large proportion of the gender wage gap and the motherhood wage penalty.[30] Paid leave programs can ensure that women remain attached to the labor force. When California implemented a paid leave program in 2004, researchers found that it doubled the overall use of maternity leave, particularly for less advantaged groups, and increased the weekly working hours and incomes for mothers with children between one and three years of age.[31]

Parental leaves also help parents care for young children. Indeed, in many countries, these policies are aimed at and primarily taken advantage of by mothers. When parental leave policies are well-paid, families can provide care for infants and toddlers without losing ties to the labor market. However, the design of the policy matters a great deal in terms of compensation, length of the leave, and whether part of the leave is reserved for fathers. When parental leaves are unpaid or poorly paid, some families may not be able to use the leave. Very short parental leaves can also be less effective

because of the difficulties in finding childcare for newborn infants. On the other hand, moderate-length paid leaves can have more positive effects, particularly when coupled with measures to increase men's caregiving. Yet when parental leaves are very long and primarily taken by women, mothers lose valuable job experience and may find little prospect for career advancement later on. The leaves may discourage employers from hiring women by placing them on a so-called "mommy track," rather than a regular career track.

Indeed, the relationship between mothers' earnings and length of leave is curvilinear.[32] Motherhood wage penalties exceed 6 percent per child in countries with less than one year or more than three years of job-protected leave, while the per child penalty is only slightly more than 1 percent in countries with moderate job-protected leave, controlling for other factors known to affect wages.[33] This suggests that while paid leaves are important to mediate the gender gap and motherhood penalty, leaves need to be designed so as to avoid long absences from the labor force.

For example, until recently, parental leave in Germany was almost three years in length.[34] While parental leaves may help women maintain links to employment, very long leaves may lead to employers placing mothers on a separate career track. As Figure Two shows, the motherhood penalty is very strong in West Germany. Although the same leave policies existed in East Germany, women were less likely to take very long leaves, given the history of women's employment, as well as better availability of childcare places in East Germany, which we discuss below.

Research based in Hungary finds that employers explicitly blame long leave policies for their attempts to screen out mothers in the hiring process.[35] Employers also channel women with childbearing aspirations into lower-level positions. In addition, employers restructure positions in order to terminate workers despite job guarantees, route returning workers into positions with lower authority, and pressure exceptional workers into taking shorter leaves.[36] This research suggests why women in countries with long parental leaves may be disadvantaged.

Countries with leaves aimed at fathers may further reduce the penalties faced by mothers, as well as the bonuses provided to fathers. For example, fathers in Sweden are entitled to two weeks of fully paid paternity leave, and two months of paid parental leave that can only be taken by fathers, referred to as "use it or lose it." As a result, as shown in Figure Two, there is a much smaller motherhood penalty in Sweden than in other countries, while the fatherhood bonus disappears. Swedish employers tend to view both men and women as caregivers; these roles are not stigmatized in the Swedish labor market.

Publicly Subsidized Childcare

In addition to leaves, research shows that publicly subsidized childcare significantly increases the wages and employment attachment of mothers, especially for those with children ages three and younger.[37] Most wealthy countries have universal preschool in place for children between ages three and six, although these programs differ by how many hours are available.[38] Research consistently shows positive outcomes from publicly subsidized childcare and educational programs, including afterschool programs and programs over vacations.[39] While publicly subsidized care for infants and toddlers varies more across wealthy countries, where it exists, employment and wages are higher and risk of poverty is lower.[40]

Countries with greater access to childcare for infants and toddlers have lesser motherhood penalties. East Germany, France, and Sweden are often noted as having better publicly subsidized childcare coverage as compared to other industrialized nations, and they indeed have lesser motherhood wage penalties than those countries, such as the U.S. and West Germany.[41] In countries with minimal publicly subsidized childcare, mothers are less likely to be employed while those who are employed see larger wage penalties. The per-child wage penalty is roughly 10 percent in countries with limited public childcare and only 4 percent in countries with generous childcare coverage, after controlling for relevant wage determinants.[42]

Another policy that is often recommended to address work-family conflict and the gender gap in pay is flexible working hours, including part-time employment. Yet we do not include this policy among our recommendations because this approach tends to relegate women to lower status positions in the labor market. For example, the Netherlands is often touted for its Work and Care Act that encourages flexible work schedules. However, many have criticized this scheme for sustaining gender wage gap and motherhood wage penalty by encouraging part-time employment among women and full-time employment among men.[43] As Figure Two demonstrates, even though we control for part-time employment, mothers in the Netherlands clearly suffer from significant wage penalty, while fathers benefit from nearly a ten percentile ranking increase in their earnings.

Conclusion

We have discussed how the motherhood penalty and fatherhood bonus together explain a large portion of gender wage disparities across wealthy countries and have highlighted the importance of specific public policies in narrowing the gaps. Research on the gender wage gap often focuses on explaining why women as a whole earn less than men, which leads to an emphasis on broad policies designed to improve employment conditions for women. However, our analysis makes it clear that policies can encourage, discourage, or sustain various gendered employment patterns that reflect not only gender, but also gendered parenthood. Understanding this nuance is critical to gaining forward momentum in the pursuit of gender wage equality.

We argue that a multi-faceted approach to achieving gender wage equality is warranted for two main reasons. First, to provide short- and long-term support for parenthood, both leave policies and the provision of publicly subsidized childcare should be discussed. Publicly subsidized childcare alone will not meet the needs of parents with newborns, while leave policies without a concomitant investment in childcare may lead to gendered divisions of care responsibilities, which may support employer perception of "juggling" mothers and committed fathers. Paying attention to the design of the policies, with an aim to equalizing the involvement of *both* parents in caregiving and employment, will lead to better outcomes.

In addition, policies need to be designed in recognition of differences in cultural contexts and attitudes toward care for children. For example, policies are most effective when the culture supports maternal employment.[44] This finding suggests that the gender earnings gap in the U.S. might shrink with the right policies in place, since Americans tend to value maternal employment.[45] Investing in early education and childcare programs, together with paid,

gender-neutral, moderate-length leaves, is likely to pay off in strong dividends regarding lower levels of gender inequality.

Understanding the different mechanisms behind gender wage gaps across these eleven countries allows us to suggest more effective policy recommendations. Countries with very large motherhood penalties should focus primarily on policy solutions aimed at addressing how gendered parenthood affects employment and earnings. This is not to suggest that policies aimed at the gender gap more broadly—such as those targeting discrimination, comparable worth, or occupational gender segregation—are not useful, as they are important mechanisms for addressing gender inequality more broadly. However, we hope this paper highlights the complexity of mechanisms behind the gender wage gap and suggest that future studies and policy analyses consider the differential impact of gendered parenthood on wages.

Notes

1 Michelle J. Budig and Melissa Hodges, "Differences in Disadvantage: Variation in the Motherhood Penalty Across White Women's Earnings Distribution," *American Sociological Review* 75, no. 5 (8 October 2010), 705-728; Budig and England; Deborah J. Anderson, Melissa Binder, and Kate Krause, "The Motherhood Wage Penalty Revisited: Experience, Heterogeneity, Work Effort, and Work-Schedule Flexibility," *Industrial and Labor Relations Review* 56, no. 2 (2003), 273-294; Jane Waldfogel, "The Effect of Children on Women's Wages," *American Sociological Review* 62, no. 2 (1997), 209-217; Shelley J. Correll, Stephen Benard, and In Paik, "Getting a Job: Is There a Motherhood Penalty?," *American Journal of Sociology* 112, no. 5 (2007), 1297-1339; Rebecca Glauber, "Race and Gender in Families and at Work: The Fatherhood Wage

Premium," *Gender & Society* 22, no. 1 (February 2008), 8–30; Killewald and Gough; Wendy Sigle-Rushton and Jane Waldfogel, "Motherhood and Women's Earnings in Anglo-American, Continental European, and Nordic Countries," *Feminist Economics* 13, no. 2 (2007), 55–91; Rebecca Glauber, "Marriage and the Motherhood Wage Penalty Among African Americans, Hispanics, and Whites," *Journal of Marriage and Family* 69, no. 4 (November 2007), 951–961.

2   Budig and England.

3   Mary C. Noonan, "The Impact of Domestic Work on Men's and Women's Wages," *Journal of Marriage and Family* 63, no. 4 (2001), 1134–1145; Shelly Lundberg and Elaina Rose, "Parenthood and the Earnings of Married Men and Women," *Labour Economics 7*, no. 6 (November 2000), 689–710; Hyunbae Chun and Injae Lee, "Why Do Married Men Earn More: Productivity or Marriage Selection?" *Economic Inquiry* 39, no. 2 (April 2001), 307–319.

4   Noonan.

5   Lundberg and Rose.

6   Glauber (2007).

7   Chun and Lee.

8   Glauber (2008), 22.

9   Ibid.

10   Ibid., 25.

11   Irene Browne and Ivy Kennelly, "Stereotypes and Realities: Images of Black Women in the Labor Market," in *Latinas and African American Women at Work*, ed. Irene Brown (New York: Russell Sage Foundation, 1999), 302–326.

12   Correll, Benard, and Paik, 1323.

13   Ibid, 1330.

14   Killewald and Gough.

15   Ibid.

16   For research focused on the motherhood penalty, see Michelle J. Budig, Joya Misra and Irene Boeckmann, "The Motherhood Penalty in Cross-National Perspective: The Importance of Work-Family Policies and Cultural Attitudes," *Social Politics: International Studies in Gender, State & Society* 19, no. 2 (17 May 2012), 163–193; Joya Misra, Michelle J. Budig and Stephanie Moller, "Reconciliation Policies and the Effects of Motherhood on Employment, Earnings and Poverty," *Journal of Comparative Policy Analysis Research and Practice* 9, no. 2 (2007), 135–155; Sigle-Rushton and Waldfogel (2007). For research that investigated the fatherhood bonus, see Irene Boeckmann and Michelle J. Budig, "Fatherhood, Intra-household Employment Dynamics, and Men's Earnings in a Cross-National Perspective" (LIS working paper series, no. 592, June 2013).

17   Boeckmann and Budig (2008).

18   Budig, Misra, and Boeckmann (2012); Misra, Budig, and Moller (2007); Joya Misra, Michelle Budig, and Irene Boeckmann, "Work-family Policies and the Effects of Children on Women's Employment Hours and Wages," *Community, Work & Family* 14, no. 2 (May 2011), 139–157.

19   Ann Orloff, "From Maternalism to 'Employment for All': State Policies to Promote Women's Employment across the Affluent Democracies," in *The State after Statism*, ed. Jonah D. Levy (Cambridge, MA: Harvard University Press, 2006), 230–268.

20   Doris Weischelbaumer and Rudolf Winter-Ebmer, "International gender wage gaps: The effects of competition and equal treatments laws on gender wage differentials," *Economic Policy* (April 2007), 235–287.

21   Kevin Stainback and Donald Tomaskovic-Devey, *Documenting Desegregation* (New York, NY: Russell Sage Foundation, 2012).

22   Joel P Rudin and Kimble Byrd, "U.S. Pay Equity Legislation: Sheep in Wolves' Clothing," *Employee Responsibilities and Rights Journal* 15, no. 4 (December 2003), 183–190.

23   Asaf Levanon, Paula England, and Paul Allison, "Occupational Feminization and Pay: Assessing Causal Dynamics Using 1950-2000 U.S. Census Data," *Social Forces* 88, no. 2 (December 2009),

865-891; Maria Charles and David B. Grusky, *Occupational Ghettos: The Worldwide Segregation of Women and Men* (Palo Alto: Stanford University Press, 2004); Donald Tomaskovic-Devey and Sheryl Skaggs, "Sex Segregation, Labor Process Organization, and Gender Earnings Inequality," *American Journal of Sociology* 108, no. 1 (2002), 102–128.

24 Rudin and Byrd; Joan Acker, *Doing Comparable Worth* (Philadelphia: Temple University Press, 1989); Levanon, England, and Allison; Paula England, "Uneven and Stalled," *Gender & Society* 24, no. 2 (2010), 149–166.

25 "Maternity at Work: A Review of National Legislation" (ILO report, Geneva: 2010), http://www.ilo.org/wcmsp5/groups/public/@dgreports/@dcomm/@publ/documents/publication/wcms_124442. pdf.

26 Anne Gauthier, "Family Policies in Industrialized Countries: Is There Convergence?," *Population* 57, no. 3 (2002), 447–474; J.C. Gornick and M.K. Meyers, *Families That Work: Policies for Reconciling Parenthood and Employment* (New York: Russell Sage Foundation, 2005).

27 Becky Pettit and Jennifer L. Hook, *Gendered Tradeoffs: Family, Social Policy, and Economic Inequality in Twenty-One Countries* (New York: Russell Sage Foundation, 2009); Misra, Budig and Boeckmann, (2011); Boeckmann, Misra and Budig, "Mothers' Employment in 19 Wealthy Western Countries: How Do Cultural and Institutional Factors Shape the Motherhood Employment and Working Hours Gap?" (conference draft, New Orleans: April 2013).

28 Regarding Australia's recent adoption of paid maternity leave, see Ray Broomhill and Rhonda Sharp, "Australia's Parental Leave policy and Gender Equality: An International Comparison" (Australian Workplace Innovation and Social Research Centre, The University of Adelaide, Australia: 2012), http://www.adelaide.edu.au/wiser/pubs/WISeR_Parental_Leave_Policy_and_Gender_Equality_an_international_comparison_report.pdf.

29 Naomi Gerstel and Amy Armenia, "Giving and Taking Family Leave: Right or Privilege?," *Yale Journal of Law & Feminism* 21, no. 1 (2009), 161–184.

30 Waldfogel; Budig and England.

31 Mary Rossin-Slater, Christopher J. Ruhm, and Jane Waldfogel, "The Effects of California's Paid Family Leave Program on Mothers' Leave-Taking and Subsequent Labor Market Outcomes," *Journal of Policy Analysis and Management* 32, no. 2 (2013), 224–245.

32 Pettit and Hook; Michelle J. Budig, Joya Misra, and Irene Boeckmann, "The Wage Penalty for Motherhood in a Cross-National Perspective: Relationships with Work-Family Policies and Cultural Attitudes" (Population Association of America conference paper, April 2010), 21.

33 Ibid.

34 This source includes data on the lengths of leaves. Irene Boeckmann, Michelle Budig and Joya Misra, "The Work-Family Policy Indicators" (Sociology Department, University of Massachusetts-Amherst: 2010), 4, http://www.lisdatacenter.org/wp-content/uploads/resources-other-work-family-policy-indicators.pdf.

35 Christy Glass and Eva Fodor, "Public Maternalism Goes to Market: Recruitment, Hiring, and Promotion in Postsocialist Hungary," *Gender & Society* 25, no. 1 (20 January 2011), 5–26.

36 Ibid.

37 Misra, Budig, and Moller; Misra, Budig, and Boeckmann (2011); Budig, Misra, and Boeckmann, (2012); Pettit and Hook; Budig, Misra, and Boeckmann (2010).

38 Jane Lewis, *Work-Family Balance, Gender, and Policy* (Northampton, MA: Edward Elgar, 2009).

39 Gornick and Meyers; Pettit and Hook.

40 Misra, Budig, and Boeckmann (2011); Misra et al., "Family Policies, Employment and Poverty Among

Partnered and Single Mothers," *Research in Social Stratification and Mobility* 30, no. 1 (March 2012), 113–128; Misra, Budig, and Moller (2007); Budig, Misra, and Boeckmann (2010); Budig, Misra, and Boeckmann (2012); Boeckmann, Misra, and Budig (2013).

41 Irene Boeckmann, Michelle Budig, and Joya Misra, "The Work-Family Policy Indicators" (Sociology Department, University of Massachusetts-Amherst: 2010), 4, http://www.lisdatacenter.org/ wp-content/uploads/resources-other-work-family-policy-indicators,pdf.

42 Budig, Misra, and Boeckmann (2010), 21.

43 Janneke Plantenga and Chantal Remery, "The Provision of Childcare Services: A Comparative Review of 30 European Countries" (report, Office for Official Publications of the European Communities, Luxembourg: 2009).

44 Budig, Misra, and Boeckmann (2010).

45 Ibid., 172.

Is Anti-Aging Medicine the New Ageism?

Arlene Weintraub

When I was reporting my book (New York: Basic Books, 2010), I traveled to Boston to interview Dr. Thomas Perls, a professor at Boston University School of Medicine and founder of the New England Centenarian Study (NECS). The study began in 1995, researching the genetic makeup of Bostonians who are more than 100 years old. Today, NECS has become the largest comprehensive study of centenarians in the world.

As anti-aging medicine was catching fire in the mid-90s, Perls told me, he happened upon the website of one of the new anti-aging societies—and he was flabbergasted. "I was finding my work quoted by these characters who were saying they could stop and reverse aging," Perls recalled. "They had this very pernicious view of elderly people. They had pictures of old people sitting in wheelchairs and staring at nursing home walls, and they were saying, 'This is what getting old is all about.'"

There are no long-term, placebo-controlled studies proving that hormones extend life.

The deeper I dug into the anti-aging industry, the more I came to believe that Perls was right. By the very nature of their work, anti-aging doctors propagate a new form of ageism. It's not that they're opposed to the idea of people living long lives. But they're deeply committed to the idea that the typical symptoms of growing old—hot flashes, loss of energy, creaky joints, what have you—can and should be avoided.

A Premise Unproven

The basic premise of anti-aging medicine seems logical: hormones decline as we age; therefore, all we have to do to avoid aging is restore our hormones to the levels they were when we were 30 or even younger. Anti-aging doctors promote human growth hormone (HGH), testosterone and "bioidentical" estrogen and progesterone to people who are otherwise healthy.

Hormones are the cornerstone of the anti-aging credo, which one doctor described to me as rectangularization (mortality compression). The idea, he said, is that patients should not have to age like their parents did, suffering a gradual increase in frailty and slow descent towards the nursing home—*triangularization* if you will. Instead they can use hormones to stay strong and healthy throughout their lives, and then "fall off a cliff fast," he said.

I find that sad. The fact is, there are no long-term, placebo-controlled studies proving that hormones extend life and that they're safe for healthy people to take long-term.

Consider the story of Hanneke Hops, who told the *San Francisco Chronicle* (November 2003) that daily injections of HGH were making her strong enough to run marathons, ride horses and fly planes. Three months later she died of liver cancer. She was 56. No one will ever know if the growth hormone played a role.

Glossing Over the Risks

If patients were aware of the concerns about anti-aging medicine, many would choose to bypass these unproven therapies for the chance of attending a grandchild's wedding at age 80, even if it meant being there in a somewhat frail state.

The industry preys upon vulnerabilities of certain segments of the over-50 population.

One of the most alarming aspects of the anti-aging industry is that it preys upon vulnerabilities of certain segments of the over-50 population. Take, for example, women in menopause who are suffering from hot flashes and other symptoms that make them desperate for relief.

When the Women's Health Initiative, a federally funded study, tied the popular menopause drug PremPro to an increased risk of breast cancer, the anti-aging industry stepped in and persuaded millions of women they could take estrogen from natural sources, like soy and yam. They'd be perfectly safe, the doctors said, because such bioidentical hormones are exact copies of what women's own bodies made in their younger years.

In my experience, many women simply don't understand that bioidentical hormones actually contain estrogen—and that all estrogens, regardless of the source, are thought to raise the risk of breast cancer, blood clots, heart attacks and strokes.

Why does the anti-aging industry gloss over the risks of the therapies they promote? I have to believe it's because if physicians who practice this specialty were forthright about the risks, with themselves and with their patients, they might not have anything left to promote at all. That makes anti-aging medicine one of the most disturbing examples of ageism in modern society.

Journalist Arlene Weintraub is the author of Selling the Fountain of Youth *(New York, N.Y.: Basic Books, 2010). She has more than 15 years of experience writing about healthcare pharmaceuticals and biotechnology.*

A Midlife Transition

Heather Lamborn

It's two o'clock in the morning, and I am once again filling my pillow with tears. For many nights, I have been unable to sleep, as my mind is filled with a terrible grief. Grief for what? I have been grieving the loss of my identity, my spirit, my soul. I feel trapped, with no room to turn, no place to hide my obligations to my elderly mother and my children. I feel exhausted, without the strength to continue life.

These were the thoughts that were becoming more intense every day. It was like a dam that had burst. I was no longer able to suppress my emotions—emotions that I had been able to keep under control for most of my fifty-four years. I had never before allowed myself to love deeply, to hate with passion, to cry in misery, or to laugh with the sheer exhilaration of living. I had always kept myself busy in order to crowd out thoughts about myself. Now, all these defenses had crumbled, and I felt lost and frail.

Except for a brief period during my early childhood, I had spent my life trying to live up to the expectations of others. Their interests always seemed to be more important than my own. How could I tell anyone my deepest, darkest secret? How could I possibly tell anyone that for my entire life I have hated the male body of my birth. What a cruel joke nature had played on me by not giving me the female body for which I had longed since earliest childhood!

At the age of four, I was allowed to wear my cousin's old dresses and to play as a girl. When I started school, however, all that changed. I was no longer allowed to wear my cousin's clothes. At school I avoided girls so that I would not be called a sissy, but at home my closest friends were girls. At school, I was unable to identify with the boys and join in their rough play, and I couldn't play with the girls for fear of teasing by the boys. I felt so alone.

After puberty, things got worse. The girls were always talking about boys, which excluded me from their circle. The boys were rougher than ever, and seemed to talk only about sex, sports, and cars. I was interested in none of these things and had no male friends. I followed quieter pursuits, although my lack of interest in sex bothered me. Was I homosexual? I didn't think so, but if not, why did I have this overwhelming desire to be a girl? I was confused. High school was the loneliest time of my life.

Those years were the mid fifties, and transsexualism was a word that was not yet in common usage. I didn't think of myself as a transvestite either; I just wanted to be a girl. Christine Jorgensen had recently made the headlines, but I thought of her sex change as some kind of unique experiment. I felt that I was alone in the world. I believed that I must be suffering from some sort of insanity.

For the next twenty years I struggled to control my "insanity" and not let anyone find out about my true feelings. I joined the army and served two years in peacetime Korea. I married a Korean woman because my family expected that I should marry, and I was less intimidated by Korean women than by American women. I got a civilian job at the Naval Air Station in Oakland, California, where we bought a house and raised three children. To all outward appearances, I was moderately successful, and was living a normal, uneventful life. In my own mind, however, things were far from normal and uneventful. I was still under the assumption that I was suffering from some form of insanity. The act of love with my wife was possible only if I fantasized that I was a woman. I acted out the male sex role as a duty to my wife; I felt like a circus animal performing on command. I became a workaholic. I watched television until late hours. I did anything and everything to keep my mind occupied. It took all my effort to remain "normal."

Despite my efforts, I would, on rare occasions, dress up in feminine attire. When dressed in this manner, I could create the fantasy that I really was a woman. This activity also carried a heavy price—guilt. I had always felt guilt about my feelings of femininity, but when I succumbed to them and actually crossdressed, my feelings of guilt and shame were overpowering. I must have bought five or six outfits in my desire to be a woman, and thrown them away again because I felt guilty.

I was about thirty-five years old, and had been married for ten years, when I chanced upon a book at the public library. The author claimed that about five percent of men enjoy dressing up in women's clothing. What a revelation! The sexual aspects of transvestism didn't seem to fit my own situation, but I decided that I must be a transvestite. At least there were other men with similar problems, and that made me feel better. I still had not heard of transsexualism. I didn't want my family to find out, though. I was sure that my wife would not understand, and I didn't want to tarnish the image that I presented to my children, especially our youngest son.

In 1985 my wife and I divorced. There were several reasons for our divorce, but I believe that my discomfort with trying to fulfill the male sexual role was the root cause. It made me very sad to see our marriage of twenty years end this way. At least we are still friends and we see each other often.

In the years following the divorce, the talk shows began airing shows about transsexualism. Now here was something I could relate to! Every week I would scan the television listings to see which show was featuring transsexuals. The guests described their feelings and how they coped with life in the opposite gender role. I learned much about myself in this manner, but I was becoming more depressed with my own situation.

After my son graduated from high school and went away to attend college, I decided to take a bold step; I disclosed my lifelong secret to my family and some close friends. As I told my story to each in turn, the release from emotional tension was profound. The flood of tears seemed to wash away a lifetime of guilt and shame. Now the secret was out, and I was free to be myself!

One of my friends suggested that I seek professional help. I believe she thought that a therapist could return me to the person that she knew. She, along with many of my other friends, believed that I was following a path to self-destruction. When they tried to convince me to stop what I was doing, they were acting out of love and concern for me. I do not blame them for what they tried to do. There is no possible way for them to understand that I am not simply making a choice between being male or female. They must take it on faith that, in my mind, I have always been female, and that I have no choice but to live the remainder of my life in my true gender. To my delight, my entire family and all but one friend finally accepted me for who I am. Perhaps that one friend will someday accept me as well.

My sessions with the therapist were, in the beginning, always tearful. Here I was, late middle-aged and only now coming to terms with my own feelings. I cried with grief over the fact that I had not begun my transition much earlier in life. I mourned the lost years I had spent in my hated male gender role. I wanted to proceed with my transition as quickly as possible in order to make up for the years that I had lost. It took many months of therapy for me to shake this feeling of lost time.

I am now almost two years into my transition. I have changed my name to Heather Jean, and now go about my social and business life in the female gender role. People generally accept me as a woman, and I feel comfortable. I have a wider circle of friends than ever before, and my social life has taken a dramatic upturn. My friends tell me that they can see a difference in me; I have changed from a passive male to an assertive, happy female who stands up for what she believes.

I now realize that I am a mixture of the old and the new. I do not grieve what has been lost. My past life was good in many ways, and I have no regrets about what I have accomplished. I can now integrate the good from the past into my future life. I am still the same person that I have always been, but now life has opened up to present experiences and challenges that were previously beyond my reach.

I had Genital Reassignment Surgery prior to my fifty-sixth birthday. At my age, I have no grand illusions about getting married, although I do date. Now that my life experiences include passing through transition, I consider myself to be fulfilled and successful.

Reflexive Questions

1. What underlying values and beliefs support the gender wage gap in the United States and worldwide? How do racism, sexism, ableism and ageism intersect to widen the gap?

2. What barriers need to be lifted for women to have equal access to high-powered jobs and equal pay, promotions, and advancement to men?

3. What factors (think of at least three) create the glass ceiling for girls and women and people from minoritized groups, in contrast to the glass escalator that exists for boys and men, especially White affluent men? How are these factors exacerbated in countries from the Global South, where greater disparities exist?

4. Why do you think it is legal for gender-based discrimination in pay? What will it take for policies to change? How will societies benefit? How will individuals and families benefit?

5. What values, beliefs, and attitudes are embedded in the term "anti-aging"? What would it mean for individuals, as well as society, to think in terms of "pro-aging"?

6. How do the beauty and anti-aging medicine industries prey on the insecurities of everyone, regardless of age? Why are middle-aged adults especially vulnerable to propaganda related to youth?

7. Why do you think advertising promoting surgical beauty interventions (Botox, plastic surgery, laser and chemical peels) is targeting younger women in their 20s? What are the causes and effects of this, especially over time?

8. What would it be like for you if you were not allowed to live as your "true" or preferred gender? What would you do? What would it mean for you and your family if you had gender affirming healthcare and intervention?

9. When considering the fluidity and complexity of biological sex and gender, why does the sex/gender binary continue to be reinforced? What social factors keep it in place?

10. How does the gender binary prevent the acceptance of gender-related diversity (i.e., intersex, transgender, nonbinary, gender-expansive people)? What would it mean if we no longer felt the need or pressure to perform our gender assigned to us at birth?

CHAPTER 10

Late Adulthood

Introduction

When you think of someone being old, what do you think of? What are your beliefs and stereotypes? What images come to mind? Do you think of all older people in the same way? Did you know that there are different types of "old" based on chronological age? In general, people who are between the ages of 60 and 75 are considered *young-old*, between the ages of 75 and 85 *old-old*, and people over 85 are considered *oldest-old* (Garfein & Herzog, 1995). As we know, however, a person's chronological age does not always accurately reflect a person's overall health and level of subjective well-being. Late adulthood has the greatest variability than any other life stage (Berger, 2019). There are vast differences in people's health, strength, and vitality in their older years. For example, someone in their 70s who is active, fit, and overall healthy could have the same vitality as another person in their 50s. Conversely, someone in their 40s who has overall poor health, overconsumes food and alcohol, and lives a sedentary lifestyle might think, act, and feel like someone in their 60s. As mentioned in chapter 9, chronological, psychological, and biological aging, as well as social determinants of health, are all strongly interconnected. These factors help explain life quality of life and life expectancy.

According to Roser, Ortiz-Ospina, and Ritchie (2020), life expectancy is important to study because it is the most important metric for understanding the health of a population. They state that before the modern world, life expectancy was about 30 years of age in every region of the world; however, since the Age of Enlightenment (1715–1789), people live longer, especially in early industrialized countries. The dramatic increase in those countries compared to non-industrialized countries led to high inequality in how health was distributed worldwide, with people in richer countries getting healthier and living longer than those in poorer countries. Overall, there has been dramatic improvement over the years. Life expectancy has more than doubled since the early 1900s, with people living on average until 72 years of age—74 for women and 70 for men. Currently, on average in the United States, women live to be 81 and men 76. Although we are living longer as a whole, international statistics do not reflect nuanced within-group differences (within each country), which are often based on race/ethnicity, socioeconomic status, geographic location, cis or transgender identity, and ability status, among other factors.

Grave inequalities in life expectancy persist across and within countries, ranging from 53 years in the Central African Republic, to 83 years in Japan. According to the World Health Organization (www.who.int/gho/mortality), the life expectancy in African regions is approximately 61 years of age, compared to people from European regions living to 78 years of age. The population of the richest countries in the world have life expectancies over 80, including the United States, with Japan consistently having the greatest longevity and health among older adults. The maximum life span is approximately 122 years, but that is extremely rare. Gloria Gutman, past president of the International Association of Gerontology, wrote about the oldest-old and centenarians for the American Society on Aging website (https://www.asaging.org/blog/global-look-oldest-old-and-centenarians-it-genes-diet-luck-or-all-combined), stating that there are currently more centenarians (people over the age of 100) and super-centenarians (those over the age of 105) than ever before. The United States has the highest number of centenarians, followed by Japan, England, and Wales. According to Guinness World Records (https://www.guinnessworldrecords.com/news/2019/3/worlds-oldest-person-confirmed-as-116-year-old-kane-tanaka-from-japan/), the "officially" oldest currently living person in the world is Kane Tanaka, age 116, from Fukuoka, Japan, and the oldest person to have lived (with official birth record) is Jeanne Calment from France, who died in 1997 at the age of 122. Gutman states that most centenarians have been remarkably healthy throughout the course of their lives and have experienced a rapid terminal decline in later life, as opposed to a long, drawn-out decline. Reasons for this suggest a strong interconnectedness of genes and epigenetic processes, which help regulate longevity and are related to one's lifestyle, environment, and stress response (Moskalev, Aliper, Smit-McBride, Buzdin, & Zhavoronkov, 2014).

It is also well documented that lifestyle and activity level can make a significant difference in quality of life. Researchers Lemon, Bengston, and Peterson (1972) tested the activity theory of aging, which suggests a positive association between a person's level of activity and maintenance of roles with their level of life satisfaction. According to Andrieieva et al. (2019), their study of 63 adults whose ages ranged from 60 to 73 found that regular physical exercise can delay age-related physical changes and help maintain good health and vitality. They found that the aging process was slowed by 10.5% for respondents in the experimental group and was accelerated by 5.7% for the respondents of the control group. Physical activity slowed down the aging process, and lack of activity accelerated the aging process for those in their study.

When considering the effects of psychosocial factors, it is also well documented that a combination of physical activity, psychological flexibility, positivity, and being a life-long learner positively affects well-being as we age. In a study conducted by Ryu and Heo (2018), they examined 188 adults in Korea between the ages of 60 and 90. They examined the relationship between specific types of leisure activities and well-being variables, such as health perception, life satisfaction, and optimism. They found that home-centered and social activities were associated with positive outcomes, suggesting the importance of promoting positive social interactions in social settings and volunteer experiences for successful aging among older adults.

In another study, Fuller-Iglesias and Antonucci (2016) studied the cultural value of familism (commitment and loyalty to family) and how social networks affected well-being among older adults from Mexico in late life. In a sample of 556 adults between the ages of 50 and 99, they found that familism may be a protective factor for decreasing depressive symptoms and increasing life satisfaction among older adults. Although there were some caveats, they recommend older adults having a balanced and diverse social network with frequent contact with supportive family and people who care for them. This recommendation, as well as being physically active and having a positive outlook, is certainly optimal; however, there is a multitude of reasons why this is not always possible for everyone. A person's social location, as well as physical location, matters. Where one lives and where one ages have a profound impact on quality of life (Cashin, 2014).

Critical geographer Edward Soja (2010) has carefully studied the effects of geographic location and social inequalities and contends that spatial justice is social justice. Where and how we live is important at every age, but it is especially important for older adults who may have experienced a lifetime of advantage or disadvantage based on where they lived, worked, raised their children, and developed a sense of community. In light of this critical perspective, what does this mean for older adults who have aged in place?

There has been an increase in research related to maximizing the benefits of naturally occurring communities (NORCs) and aging in place. Aging in place is the ability for adults to remain in their home and community safely, independently, and comfortably, regardless of age, income, or abilities (Centers for Disease Control and Prevention, 2009). In a study conducted in the United States by Martin, Long, and Kessler (2019), they found that older adults preferred to live at home; however, it was essential that they were able to maintain their sense of identity by having independence, control, and well-being. In another study conducted by Liu, Dijst, and Geertman (2017), they examined the subjective well-being and the role of the home environment and personal resources of 1035 older adults in urban and rural areas of Shanghai, China. They found good-quality housing, accessibility to medical and financial resources, higher neighborhood economic status, and a mixed-aged neighborhood are important correlates of the adult subjects' well-being. Overall, participants stated that comfort was their most important need, and physical needs were more important than social needs. These findings have important implications, especially when considering the alternative. This then begs the question: What does it mean to age in place if where you live is dangerous or unhealthy?

Not all older adults perceive their old age to be their "golden years." While some will be financially comfortable and live in safe and pleasant neighborhoods, others will continue to struggle as in their younger years, while others' lives will become progressively worse. A study conducted by Ailshire and Garcia (2018) found that the social, economic, and physical environments were crucial in an older adult's ability to have a healthy, active, and engaged life. Overall, there is great inequity in living environments. Racial and ethnic minorities disproportionately live in neighborhoods characterized by poverty, disorder, pollution, and lack of social cohesion. They contend that neighborhood inequality is a significant burden to older adults and contributes to disparities in aging.

In another study, researchers Finlay, McCarron, Statz, and Zmora (2019) offer a critical understanding of the concept of aging in place. They interviewed 125 independent-dwelling adults with the mean age of 71 and 10 community policymakers and community service providers. They asked them what strengthened or weakened their desire and ability to age in place. Overwhelmingly, participants stated the need for accessible, affordable housing, reliable services and amenities, access to healthcare, and transportation and mobility. The researchers challenged the current literature related to aging in place for being highly individualistic, resourced, and ableist and failing to consider the adversity caused by a lack of affordable, safe, and healthy housing and a reduction in governmental social services. They offer a more realistic notion of aging in place and urge us to think about this concept in more inclusive and socially just ways. They also urge researchers, policymakers, and diverse community stakeholders to invite people from marginalized groups to collaborate in planning processes to advance opportunities for naturally occurring retirement communities and aging in place in just, equitable ways.

In sum, older adults, regardless of their gender, sexual orientation, race/ethnicity, nationality, or social class, will reflect on their lives and evaluate, interpret, and reinterpret their experiences. Erikson stated that they will either perceive their past as though it has been positive (integrity) or not well-spent (despair). It is likely that most older adults will experience a mixture of both. Nevertheless, it is important for us to listen to their life narratives and help them frame them in the most empowering and positive way possible. While their bodies may be declining in strength, abilities, and functioning, due to the paradox of aging, they will often prefer to focus on positive stimuli, as noted with the positivity effect (Zhou, Lu, Chen, Dong, & Yao, 2017). They will also need support in combatting the effects of ageism and internalized ageism (Bodner, 2009). In light of the social science literature, it is important for everyone to reject ageist ideologies and practices, validate older adult's struggles and worries, protect them from loneliness, abuse, and exploitation, and offer tangible support. The readings in this chapter will offer some greater insight related to social determinants of health among older adults, policies that can positively affect LGBTQ older adults, and the lessons we can learn from Japan in terms of positive and healthy aging.

Summary of Readings

In the reading "**Equity and Social Determinants of Health Among Older Adults**" (2014), Steven Wallace explores how race, income, education, and health literacy affect the health of older Americans. Wallace discusses the results of the 2014 edition of the National Healthcare Disparities Report, which shows both Latinos and African Americans receive lower-quality healthcare in 40% of the measured indicators. Wallace argues that policies can mitigate health inequality due to avoidable differences based on inequity. They contend that the medical system, as well as social and political factors, leads to health inequality and should be targeted. Both race and class are determinants of health in the United States, with racial minorities, especially African Americans, and individuals with lower socioeconomic status having more health issues and less access to adequate medical care. Education is also a determinant of health, as having a higher education correlates with longer life expectancy and lower rates of most health conditions.

Wallace states that many older adults, as well as politicians and policymakers, lack the health literacy necessary to make important health-related decisions. Wallace contends that "structural discrimination creates patterns in life chances through 'neutral' policies and practices that impact groups differently." To improve the health of older Americans, Wallace reiterates the need for legislation that creates healthy environments for everyone, not just for those who can afford health-care or to eat, breathe, sleep, and live well. Reducing poverty increases health equity for everyone, but especially for older adults- some of the most vulnerable people in society. Wallace states, "elders will be emotionally and physically healthier when they and their families make a living wage, have decent and affordable housing, and reside in safe and health-promoting neighborhoods."

In the reading "**Protecting and Ensuring the Well-Being of LGBT Older Adults: A Policy Roadmap**" (2016), Robert Espinoza discusses the report in 2015 released by the *White House Conference on Aging*, which outlined policy imperatives on aging sectors. Espinoza states that despite the growing numbers of lesbian, gay, bisexual, and transgender (LGBT) older adults in the United States, they were hardly mentioned in the 2015 report. This lack of attention speaks to an ongoing need to document the needs of LGBT older adults. Espinoza suggests ways to remedy this inattention and asserts that future policies targeting LGBT older adults call for change in two areas: 1) specifying LGBT older people in governmental regulations that fund long-term care and housing and 2) improving data collection on their lives. Widespread discrimination decreases the long-term caregiving systems available to LGBT older adults as well as their access to affordable and safe housing. Espinoza recommends several policy areas to improve housing stability for LGBT people, including 1) creating overt legal protections against housing discrim-ination; 2) including questions related to sexual orientation and gender identity in surveys at the US Department of Housing and Urban Development (HUD); 3) commissioning HUD-funded research on housing instability among LGBT older people; and 4) encouraging the funding of affordable, LGBT-friendly senior housing developments.

Lastly, more research on LGBT older people is needed to quantify the challenges these com-munities face and design effective policies targeting them. Espinoza notes that the U.S. Census does not have questions about sexual orientation. If these questions were standardized, this data could illuminate the nature of health disparities among LGBT elders, create better practices in program design, and quantify the challenges these communities face. In sum, future policy should include mandated LGBT cultural competence training for everyone in the long-term-care system, creating safer and more affordable housing options, expanding nondiscrimination protections nationwide, and funding a broad range of support services for LGBT older people.

The last reading in this chapter, titled "**America's Aging Society Problem: A Look to Japan for Lessons on Prevention**" (2014), is by Ender Ricart. The author posits that by enacting policies similar to those in Japan, the United States can manage the care of its rapidly aging population. By 2050, 21% of Americans will be over the age of 65, and the United States will be in need of care for "epidemic levels of elderly." With a quarter of its population over the age of 65, Japan already has developed effective national long-term-care insurance (LTCI) to effectively care for its older population. LTCI revisions in Japan established nationwide support networks for aging residents known as *community comprehensive support centers*. Working with regional governments, these centers manage early detection and prevention of light conditions and diseases and run community-based programs for seniors. These centers focus on increasing services to improve health, exercise, nutrition, and "mental training" education as a means of social interaction with other older adults.

The United States can learn lessons from Japan. Whereas Japan has enacted an effective, nationwide form of elder care, Ricart states that the United States lags behind. American elder support systems rely on fragmented, local initiatives that often fail after a few years. It should be noted that the Patient Protection and Affordable Care Act (PPACA) has expanded Medicare and Medicaid coverage to include the prevention and treatment of some lifestyle diseases; however, the United States remains focused on cost and predicting who may need these programs instead of focusing on prevention through lifestyle changes in health, education, exercise, community, diet, and health screening. The author contends that the United States can and should do better for older adults.

References

Ailshire, J., & Garcia, C. (2018). Unequal places: The impacts of socioeconomic and race/ethnic differences in neighborhoods. *American Society on Aging, 42*(2), 20–27. doi:10.2307/26556356.

American Society on Aging. https://www.asaging.org/blog/global-look-oldest-old-and- centenarians-it-genes-diet-luck-or-all-combined

Andrieieva, O., Hakman, A., Kashuba, V., Vasylenko, M., Patsaliuk, K., Koshura, A., Istyniuk, I. (2019). Effects of physical activity on aging processes in elderly persons. *Journal of Physical Education and Sport, 19*, 1308–1314. doi:10.7752/jpes.2019.s4190

Berger, K. S. (2019). *Invitation to the life span (4th ed.)*. Worth Publishers.

Bodner, E. (2009). On the origins of ageism among older and younger adults. *International Psychogeriatrics, 21*(6), 1003–1014. doi:10.1017/S104161020999055X

Centers for Disease Control and Prevention. (2009). *Healthy places terminology*. Retrieved from https://www.cdc.gov/healthyplaces/terminology.htm

Cashin, S. (2014). *Place, not race: A new vision of opportunity in America*. Beacon Press.

Finlay, J. M., McCarron, H. R., Statz, T. L., & Zmora, R. (2019). A critical approach to aging in place: A case study comparison of personal and professional perspectives from the Minneapolis metropolitan area, *Journal of Aging & Social Policy*, (Dec.), 1–25. doi:10.1080/08959420.2019.1704133

Fuller-Iglesias, H.R., Antonucci, T.C. (2016). Familism, social network characteristics, and well-being among older adults in Mexico. *Journal of Cross-Cultural Gerontology, 31*, 1–17. doi:10.1007/s10823-015-9278-5

Garfein, A. J., & Herzog, A. R. (1995). Robust Aging among the young-old, old-old, and oldest-old. *The Journals of Gerontology: Series B, 50B*(2), 77– 87. doi:10.1093/geronb/50B.2.S77

Guinness World Records. https://www.guinnessworldrecords.com/news/2019/3/worlds-oldest-person-confirmed-as-116-year-old-kane-tanaka-from-japan/

Lemon, B. W., Vern. M. A., Bengtson, L., Peterson, J. A., (1972). An exploration of the activity theory of aging: Activity types and life satisfaction among in-movers to a retirement community. *Journal of Gerontology, 27*(4), 511–523. https://doi.org/10.1093/geronj/27.4.511

Liu, Y., Dijst, M., & Geertman, S. (2017). The subjective well-being of older adults in Shanghai: The role of residential environment and individual resources. *Urban Studies, 54*(7), 1692–1714. doi:10.1177/0042098016630512

Martin, D., Long, O., & Kessler, L. (2019). Planning for aging in place: Incorporating the voice of elders to promote quality of life., *Journal of Housing for the Elderly, 33*(4), 382–392. doi:10.1080/02763893.2019.1593280

Moskalev, A., Aliper, A., Smit-McBride, Z., Buzdin, A., & Zhavoronkov, A. (2014). Genetics and epigenetics of aging and longevity. *Cell Cycle, 13*(7), 1063–1077. doi:10.4161/cc.28433

Roser, M., Ortiz-Ospina, E., & Ritchie, H. (2020). Life expectancy. *Published online at OurWorldInData.org.* Retrieved from: https://ourworldindata.org/life-expectancy

Ryu, J., & Heo, J. (2018). Relationships between leisure activity types and well-being in older adults. *Leisure Studies, 37*(3), 331–342. doi:10.1080/02614367.2017.1370007

Soja, E. (2010). *Seeking Spatial Justice.* Globalization and Community Series. University of Minnesota Press.

World Health Organization. Published online and retrieved from https://www.who.int/gho/mortality_burden_disease/life_tables/situation_trends_text/en

Zhou, L., Lu, J., Chen, G., Dong, L., & Yao, Y. (2017). Is there a paradox of aging: When the negative aging stereotype meets the positivity effect in older adults. *Experimental Aging Research, 43*(1), 80–93. doi:10.1080/0361073X.2017.1258254

Equity and Social Determinants of Health Among Older Adults

Steven P. Wallace

What creates health disparities and what policy options are available for ameliorating them?

Attention to the challenges faced by older adults of color in the United States was first highlighted by a report in 1964 from the National Urban League, *Double Jeopardy: The Older Negro in America Today* (National Urban League, 1964). At the time, it was groundbreaking just to document the gap in health and wealth between older African Americans and whites, a gap that was particularly acute in old age. In the subsequent half-century, we have expended a lot of effort to further specify the existence of health disparities by race and ethnicity.

African Americans and Latinos receive lower quality healthcare in 40 percent of the indicators measured in the **National Healthcare Disparities Report.**

The 1985 United States Department of Health and Human Services (HHS) *Secretary's Taskforce Report on Black and Minority Health* was the first signal of top governmental-level concern with health differences by race, with the clearest documentation being the mortality gap for African Americans. Forty-two percent of cumulative deaths by age 70 among African Americans were shown to have been avoidable if African Americans' mortality profile matched that of whites (Heckler, 1985). And in 2003, the Institute of Medicine report, *Unequal Treatment: Confronting Racial and Ethnic Disparities in Health Care*, clearly documented the health-care system's under-treatment and poorer treatment of African Americans (Smedley, Stith, and Nelson, 2003).

We now have the annual *National Health-care Disparities Report*, mandated by Congress, that provides snapshots of access and quality inequities by race and ethnicity. The most recent edition shows that African Americans and Latinos receive lower quality healthcare in 40 percent of the indicators measured, American Indians/Alaska Natives in one-third of the indicators, and Asian Americans in one-quarter. There were many more than 100 quality points tracked, such as the receipt of colon cancer screening by those older than age 50 and hospital admissions for uncontrolled diabetes (Agency for Healthcare Research and Quality [AHRQ], 2014).

Reducing Health Inequities with Prevention

Health inequities are the result of *avoidable* differences between populations that affect less powerful groups in society. They stem from a pattern of health determinants, outcomes, and resources associated with broader social inequities. When patterns of social exclusion, blocked opportunities, or unequal returns on effort are common to a population, the resulting differences in health status and healthcare are inequitable (Wallace, 2012).

Most attention to the causes of health inequities among older adults has focused on the medical system, which has its greatest impact on health outcomes after a person becomes ill. But preventing illness has the greatest potential for reducing health inequities, as well as for reducing the need for expensive medical care. Because exposures to many risk factors for disease and disability are unequally distributed across groups, it is important to address social and political factors. Heart disease is the leading cause of death in old age for all groups and there are clear differences in cardiovascular disease rates by income and race or ethnicity. Policy efforts to reduce the average sodium content of commonly consumed packaged foods are one cost-effective approach for reducing blood pressure and cardiovascular disease at the population level (Morrison and Ness, 2011). Similarly, policy efforts exist to improve population-level physical activity, promote balanced diets, and reduce smoking, each of which has a salutatory impact on the risks for cardiovascular disease as well as multiple other health conditions.

Experiences of discrimination and bias lead to increased stress and unhealthy adaptive behaviors across all socioeconomic statuses.

Efforts to promote health are not adopted evenly across populations, and groups at the highest risk often are the last to benefit from the societal changes and new technologies. Smoking rates are a good example of the trend of more advantaged populations benefitting first from new knowledge and social patterns. Smoking rates peaked in the mid-1960s in the United States, just before the Surgeon General's report confirming that tobacco smoking led to cancer and other health problems. In 1966, smoking rates were similar by education, with about 43 percent of the adult population smoking. The most educated group (with sixteen or more years of education) was somewhat less likely to smoke, at 35 percent.

By 1987, the smoking rate for the most educated had fallen by half (to 17 percent), while those with the least education (less than high school) had fallen only by a quarter (from 42 percent to 34 percent) (Centers for Disease Control and Prevention [CDC], 1994). The trend continued from 1985 through 2011, with smoking by college graduates falling in half again to 7.5 percent, while those without a high school diploma declined to 27.4 percent, leaving a large inequity in this significant disease risk factor. This highlights the importance of focusing on different groups in society that are often marginalized due to their exclusion from power and resources.

Race as a Social Determinant of Health

The social and political forces that shape health risks often work through race or ethnicity, gender, and class, each of which has a separate dynamic in determining health status, in addition to interacting with each other. Race long has been known to be a social determinant of health status. Older African Americans consistently have higher rates of major health problems (including hypertension, diseases of the circulatory system, and diabetes) than do non-Latino whites. They also have the highest rates of functional limitations. While the gap in disease and disability rates diminishes when studies control for black–white population differences in wealth and other socioeconomic characteristics, most studies continue to find that race has an independent effect on poor health.

Race affects the health of minorities throughout their life course through both perceived and structural mechanisms. Experiences of discrimination and bias lead to increased stress and unhealthy adaptive behaviors across all socioeconomic statuses (Zarit and Pearlin, 2005). Structural discrimination creates patterns in life chances through "neutral" policies and practices that impact groups differently. Social Security, for example, has a gender-neutral set of criteria for earning service benefits that has the effect of leaving an inequitable number of older women struggling economically in old age.

The pattern of racial inequities for Latino older adults is more complex because their disease rates do not reflect their low economic position as clearly as do the disease rates of African Americans. Most evidence suggests that Latino men have a lower prevalence of heart disease and major cancers than whites, but it is not clear why. Older Latinos clearly are disadvantaged socioeconomically, have very high rates of diabetes and obesity, and engage less in exercise than non-Latino whites. In addition, hypertension is at least as prevalent among Mexican American older adults as it is among the general older adult population. Smoking and alcohol consumption rates among Latino males also are high. Any advantages in diseases of the heart and cancer among Latino males cannot be explained by known risk factors.

The most likely explanation is that immigration to the United States selects for the healthiest persons, while some of those who fall ill or face the worst settlement experiences return to their homeland (Markides, Rudkin, and Wallace, 2007). This suggests that immigrants arrive with a "health capital" that is important to protect and promote so that they can remain healthy. As future generations of Latino elders who are mostly U.S.-born may not benefit from that health capital, making investments in the health of younger Latinos is particularly important so that they will be less affected by a cumulative disadvantage when they reach old age.

Economic Resources as a Social Determinant of Health

Economic resources are a well-documented social determinant of health (Hajat et al., 2011). Mortality rates increase as poverty increases, with the effect being most dramatic in ages 24 to 44 and ages 45 to 64. A similar, but smaller, increase in mortality rates occurs for older adults living in neighborhoods with high poverty rates (Rehkopf et al., 2006).

It is likely that the higher total mortality in older ages washes out some income effects, in addition to those most vulnerable to the disadvantages of low incomes having died at younger ages. Disability rates also vary among older adults by income, even after controlling for age, gender, education, and race (Schoeni et al., 2005). Self-reported health also is related to income, and those with low incomes experience health declines at earlier ages than wealthier individuals (Crimmins, Kim, and Seeman, 2009). The association between poverty and poor health in old age is reciprocal—poverty causes poor health (social causation) and poor health causes low incomes (social selection)—but social causation is the dominant direction.

Economic resources are considered a "fundamental" cause of health because they are necessary to obtain all goods and services needed in a healthy life. In addition to individual resources, collective resources impact access to the conditions that promote a healthy life course. Residential neighborhoods are strongly segregated by income (and race), limiting access of the poor to healthy housing. Higher income neighborhoods are more likely to be away from the pollution of freeways and factories, are convenient to affordable and healthy food, have access to quality medical and other services, and promote physical activity by being safe and attractive for walking. Those with lower incomes also are subject to social exclusion by having less access to steady employment, suffering from inferior public services, and having little voice in public policy decisions. This suggests that reducing poverty is an effective way to reduce health declines and improve health equity in old age.

Residential neighborhoods are an important life space for older adults because they spend more time in their neighborhoods than do employed younger adults. Neighborhoods are highly segregated by race and socioeconomic status, and neighborhood socioeconomic status is associated with mortality, disability, and self-assessed health. The conditions that are likely to affect older adults in lower income neighborhoods include determinants of health such as fewer grocery stores and alternatives to fast food. Low-income communities also have fewer and lower quality sources of medical care, higher crime rates, lower quality housing, and weaker social support networks (Wallace, 2012).

Improvements in life expectancy at the national level are driven by broad-based economic growth when growth works to reduce poverty (e.g., in South Korea), or by the expansion of supports even without economic growth, as in when basic health-enhancing services reach all residents (e.g., in Costa Rica) (Sen, 1998). In contrast, when economic growth goes largely to people who are already well off, and where public services for individuals with low incomes are inadequate, economic growth has a marginal impact on national health outcomes. Within countries, inequality influences both mortality and self-assessed health after a threshold level of income is reached, especially at the highest levels of inequality. The inequality effect for mortality is most apparent for people younger than age 65, where the leading causes of death include unintentional injury, suicide, homicide, and HIV—all conditions that are particularly sensitive to social conditions (Backlund et al., 2007).

We often try to assess and improve the health literacy of older adults and caregivers, forgetting that public officials and service providers also have constraints on their health literacy.

Steps for Improving Health Literacy

Education is a powerful determinant of social and economic position. People with higher education have longer life expectancies, lower rates of most health conditions, and lower levels of disability—independent of their income and health insurance. The health status gap between those with the highest and lowest educational levels has been increasing for the past several years, indicating that the advantages of more education (and disadvantages of less education) are of growing importance in health inequities. The educational gap in mortality rates increased between 1990 and 2000 for older adults. Mortality rates during that period changed little for those with a high school education or less, while death rates declined among those with more than a high school education. The educational disparity in smoking rates and other protective health behaviors, such as larger social networks, is a likely contributor to these widening mortality differences (Meara, Richards, and Cutler, 2008).

Related to education is the issue of health literacy. There is a growing concern that many older adults do not have sufficient knowledge—or the skills to use knowledge—to make healthy decisions and to be active participants in their healthcare. Typically, people with more years of education have both better cognitive processing skills to use new complex information effectively, as well as more baseline knowledge relevant to health. To the extent that we provide people with *useable* knowledge about how their behavior affects their health (e.g., how physical activity can reduce the risk of falls), and how to assess medical advice (e.g., benefits and risks of particular medications), we are improving the conditions under which they can be healthy.

But we too often stop with trying to assess and improve the health literacy of older adults and their caregivers, and forget that public officials and service providers also have constraints on *their* health literacy. When transportation planners only consider the least expensive options in designing regional transportation, they are demonstrating low levels of health literacy because they also are not factoring in the health benefits of lowered pollution, greater physical activity, and increased access to services by older adults that might come from alternative designs.

The Age-Friendly Cities effort, led by the World Health Organization (WHO) and embodied in a number of U.S. initiatives, provides a series of policy-level analyses for how communities can provide a context that promotes healthy aging through policies across multiple sectors (AARP, 2014; WHO, 2007). In the United States, this has been discussed as prioritizing "health in all policies." These efforts show how policy makers and others who shape the life-spaces of older adults need to improve their health literacy to promote health equity for older adults. A new initiative by the Robert Wood Johnson Foundation to foster a "culture of health" in communities and institutions is one means for improving the health literacy of policy makers (Lavizzo-Mourey, 2014).

Given the earlier discussion of the key role of economic resources in shaping the health of older adults, improving health literacy among policy makers will involve improving their understanding of the basic resource needs of the older population. Currently, when policy makers and other key stakeholders consider the economic status of older adults, the most common indicator of economic need that they use is the Federal Poverty Level or FPL (officially called the federal poverty guideline or threshold). Many public programs are linked to the FPL, such as food stamps, housing subsidies, Medicaid, and assistance with Medicare costs. For policy makers to be fully health literate, they need to understand that the FPL does not provide an adequate measure of the resources needed for older adults to maintain the minimum decent standard of living required for health.

The FPL was designed in the 1960s and based upon an average national 1950s standard of living for young families, not older adults. It is the same amount everywhere in the country (Wallace, Padilla-Frausto, and Smith, 2013). As such, it does not account for the wide variation in housing costs by state and county, is insensitive to the costs of medical care faced especially by older adults, and has not kept up with the standard of living. To provide adequate resources for older adults requires a measure of need based on 21st century regional costs, such as the Elder Economic Security Standard Index (Elder Index). Based upon the actual cost for older adults for basic housing, healthcare, food, transportation, and other needed spending at the county level, it incorporates the characteristics of a measure most wanted by state policy makers, but is not often used because of institutional barriers (Padilla-Frausto and Wallace, 2012). This suggests that cultural competency to promote the health of low-income and minority older adults by key stakeholders involves not only knowledge, but also the ability and incentives to act on that knowledge.

As we work to reduce health inequalities in our country, it is important to remember that while linguistic and cultural competence are crucial for working with older adults, broader societal patterns that disadvantage elders of color, those with low incomes, and women create conditions that make it difficult for them to enjoy a healthy old age. To reduce health inequities among older adults we need to create supportive institutions and laws that create healthy environments for older adults, and make the healthy choice the *easy* choice for health behaviors. From a life-course perspective (Ferraro and Shi, 2009), diverse elders will be emotionally and physically healthier when they and their families make a living wage, have decent and affordable housing, and reside in safe and health-promoting neighborhoods in a society that values diversity.

References

AARP. 2014. "Liveable Communities." www.aarp.org/research/ppi/liv-com.html. Retrieved August 1, 2014.

Agency for Healthcare Research and Quality (AHRQ). 2014. *National Healthcare Disparities Report 2013*. Rockville, MD: AHRQ.

Backlund, E., et al. 2007. "Income Inequality and Mortality: A Multi-level Prospective Study of 521,248 Individuals in 50 U.S. States." *International Journal of Epidemiology* 36(3): 590–6.

Centers for Disease Control and Prevention (CDC). 1994. "Surveillance for Selected Tobacco-use Behaviors—United States, 1900–1994." *Morbidity and Mortality Weekly Report* 43(SS-3). Atlanta, GA: CDC.

Crimmins, E. M., Kim, J. K., and Seeman, T. E. 2009. "Poverty and Biological Risk: The Earlier 'Aging' of the Poor." *The Journals of Gerontology, Series A: Biological Sciences and Medical Sciences* 64(2): 286–92.

Ferraro, K. F., and Shi, T. P. 2009. "Aging and Cumulative Inequality: How Does Inequality Get Under the Skin?" *The Gerontologist* 49(3): 333–43.

Hajat, A., et al. 2011. "Long-term effects of Wealth On Mortality and Self-rated Health Status." *American Journal of Epidemiology* 173(2): 192–200.

Heckler, M. M. 1985. *Report of the Secretary's Task Force on Black and Minority Health*: Washington, DC: United States Department of Health and Human Services.

Lavizzo-Mourey, R. 2014. "Building a Culture of Health." Princeton, NJ: Robert Wood Johnson

Foundation. www.rwjf.org/en/about-rwjf/annual-reports/presidents-message-2014.html. Retrieved August 1, 2014.

Markides, K. S., Rudkin, L., and Wallace, S. P. 2007. "Racial and Ethnic Minorities." In J. E. Birren, ed., *Encyclopedia of Gerontology* (2nd ed.). San Diego, CA: Elsevier.

Meara, E. R., Richards, S., and Cutler, D. M. 2008. "The Gap Gets Bigger: Changes In Mortality and Life Expectancy, by Education, 1981–2000." *Health Affairs* 27(2): 350–60.

Morrison, A. C., and Ness, R. B. 2011. "Sodium Intake and Cardiovascular Disease." *Annual Review of Public Health* 32(1): 71–90.

National Urban League. 1964. *Double Jeopardy: The Older Negro in America Today.* New York: National Urban League.

Padilla-Frausto, D. I., and Wallace, S. P. 2012. *The Federal Poverty Level Does Not Meet Data Needs of the California Legislature* (Health Policy Brief). Los Angeles, CA: UCLA Center for Health Policy Research.

Rehkopf, D. H., et al. 2006. "Monitoring Socioeconomic Disparities in Death: Comparing Individual-level Education and Area-based Socioeconomic Measures." *American Journal of Public Health* 96(12): 2135–8.

Schoeni, R. F., et al. 2005. "Persistent and Growing Socioeconomic Disparities in Disability Among the Elderly: 1982–2002." *American Journal of Public Health* 95(11): 2065–70.

Sen, A. 1998. "Mortality As an Indicator of Economic Success and Failure." *The Economic Journal* 108(446): 1–25.

Smedley, B. D., Stith, A. Y., and Nelson, A. R. 2003. *Unequal Treatment: Confronting Racial and Ethnic Disparities in Health Care.* Washington, DC: The National Academies Press.

Wallace, S. P. 2012. "Social Determinants of Health Inequities and Healthcare in Old Age." In T. Prohaska, L. Anderson, and R. Binstock, eds., *Public Health for an Aging Society.* Baltimore, MD: The Johns Hopkins University Press.

Wallace, S. P., Padilla-Frausto, D. I., and Smith, S. 2013. "Economic Need Among Older Latinos: Applying the Elder Economic Security Standard Index." *Journal of Cross-Cultural Gerontology* 28(3): 239–50.

World Health Organization (WHO). 2007. *Global Age-Friendly Cities.* Geneva, Switzerland: WHO.

Zarit, S. H., and Pearlin, L. I., eds. 2005. "Health Inequalities Across the Life Course." *Journals of Gerontology, Series B: Psychological Sciences and Social Sciences* 60B (special issue).

Protecting and Ensuring the Well-Being of LGBT Older Adults

A Policy Roadmap

Robert Espinoza

Concrete suggestions for remedying government and research oversight of LGBT elders.

In December 2015, the White House Conference on Aging released a final report summarizing its decennial gathering, held earlier that year (White House Conference on Aging, 2015). In previous conferences, this report has mapped policy imperatives for the aging and long-term-care sectors.

In this spirit, the 2015 report outlined a variety of public and private sector recommendations, actions, and public input across four areas: retirement security, healthy aging, long-term services and supports, and elder justice. Though the numbers of lesbian, gay, bisexual, and transgender (LGBT) older adults is rapidly growing and uniquely affected across all four areas, such elders were mentioned only twice in the report: in an acknowledgement that LGBT elders deserve age-friendly communities, and in a description of an initiative to assess how the aging network can best reach LGBT older people through the Older Americans Act (OAA). The Act funnels significant resources to the

aging network nationwide, yet never mentions LGBT elders.

While narrow in scope, this lack of attention embodies how the federal government construes LGBT older people. The notion of age-friendly communities for LGBT people affirms that equity and inclusion are part of an increasingly popular policy aspiration to create accessible, city-wide environments with robust home- and community-based services and supports (World Health Organization, 2007). The OAA initiative speaks to the ongoing charge to document the needs of LGBT elders across a range of physical, economic, and social factors—a national project structurally underfunded in the private and public sectors.

Although researchers and practitioners consistently describe LGBT elders as exhibiting smaller support networks, aging with higher rates of disability and chronic illness, and experiencing discrimination across long-term care, the systems interfacing with LGBT elders rarely designate them in policy reforms or as funding priorities (Fredriksen-Goldsen et al., 2011; National Academy on an Aging Society and Services and Advocacy for GLBT

Elders [SAGE], 2011). Moreover, LGBT elder advocates are asked routinely to substantiate their widespread challenges through rigorous, quantitative research and intensive evaluations to garner government support—despite the dearth in large-scale data, research, and program evaluations on LGBT people, especially in the context of aging.

This dilemma places LGBT aging at an important policy crossroads. The next era of policy change for LGBT elders calls for progress in two broad areas: specifying LGBT older people in the regulations that govern and fund long-term care, housing, and community-based services; and a creating a dedicated project to study and improve data collection on the lives of LGBT older people. Future policy opportunities include mandating LGBT cultural competence throughout the long-term-care system, creating safer and more affordable housing options, expanding nondiscrimination protections nationwide, and funding a broad array of supports and services for LGBT older people.

Early Advocacy in LGBT Aging

In 2000, the National Gay and Lesbian Task Force published *Outing Age*, a landmark publication delineating the general lack of protections for LGBT people in areas such as Medicare, Medicaid, and housing, among others, while positing that LGBT elders suffer the dual consequences of ageism within the LGBT community and heterosexism within the aging and long-term-care sectors, marginalizing this cohort in both spheres (Cahill, South, and Spade, 2000).

In 2010, the Movement Advancement Project and SAGE released *Improving the Lives of LGBT Older Adults*, a comprehensive report enumerating more than fifty recommendations across

areas such as Social Security, Medicare, Medicaid, veterans benefits, visitation, and medical decision-making (MAP and SAGE, 2010). This report elicited endorsements from influential national aging organizations including the Center for American Progress, AARP, the American Society on Aging, and the National Senior Citizens Law Center (now Justice in Aging)—a first for the LGBT aging movement. It also complemented the opening of an office in Washington, D.C., for SAGE, the country's premiere organization for LGBT older people, which provided a dedicated voice to lobby for concrete federal changes (Espinoza, 2013a).

That same year, the U.S. Department of Health and Human Services (HHS), through its Administration on Aging, announced a grant to seed the National Resource Center on LGBT Aging, which would ultimately train thousands of aging providers on LGBT cultural competence, among other strategies, and exponentially elevate LGBT issues in the policy world (Meyer, 2011). Together, these developments engendered the focus, visibility, and collaboration to build a superior advocacy agenda and network of champions in the years to come.

From 2010 to 2014, three developments characterized the LGBT aging policy field: the production of seminal LGBT aging–themed policy reports, a growing national infrastructure of organizations committed to LGBT older people, and early (but important) interest from the federal government around partnering with LGBT organizations. In that five-year span, policy reports were issued on the OAA, trans-gender aging, health equity, LGBT elders of color, and HIV and aging (SAGE, 2011; SAGE and National Center for Transgender Equality, 2012; SAGE, 2013; Cahill et al., 2010).

Also, national aging organizations issued publications covering the testimonials of discrimination in long-term-care facilities, the realities of being a LGBT Latino older adult, and housing discrimination aimed at same-sex elder couples (Equal Rights Center [ERC], 2014). In 2012, at the Gerontological Society of America conference, the National Academy on an Aging Society issued the first policy report about LGBT elders written by a group in the field of aging, in partnership with SAGE (National Academy on an Aging Society and SAGE, 2011).

This surge in policy analysis was matched by nonprofit infrastructure growth and government attention. In 2010, seven national "minority aging" organizations formed the Diverse Elders Coalition to advance federal goals for older people marginalized by racial, gender, and economic inequalities. LGBT older people surfaced as a top priority for this coalition, greatly expanding this population's legitimacy, and the coalition collectively convinced the Leadership Council of Aging Organizations to adopt numerous resolutions in support of these communities through the OAA (Espinoza, 2011).

Nationwide, advocates increasingly were forming organizations, task forces, coalitions, and roundtables to assess the needs of LGBT elders and provide services, training, and advocacy for LGBT elders in their communities and at the federal level. A watershed moment for local LGBT elder advocacy occurred when New York City's Department for the Aging (coupled with city-wide funding) seeded the country's first LGBT senior center, a policy inspiration for other parts of the country to mobilize dollars from city officials for LGBT elder services.

Earlier, I had described the multiple ways in which the federal government increased its attention on LGBT elder issues (Espinoza, 2013a), which included working with national organizations to host a first-ever White House LGBT Conference on Aging in February 2015—a day dedicated to LGBT elder housing advocacy—and spearheading various congressional hearings and briefings on this community. Federal leaders also began integrating LGBT elders into their legislative proposals, including a 2012 bill aiming to name LGBT older people as a population of "greatest social need" in the OAA, and making executive orders and administrative changes that heeded the policy guidance of LGBT policy analysts.

Two illustrative examples include 2010 guidance from the Administration for Community Living (ACL) that LGBT older people could be considered a population of "greatest social need" in local planning initiatives, and a 2013 reform from the Social Security Administration allowing transgender people to modify their Social Security records to reflect their gender identities. The June 2015 decision by the U.S. Supreme Court to grant full marriage rights to same-sex couples effectively dismantled most, though not all, of the marriage-based legal barriers for married same-sex couples, including inequities in Medicaid, Medicare, and Social Security. This ruling—and the years of policy advocacy preceding it—opens the door to a policy agenda in five areas affecting LGBT older people: long-term care, housing, nondiscrimination protections, community-based services, and LGBT aging data and research.

Long-Term Care, Housing, and Community Services

LGBT people, as with most people, want to age independently, in good health, and be financially secure in their homes and communities (SAGE, 2014). Yet aging independently in one's community often requires caregiving support, especially when dealing with physical, cognitive, and mental impairments, and the increased frailty and mobility concerns connected with aging.

Three trends exacerbate these conditions. First, most forecasts show that the population ages 65 and older will nearly double to more than 80 million between 2013 and 2040. Second, new research by the National Alliance for Care-giving and AARP Public Policy Institute (2015) describes how people are living longer, and with higher rates of chronic illness, which heightens the need for caregiving assistance. Finally, as these shifts occur, family caregivers increasingly are strained to provide care for aging loved ones, which incurs considerable psychological and financial implications—and, based on current projections, the supply of paid caregivers (i.e., direct care workers), likely will not meet projected demand.

For LGBT older adults, the ecosystem of available caregivers further shrinks because of smaller support systems and widespread discrimination (SAGE, 2014). Research shows that many long-term-care professionals lack knowledge of the unique needs of LGBT people; this can compromise the quality of care for LGBT elders and limit their ability to age and thrive in their homes and communities (Meyer, 2011).

In summer 2015, the Centers for Medicare & Medicaid Services (CMS) updated its rules in two areas central to long-term care: Medicaid managed care (a new paradigm for care delivery in Medicaid-funded services at the state level), and long-term-care residential facilities. Given the number of low-income people entering this system, including LGBT people with higher poverty rates, these rules provide ample opportunities to improve policies for LGBT older people. CMS and state leaders could require that marketing and outreach activities to Medicaid enrollees and facility residents represent

and reach all LGBT people. As well, they could require caregiver assessments and care planning procedures to include LGBT people's primary caregivers in their plans, which could include friends and family members of choice (not necessarily spouses), children, or biological family members; these primary caregivers might also serve as primary representatives for enrollees and residents in formal assessments. CMS and state leaders could track the extent to which plans and facilities serve LGBT people, as well as document and report their experiences through regular data collection and research. They also could mandate LGBT cultural competence training for all direct care workers (including nursing aides, home health aides, and personal care aides), mandating and increasing training requirements across occupations as needed, while providing funding and other incentives for this training to be administered.

CMS could require state plans to list providers in their directories who specialize in and have been trained in LGBT issues, including experts in geriatrics. Nursing home staff could be required to offer relevant information on LGBT-friendly resources in their communities, as part of a resident's transition to home- and community-based care. In all of these recommendations, CMS should distinguish transgender care from an all-encompassing LGBT approach, ensuring that gender identity and transgender status receive deserved attention.

As with long-term care, housing for LGBT elders has increased in salience in recent years. Safe, affordable housing allows older people to live in their communities for as long as possible; unfortunately, LGBT older adults face significant barriers to this reality. A recent ten-state housing investigation of same-sex couples found that nearly one in two couples experienced discrimination when seeking housing (ERC, 2014). Moreover, a national market research study of LGBT adults ages 45 and older found that one in eight older LGBT adults and one in four older transgender adults report discrimination when searching for housing, on the basis of their sexual orientations and gender identities, respectively (SAGE, 2014). In response, organizations across the spectrum have launched multi-pronged housing initiatives for LGBT older people, including policy-focused projects (SAGE, 2014).

I recommended the following six policy areas for improving housing stability for LGBT older people: enacting explicit legal protections for LGBT people against housing discrimination at the federal, state, and local levels; funding local public education so that LGBT older people comprehend their rights under a federal "Equal Access Rule"; inserting questions on sexual orientation and gender identity in all relevant surveys at the U.S. Department of Housing and Urban Development (HUD), plus commissioning HUD-funded research on housing instability among LGBT older people; requiring HUD grantees to be trained in LGBT cultural competence, and to develop outreach materials to LGBT people; encouraging the funding and development of LGBT-friendly affordable senior housing developments nationwide; and ensuing grant recipients under HUD's Section 202 program recognize that LGBT people in this program are protected against discrimination in housing (Espinoza, 2015).

Central to these recommendations, and to the ideas offered in the long-term-care section of this article, is the profound need to expand LGBT nondiscrimination protections at the federal, state, and local levels, with specific attention to public accommodations (Human Rights Campaign, 2015). Unfortunately, many LGBT people live in communities where they can be legally fired and denied housing, simply because of their sexual orientation and gender identity.

In addition to long-term care and housing, LGBT older people merit targeted community services that improve their physical and mental health and keep them actively engaged in their communities. The OAA provides more than $2.3 billon to aging services nationwide, yet few of these dollars fund LGBT-specific programming. Given the magnitude of this legislation—and its subsequent authorization this past April—policy makers had proposed delineating LGBT older people in the OAA, which would strengthen funding for LGBT-friendly supports around the country. Funding for such programming can also stem from city and state sources. In recent years, advocates have launched commissions and task forces to enhance policies for LGBT older people, and community-based organizations have successfully advocated for the funding to launch housing developments in cities around the country and resource a wide array of health and social offerings for LGBT elders.

Improving Data and Research on LGBT Elders

Transforming long-term care, housing, and the spectrum of community-based services to better serve LGBT older people would benefit from more data and research on this population—both to cull best practices in program design and to quantify the challenges facing these communities. Unfortunately, the marginal amount of quantitative data on LGBT older adults limits researchers from effectively studying this population, and prevents advocates from quantifying the scope of challenges facing LGBT elders—a request frequently made by government officials who weigh policy proposals or funding requests on current statistics (Espinoza, 2013b).

It also is important to recognize the progress in LGBT research with the National Institutes of Health and the National Institute on Aging; in 2009, they funded the first federally funded research project, *Caring and Aging with Pride*, on LGBT aging, health, and well-being (Fredriksen-Goldsen et al., 2011, 2013).

The research project was recently expanded and is now called *Aging with Pride: The National Health, Aging, Sexuality and Gender Study*—the first longitudinal study to track LGBT elders' aging, well-being, and health trajectories over time, as well as studying their families, caregivers, and communities. Yet the U.S. Census, and the broad array of federal surveys on health, retirement, and long-term care rarely include questions on sexual orientation, gender identity, or transgender status. Moreover, these types of questions are insufficiently tested among older people for clarity and accuracy, which might mean measurement errors in related research. Where these data exist, samples of people ages 60 and older are limited and often skew toward those with higher income, and who are white and more educated, as recently emphasized by a team of transgender aging advocates (SAGE and National Center for Transgender Equality, 2012).

In clinical settings, healthcare and long-term-care entities rarely pose these questions in the patient-intake process, despite evidence that knowing a patient's sexual orientation and gender identity can enhance person-centered care, largely by increasing candor and communication between LGBT people and their providers (The Fenway Institute and Center for American Progress, 2013). Moreover, if these questions were standardized, and the responses were aggregated and reported, these data could further uncover the nature of health disparities among LGBT people as they age. Similarly, state and area agencies on aging are not required to measure the extent to which they serve LGBT people, and the regulations that govern Medicaid managed care and long-term residential facilities, as two examples, contain no requirements to track and measure LGBT people as consumers, beneficiaries, and residents. In numeric terms, it remains unclear whether LGBT people are served effectively by community supports in aging and long-term-care systems nationwide.

Various policy recommendations would help remedy this dearth in knowledge. HHS could include questions on sexual orientation and gender identity in their national survey instruments, across relevant agencies, which includes testing their validity among older people. The Office of the National Coordinator for Health Information Technology could update its meaningful use standards to include these questions. State health departments could insert questions on sexual orientation and gender identity in their patient-intake and care-planning systems and tools, following the lead of states such as New York (Espinoza, 2013b).

In clinical settings, these questions must be accompanied by mandates regarding training, confidentiality protocols, and consumer rights resources so that LGBT people are protected against bias and discrimination from professionals gathering this information. Finally, the ACL could require that state and area units on aging collect data on the extent to which LGBT people are effectively served in their communities—an initiative noted in the 2015 White House Conference on Aging report.

Conclusion

The World Health Organization (2007) outlines the tenets of age-friendly communities: proper transportation, accessible public spaces, affordable housing, meaningful social participation, respect and social inclusion, civic engagement and employment, communication and information, and community and health services. This constellation of services relies on a system that effectively offers long-term care to all beneficiaries, provides housing options across the life span, and invests significant resources in services, programs, and initiatives across various dimensions of civic and social life.

Unfortunately, LGBT older people too often encounter discrimination in all of these areas, and are rarely studied by researchers or practitioners in ways that would yield meaningful data and solutions. Policy reform on LGBT aging should focus on developing the skills and knowledge of professionals working in long-term care, widening housing options, and funding local aging resources specific to LGBT elders.

It should include questions on sexual orientation and gender identity in federal surveys and clinical settings across the aging and long-term-care fields, as well as in the national network of state and area agencies on aging. Together, a transformation in practice and institutional knowledge will create a vibrant environment that re-imagines aging for generations of LGBT people.

References

Cahill, S., South, K., and Spade, J. 2000. *Outing Age: Public Policy Issues Affecting Gay, Lesbian, Bisexual and Transgender Elders.* New York: The Policy Institute of the National Gay and Lesbian Task Force.

Cahill, S., et al. 2010. *Growing Older with the Epidemic: HIV and Aging.* New York: Gay Men's Health Crisis.

Equal Rights Center (ERC). 2014. *Opening Doors: An Investigation of Barriers to Senior Housing for Same-Sex Couples.* Washington, DC: ERC.

Espinoza, R. 2011. "The Diverse Elders Coalition and LGBT Aging: Connecting Communities, Issues, and Resources in a Historic Moment." *Public Policy & Aging Report: Integrating Lesbian, Gay, Bisexual, and Transgender Older Adults into Aging Policy and Practice* 21(3): 8–12.

Espinoza, R. 2013a. "Five Years of Political Progress for LGBT Older People—But More Remains." *SAGE Blog.* http://blog.sageusa.org/blog/2013/07/five-years-of-politicalprogress-for-lgbt-older-people but-more-remains-1.html#sthash.I6fGohGz.dpuf/. Retrieved January 4, 2016.

Espinoza, R. 2013b. "The Unmeasured LGBT Life." *Huffington Post.* www.huffingtonpost.com/robertespinoza/the-unmeasured-lgbtlife_b_4261203.html. Retrieved January 14, 2016.

Espinoza, R. 2015. *Welcome Home: Improving Housing Security for LGBT Older Adults.* New York: SAGE.

Fenway Institute and Center for American Progress. 2013. *Asking Patients Questions about Sexual Orientation and Gender Identity in Clinical Settings: A Study in Four Health Centers.* Boston, MA: The Fenway Institute.

Fredriksen-Goldsen, K. I., et al. 2011. *The Aging and Health Report: Disparities and Resilience among Lesbian, Gay, Bisexual, and Trans-gender Older Adults.* Seattle, WA: Institute for Multigenerational Health.

Fredriksen-Goldsen, K. I., et al. 2013. "The Physical and Mental Health of Lesbian, Gay Male, and Bisexual (LGB) Older Adults: The Role of Key Health Indicators and Risk and Protective Factors." *The Gerontologist* 53(4): 664–75.

Human Rights Campaign. 2015. "Infographic: The Need for Full Federal LGBT Equality." www.hrc.org/blog/

infographic-the-needfor-full-federal-lgbt-equality. Retrieved January 4, 2016.

Meyer, H. 2011. "Safe Spaces? The Need for LGBT Cultural Competency in Aging Services." *Public Policy & Aging Report: Integrating Lesbian, Gay, Bisexual, and Transgender Older Adults into Aging Policy and Practice* 21(3): 24–7.

Movement Advancement Project (MAP) and SAGE. 2010. *Improving the Lives of LGBT Older Adults.* Denver, CO: MAP.

National Academy on an Aging Society and SAGE (Services and Advocacy for GLBT Elders). 2011. *Public Policy & Aging Report: Integrating Lesbian, Gay, Bisexual, and Transgender Older Adults into Aging Policy and Practice.* Boston, MA: The Gerontological Society of America.

National Alliance for Caregiving (NAC) and AARP Public Policy Institute. 2015. *Caregiving in the U.S.* 2015. Washington, DC: NAC and AARP Public Policy Institute.

SAGE. 2011. *LGBT Older Adults and Reauthorization of the Older Americans Act.* New York: SAGE.

SAGE. 2013. *Health Equity and LGBT Elders of Color: Recommendations for Policy and Practice.* New York: SAGE.

SAGE. 2014. *Out & Visible: The Experiences and Attitudes of LGBT Older Adults, Ages 45–75.* New York: SAGE.

SAGE and National Center for Transgender Equality. 2012. *Improving the Lives of Transgender Older Adults: Recommendations for Policy and Practice.* New York: SAGE.

White House Conference on Aging (WHCOA). 2015. *2015 White House Conference on Aging Final Report.* Washington, DC: WHCOA.

World Health Organization. 2007. *Checklist of Essential Features of Age-Friendly Cities.* www.who.int/ageing/publications/Age_friendly_cities_checklist.pdf. Retrieved January 4, 2016.

America's Aging Society Problem

A Look to Japan for Lessons on Prevention

Ender Ricart

It is estimated that by 2050, 21% of the U.S. population will be over the age of 65. With approximately 70% of this population expected to require some form of long-term care for at least three years, along with an estimated 91% of older adults with one chronic condition and many more with functional limitations, the United States is poised for epidemic levels of elderly in need of care. The government, industry, and individuals are asking: "How are we going to provide and pay for this care?"

America is not alone in asking this question. In the last two decades, Japan has seen a dramatic decline in birth rates, a rise in life expectancy, and the retirement of its own baby boomer generation. With a quarter of its population over the age of 65, Japan is one of the world's leading aged nations, and has already crossed the demographic threshold that is still looming for the U.S. Since the enactment of national and socialized long term care insurance (LTCI) in 2000, old-age care has increasingly become synonymous with "dependence on LTCI." As Japan's future economic and demographic situation continues to grow bleaker, limiting the number of elderly in need of care has gained increasing precedence.

Given the Confucian cultural tradition of family-based care for elders, the government's initial assumption was that the use of LTCI services would be low, giving them time to build-up the necessary care-infrastructure to support future growth. But, within the first few years, LTCI enrollment was off the charts, incurring higher than expected total costs. The primary enrollees were seniors with relatively light conditions, requiring minor assistance with activities such as food shopping, bathing, and cooking. Gerontological research demonstrated that many of these light conditions were gateways for further mental and physical decline, leading to heavier care burdens, but also that with proper diet and exercise, those conditions could be improved, or even prevented. The national government has dedicated significant funds to gerontological research on the first-causes of physical and mental decline in old age, means of intervention, and innovations in community-based care-prevention delivery systems. Subsequent LTCI policy revisions in 2006, 2012, and 2015 have all focused on old-age related disease and disability prevention.

Japan's LTCI revisions decreed the nationwide establishment of support networks for aging residents, termed Community Comprehensive Support Centers (*chiiki hōkatsu shiensentā*) in each municipality. Together with regional governments, they are responsible for establishing and managing the early-detection and intervention system of care-prevention. In the most recent LTCI reform of April 2014 (2015 enactment), a separate policy system for prevention, "New Care-Prevention System," was established, formalizing the responsibility of the regional, as opposed to the national, government to design, promote, and run community-based prevention programs for resident seniors.

The New Care-Prevention System utilizes annual surveys distributed by the local government to identify resident elderly "at risk of enrolling in LTCI," and solicits them to take community- based courses for health promotion, exercise, and social participation. For example, a senior who has difficulty walking to the store each day to go food shopping is considered at risk for enrolling in LTCI, and is targeted for participation in a community strength-building exercise class. The Community Comprehensive Support Centers offer exercise courses and educational courses on proper nutrition for seniors, oral health, and continued education to promote "mental training." The centers also function as social venues for seniors to gather and talk over tea and treats. Regional governments provide funding for the creation of community spaces, buying out commercial or private buildings to create designated social-spaces called "Salons" for community events. Major participants in such venues include seniors as they have the free time to dedicate to such activities. A community that fosters opportunities for seniors to socially engage, also builds social capital, fosters a sense of self-worth, and encourages the regular use of one's body and mind. For Japanese gerontologists and seniors, continued activity in old age is the key to mental and physical well being and quality of life.

The current healthcare environment in the U.S. is beginning to implement prevention-based healthcare policy to combat lifestyle diseases. The Patient Protection and Affordable Care Act (PPACA) has made various policy changes to Medicare and Medicaid, expanding coverage to include the treatment and prevention of some lifestyle diseases. While awareness and use remains low, Medicare will reimburse costs for health screenings during Annual Wellness Visits (AWV), encouraging early detection and intervention in potentially disabling age-related diseases. Unfortunately, concern for the aging society problem in America is confined to aging- studies specialists. The problem-consciousness among American policymakers of the issues associated with an aging society remains a matter of entitlement debates and cost-containment for Medicare and Medicaid expenditure, and not a question of how such spending might be reduced through targeted lifestyle intervention among seniors.

If we look to Japan as an example, America could benefit from enacting like-minded policies that target and empower older adults aged 65 and over to make lifestyle choices that will prevent behaviorally caused diseases such as frailty, obesity, depression, diabetes, and high blood pressure. These diseases can successfully be avoided in large numbers of elderly through health education, regular exercise, social activity, dietary changes, and the more routine use of health screening. Notable innovative community initiatives have been organized by non-profit organizations such as the Community Partnership for Older Adults under the Robert Wood Johnson Foundation and the various programs organized by the National Council on Aging. However, without top-down directives for state-level implementation of community-based prevention and support systems for seniors, the development and spread of such an infrastructure will depend upon fragmented bottom-up local initiatives, many of which fail within a few years due to unstable management, weak networking, and low participation.

Japan utilized the already existing social welfare infrastructure of municipal governments and community centers to build hubs for the New Care-Prevention System. They reached out to local businesses, care providers, and non-profit organizations to expand service and coverage to cater to the needs of at-risk seniors. To increase public awareness the national government employed TV, newspapers, regional health centers, and care providers to educate the general population about old-age lifestyle disease prevention. With the ACA, the focus of healthcare policy in the U.S. has indeed begun to shift from disease-centered treatment to include disease- prevention. A focused public-health campaign to combat old-age lifestyle diseases is a natural next step. With isolated old-age health promotion initiatives already underway and the turn to lifestyle-disease prevention in America's medical approach, what is needed now are coordination centers to ensure the targeted creation, continuation, and expansion of old-age disease prevention services and support for America's aging baby boomers.

There are a few linkages between the U.S. and Japan that can serve as starting points for future collaboration and coordination about old-age lifestyle disease prevention. Aging studies scholars and gerontologists at University of Hawai'i collaborate with the Okinawa Research Center for Longevity Science, and Michigan State University with Tokyo University and the Tokyo Metropolitan Institute of Gerontology. Research exchange remains focused on old-age care and care delivery methods and not specifically prevention, but it is possible to use these existing networks for such purposes.

Reflexive Questions

1. How old is your oldest living relative? How does their biological and psychological age align with their chronological age? How would you describe their quality of their life? When thinking from biopsychosocial perspectives, what factors have contributed to or detracted from their health, joy, and well-being?

2. Overall, what factors do you think are most important when it comes to subjective well-being and quality of life in old age? Are these factors realistic and available to everyone? If not, why not? Explain.

3. How long do you think you will live? Does longevity run in your family? What lifestyle changes would you have to make and maintain in order to live a long healthy and happy life? What could derail you from well-being in old age?

4. If personality traits remain fairly stable, what do you predict your personality and lifestyle would be like in old age? Would you be more like a parent, another older adult in your life, or entirely different? Explain.

5. What attitudes, beliefs, and actions would have to change in order to decrease vulnerabilities for older people in the United States?

6. Considering larger structural and institutional systems (i.e., legal, education, financial, medical, industrial, etc.), what would have to change to create more affordable, good, safe housing for all older adults?

7. Why does housing discrimination continue? How does this discrimination affect quality of life, especially in old age?

8. Imagine if you were to "age in place" in the first home you moved to after college, living there until your old age (80s or 90s). What do you think it would be like for you? What would you hope for if you did not have the ability to move?

9. Do you think programs like the community support centers in Japan should be implemented in the United States? Why or why not?

10. Describe why race, gender, and sexual orientation are socioeconomic determinants of health.

11. Why is it that education is considered a social determinant of health in the United States? Why does it correlate with longer life expectancy and lower rates of most health conditions?

12. Knowing what we know about inequality in education, how does this affect our ability to receive health education/literacy as we age?

CHAPTER 11

End of Life, Loss, and Bereavement

Introduction

My first memory of someone close to me dying was my godmother, who lived in Honduras. I was very close to my "*madrina* Joaquina," who was an amazing woman. It is hard to recall now how old I was when she died. I think I was a young adult, still in college. I was not able to go to her funeral, and I was deeply saddened by her passing. What was especially upsetting to me was that my mother said that she died from cancer but that my godmother did not know it. In disbelief, I asked why her doctor or family members did not tell her about her illness or how long she had to live. My mother said that they did not tell her because they did not want to upset her. They wanted her to die peacefully. Given that I was raised in the United States, I could not believe that the medical personnel were not transparent about the process. "It was her right to know," I told my mother. "She wasn't given the opportunity to say her goodbyes!" It was then that I realized how different my worldview was from my family members there. Open and direct communication and the right to be informed was an expectation I had based on my "American" cultural beliefs.

Death and dying are topics that most people do not want to think about and often actively avoid. As I write this book, the world is collectively experiencing grief related to a global pandemic due to COVID-19. The pandemic has devastated countries worldwide, and the death toll has been especially high in the United States. A writer from *Time Magazine*, W. J. Hennigan (2020), reported on the suffering experienced in New York City:

> The makeshift morgue is just one stop in a citywide cavalcade bearing an unfathomable number of bodies. Since March 14 [two months' time], COVID-19 has killed some 20,000 in New York City; at the height of the pandemic on April 7, two dozen people were dying every hour. But those figures don't capture the competing challenges that the scale of death has created on the ground. The first is logistical: How do you handle that many dead bodies in a safe and hygienic manner? The pandemic has overwhelmed the network of funeral parlors, mortuaries and morgues designed to process the dead. At the worst moments, hospitals loaded corpses onto refrigerated trucks with forklifts. Medical examiners set two-week limits to claim bodies before they were sent in pine boxes to paupers' graves on Hart Island. Funeral homes stacked caskets in spare rooms, hallways and private chapels. Crematories' brick ovens collapsed because of overuse.

This tragedy is truly unfathomable—so many families are experiencing intense loss and grief on multiple levels. What is even more incomprehensible is that the United States led the world with COVID-19-related deaths. By the end of April 2020, in less than four months' time, more than 100,000 Americans lost their lives to COVID-19. According to the Centers for Disease Control and Prevention (https://www.cdc.gov/nchs/covid19/mortality-overview.htm), from February 2020 to February 2021, over 500,000 people died due to the virus—just one year after the pandemic was evident in the United States. The death toll is catastrophic! How is this possible in one of the wealthiest, most resourced, powerful countries in the world? Although we may never be certain about the accuracy of other countries' reporting of COVID-19-related deaths, we are certain about the staggering death toll in the United States.

As the country is in a state of shock, grief, denial, fear, anxiety, there are so many unanswered questions. Why were we not better prepared? What were the socioeconomic, political, structural, and institutional factors that exacerbated the ability to manage this health crisis? Worldwide, people lost their jobs, access to healthcare, ability to buy food and pay their bills, and were displaced from their homes, sheltered in place, and quarantined under difficult circumstances. For those who have lost a loved one, how are they coping with their devastating loss, especially at a time when burial and grieving rituals are not possible? What resources do they have (internal, interpersonal, and material) to manage the immediate and long-term response? Not surprisingly, women (https://www.un.org/sustainabledevelopment/gender-equality/) and people of color (https://www.cdc.gov/coronavirus/2019-ncov/community/health-equity/race-ethnicity.html) are suffering the greatest brunt of this health and economic crisis. And if the grief and loss related to the COVID-19 were not enough, at the time of writing this book, the United States was simultaneously experiencing sociopolitical division and extreme unrest and protests across the country in response to the murder of George Floyd, an African American man who died at the hands of police. His death, as well as the murders of Ahmaud Arbery and Breonna Taylor, among many others, are stark reminders of the brutal and fatal realities of the interlocking systems of oppression and power produced by a culture of violence, male dominance, white supremacy, racism, and poverty in the United States (Collins & Bilge, 2016). Currie (2017) urges us as a society to examine the structural roots of racially different patterns of life and death among Whites and African Americans and to confront these inequities. As long as gross power imbalances and socioeconomic disparities continue, so will the mounting resentment and risk to those most vulnerable to injustice. The nation, and indeed the world, is grieving on so many levels.

Although we expect death to be a part of life, who, when, where, how, and why someone dies makes a difference in how we cope with the loss. Most of us are taken aback by untimely death. We are especially grief stricken with a miscarriage; when a baby, child, or young person dies; or when death happens suddenly due to natural disasters, war, illnesses, and senseless deaths related to injustice, violence, genocide, terrorism, mass shootings, murder, and preventable accidents. The cause (specific illness or injury that leads to death), the manner of death (natural, homicide, suicide, accident, undetermined), and the timing of the death (age of person who died and is grieving) will often affect the intensity and extent to which we grieve (Corr, Corr, & Doka, 2019). Although somewhat challenged now, Elisabeth Kubler-Ross's (1969) model offered an important foundation for the study of grief, which she postulated happened in five stages: denial, anger, bargaining, depression, and acceptance. Although not everyone experiences these responses, and certainly not in sequence, grief is complex and affects us all differently. In a study conducted by Arizmendi and O'Conner (2015), the researchers identified four distinct paths for grief: resilience, chronic grief, depressed-improved, and chronic depression. They noted that some people continue to experience severe disruption to their lives years after their loss, which is known as complicated grief. People will also react differently based on the type of loss and grief (Houck, 2008; Hill, Cacciatore, Shreffler, & Pritchard, 2017).

When we consider loss throughout the lifespan and across multiple contexts, we know that loss, as an experience, extends beyond the loss of life. For example, the loss experienced due to the death of a loved one is experienced differently than the loss of a romantic relationship, a job, a way of life, a home, a car, etc. Additionally, some losses are ambiguous losses, as suggested by well-known scholar and family therapist Pauline Boss (1999; 2007; 2016). Her research has identified two types of ambiguous loss: one that is based on physical absence with psychological presence (e.g., war, kidnapping, missing body, divorce, incarceration, desertion, immigration) and the other psychological absence with physical presence (e.g., dementia, autism, chronic mental illness, addiction, depression, obsessions, gender transition). Boss states that ideally, practitioners will help people cope with the effects of this loss by strengthening their resilience. Although we know that individual, family, and community resilience is essential to well-being (Walsh, 2016), other scholars (Hart et al., 2016) contend that "it is time for resilience to go beyond understanding how individuals cope with adversity to challenge the structures that create disadvantages in the first place" (p. 5). This social justice approach necessitates that scholars, policymakers, and practitioners take the wider socioeconomic and political landscape into account as they support those most vulnerable within societies.

People from minoritized and oppressed groups are disproportionately negatively impacted by loss (Aday, 1994). By definition, vulnerable populations are social groups who have limited resources and are at an increased risk for death and premature death (Flaskerud & Winslow, Betty 1998). They are more likely to die from preventable deaths such as homicide, femicide, genocide, starvation, police brutality, homelessness, xenophobia, homophobia, and treatable diseases. People occupying multiple subjugated identities (i.e., trans women of color, people of color with disabilities, uneducated people living in rural areas and the Global South) are at even higher risk for social inequalities, abuses, and compounded loss and grief. Collins and Bilge (2016) contend that intersectionality provides an analytical framework for explaining how social divisions of our multiple identities (race, class, gender, etc.) situate people differently in terms of insecurity. For example, in their study of the devastating effects and the post-tsunami recovery of Indian island communities in South Asia in 2004, Gupta and Sharma (2006) found that remote and most vulnerable communities took the longest to recover. People in those regions, especially from the most vulnerable sectors and displaced communities, were especially devastated, with women and children suffering the worst. This was also evident with Hurricane Katrina in 2005 in New Orleans; the earthquakes in Chile and Haiti in 2010 and Japan in 2011; and Hurricane Maria in 2017 in Puerto Rico, Dominica, and St. Croix. The death toll and economic impact was catastrophic. To date, they have not fully recovered and will likely be experiencing effects of loss for decades to come. Overall, people from countries that are plagued by corruption, unstable economies, weak infrastructures, chronic poverty, and violence are especially vulnerable in ways that those from more resourced and equitable countries are not (Naudé, Santos-Paulino, & McGillivray, 2009). This vulnerability can hinder resilience and one's ability to overcome the effects of chronic and cumulative loss over time.

In sum, our social location and sociocultural/religious contexts greatly affect how we perceive and manage our responses to death, loss, and grief. As such, our worldviews greatly shape the way we approach certain topics such as abortion versus reproductive rights, euthanasia or assisted suicide/death, being on life support, being buried versus cremated, having an open casket versus no casket at all, and how we manage the remains or ashes of a loved one. Despite the multitude of diverse perspectives, most cultures have norms, rituals, and traditions to help us with the grief process. The following readings provide a snapshot of how age and gender affect our reactions to our parents' deaths and how burial and grieving rituals are performed in China and Mexico.

Summary of Readings

The first reading, "**Parents' Death and Adult Well-Being: Gender, Age, and Adaptation to Filial Bereavement**" (2015) by Thomas Leopold and Clemens M. Lechner, examines the profiles of life satisfaction for 2,760 adult children, ages 17 to 70 from Germany who were anticipating, reacting to, or adapting to a parent's death. Although the vast majority of people lose their parents as middle-aged or older adults, few studies have targeted filial bereavement and subjective well-being among adults. This study aimed to fill this gap by examining how age and gender affect the bereavement process. The findings showed gender and age differences in life satisfaction. Adult daughters who lost their mothers experienced the greatest decline in life satisfaction and took 4 to 5 years to adapt to this life change. The researchers found that the circumstances and timing of the parent's death affected filial bereavement. For example, if a parent died at an older age due to natural causes, their adult child experienced on-time filial bereavement and had less adverse effects. In contrast, younger adults who experience the death of a parent "off-time" under unusual or untimely circumstances had a great decline in life satisfaction. Daughters who lost their mothers in young adulthood did not fully adapt even several years after the death. They suffered significant turmoil as they learned to adapt to changing family roles and loss of instrumental support.

The second reading, "**Kin and Kindred: Death and Social Relations**" (2004) by Tong Chee-Kiong, examines how funerary rituals of Chinese Singaporeans are intended to demonstrate family unity and delineate the status of individual family members. Families often display unity and solidarity by performing death rituals as a group. Moreover, death rituals differentiate relatives of the deceased from outsiders, which is important. For example, during the funeral, outsiders cannot see the deceased, and ritualized weeping is performed by kin but not visitors and friends. The social stratification of Chinese culture also manifests itself in death rituals that differentiate one's relationship with the deceased based on gender and age, among other things. Sons will often stand closest to the coffin, the eldest sons before his siblings, then followed by daughters-in-law, daughters, etc. This underscores the patriarchal values of Chinese culture. Lastly, Chee-Kiong emphasizes that, while many studies highlight Chinese culture's emphasis on the collective over the individual, ethnographic evidence suggests ritual sponsors have their own individual interests in performing the rituals, which can create conflict between siblings. However, these conflicts are often covert and masked by the family performance of unity and cohesion during the funerary process.

"**Origins and Celebrations of El Día de los Muertos**" (2008) by J. Rhett Rushing examines the origins of this holiday, its evolution, and its current rituals and traditions. *El Día de los Muertos* (Day of the Dead) began as a harvest festival during the fall equinox. Agricultural societies around the world would celebrate the symbolic "death" of the crops as well as their human dead, who received offerings and prayers. After the arrival of the European conquistadores, Roman Catholicism changed the nature of the harvest festival, de-emphasizing the harrowing aspects of the season and making it a day of celebrating saints. Today, November 1 is All Saints Day, which celebrates the communion of saints and those who have died. November 2 is All Souls Day, or *El Día de los Muertos* in Mexico and other parts of Latin America, and has become a day for families to celebrate their deceased loved ones.

While there are no official guidelines to celebrating *El Día de los Muertos*, there are common traditions. People will often create and decorate *altares* (altars) with images of the deceased and give offerings, or *ofrendas,* with bread called *pan de muerto (bread of death)*, candies, candles, favorite foods, and an abundance of marigolds, among other things. *Calaveras* are cartoon-like skeleton figurines that are sometimes placed on altars to remind people of our shared humanity and how all people are equal in death. One of the most traditional activities is visiting the cemetery. Families will often clean the gravesite of deceased relatives, take flowers, usually marigolds, eat a meal and spend time there as a family. Ultimately, *el Día de Los Muertos* is not only a day of remembrance, but it is a time to celebrate life and reinforce and reestablish family unity.

References

Aday, L. A. (1994). Health status of vulnerable populations. *Annual review of public health, 15*(1), 487–509.

Arizmendi, B. J., & O'Connor, M. (2015). What is "normal" in grief? *Australian Critical Care, 28*(2), 58–62. doi:10.1016/j.aucc.2015.01.005

Boss, P. (1999). *Ambiguous loss: Learning to live with unresolved grief.* Harvard University Press.

Boss, P. (2007). Ambiguous loss theory: Challenges for scholars and practitioners. *Family Relations, 56*(2), 105–111. doi:10.1111/j.1741-3729.2007.0044.x

Boss, P. (2016). The context and process of theory development: The story of ambiguous loss. *Journal of Family Theory & Review, 8*, 269–286. doi:10.1111/jftr.12152

Centers for Disease Control and Prevention. (2021). COVID-19: Health equity considerations and racial and ethnic minority groups. https://www.cdc.gov/coronavirus/2019-ncov/need-extra-precautions/racial-ethnic-minorities.html

Centers for Disease Control and Prevention. (2021). COVID-19 mortality overview. (https://www.cdc.gov/nchs/covid19/mortality-overview.htm).

Corr, C. A., Corr, D. M., & Doka, K. J. (2019). *Death & dying, life & living (8th ed.)*. Centage.

Currie, E. (2017). Confronting the North's South: On race and violence in the United States. *International Journal for Crime, Justice and Social Democracy, 6*(1), 23–34. doi:10.5204/ijcjsd.v6i1.382

Flaskerud, J. H., &nWinslow, B. J. (1998). Conceptualizing vulnerable populations Health- Related Research, *Nursing Research, 47*(2), 69–78.

Gupta, M., & Sharma, A. (2006). Compounded loss: The post tsunami recovery experience of Indian island communities. *Disaster Prevention and Management, 15*(1), 67–78. doi:10.1108/09653560610654248

Hart, A., Gagnon, E., Eryigit-Madzwamuse, S., Cameron, J., Aranda, K., Rathbone, A., & Heaver, B. (2016). Uniting resilience research and practice with an inequalities approach. *SAGE Open, 6*(4). doi:10.1177/2158244016682477

Hennigan, W. J. (2020, May 21). "We do this for the living." Inside New York's citywide effort to bury its dead. *Time Magazine*. https://time.com/5839056/new-york-city-burials-coronavirus/

Hill, P. W., Cacciatore, J., Shreffler, K. M., & Pritchard, K. M. (2017). The loss of self: The effect of miscarriage, stillbirth, and child death on maternal self-esteem. *Death Studies, 41*(4), 226–235. doi:10.1080/07481187.2016.1261204

Houck, J. A. (2007). A comparison of grief reactions in cancer, HIV/AIDS, and suicide bereavement. *Journal of HIV/AIDS & Social Services, 6*(3), 97–112. doi:10.1300/J187v06n03_07

Kubler-Ross, E. (1967). *On death and dying*. Macmillan.

Naudé, W., Santos-Paulino, A. U., & McGillivray, M. (Eds.) (2009). *Vulnerability in developing countries*. United Nations University Press.

United Nations. The impact of COVID-19 on women. https://www.un.org/sustainabledevelopment/gender-equality/

Walsh, F. (2016). *Strengthening family resilience* (3rd ed.). Guilford Press.

Parents' Death and Adult Well-being

Gender, Age, and Adaptation to Filial Bereavement

Thomas Leopold and Clemens M. Lechner

The authors investigated how filial bereavement affects the subjective well-being of adult children. They used data from the German Socio-Economic Panel Study to examine temporal profiles of life satisfaction in 2,760 adult children ages 17–70 who moved through the stages of anticipation of, reaction to, and adaptation to a parent's death. Fixed effects models covering up to 11 yearly measurements per respondent revealed that the negative effects of parental loss on life satisfaction varied substantially by gender and age. First, daughters who lost their mothers experienced the deepest drops in life satisfaction. Second, negative effects were stronger if filial bereavement was "off time": children who lost a parent in younger adulthood experienced steeper declines in life satisfaction. Daughters who are untimely bereaved of their mothers did not fully adapt even several years after the death.

The deleterious impact of parental death on child outcomes is well documented (Amato & Anthony, 2014; Schafer, 2009). This literature, however, has almost exclusively focused on filial bereavement in childhood or adolescence. Although the vast majority of people in industrialized societies lose their parents in middle or older age (Watkins, Menken, & Bongaarts, 1987), only a few studies have addressed filial bereavement among adults. These studies have suggested that losing a parent in adulthood can entail long-term adverse effects on subjective well-being (Marks, Jun, & Song, 2007).

Yet, extant studies on the effects of filial bereavement on subjective well-being in adulthood provide only limited insight into the nature of these effects. Two limitations stand out. First, the evidence is largely based on cross-sectional data. The only existing longitudinal studies on subjective well-being following the death of a parent (Marks et al., 2007; Umberson & Chen, 1994) used two-wave panel designs in which gaps between both observations were large, amounting to 3 or 5 years, respectively. We still lack research that adequately traces filial bereavement as a process to answer the questions of whether, to what extent, and on what time scale bereaved adult children adapt to the loss of a parent.

Second, the study of interindividual differences in the reaction to parental death has revealed considerable variation, in particular along gender lines (Rostila & Saarela, 2011; Umberson, 2003). Less attention has been devoted to the moderating role of bereaved adults' age. This neglects a key tenet of life course theory, namely, the distinction between "off-time" and "on-time" transitions: If the timing of a parent's death fits with the script of the "normal, expectable life" (Neugarten, 1969), adverse effects on adult children might be attenuated compared with off-time filial bereavement experienced earlier in adulthood.

The present study addressed both of these limitations. Using large-scale, long-run panel data from Germany, we investigated the effects of parents' death on within-person change in life satisfaction. We pursued two goals. First, we aimed to unravel the process of adaptation to filial bereavement, tracing out temporal profiles of life satisfaction as individuals experienced the loss of their first and second parent. Second, we designed our study to capture the gendered and age-dependent nature of these effects. With regard to gender, we examined how the impact of parental loss varied with (a) the gender of the parent, (b) the gender of the adult child, and (c) the gender constellation of the parent–child dyad. With regard to age, we addressed the distinction between off-time and on-time loss of a parent, comparing the effects of untimely bereavement in younger adulthood to normative transitions experienced later in life.

Background

Filial Bereavement and Subjective Well-being

Filial bereavement is associated with substantial and long-term reductions in adult well-being (Marks et al., 2007). The literature suggests three main pathways that mediate these negative effects. First, the bereavement process itself involves significant emotional turmoil. Experiencing the death of a parent may trigger a variety of negative emotions and feelings that can overburden bereaved children and lead to a prolonged stress response. Already before the parent's death, witnessing his or her health

deteriorate can be emotionally demanding for adult children, especially if they act as caregivers (Umberson, 2003).

Second, losing a parent is a major transition of adulthood that may involve not only a reconfiguration of family roles and responsibilities but also a transformation of the child's identity, both of which can place substantial psychological burden on bereaved adults (Petersen & Rafuls, 1998). This applies to the death of the first and the second parent, although each of these transitions entails specific shifts that are important to consider. Loss of the first parent may often instigate the first life course phase of intense and prolonged grief experienced by middle-aged adults. Death of the second parent may signify a new meaning in life, as this transition "demands a realization of one's own mortality as the 'next-in-line' in a constant flux of generational turnover" (Marshall, 2004, p. 354).

Third, parents are a critical source of emotional comfort and instrumental support, not only in childhood and adolescence but also throughout adulthood (Bengtson, 2001). In modern societies, children can expect to share five or more decades of lifetime with their parents. When a parent's death disrupts these bonds, adult children lose an important and often irreplaceable source of emotional and instrumental support, which may entail permanent reductions in their subjective well-being (Umberson, 2003).

Although filial bereavement is commonly recognized as a critical transition of adult life, only a few empirical studies have investigated its consequences for adult children's subjective well-being. Most of these studies were based on cross-sectional or retrospective data and relied on small, nonrepresentative samples (e.g., Moss, Moss, Rubinstein, & Resch, 1993; Moss, Resch, & Moss, 1997). Only two studies have advanced from cross-sectional designs, drawing on large-scale prospective data from adults who lost one or both of their parents between two panel waves (Marks et al., 2007; Umberson & Chen, 1994). Despite their merits in exploring the consequences of filial bereavement for adult well-being, these studies have important drawbacks. First, similar to cross-sectional explorations, they compared adults who lost a parent to those who did not. This approach is prone to bias due to unobserved heterogeneity between individuals, such as social background characteristics, personality traits, or genetic factors that are either unobserved or only insufficiently controlled by measures of socioeconomic position. Second, and more important, two-wave designs are insufficient to fully capture parental loss as a life course transition and to unravel how these effects on bereaved adults unfold over time.

In this regard, theory and empirical research on the impact of life events has demonstrated that an extensive window of longitudinal observation is necessary to provide an adequate assessment of effects on subjective well-being. This method enables the analyst to study longer term profiles of within-person change as individuals move through the stages of (a) anticipation, (b) reaction, and (c) adaptation in the process of filial bereavement (Clark, Diener, Georgellis, & Lucas, 2008): On the one hand, anticipatory (or *lead*) effects may precede the focal event by several months or even years. In the case of filial bereavement, adult children may be aware that the death of a parent is imminent, especially if they act as caregivers (Umberson, 2003). On the other hand, research has demonstrated that the impact of major life events on subjective well-being is often transient. As suggested by *set-point theory* (Diener, Lucas, & Scollon, 2006), people adapt to life events over time, including

severe loss events such as the death of a spouse (Luhmann, Hofmann, Eid, & Lucas, 2012). In the absence of nuanced longitudinal assessments tracing the process of filial bereavement from pre- to postevent stages, it remains unknown whether the same is true for the loss of a parent. Open questions in this regard are whether, to what extent, and on what time scale bereaved adult children revert to previous levels of subjective well-being.

Gender and Age Differences in the Effects of Filial Bereavement

Gender. Extant studies have revealed substantial heterogeneity in the effects of parental death on outcomes in adult children. The most prominent moderator is gender. Previous studies have indicated that the death of a mother is more traumatic than the death of a father (Umberson, 2003; Umberson & Chen, 1994). This difference is typically attributed to the special quality of the attachment bonds between children and their mothers, who act as primary caregivers in childhood and continue to invest more in family relationships across the life span (Bowlby, 1969; Umberson, 2003).

Further evidence has suggested that the impact of filial bereavement on subjective well-being also depends on the child's gender. Regarding main effects, the evidence is inconclusive. Findings indicating that daughters suffer more from the death of a parent than do sons (Moss et al., 1997) have not been corroborated by other studies (Marks et al., 2007; Umberson & Chen, 1994). More consistent evidence has emerged for the gender *constellation* of the parent–child dyad, in particular with regard to the mother–daughter tie. In line with studies documenting the unique qualities of this bond in terms of intimacy, contact frequency, and instrumental support

(Silverstein, Bengtson, & Lawton, 1997; Troll, 1987), empirical findings have shown that the death of a mother entails particularly adverse consequences for daughters. Conversely, sons appear to suffer more from the death of a father (Umberson & Chen, 1994). Although the latter result does not correspond to the strength of emotional ties, it might indicate the importance of personal identification with same-gender parents who serve as role models well into adulthood (Umberson, 2003).

Taken together, these findings suggest that gender is an important moderator of the impact of filial bereavement. Yet the evidence is sparse and far from conclusive. In particular, there is a lack of longitudinal research into gender differences as daughters and sons move through different stages of filial bereavement, including anticipation of and adaptation to the loss of mothers and fathers.

Age. Even less is known about the moderating role of adults' age at parental death. In previous longitudinal studies on filial bereavement in adulthood, analyses of the moderating role of adults' age at the time of their parent's death were either absent (Marks et al., 2007) or complicated by data limitations in terms of a restricted age range of study samples and insufficient observation time (Umberson & Chen, 1994). From a life course perspective, adults' age at the time of their parent's death is of central interest because it indicates whether this transition occurs on time or off time (Elder, 1977). Younger adults who are confronted with an untimely death of a parent experience an off-time transition that is out of step with the predictable sequence of family transitions (Hagestad, 1996). These nonnormative events are often unanticipated and shared by few age peers to provide mutual comfort. Compared

with those who experience their parents' death in older age, untimely bereaved adults are likely to sustain more severe and longer term declines in subjective well-being. [...].

Discussion

This study asked how the death of a parent affects the subjective well-being of adult children. Using large-scale panel data, we explored temporal profiles of life satisfaction as adult children moved through the stages of anticipation of, reaction to, and adaptation to filial bereavement. Moreover, we shed new light on the moderating roles of gender and age. In doing so, we offer the first comprehensive longitudinal investigation of the impact of a parent's death on life satisfaction in adulthood.

Results from fixed effects regression models tracking change in life satisfaction across an observation period of up to 11 yearly measurements showed that the average declines following the first and second parent's death were modest in size, each amounting to approximately 0.16 *SD* of within-person variation in life satisfaction over time. However, our analysis revealed considerable variation beneath these average effects, showing that the impact of filial bereavement on adult life satisfaction is strongly gendered and age dependent.

Gender differences emerged primarily with regard to the gender constellation of the parent–child dyad. This supports one of the main conclusions drawn in Russell and Saebel's (1997) review on the distinctness of intergenerational relationships: Gender differences emerge as dyadic effects, rather than as main effects of the parent's gender or child's gender. Consistent with earlier work (Umberson, 2003), our findings direct attention to the mother–daughter tie, as daughters who lost their mothers experienced the strongest declines in life satisfaction. This also dovetails with research on the strength of intergenerational bonds, which has highlighted the unique qualities of mother–daughter ties in terms of intimacy, contact frequency, and instrumental support (Fingerman, 2001; Silverstein et al., 1997). A further notable gender difference concerned the pre-event period. Daughters displayed anticipatory drops in well-being, whereas no such lead effect was found in sons. Considering two well-established findings from the literature on intergenerational relationships, this result could reflect daughters' higher awareness of parents' health status as well as their greater exposure to the strain of (terminal) caregiving (Leopold, Raab, & Engelhardt, 2014). Indeed, the literature has associated daughters' caregiving with anticipatory grief characterized by a state of anxiety, depression, hostility, and trouble getting things done. Furthermore, the prevalence and intensity of these anticipatory reactions were positively related to levels of cohesion and affection in the relationships between givers and receivers of care (Lindgren, Connelly, & Gaspar, 1999; Waldrop, 2007).

The present results also showed a clear pattern of age differences. We found that off-time filial bereavement (i.e., losing a parent earlier in adult life) was associated with deeper drops in life satisfaction than losing a parent at an older, more typical age. Among daughters who experienced an untimely death of their mother, the estimated effect amounted to 0.5 SD of within-person change in life satisfaction over time. This ranks among the stronger declines documented in the literature on life events and subjective well-being (Clark et al., 2008; Luhmann et al., 2012). Moreover, daughters who lost their mothers off time did not fully adapt even 4 to 5 years after the death.

This sizable and lasting effect sheds new light on one of the closest of all human bonds (Troll, 1987). Research has shown that the mother–daughter bond is tightened when daughters experience important adult transitions, such as marriage and parenthood (Fischer, 1981). During this stage of life, loss of the mother may represent a traumatic disruptive event from which many daughters cannot fully recover in terms of subjective well-being.

The age-dependent impact of filial bereavement is in line with life course theory, suggesting that the timing of this transition is crucial in determining its consequences (Elder, 1977; Neugarten, 1969). It also parallels earlier findings showing that the adverse health consequences of filial bereavement are more pronounced in childhood and adolescence than in later adulthood (Rostila & Saarela, 2011). There are several possible reasons for why filial bereavement has less adverse consequences at older ages. First, parents' role as primary attachment figures in childhood loses some of its significance across adolescence and particularly in adulthood, as other social relationships (to peers, spouses, one's own children) gain in importance (Bowlby, 1969). Second, the death of a parent at a younger age may more often be unexpected, which may aggravate its adverse consequences for the well-being of the bereaved (Bur-ton, Haley, & Small, 2007; but see Carr, House, Wortman, Nesse, & Kessler, 2001). Because losing a parent at a younger age is increasingly uncommon in modern societies, untimely bereaved adults have fewer age peers who share their experience and can provide comfort. Older adults, in contrast, may not only have more time to prepare for the death of the parent and engage in anticipatory coping but also take solace from the feeling that this transition comes naturally and is shared by many.

Some limitations to our study warrant future investigation. First, there were potentially confounding variables that cannot be fully controlled for even in a fixed effects design. This concerns time-varying characteristics, such as shared environmental conditions, that may adversely affect both parental health and the subjective well-being of their adult children. It is also important to note that time-constant characteristics, such as predispositions to disease, were controlled only to the extent that their manifestation does not change over time. Although our analyses were based on a comprehensive set of time-changing covariates, we caution that conclusions regarding the causal effects of parental death on adult subjective well-being rely on the assumption that these covariates fully capture any remaining confounders.

Second, with the present data, we could address only the cognitive-evaluative dimension of subjective well-being as an outcome. A recent meta-analysis has not only suggested that major life events often differentially affect the cognitive dimension (e.g., life satisfaction) and affective dimension (e.g., positive and negative emotions) of well-being but also that rates of adaptation may diverge for both dimensions (Luhmann et al., 2012). In view of that, future studies could complement our analyses by addressing change in affective well-being as well as other relevant outcomes that may be influenced by the experience of parents' death in adulthood, such as mental health and alcohol consumption (Marks et al., 2007). In this regard, qualitative and quantitative research has shown that the effects of parental death on different outcomes may vary by bereaved adults' and parents' gender. Men, for example, may increase their alcohol consumption more often than women, especially after the

loss of their father (Marks et al., 2007); men also appear to be somewhat more vulnerable to heightened mortality following the death of a parent in adulthood (Rostila & Saarela, 2011). Women, by contrast, may show more pronounced changes in affective outcomes than men (Umberson, 2003; Umberson & Chen, 1994). Considering such possible differences, it would be desirable for future studies to use a broader range of outcome measures in order to paint a more nuanced picture of short-term and long-term effects of filial bereavement in adulthood.

Third, our data did not allow us to include information on factors other than age and gender that might moderate the impact of bereavement on well-being. Important family-internal factors include the life course history and quality of the parent–child relationship (Marks et al., 2007; Umberson & Chen, 1994), whether the adult child acted as a caregiver to the deceased parent (Burton et al., 2007; Umberson, 2003), and whether the death was expected or unexpected for the bereaved (Carr et al., 2001).

A further limitation is that the number of observations available in our data was not sufficient to study the possible moderating effects of age and gender in reactions to the second parent's death, although qualitative studies have suggested that the first and second parent's death may be experienced differently (e.g., Marshall, 2004). Finally, we note that our data comprised yearly measurements. As a result, there was a time lag between the death event and the subsequent survey wave of, on average, 6 months. Given that the negative impact of bereavement on subjective well-being is typically strongest shortly after the death (Luhmann et al., 2012), the effects reported in this study are likely to be conservative estimates of the negative impact of parental death on life satisfaction. More finely grained analyses, preferably based on monthly data, could illuminate the anticipation of, reaction to, and adaptation to parental death in higher temporal resolution.

Taken together, our findings show that although the loss of a parent in adulthood typically involves only moderate drops in life satisfaction and is followed by gradual adaptation, its impact on life satisfaction varies considerably by gender and age. This corroborates calls for greater attention to potential heterogeneity in the impact of life events on subjective well-being (Diener et al., 2006) and concurs with the claim that life events may cause change in life satisfaction that is not followed by a relatively swift return to a set point (Headey, 2010).

Although life satisfaction is an important outcome in its own right, research indicates that it is also predictive of future mental health problems, suicidality, physical health problems, and mortality, even after adjusting for other well-known risk factors (Diener et al., 2013). Our results concerning age and gender differences in filial bereavement allow identifying individuals who are at a heightened risk of experiencing potentially far-reaching consequences of parental loss in terms of long-term declines in life satisfaction and associated health problems. Our findings suggest that, in particular, daughters who experience an off-time loss of their mother could benefit from bereavement counseling and support groups that are visible and accessible. Demographic changes indicate a continuing need for such interventions: As early parental loss becomes increasingly rare, this experience is increasingly out of step with the normal, expectable life, potentially intensifying its adverse consequences and hence the need for targeted support.

Note

Replication files are available at the authors' websites: www.thomasleopold.eu (Thomas Leopold) and www.clemenslechner.eu (Clemens M. Lechner). The data used in this publication have been made available by the German Socio-Economic Panel Study at the German Institute for Economic Research, Berlin.

References

Allison, P. D. (2009). *Fixed effects regression models*. Los Angeles: Sage.

Amato, P. R., & Anthony, C. J. (2014). Estimating the effects of parental divorce and death with fixed effects models. *Journal of Marriage and Family, 76,* 370–386. doi:10.1111/jomf.12100

Bengtson, V. L. (2001). Beyond the nuclear family: The increasing importance of multigenerational bonds. *Journal of Marriage and Family, 63,* 1–16. doi:10.1111/j.1741-3737.2001.00001.x

Bowlby, J. (1969). *Attachment and loss* (Vol. 1). London: Hogarth.

Burton, A. M., Haley, W. E., & Small, B. J. (2007). Bereavement after caregiving or unexpected death: Effects on elderly spouses. *Aging and Mental Health, 10,* 319–326. doi:10.1080/13607860500410045

Carr, D., House, J. S., Wortman, C., Nesse, R., & Kessler, R. C. (2001). Psychological adjustment to sudden and anticipated spousal loss among older widowed persons. *Journals of Gerontology Series B: Psychological Sciences and Social Sciences, 56,* 237–248. doi:10.1093/geronb/56.4.S237

Clark, A. E., Diener, E. Georgellis, Y., & Lucas, R. E. (2008). Lags and leads in life satisfaction: A test of the baseline hypothesis. *Economic Journal, 118,* 222–243. doi:10.1111/j.1468-0297.2008.02150.x Diener, E., Inglehart, R., & Tay, L. (2013). Theory and validity of life satisfaction scales. *Social Indicators Research, 112,* 497–527. doi:10.1007/s11205-012-0076-y

Diener, E., Lucas, R. E., & Scollon, C. N. (2006). Beyond the hedonic treadmill: Revising the adaptation theory of well-being. *American Psychologist, 61*, 305–314. doi:10.1037/0003-066X61. 4.305

Dolan, P., Peasgood, T., & White, M. (2008). Do we really know what makes us happy? A review of the economic literature on the factors associated with subjective well-being. *Journal of Economic Psychology, 29*, 94–122. doi:10.1016/j.joep.2007.09.001

Fingerman, K. L. (2001). *Aging mothers and their adult daughters: A study in mixed emotions.* New York: Springer.

Fischer, L. R. (1981). Transitions in the mother–daughter relationship. *Journal of Marriage and the Family, 43*, doi:10.2307/351762

Hagestad, G. O. (1996). On-time, off-time, out of time? Reflections on continuity and discontinuity from an illness process. In V. L. Bengtson (Ed.), *Adulthood and aging: Research on continuities and discontinuities* (pp. 204–222). New York: Springer.

Headey, B. (2010). The set point theory of well-being has serious flaws: On the eve of a scientific revolution? *Social Indicators Research, 97*, 7–21. doi:10.1007/s11205-009-9559-x

Leopold, T., Raab, M., & Engelhardt, H. (2014). The transition to parent care: Costs, commitments, and caregiver selection among children. *Journal of Marriage and Family, 76*, 300–318. doi:10.1111/jomf.12099

Lindgren, C. L., Connelly, C. T., & Gaspar, H. L. (1999). Grief in spouse and children caregivers of dementia patients. *Western Journal of Nursing Research, 21*, 521–537.

Lucas, R. E., & Donnellan, M. B. (2012). Estimating the reliability of single-item life satisfaction measures: Results from four national panel studies. *Social Indicators Research, 105*, 323–331. doi:10.1007/s11205-011-9783-z

Luhmann, M., Hofmann, W., Eid, M., & Lucas, R. E. (2012). Subjective well-being and adaptation to life events: A meta-analysis. *Journal of Personality and Social Psychology, 102*, 592–615. doi:10.1037/a0025948

Marks, N. F., Jun, H., & Song, J. (2007). Death of parents and adult psychological and physical well-being: A prospective U.S. national study. *Journal of Family Issues, 28*, 1611–1638. doi:10.1177/0192513X07302728

Marshall, H. (2004). Midlife loss of parents: The transition from adult child to orphan. *Ageing International, 29*, 351–367. doi:10.1007/s12126-004-1004-5

Moss, M. S., Moss, S. Z., Rubinstein, R., & Resch, N. (1993). Impact of elderly mother's death on middle age daughters. *International Journal of Aging & Human Development, 37*, 1–22. doi:10.2190/QNA3-F9FY-UTRV-L8GE

Moss, M. S., Resch, N., & Moss, S. Z. (1997). The role of gender in middle-age children's responses to parent death. *Omega: Journal of Death and Dying, 35*, 43–65. doi:10.2190/W6MM-QARHPHVA-YTQD

Neugarten, B. L. (1969). Continuities and discontinuities of psychological issues into adult life. *Human Development, 12*, 121–130. doi:10.1159/000270858

Petersen, S., & Rafuls, S. E. (1998). Receiving the scepter: The generational transition and impact of parent death on adults. *Death Studies, 22*, 293–524.

Pollmann-Schult, M. (2014). Parenthood and life satisfaction: Why don't children make people happy? *Journal of Marriage and Family, 76*, 319–336. doi:10.1111/jomf.12095

Rostila, M., & Saarela, J. M. (2011). Time does not heal all wounds: Mortality following the death of a parent. *Journal of Marriage and Family, 73*, 236–249. doi:10.1111/j.1741-3737.2010.00801.x

Russell, A., & Saebel, J. (1997). Mother–son, mother–daughter, father–son, and father–daughter: Are they distinct relationships? *Developmental Review, 17*, 111–147. doi:10.1006/drev.1996.0431

Schafer, M. H. (2009). Parental death and subjective age: Indelible imprints from early in the life course? *Sociological Inquiry, 79*, 75–97. doi:10.1111/j.1475-682X.2008.00270.x

Silverstein, M., Bengtson, V. L., & Lawton, L. (1997). Intergenerational solidarity and the structure of adult child–parent relationships in American families. *American Journal of Sociology, 103*, 429–460. doi:10.1086/231213

Troll, L. E. (1987). Mother–daughter relationships through the life span. *Applied Social Psychology Annual, 7,* 284–305.

Umberson, D. (2003). *Death of a parent: Transition to a new adult identity.* New York: Cambridge University Press. doi:10.1017/CBO9780511500046

Umberson, D., & Chen, M. D. (1994). Effects of a parent's death on adult children: Relationship salience and reaction to loss. *American Sociological Review, 59,* 152–168. doi:10.2307/2096138

Wagner, G. G., Frick, J. R., & Schupp, J. (2007). The German Socio-Economic Panel Study (SOEP): Scope, evolution and enhancements. *Schmollers Jahrbuch, 127,* 139–169.

Waldrop, D. P. (2007). Caregiver grief in terminal illness and bereavement: A mixed-methods study. *Health & Social Work, 32,* 197–206. doi:10.1093/hsw/32.3.197

Watkins, S. C., Menken, J. A., & Bongaarts, J. (1987). Demographic foundations of family change. *American Sociological Review, 50,* 689–698.

Kin and Kindred

Death and Social Relations

Tong Chee-Kiong

Filial Piety and Family Continuity

Death rituals reinforce the values of filial piety and loyalty, which are important for the maintenance of family and kinship unity. In fact, filial piety is one of the most common reasons cited for ritual performance. The idea that the worship of ancestors centers on the family and is expressed through filial piety is, of course, not unique to the Chinese in Singapore. Granet, writing on traditional Chinese society, notes that:

> this piety was not only addressed to the dead; it was composed of all homage that a person should receive during his life on earth, at the moment of his death and in the course of his ancestral life.[1]

This view is later echoed by Freedman when he writes:

> A man's loyalty to the interests and wishes of his father is supposed to outweigh all other loyalties and attachments. ... The supreme act of filial piety is the performance of the mortuary and funeral ceremonies for the parents.[2]

Filial piety is a principle that Chinese parents consistently inculcate their children with, parents often telling them stories of acts of filial piety found in the Chinese classics. During the enactment of the ancestral rituals children are always present, and they are constantly reminded of their duty to the parents to enact the rituals. One mother explained to her young son, "Look at the way that I am carrying out the rituals. Remember that you must do the same for me when I pass away." Thus, the ritual care of the dead serves to reinforce to the young their duty to the ancestors and their living parents.

Throughout the funeral, the symbol of *xiao* is manifest. Large Chinese characters, such as *zhong xiao chuan jia*, which translates as "loyalty, filiality, and the provisions of sons for continuing the family name," are placed before the coffin. Pictures depicting the twenty-four acts of supreme filial piety are also prominently displayed. Similarly, in the ancestral hall, the words *zhong xiao*, literally meaning "loyalty and filiality," are affixed on the main entrance. These symbols serve two purposes. First, they act as a message to the public that the value of *xiao* is a family tradition, a virtue held in high regard by the family. Second, they serve as a constant reminder to descendants of their duty to the parents.

Filial piety is not only a highly regarded value, but because it is constantly invoked in the performance of ancestral rituals, its existence actually defines a set of obligatory behavior that is required of the individual and family. In fact, it is noted that the mourning pins worn by the descendants are actually known as *xiao bu,* the same term used to denote filial piety. Many informants expressed surprise when asked why funerals are necessary. To them the answer is simply, "Duty requires that it must be done." This is true even if the relationship between parents and sons are estranged. At one funeral, a son, who had not returned home for years after quarreling with his father, took part in the funeral. Ancestral rituals are a reciprocal response of sons in repayment of a debt, an extension of the duty that a son owes his parents through life.

There is a close connection between the ethical values which are thought to maintain social order and the enactment of death rituals. Because of this, ethics provide a moral sanction for social and religious behavior. They take on a transcendental quality and become a powerful motivator of social behavior. In fact, they assume an obligatory nature where failure to perform prescribed rituals open the descendants to strong moral sanctions, both from society as well as from the transcendental beings—the ancestors. As Weber suggests, "... the system of inviolable norms is considered sacred, and infraction of them would result in magical or religious evils."[3]

Informants maintain that the perpetuation of the family name is of utmost importance, and even today, most Chinese parents in Singapore claim that they prefer male children in order to continue the family name. Citing classical injunctions, one informant said, "Of the three unfilial acts, the greatest is the lack of posterity." The idea is that the failure to provide sons would mean an end to the family name. In extreme circumstances, parents of a dead unmarried son would conduct a "ghost marriage" on the son's behalf in order to gain sons to continue the family line.[4] More commonly, a son is adopted for the same reason. During the funeral, the importance of family continuity is exemplified by raising the status of the eldest grandson to that of son of the deceased. In the graveyard, the personal name of the deceased on the gravestone is painted green, to signify death. The family name, however, is always inscribed in red, symbolizing that it never dies but is perpetuated by the descendants.

Death Rituals and Social Differentiation

Death rituals distinguish the kin group from outsiders, and informants have clear ideas about who can and cannot participate in the funeral rituals. Only relatives of the deceased, that is, those within the *wu dai* or five generations, are allowed to take part in the rituals. They have the privilege and obligation to wear the mourning garments. For non-kin to don a mourning garment would not only be construed as silly but foolhardy, as it would place the person in danger of attacks by the deceased. Funeral rituals therefore have the effect of consolidating the family unit and affirming the social relations within the group by juxtaposing the "us" against the "them." This social boundary is often articulated in terms of the cosmology of ancestors versus ghosts. Ancestors are considered as *zi ji ren,* or literally "one's own people." Other people's ancestors, however, are regarded as dangerous ghosts. The differentiation between family members and outsiders is also manifested in the strict rules regarding the placement of ancestral tablets on the family ancestral altar. Only family members in the patrilineal line of descent have a right to have their ancestral tablets erected there. Freedman suggests that tablets of non-kin can be found on the domestic ancestral altar[5] but informants met this suggestion with skepticism.

Death rituals highlight the exclusiveness of the kin group by clearly displaying their membership and setting them against outsiders, separating the family from the community. This point is most clearly exemplified by the placement of a screen before the coffin (see Plate 11.1). At the funeral, the coffin is surrounded on three sides by canvas sheets, effectively blocking it from public view.[6] The screen acts as a symbolic as well as a physical barrier between family members and outsiders, between those who can come into direct contact with the dead and those who cannot. Similarly, ritual precautions, such as the giving of red threads and candles to ward off the evil influences of death, are only necessary for visitors, and not required for the kin of the deceased.

PLATE 11.1 The Ritual screen and the altar to the deceased.

Death rituals demarcate the kin group against outsiders, and illuminate formal kinship relations by highlighting segmentations and hierarchies within the group. The assumption is that every social relationship in Chinese society is, by definition, unequal. Anderson notes, for example:

> The fundamental conceptions about social groups (among the Chinese) are centripetal and hierarchical, rather than boundary oriented and horizontal.[7]

The social relationships between every person in Chinese society, at least on the public level, are clearly ordered and characterized by strategic stratifications. According to Confucius, there are five universal principles: those of the relationship between ruler and minister, father and son, husband and wife, elder and younger brother, and between friends. It is important to note that, except for the last one, they are all asymmetrical. Properly observed, in an ideal world there can therefore be no conflict within Chinese society since these principles bind everyone to one another by a set of duty and obligations. Furthermore, this hierarchy is not only reflected in the society's idea of reality; it is also cosmologically oriented, as status differentiations are embedded in the rituals. In fact, grades of mourning in traditional Chinese society are institutionalized and written into the law of the state, which imposes a duty of mourning upon the people, sanctioned by punishment by the courts.[8] The wearing of mourning garments clearly demonstrates the hierarchical nature of Chinese society. It is not only a symbol that the family is in mourning; it also highlights the social divisions within the group.

As described earlier, the mourning garments are differentiated by the type, coarseness, and color of the garments. Thus, by looking at the mourning garments, any observer can immediately deduce the relationship between a particular mourner and the deceased, since mourning grades are based on the formal consanguinal and affinal ties to the deceased. The coarser the clothes, the closer the person is to the dead and to death. Moreover, there is an array of proper behaviors expected of each group of mourners, ranging from the amount of grief a person must show to the number of hours he must spend in the presence of the dead at the funeral vigil. Behavior that does not fulfill the expectations of the mourning grade opens the person to criticism and gossip. In one case, for example, one of the sons spent his nights sleeping instead of keeping watch over the coffin. This was considered to be extremely irresponsible and he was accused by other siblings of being an unfilial son. Fourth and fifth order mourners, however, are not required to observe the overnight vigil although, if they do so, they are often singled out for praise.

The hierarchical nature of Chinese society is reinforced by the conventions of social distance between the living and the dead. At every point in the ritual performance, there are strict rules regarding the physical distance required between an individual and the deceased. Sons always stand nearest to the deceased, the eldest son before his siblings. They are followed by daughters-in-law, daughters, etcetera, staggered according to the degree of consanguinal and affinal relations to the deceased.[9] The generation-agesex principle which operates in the organization of family and social relations in Chinese society is thereby made manifest in the death rituals. Formal kinship distinctions become apparent, since the position of any person in the ritual hierarchy is a reflection of his status in the family hierarchy. Again, there is much obligatory behavior accompanying the right to be close to the dead.

This hierarchical contrast is also concretized by the placement of ancestral tablets on the family altar. At one level, through the rules of admissions, the altar acts as a boundary between family and non-family members. At another, by the rules of placement, it also differentiates the family. The ancestral tablets of the elder generation are placed before the younger generation, the older having precedence over the younger if they are from the same generation, and males are placed on the right side, females on the left. [...].

Tensions Between the Individual And the Social Group

Many studies on the Chinese have emphasized the dominance of the collectivity over the individual. Baker, for instance, stressed the ascendancy of the family:

> The individual alive is a personification of all his forebears and all his descendants yet unborn. His existence as an individual is necessary but insignificant besides his representative of the whole.[10]

The ethnographic evidence, however, suggests that ritual sponsors have vested interests in performing the rituals, resulting in conflict and competition between siblings. This is not, however, to say that an individual is only interested in a rational, premeditated selfish evaluation of his personal interests above all else, regardless of the interests of others in the family and community. Instead, what is suggested is that there is a constant tension between the desires of an individual and the needs of the social group. In other words, among the egoistical wishes of individuals, an important part comprises their quest for and conception of the symbolic order, of the good society. This quest constitutes a basic, although differentiated, component of the whole panorama of social and cultural activities, orientations and goals.[11] Consensus and conflicts coexist in the ritual process, just as in social life in general.

Conflict and competition, however, are generally kept from the public view. For instance, the reason given for storing the father's ancestral tablet in a Mahayana Buddhist temple rather than in the home of the eldest son was that the ancestor would be happier in the temple since the priests would chant prayers for him daily. Similarly, the rationale for having many bands at the funeral is to create a festive atmosphere for the deceased. Being hidden, however, does not mean that these representations are not known. Obviously, any person who has had a death in his family is aware of the conflicts that often arise during the ritual process. This known yet misrepresented, seen yet hidden, attribute of death rituals is an important feature of Chinese social life, most clearly illustrated in the idea of gift-giving. When a person gives a gift, for example at a wedding, the gift of money must be placed inside a *hong bao* or red packet; that is, it is hidden from view. Moreover, the gift is given unobtrusively, pressed into the palm of the hand during the handshake or quickly slipped into the groom's pockets.

By hiding the gift, the amount of money given is supposedly unknown. However, it is clear that there are unwritten rules regarding how much money is expected.[12] To give an insufficient amount opens that particular person to gossip and ridicule. Giving too large a gift is disruptive as it obliges the recipient to reciprocate on other occasions with an even larger gift. In sum, there is an internal message to death ritual enactment. Everyone is aware that conflict and competition exist in the private sphere, but there is a mutual hiding of these conflicts under the cover of ethical imperatives.

Notes

1 Marcel Granet, *The Religion of the Chinese People,* p. 82.

2 Maurice Freedman, *Chinese Lineage and Society,* p. 118.

3 Max Weber, "The social psychology of world religions," *From Max Weber: Essays in Sociology.* Edited by C.W.Mills and translated by H.H.Gerth, New York: Oxford University Press, 1958, p. 296.

4 A description of "ghost marriages" can be found in Chapter 7.

5 Maurice Freedman, *Chinese Lineage and Society,* pp. 153–4.

6 Chapter 5 will show that this has also to do with the management of death pollution and blocking off the negative effects of death.

7 Benedict Anderson, *Imagined Communities: Reflections on the Origins and Spread of Nationalism.* London: Verso Press, 1983, p. 22. The basically hierarchical nature of Chinese society has also been noted by Maurice Freedman, *The Study of Chinese Society,* p. 353, and Hugh Baker, *Chinese Family and Kinship,* p. 11.

8 Hugh Baker, *Chinese Family and Kinship,* p. 108.

9 The only person to break this convention is the eldest grandson, who in his mourning grade and physical distance to the dead, takes on the status of a son. This elevation in status is linked to the emphasis on family continuity.

10 Hugh Baker, *Chinese Family and Kinship,* pp. 26–30.

11 See S.N.Eisenstadt's "Introduction" in Max Weber, *On Charisma and Institution Building, Selected Papers.* Edited and with an Introduction by S.N. Eisenstadt, Chicago: University of Chicago Press, 1968, p. xii.

12 At the time of writing, the amount is about S$80 for friends attending a wedding; S $ 120–200 if they are close friends. Relatives and close relatives give larger amounts. Weddings are expensive affairs and the money given is needed to defray the costs. Interestingly, even at very large weddings, informants can often recall later how much money each person gave.

Bibliography

Anderson, Benedict. *Imagined Communities: Reflections on the Origins and Spread of Nationalism.* London: Verso, 1983.

Baker, Hugh D.R. *Chinese Family and Kinship.* London: Macmillan, 1979.

Freedman, Maurice. *Chinese Lineage and Society: Fukien and Kwangtung.* London: Athlone Press, 1966.

Granet, Marcel. *The Religion of the Chinese People.* Translated, edited and introduced by Maurice Freedman. Oxford: Basil Blackwell, 1975.

Weber, Max. *From Max Weber: Essays in Sociology.* Translated and edited by H.Gerth and C.W.Mills. Oxford: Oxford University Press, 1958.

Weber, Max. *On Charisma and Institution Building. Selected Papers.* Edited and with an introduction by S.N. Eisenstadt. Chicago: University of Chicago Press, 1968.

Origins and Celebrations of El Día de Los Muertos

J. Rhett Rushing

Harvest time. The crops are in and the fields are torn and broken from giving their all. What has been nurtured and tended since the first warming winds of spring is now cold and dead and spent. Ghosts roam here as the line between the living and the dead is blurred and any door separating them stands ajar. This is the liminal time of transition and uncertainty. This is *Samhain.*

In Northern European history when the ancient Celts farmed and struggled—before the Christians and even before the Romans—*Samhain* was the end of the harvest time when farmers gave thanks for the bounty and prepared for the long winter to come. It was a time of celebration, but equally a time of caution. The normal rules and behaviors were suspended and time seemed to stand still.

For agricultural peoples the world over, the fall equinox signaled the end of the year, the onset of the Harvest Moon (when many farmers worked by full moonlight to gather crops before the weather turned bad), and the beginning of winter. The symbolic "death" of the crops was celebrated with feasting, with the ritual burning of the "Wicker Man" made of stalks and stems left over from the harvest, and the scattering of ashes over the fields to ensure fertility in the coming seasons.

It was time of remembering the human dead as well, including the offering of foods and prayers. And since the dead were free to wander the earth, the living stayed close to their homes. If anyone had to be out at night, they were careful to wear a mask so as to confuse the ghosts who might be seeking them. In Ireland, travelers carried small lanterns carved from turnips to light their way, and those turnips were frequently carved with spooky faces as well.

Roman conquest did little to alter *Samhain* celebrations, but the coming of Christianity and organized Catholicism made a mark still in evidence today. For a thousand years all across Christendom, the church worked to supplant "pagan" rituals with Christian characters and themes, and by the conquest of the New World, Roman Catholicism had turned the harvest festival from harrowing to holy.

In an attempt to de-emphasize the spooky and liminal aspects of the season, it was decided that a day of celebration for all the hallowed saints would satisfy the farmers' need for a celebration while shepherding it into a religious event. For the most part this was a successful conversion, but it did not address the people's need to "blow off steam" after the hard work of harvesting. *Samhain* had allowed for a period of ritualized misbehavior and a suspension of the normal rules governing daily life. Simply retooling the feast did not cure the social restlessness, and being as creative as only humans can be, the night before All Hallows Day became the target for eeriness and mischief—All Hallows Eve, or Halloween.

Coming to the New World, Catholic conquerors again encountered harvest festivals where agricultural populations celebrated with feasting and a time of reverence for the dead returning to share the harvest. For untold centuries, Toltecs, Mayans, and Aztecs typically dedicated an entire month to the dead, and enjoyed a corn harvest fully intended to be shared among the living and the deceased. Again incorporating indigenous practices under the blanket of Catholic belief, All Saints Day took root in New Spain as a day of veneration and remembrance for those gone on. Initially, November the first was dedicated to recognized Catholic saints, but since children could die in a state of grace, the "little saints" were included as well. November the second (All Souls Day, or as it is known in Mexico and the American Southwest, *El Día de los Muertos*) developed as a formal time for remembering deceased adults.

are often decorated with images of the deceased and filled with *ofrendas,* or offerings. These offerings frequently include *pan de muerto,* bread baked only during this season, in the shapes of the *Virgen de Guadalupe* or other religious figures, skulls, skeletons, or little animals if intended for *los angelitos* (deceased children). Other offerings include candies, sugar skulls, candles, toys, favorite foods, beer or tequila, and marigolds by the score.

Oftentimes, cartoon-like skeleton figurines known as *calaveras* are placed on the altar. These serve as humorous reminders of our shared humanity. Stripped of all pomp and pride down to bare bones, these clown-like figures sing and dance and remind us that no matter how important we feel ourselves to be in life, we are all equal in death.

FOOD OFRENDAS commonly left for the dead

A colorful skeleton figurine to be left at an altar

There are no formal guidelines for celebrating *El Día de los Muertos,* but there are several hallmarks of the holiday. Altars, whether constructed in the home or in larger, shared spaces,

Perhaps the most traditional of *El Día de los Muertos* activities is the visit to the graveyard.

Families will often eat breakfast and visit the church to light a candle before packing rakes, hoes, flowers, paint, tools, and a selection of foods. Outside the gates of the cemetery vendors crowd the streets selling marigolds, *milagros,* religious images, foods of all sorts, candles, and every sort of flower vase and picture frame.

Arriving at the *campo santo* (cemetery) the family will pull weeds, align grave decorations, repaint faded items, water grass or flowers, sprinkle water over bare earth, and sweep and generally clean up the gravesite in honor of the deceased. Afterwards, a cloth or blanket may be spread over the grave and the family will enjoy a meal.

In some locations and among some families, visits to the grave take place the night before All Souls Day so that family and friends can drop by and spend the night "remembering" the deceased with songs and stories, food and drink. The living are brought together, the dead are remembered, and the family is whole. As with most Tejano celebrations, the ultimate goal of each gathering is to reinforce and reestablish family unity. It may be easier to understand this social function in terms of memory, for as long as one is remembered by the family, one still has "life" in the family. *El Día de los Muertos* is entirely about life and death and remembering.

A display of altar items at UTSA's Institute of Texan Cultures

Reflexive Questions

1. What are your beliefs about death? What emotions are evoked when you think of yourself dying or someone close to you dying?

2. Do you believe in an afterlife? What informs your beliefs?

3. What cultural/religious values inform your perspectives about the dying process and death?

4. How do you think the grieving process is different based on the timing (young, middle age, older) and manner of death (natural, homicide, suicide, accident, unknown, war) of the deceased person?

5. Developmentally, how do you think a person's age affects their grieving process?

6. How do you think the untimely death of a parent affects a child and vice versa?

7. How does the untimely death of a child affect a person, marriage, and/or family? What can they do to strengthen and overcome challenges?

8. What are death and burial rituals in the United States? Why is it that we do not take time off for grief and bereavement? What values are embedded in this? What are the consequences?

9. What are some symbolic forms of death or loss (e.g., the death of childhood, a dream, a way of life, a sense of security or peace)? What effects can they have on us?

10. What are losses that you have experienced in your life and how did you grieve them?

11. If you could create a ritual for a loss, what would you create? How do you think it could help you or others?

12. When you die, how do you want to be remembered? What actions or attitudes do you have to maintain, change, or adopt to work toward this ideal?

CHAPTER 12

A Call to Action

Being an Agent of Change

Introduction

Throughout this text, you have read about how our social identities and contexts shape our lives across the life span. These readings highlight the nuance of developmental stages when viewed through intersectional, contextual, and sociocultural perspectives. My hope is that the content of this text has opened more space for you to think critically about your own influences and development. I hope that you are closer to understanding the intersections of your own identity, socialization, and cultural contexts as well as those of others who occupy different spaces and contexts than you. It is essential for us to engage critically with scholarly work and other bodies of knowledge and to use them to advocate for change. I echo the sentiment of countless writers and activists that have come before me who have created the space for us to continue to do the work of social justice. In doing so, each one of us, in our own ways, can work toward dismantling oppressive systems and structural barriers leading to inequity and injustice. In response to the questions posed in the introduction of this text as to what constitutes "optimal development" and how people achieve it, I share my concluding thoughts.

To answer these questions, it is essential to consider how optimal development is often linked to gender, race, class, sexuality, and other social identities bound within power, privilege, and oppression. These aspects of identity cannot be examined in isolation from one another or void of their contexts (Lorde, 2007). As mentioned earlier, power relations are deeply entrenched in social identities that intersect in complex ways. For example, the power, privilege, and oppression from racism and sexism cannot be understood in isolation from one another (Collins and Bilge, 2016). Consider school achievement and social class. Although researchers continue to find a relationship between affluence and academic achievement, this relationship is influenced by factors such as school location and the social identities of the students and families (Sirin, 2005). Without considering how these factors and systems intersect, scholars and policymakers focus prevention and intervention strategies at the individual level, instead of at structural and systemic levels. Although individuals play a role in their success, assuming they are solely responsible for their success fails to consider how systems of oppression and privilege (e.g., classism, racism, sexism, heterosexism, etc.) intersect and become institutionalized in ways that limit or grant access and opportunity. Therefore, the question of what is *optimal* development introduces two new questions: 1) who defines *optimal* development and 2) who has the access and means to *optimally* develop? If intersectionality is to be the future of mainstream human development and family science (Few-Demo, 2014), then social scientists must attempt to answer such questions and in doing so, create the space for equity and social justice to be enacted. This not only advances science in necessary and important ways, but benefits people consuming the science—policymakers, lawyers and judges, those working in law enforcement, medical personnel, teachers, and students, among others. These necessary and urgent advancements are especially evident when scholars and practitioners see their work as forms of praxis.

What is praxis and why is it important? Praxis is having a critical consciousness and putting it into action in order to make necessary changes (Freire, 1970). It is important because dismantling systems of oppression requires it. Patricia Hill Collins (1990) contends that praxis requires that we acknowledge that we are all responsible for resisting harmful and constraining ideologies, actions, and inequitable institutions. Praxis is actively challenging and disrupting social structures that keep people from minoritized groups from having equity. Taking action is a risk. This work is not easy. As Cornel West (2009) suggests, taking action requires courage and it requires us to get into good and necessary trouble, as stated by Representative John Lewis. Being an agent of change requires one to resist systems of oppression and inequality, especially as members of the dominant group who benefits from them.

According to family scholars Katherine Allen (2000) and April Few-Demo (2014), a call to action requires us to be reflexive, responsive, and to hold ourselves accountable for what we say and do, and what we do not say and do. We might ask ourselves, "Why is this important?" or say, "I didn't do anything to cause the pain or injustice of others." "I didn't ask for my unearned privilege." The call to action is especially important for members of society who have been afforded the socially sanctioned power to affect change (Goodman, 2011). This awareness is important for all of us, because if you are reading this, you have more power than you know. Your power may be invisible to you, but it is precisely this invisibility that makes your power a privilege. While you may not be aware of how you have benefited from White, male, heterosexual, or class privilege per se, it is evident to others who do not experience power and privilege in the same way. Many people are denied access that affords greater opportunity because of their social location; and to whom much is given, much is expected. It is the responsibility of those with unearned privilege due to their social location (i.e., skin color, gender, wealth, ability status, sexual orientation, immigration status, religion, etc.) to disrupt what is unjust (Goodman, 2011).

The fact that those of us who are in a position of power *choose* to act or not act is a sign of our privilege—our privilege to remain uninformed or uninvolved in the fight for social justice. For example, it would be tempting for men to ignore the news related to the "#MeToo" movement; a White person to not understand the urgency related to the "Black Lives Matter" movement; a heterosexual person to not need to care or be informed about the rights of LGBTQ people; and a U.S. citizen to not care about the atrocities happening to undocumented Latinx people at the U.S.–Mexico border. After the murder of George Floyd on May 25, 2020, by a Minneapolis police officer, someone posted a tweet that included the words of civil rights activist Ella Baker: "'Until the killing of black men, black mothers' sons, becomes as important to the rest of the country as the killing of a white mother's son, we who believe in freedom cannot rest until this happens.'

#blacklivesmatter #JusticeForGeorgeFloyd." This sentiment expresses a call for all of us to take action as agents of change. It calls on us to accept accountability for changing systemic racism, sexism, violence and oppression (Tourse, Hamilton-Mason, & Wewiorski, 2018). This leads us to another question- why is accountability important?

Anne Russo (2019) writes about what it means to engage in a praxis of accountability. She states that intersectionality is the bridge to accountability and makes the structural and systemic inequities open to ongoing collective scrutiny, intervention, and transformation. She states that by cultivating critical, compassionate consciousness and acquiring tangible skills, we can work to transform, rather than to deepen systems of oppression and violence. When looking back at the literature related to child, adolescent, and adult development, we know this work is necessary and urgent. This work helps us create spaces where we can create the world we envision. It is what McDowell (2015) and McDowell, Knudson-Martin, & Bermudez (2018) refer to as the need to move from third-order thinking to third-order change.

This work seems overwhelming. Many of us feel like we cannot make a difference or that what we do is not enough to effect change. I strongly believe that all of us can and do make a difference. We can continue to work within our own spheres of influence to lead by example to denounce oppression and all the "isms" and stand on the side of equity and social justice. Each one of us can demonstrate that we are actively trying to be an anti-racist, anti-sexist, anti-misogynous, anti-homophobic, anti-xenophobic, anti-transphobic, for people at every age and stage of their lives—from infancy to old age. We might not have all the answers or walk on this path with ease, but as Tatum (1997) suggests, at the very least, we can have the courage to engage in difficult dialogues about race and the effects of oppression. To help move us toward action, we turn to the final reading.

Summary of Readings

In the classic essay "**Where Do We Go from Here?**" (2012), Patricia Hill Collins explores the conceptualization of, and possible ways to implement, intersectionality. Collins asserts that intersectional scholarship champions an important conceptual shift from viewing social categories as discrete, exclusive phenomena and more toward viewing the relationships among them, which produces more robust analyses of systems of power. By focusing on how intersecting and interlocking systems of power influence institutions and our everyday lives, intersectionality focuses its attention on structures of power over the subjective experiences of the individual. As intersectionality continues to be integrated into academic fields, Collins cautions scholars against parsing intersectionality from its social justice origins. Social justice should be at the heart of intersectional frameworks. While understanding one's position on an issue is a necessary step toward social change, Collins asserts much more is needed when dismantling social inequality. Instead of focusing on individual consciousness, attention must be refocused on coalitional politics and social activism. In response to her question (Where do we go from here?), she states that we must *move forward* with an intersectionality-informed commitment to coalitional politics as a way to take action and enact social justice.

References

Allen, K. (2000). A conscious and inclusive family studies. *Journal of Marriage and Family, 62*(1), 4–17.

Collins, P. H., & Bilge, S. (2016). *Intersectionality.* Polity Press.

Few-Demo, A. L. (2014). Intersectionality as the "new" critical approach in feminist family studies: Evolving racial/ethnic feminisms and critical race theories. *Journal of Family Theory & Review, 6*(2), 169–183.

Freire, P. (2007). *Pedagogy of the oppressed* (M. B. Ramos, Trans.). Continuum. (1970).

Goodman, D. J. (2011). *Promoting diversity and social justice: Educating people from privileged groups (2nd ed.).* Routledge-Taylor & Francis Group.

Lorde, A. (2007). *Sister outsider: Essays & speeches by Audre Lorde.* Crossing Press.

McDowell, T. (2015). Applying critical social theories to family therapy practice. AFTA Springer Series.

McDowell, T., Knudson-Martin, C., & Bermudez, J. (2018). *Socioculturally attuned family therapy: Guidelines for equitable theory and practice.* Routledge.

Russo, A. (2019). *Feminist accountability: Disrupting violence and transforming power.* New York University Press.

Sirin, S. R. (2005). Socioeconomic status and academic achievement: A meta-analytic review of research. *Review of educational research, 75*, 417–453. doi.org/10.3102/00346543075003417

Tatum, B. D. (1997). *Why are all the Black kids sitting together in the cafeteria?: And other conversations about race.* Basic Books.

Tourse, R. W. C., Hamilton-Mason, J., & Wewiorski, N. J. (2018). *Systemic racism in the United States: Scaffolding as social construction.* Springer.

West, C. (2009). *Hope on a tightrope: Words and wisdom.* Smiley Books.

Where Do We Go from Here?

In Search of New Knowledge: Intersectionality

Patricia Hill Collins

Initially, the question "How can we reconceptualize race, class, and gender as categories of analysis?" seemed straightforward. Yet, grappling with the complexities of intersecting social inequalities has stimulated far more expansive knowledge projects than I initially envisioned. *Intersectionality* is currently the umbrella term that best incorporates this emerging field of study. My initial questions about race, class, and gender are now part of a much larger body of intersectional scholarship that examines multiple connections, for example, how ability and age are interrelated or how sexuality operates within and across ethnic groups.

Within American higher education, the contributions and challenges of intersectional scholarship have become increasingly visible and accepted across several fields of study. Because my work on Black feminism has been necessarily interdisciplinary, I have encountered a broad array of scholars in other disciplines, across varying national settings, and from diverse backgrounds who are also intrigued with how their intellectual projects might be enhanced by a greater emphasis on examining the intersections of race, class, gender, sexuality, age, ability, and citizenship status. In this sense, intersectional frameworks are simultaneously universal and particular. They transcend any one discipline, national setting, or level of analysis (e.g., micro or macro).

Looking back, I see deeper understandings within intersectional scholarship in answering my first question. First, we now know far more about the saliency of race, class, and gender as categories of analysis in varying social contexts. Because these categories are organized differently from one setting to the next, they are not deterministic, master categories that explain all social inequalities. Race, class, and gender are categories that are more salient in the U.S. context than in other national, cultural, and regional settings, where other categories, such as sexuality, age, ability, citizenship status, and religion, may be equally, if not more, prominent. The constellation of all of these categories shifts such that specific combinations become more visible or muted across varying geographic locations, political units, and time periods.

Second, intersectional scholarship has identified an important conceptual shift away from seeing race, class, and gender as discrete phenomena and toward viewing the *relationships* among them as the focus of attention. Power relations of racial and gender segregation as well as those of colonialism rely on categorical thinking that divides the world, and knowledge itself, into separate entities, each having a specific place. Much as the books in a library are shelved with only one number, systems using racism, heterosexism, class exploitation, and sexism also separate and categorize people. In contrast, contemporary relationships of desegregation, decolonization, and recolonization are far more fluid. Just as books can carry multiple keywords, rather than a single number, we now know that individuals have multiple identities; many people hold dual citizenship, for example. When it comes to contemporary power relations in a decolonizing world, intersectional frameworks suggest that there are no pure oppressors or oppressed and that, instead, most social phenomena reflect a tangled set of relationships of privilege and penalty. By replacing "either/or" understandings of the world with a "both/and" lens, intersectional scholarship has focused attention on the processes of relationality.

Third, this shift toward relationality has enabled intersectionality to produce more robust analyses of power. Specifically, we now have a much better sense of how oppressions mutually construct one another within relations of structural power. Many of us have improved our capacity to think outside the boxes of heterosexual-only, or West/North-only, or Christian-only, and similar kinds of thinking that aim to impose a monocategorical, and therefore monocausal, framework on what is obviously a complex and ever-changing set of power relations. Similarly, intersectional analyses have broadened prevailing understandings of identity beyond individual experiences. Instead, focusing on how intersecting systems of power shape a host of constructs, such as personal and group identities, the experiences that accompany such identities, and the social problems faced by people holding those identities, reverses attention from the subjective experience of individual identity to structures of power.

Despite these contributions, intersectional scholarship faces new challenges. Becoming a named discourse has been important for reasons of academic legitimacy, yet the acceptance of intersectionality within the academy raises the question of its connections to its origins in social justice initiatives. The challenges of intersectionality resemble those facing U.S. Black feminism as a social justice project, namely (1) refocusing U.S. Black feminism on the everyday realities of Black women's lives; (2) paying careful attention to how the language of Black feminism is being used, often in ways that are antithetical to Black feminist politics; and (3) developing new standards for evaluating the effectiveness of Black feminism as a social justice project within a greatly changed political environment (for an extended discussion of these points, see Chapter 5). In a similar fashion, the more legitimate that intersectional scholarship becomes in colleges and universities, the more abstract and disengaged it can become from actual social relations. This disengagement may move the discourse away from its origins in social justice projects and their focus on human freedom. Intersectional scholarship may gain legitimacy while losing its very reason for existing. [...].

Where Do We Go from Here?

In this essay, I have sketched out how a revitalized commitment to coalitional politics that is informed by an intersectional understanding of community might suggest new visions and accompanying courses of action. But where do we go from here? Three implications of my argument thus far suggest some future directions.

First, this essay shows the limitations of social change as a vision for coalitional politics. Thus far, I have emphasized themes of barriers and coalition building, the nuts and bolts of moving toward a vision. At the same time, I have neglected the assumption from "Toward a New Vision" that the objective of coalitional politics is "social change." A belief in social change may be a good starting point for coalition building, but this idea cannot sustain coalitional politics. Social change is neither a philosophy nor an ethical position. It is a tool, a technique, a description of variation across time toward or away from some goal. Social change begs the question of what goals are desirable as well as the standards used to move toward them.

The construct of social justice might offer a richer overarching framework that can guide and evaluate the success of coalitional politics. For many of us engaged in intellectual activism, social justice has become a far more useful concept than amorphous notions of social change. A renewed emphasis on social justice might also benefit intersectional scholarship. An ethics of social justice might help to clarify the purpose of intersectional scholarship, its intended audiences, its content, and the forms that such scholarship might take. This shift toward social justice highlights the necessity of principled positions for both coalitional politics and intersectional scholarship. A question more suitable for today might read: *How can we transcend the barriers created by our experiences within intersecting systems of oppression to build coalitions that foster social justice?*

A second implication of this essay concerns the need for more complex analyses of collective action. In "Toward a New Vision," I issued a call to action, suggesting that a changed consciousness within each individual was essential for building coalitions. I ended that earlier essay by charging readers to "examine their own position." Developing an understanding of one's own position is necessary, but it is far from sufficient for social justice projects. Individuals

can understand their own positions, yet, if they are disconnected from social justice commitments, they may be ineffective in contesting social inequalities. I now reject the notion that the "revolution" is buried deep within each of us and that all we need to do is "find" it, like a hidden treasure. This may be the case for many people, but when it comes to social inequalities that stem from intersecting systems of power, much more is needed than assessing our own individual consciences.

Refocusing attention on coalitional politics and on the skill set needed to engage in such politics pushes back against a narcissistic individualism that encourages each of us to hunt for our own "private revolutions." We need to develop a more robust understanding of social groups; coalitional politics; and the reasons why some individuals engage in activism, whereas others, armed with the same information and undergoing similar experiences, do not. This essay's discussion of coalition building, both within and among communities of color, suggests that, although individuals are the foundation of any political action, we need better analyses of how social groups are organized and operate. Moreover, intersectional analyses that remain attentive to the social justice implications of scholarship may be positioned to make important contributions to coalitional politics.

Finally, claiming an ethics of social justice and linking it to a more robust understanding of coalitional politics creates space for coalitions of conscience. Such coalitions would be grounded in an ethical framework of the sort suggested by a commitment to social justice. Conscience would be expressed not solely through an individual's consciousness but also via group-based, principled commitments. My earlier discussion of communities and coalitional politics was designed to broaden our thinking about forms of political organization and democratic processes. Building on this analysis, here I suggest that communities might also be sites of "conscience," where group members take principled positions on the social injustices that result from intersecting systems of power. Ethical frameworks that inform such communities need not emerge primarily from *a priori* abstractions about the meaning of social justice. Rather they are constantly reworked within social justice projects that are honed in the crucible of experience. My earlier discussion of coalition building, both within and across communities of color, sketched out some of the issues associated with engaging in this form of robust community politics.

Many of us have had glimpses of coalitions of conscience and may have been members of communities that housed them. We can find many examples of coalitions of conscience in everyday life. Coalitions of conscience do not usually form the focus of scholarship, but when they do, they offer important lessons. For example, in their conversations as recorded in *We Make the Road by Walking,* Paulo Freire and Myles Horton discuss their road into activism and their shared view of literacy as foundational to empowerment. Similarly, Mark Warren does us a real service in his volume *Fire in the Heart,* a nuanced study of how whites who are committed to racial justice initiatives actively chose to engage in coalitions of conscience. Dawne Moon's book *God, Sex and Politics: Homosexuality and Everyday Theologies* thoroughly explores the internal politics of building coalitions of conscience among individuals within faith communities. These examples illustrate how building coalitions of conscience can be exciting, exasperating, and empowering for community members and show that scholarship about coalitions of conscience

that reflects intersectional analysis can have a far-reaching effect.

For me, coalitions of conscience do not exist in my imagination—rather, they have taken tangible forms as I have traveled the path of my own intellectual activism. Whether drawn from my engaged scholarship on Black feminism, intersectionality, the sociology of knowledge, or critical education, I have a lifetime of experiences that remind me of the value of coalitions of conscience and the hard work it takes to bring them about. Where do I go from here? I have not yet walked away, so it seems I'll keep on trying. Where do we go from here? The answer to this question is in your hands.

Additional Resources

Bell, Brenda, John Gaventa, and John Peters, eds. 1990. *We Make the Road by Walking: Conversations on Education and Social Change,* by Myles Horton and Paulo Freire. Philadelphia: Temple University Press.

Cohen, Cathy J. 2010. *Democracy Remixed: Black Youth and the Future of American Politics.* Chicago: University of Chicago Press.

Collins, Patricia Hill. 1993. "Toward a New Vision: Race, Class, and Gender as Categories of Analysis and Connection." *Race, Sex and Class* 1:25-45.

———. 2009. *Another Kind of Public Education: Race, Schools, the Media and Democratic Possibilities.* Boston: Beacon Press.

———. 2010. "The New Politics of Community." *American Sociological Review* 75(1): 7-30.

Moon, Dawne. 2004. *God, Sex and Politics: Homosexuality and Everyday Theologies.* Chicago: University of Chicago Press.

Warren, Mark R. 2010. *Fire in the Heart: How White Activists Embrace Racial Justice.* New York: Oxford University Press.

Reflexive Questions

1. How would you describe your thoughts and feelings after reading this book?

2. How have the readings affected your perspectives and outlook on the future? Are you more hopeful, optimistic, anxious, worried, hopeless, or something else?

3. What have you learned about your own social location that you were not fully aware of before? What knowledge about yourself was strengthened?

4. What does it take for everyone, from every background, to have an equal opportunity to thrive and live their best life?

5. What socioeconomic and cultural forces are currently blocking or preventing equity among people of different genders, races, abilities, nationalities and sexual orientations?

6. What would you tell someone who thinks inequality, such as White supremacy and male privilege and domination, are good, especially for families, employers, and the government?

7. What prevents us from having difficult dialogues about race, class, gender, sexual orientation, and social class? What prevents us from standing up to oppression and each one of the "isms"?

8. How does inequity affect us? Who benefits at the expense of others?

9. How do you enact praxis? What are specific causes that you care about and want to see change? What are the things that you are currently doing or would like to start doing to work toward social justice and change?

10. What gives you hope? What collations can you join or create to work toward positive change?

About the Author

J. Maria Bermudez has been a scholar of human development and family studies and a practicing marriage and family therapist for over 25 years. She has published over 60 scholarly articles and book chapters and is the co-author of the book *Socioculturally Attuned Family Therapy: Guidelines for Equitable Theory and Practice* (2018). She first developed her appreciation of culture and diversity as a child when she would visit her native country of Honduras. She grew up in Houston, Texas, where she earned a Bachelor of Arts in psychology at the University of Houston, a Master of Science in child and family development and marriage and family therapy at Purdue University, and a Ph.D. in human development and marriage and family therapy at Virginia Tech. She is an associate professor in the Department of Human Development and Family Science at the University of Georgia and affiliate faculty of the Interdisciplinary Women's Studies Program and Latin American and Caribbean Studies Institute. Her work is anchored in feminist-informed, socioculturally attuned, and culturally responsive approaches to research, teaching, and clinical practice. Dr. Bermudez has taught courses on diversity and human development for her entire career. She greatly enjoys teaching and helping students connect the material to their own personal and professional lives.

CPSIA information can be obtained
at www.ICGtesting.com
Printed in the USA
BVHW010028030921
615898BV00011B/260